HUMAN RESOURCE PRACTICE

5th edition

Malcolm Martin
Fiona Whiting
Tricia Jackson

Published by the Chartered Institute of Personnel and Development,
151, The Broadway, London, SW19 1JQ

This edition first published 2010
First published 1997
Reprinted 1998, 1999
Second edition published 2000
Reprinted 2000
Third edition published 2002
Reprinted 2002, 2003, 2004 (twice)
Fourth edition published 2005
Reprinted 2006, 2007, 2008, 2009
Fifth edition published 2010
Reprinted 2011

Typeset by Fakenham Photosetting Ltd, Norfolk

Printed in Great Britain by Charlesworth Press

British Library Cataloguing in Publication Data
A catalogue of this publication is available from the British Library

ISBN 978 1 84398 253 1

The views expressed in this publication are the authors' own and may not
necessarily reflect those of the CIPD.

The CIPD has made every effort to trace and acknowledge copyright holders. If any source has been
overlooked, CIPD Enterprises would be pleased to redress this in future editions.

Chartered Institute of Personnel and Development, CIPD House,
151, The Broadway, London, SW19 1JQ

Tel: 020 8612 6200

Email: cipd@cipd.co.uk

Website: www.cipd.co.uk

Incorporated by Royal Charter

Registered Charity No. 1079797

Contents

List of Figures and Tables

Acknowledgements

We recognise that directly or indirectly those with whom we work, and have worked, help create such practical knowledge and skill as we have. Preparation of the revised material in this fourth edition has been greatly helped by comments, informed suggestions and contributions from students, delegates, business clients, our fellow tutors, associates and publisher. These have been invaluable in providing insights into current trends and organisational procedures and practices. We would like to thank them all for their assistance.

Finally, Malcolm, Fiona and Tricia would like to thank their respective partners, Christina, Derek and David, for their continuing understanding and support during the fifth revision of this book.

CHAPTER 1

Introduction and overview

OUR PURPOSE

Our purpose is to set out a practical approach to human resource (HR) practices. We hope that anyone wanting a good working understanding of HR practices will find that this book meets their needs. Students on a variety of HND, undergraduate and certificate programmes should find it valuable as an introduction and as a supporting text that provides a practical perspective to the issues that they are studying.

The structure of the book follows the rationale set down in the Chartered Institute of Personnel and Development (CIPD) Professional Standards for the Certificate in HR Practice (CHRP). This programme is self-standing but also provides an access route to the Professional Development Scheme (PDS). CHRP students, enrolled at a CIPD-approved centre, will find that this book provides essential background reading to reinforce their learning.

The central purpose of the CHRP is to develop competence in a range of core HR and development skills together with the acquisition of underpinning knowledge and understanding. Many line managers also need these skills, knowledge and understanding. This book has been written to provide a variety of readers with a grounding in the basics of HR activities. It therefore considers the breadth of knowledge and range of skills necessary for the effective performance of HR work, while taking into account the organisational culture and environment.

A summary of the book's structure and an overview of its contents follow. But first we consider the type of reader most likely to benefit from the book and the learning sources you should use.

YOU, THE READER

This book's focus on the core skills required in managing and working effectively with people makes it suitable for a large range of potential readers. The CHRP programme is widely regarded as an ideal course for all newcomers to the profession, but we expect that readers will belong to one or more of the following groups:

- HR officers and managers who are newly appointed to the role and who lack previous generalist experience (you may be the sole HR practitioner within your organisation, or your post may be a newly established one)
- HR assistants, administrators and secretaries who support more senior HR staff
- students on the Certificate in HR Practice programme
- students on any of a variety of management, business and supervisory programmes with an HR unit or module
- employees working for new but rapidly expanding organisations who acquire responsibility for establishing and formalising HR policies, procedures and practices
- staff who work in HR-related areas – for example, a personal assistant to a managing director or a payroll supervisor
- staff who work in specialist areas of HR practice, such as training, employee relations or job evaluation, who wish to progress into or have more knowledge of generalist roles
- line managers or supervisors who have responsibility for HR activities
- owners or managers of small businesses who have overall responsibility for the 'people element' within them.

We've sought to achieve an easy personal writing style that we hope will encourage readers to engage in the subject.

Please note: We use the title 'HR practitioners' throughout this book as a generic term to cover all the above types of job and all levels of HR work, including those for whom the activities may be only part of wider responsibilities.

LEARNING SOURCES

This book has been written by three authors, all experienced in the field of HR but with very different experiences, styles and, sometimes, perspectives. In order to understand each of the issues tackled within your own organisational circumstances, you will need to draw upon your own experience and perspective. Much of what we offer is considered 'good practice'. We also provide good coverage of relevant legal issues.

A further component is the commercial or political reality of your organisation that you will confront on a regular basis. Commercial and political realities vary in their effect enormously from organisation to organisation. While we touch on these where we can, you will need to use your experience of working in your organisation to fully understand the commercial and political reality. Striking a good balance between good practice, the law and commercial/political realities will be important if you are to be effective.

To gain the maximum benefit from the book you will find it valuable to discuss the issues raised with appropriate people, particularly if you are relatively inexperienced in the areas under consideration.

These people or 'learning sources' may include:

- senior colleagues, such as HR specialists and line managers, peers and subordinates who have knowledge and experience of the organisation and how it operates
- HR managers and officers from sister, parent and outside organisations
- specialists within your organisation such as company solicitors, health and safety officers, computer programmers/analysts, medical personnel and occupational health advisers
- members of your local CIPD branch and other networking bodies
- college tutors and fellow students
- other contacts that you have made through live networking activities
- appropriate contacts that you might make through social networking
- employees of advisory bodies such as the Advisory, Conciliation and Arbitration Service (Acas), the Health and Safety Executive (HSE) and the Commission for Equality and Human Rights, and representatives of employers' organisations and trade union bodies.

You should establish contacts with these learning sources and make use of them to facilitate your learning experience. We shall be making periodic reference to your 'learning sources' throughout this book, so – bearing in mind the above list – choose those sources that are going to be of most benefit to you in terms of their knowledge, availability and willingness to help.

In addition to these 'people resources' there is also a range of publications available that provide general guidance and practical help. If you are a member of the CIPD you should already have booklets on the following:

- the CIPD Professional Standards
- continuing professional development (CPD)
- the CIPD Code of Professional Conduct
- any relevant CIPD Infosource documents – eg survey reports.

Acas has also produced a series of advisory booklets that provide invaluable assistance in a wide range of people management activities. We recommend that you acquire, or download, copies of these booklets either for your personal use or for the whole of the HR department.

It is also worthwhile becoming familiar with a number of useful websites, such as the CIPD, Acas, Business Link, and various government departments, such as the Department for Business, Innovation and Skills (BIS). If you create a database of favourite sites, you will be able to discover up-to-date information on almost any topic of interest. There are also bookmarking services such as Delicious that you might use. Other suggestions are made in Chapter 10.

In order to keep up to date with changes in the world of HR management, employment legislation and case law, you might also want to encourage your organisation to subscribe to a reputable information service such as those provided by the CIPD (eg HR-inform), Croner's or XpertHR. Subscriptions provide online reference material which is kept regularly up to date.

THE STRUCTURE

We have designed this book to make it easy for you to 'dip in' to chapters and sections that are of particular interest. It is divided into 12 chapters (including this one). The subject areas represent the major activities associated with HR work, and we highlight the links between these activities throughout. We also provide brief details of the contents of each chapter in the *Overview* section below, including the changes that have been made in writing the fifth edition of this book, superseding the fourth edition called *Personnel Practice*.

The next two chapters set the scene for what follows. We examine the internal and external factors that exert an influence on an organisation along with their effect on the work of HR practitioners, and we look at the legal background to HR practice.

While we see these two as setting the scene, each chapter can be read independently, and cross-references between chapters are intended to assist this and to minimise duplication of material.

Each chapter contains the following features, where appropriate:

- learning objectives
- an introduction
- an explanation of why the topics covered are important to HR practitioners
- the main body of information
- case study material to reinforce key issues and demonstrate points of good and poor practice
- the many and varied roles played by HR practitioners
- a summary
- activities to encourage the acquisition and application of knowledge in an organisational setting and the planning of work experiences aimed at skills development
- a section covering references, legislative Acts and codes of practice, further reading and recommended websites.

The last two features highlight our desire to change your learning experience from a passive to an active one. You are recommended to tackle at least two activities from each chapter.

In this new edition we have incorporated recent and forthcoming legislative changes throughout the book (but particularly in Chapter 3). Recent trends in HR-related matters have been noted and commentary provided on the changing nature of employment and the changing organisational context of HR. New methods of communication in the form of email and Web 2.0 are examined in a revised chapter and recognised throughout the book. We have also updated the suggested further reading and the references. These and other changes are highlighted in the *Overview*.

OVERVIEW

Chapter 1 Introduction and overview

As you will have seen, here we cover our purpose and the types of reader borne in mind when compiling this book, the wide range of learning sources available to you, the book's structure, an overview of its contents and an indication of the main changes in content from previous editions.

Chapter 2 The organisational context

We consider the broader aspects surrounding the HR function, as well as the wide range of activities involved in its execution. We pay attention to the different types of organisation and organisational structures in which practitioners may work, as well as including the concepts of customer care and stakeholders. The effects of the internal corporate culture and the external corporate environment are summarised, noting the types of action that practitioners can take. This latest edition:

- expands and updates the section on public sector organisations
- introduces the 'third sector' comprising charities, social enterprises, etc
- adds a section on the organisation of the HR function and the shared services environment
- updates the section on skills shortages.

Trade unions and their role in formulating collective agreements are described, and there is a brief examination of the role of the Advisory, Conciliation and Arbitration Service (Acas).

Chapter 3 The legal background

Building on the external influences on organisations that we examine in Chapter 2, in this chapter we address the complex area of legislation. We concentrate on the employment law aspects and provide a summary of the relevant legislation under four main headings:

- civil law and, in particular, contracts of employment
- employment protection rights, concentrating on the important issues of unfair dismissal and equal opportunities
- other statutory legislation, covering the broad areas of health and safety and human rights (data protection is covered in Chapter 10 *Information and communication technology in HR*)
- trade unions and their role in formulating collective agreements.

Now we start the process of homing in on specific groups of HR activities.

Chapter 4 Job analysis

This is a new chapter for this fifth edition in which we examine the importance of good job analysis in relation to HR activities before considering jobs in three categories. We look at the most commonly used approaches to job analysis and job design. Also in this chapter we describe job evaluation in a new level of detail for this new edition and look at the process for and some of the implications of using job evaluation.

Chapter 5 Recruitment and selection

Taking into account the legal setting, we consider the processes of:

- recruitment – job analysis (job descriptions, person specifications and competency frameworks) and advertising, including Internet advertising
- selection – collecting information on candidates via application forms, various types of interviews, aptitude and personality tests and assessment centre performances, and assessing and comparing candidates (with specific guidance on good interviewing practice)
- making an offer – conditional offers and employment checks
- induction – of new starters
- evaluation – of the whole process.

In this latest edition, we have provided more information on the changing nature of the workforce affected by such things as demographic change and the variety of resourcing options this presents to employers, and have covered the growing area of employment checks as well as updating legislative references.

Chapter 6 Performance management

First we consider what performance management is and examine the differences between performance appraisal and the broader concept of performance management. In this latest edition we have updated the references to recent trends in performance management practices in UK organisations, including dealing with poor performance. We use a case study to demonstrate the need for all performance management systems to be closely integrated and directed towards achieving business goals. Performance appraisal is looked at in some detail: its purposes, motivational effects, history and trends, and the various components requiring consideration when designing a new scheme. We also address various theories of motivation. We include a section on giving and receiving feedback. Although we touch on payment systems, including financial and non-financial rewards, more information on this is contained in the new chapter on reward (see below). The legal references have also been updated.

Chapter 7 Reward

This is another new chapter for this fifth edition, and in it we look at definitions of reward and why it is such an important issue. We consider the different types of pay systems and structures in some detail, and explore the use of flexible benefits. We also look at non-pay reward and pensions. We examine the link between pay and performance and pay and motivation. We take a detailed look at the legal aspects of reward, including equal pay concerns. Finally we consider the different things that impact on decisions about pay in organisations and where supporting information can be found.

Chapter 8 Employee relations

In this chapter we survey the changing nature of employee relations and examine individual conflicts, looking at disciplinary rules and grievance procedures against the backdrop of relevant employment legislation. We update the situation following the demise of the statutory procedures and we look at the new Acas Code. We provide tips on good practice in carrying out disciplinary, capability and grievance interviews, and highlight the need for an organisation to follow the correct procedures at all times. We stress that poor handling of conduct or capability cases increases the risk of claims to employment tribunals of unfair dismissal, and that employee relations problems may result from the mismanagement of formal grievances. A section on absence management tools is also featured in this chapter. We additionally include a new section on bullying and harassment.

The importance of employee involvement is emphasised when considering triggers for potential collective conflicts, in both unionised and non-unionised environments. As in Chapter 3, we cover the impact of the information and consultation regulations, and we provide further information on the role of the psychological contract in employee relations.

Chapter 9 Learning and development

In this chapter we look at definitions of learning and development and then work through the stages of the training cycle, starting with the identification of learning needs and proceeding through the stages of planning, implementing and evaluating. We consider important issues such as the range of available learning and development techniques and individuals' preferred learning styles. In addition, we consider national initiatives such as Investors in People and National Vocational Qualifications. Other sections reflect the relevance of competencies, changing technology and e-learning. This latest edition explains the relevance of the chapter content to HR, updates some of the terminology, and cites new learning opportunities; these opportunities should be read in conjunction with Chapter 10.

Chapter 10 Information and communication technology in HR

This chapter has been extensively revised and expanded for this new-titled edition to reflect the increasing knowledge and net-awareness of our readers. The implications of the data protection code are spelled out in stressing the importance of keeping accurate HR records (manual and/or computerised). The chapter contents reflect technological changes and the increasing importance not just of the Internet but also of Web 2.0 and the read-write capabilities of the World Wide Web. The section on email and Internet use has been expanded and a new section on confidentiality, openness and Web 2.0 added, highlighting the implications of these developments for HR practitioners.

Chapter 11 Change in organisations

This is a new chapter for this fifth edition. In it we look at why change is important and why organisations need to change. We reflect that change has become almost a constant state for many organisations in a fast-moving world and as such will be something all HR practitioners will become experienced in dealing with. We consider different tools, techniques and approaches for managing change and then move on to consider in some detail the impact of change on individuals. We also look at individual responses to change and consider the different behaviours that those affected by change might display. We examine the impact of change on the psychological contract and look at different approaches to supporting employees through change.

Chapter 12 Personal effectiveness

The final chapter, incorporating minor revisions, seeks to provide further guidance on the variety of skills necessary for effective performance in an HR role. We examine the broad issue of self-development before covering the following skills areas:

- communication – report-writing, making presentations and making a business case for introducing change
- negotiating, influencing and persuading – in formal and informal situations
- counselling – for example, in handling redundancies, early retirements, sickness absence and personal problems
- time management – in and outside the workplace
- assertiveness – in work-related and personal situations.

Finally, we refer to the emphasis placed nowadays by a large number of professional associations such as the CIPD on the concept of continuing professional development (CPD). The main focus of this concept is the proposition that learning (and the acquisition of knowledge and skills) is not a one-off process but one that should carry on throughout your working life. We have tried to reinforce this message, and hope that it is one you take to heart at this, the beginning of a new learning experience.

CHAPTER 2

The organisational context

LEARNING OUTCOMES

After reading this chapter you will:

- appreciate the type of activities in which HR practitioners may be involved
- recognise the type of organisation for which you work and the main implications for you as a practitioner
- recognise how the HR function is structured in your organisation
- grasp the main principles of the customer care and the stakeholder concepts
- know the behaviours involved in good customer care
- be able to distinguish administrative, advisory and executive tasks as carried out in the HR function
- be able to develop links with your management team, your employees and the community
- have a broad understanding of the role of trade unions and be aware of the services of Acas
- be able to understand the key roles and tasks of the HR function and its contribution to organisational success
- understand the concept of outsourcing functions and services.

INTRODUCTION

Because the HR function operates within an organisational context, we shall be considering the nature of organisations and the relationships that HR practitioners need to establish with managers, trade unions and employees. The corporate environment is also important, and this includes the effect of changes that occur in that wider environment.

We believe that the HR role is the most interesting and exciting one in any organisation. It may be a cliché that people are an organisation's greatest asset, but no organisation exists without people and nothing is achieved except through their efforts. HR practices therefore go to the heart of the organisation and potentially have a role in every facet of its activities. As an HR practitioner, you could conceivably be called on to help solve very personal individual problems.

Equally, you could be asked to contribute to major strategic policy decisions in the boardroom. Quite possibly, both could happen on the same day.

Organisations of different sizes and in different sectors organise and structure HR in different ways and use different models of service delivery. We will touch on some of this throughout the chapter, including the concept of HR shared services and also the importance of customer care within the context of HR services. Because we consider it important for you to understand your role, each chapter in this book will comment on the HR practitioner's role in the context of the material covered by that chapter. Here we are taking an overview of HR practice within the context of the organisation.

We will start by looking at the environment in which your organisation exists.

EXTERNAL ENVIRONMENT

We do not need to look far to see tremendous change in our society. Indeed, change is the third great certainty – the other two being death and taxes! Look back over the last 10 years and consider the increase in the number of smaller businesses created in that period. Reflect on the effect that the Internet and social networking has, and on the implications for your employer, for society and for yourself. Look at the impact of European legislation where regulation of equality and health and safety are just two effects in the employment area alone. How many employees have experienced redundancy? To what extent have 'green' issues come to the fore?

The environment in which organisations operate is wide, and change originates from six areas which may be summarised with the mnemonic PESTLE. The areas are:

- **P**olitical – changes brought about by powerful bodies such as governments, the European Union (EU), the trade union movement and regulatory bodies
- **E**conomic – economic climate, interest rates (which affect the cost of borrowing and, potentially, company profitability), skills shortages, consumer debt, demand for goods, import tariffs and the creation of the euro
- **S**ocial – one-parent families, an ageing population, consumer expectations, demographic changes (changes in the structure of the population), immigrant workers, lifestyles, consumer attitudes to social, environmental and other issues
- **T**echnological – developments in medicine, mobile phones, energy sources, the Internet
- **L**egal – new laws originating from Acts of Parliament, interpretations of the law by the courts (both domestic and European), international laws (for example, covering disposal of waste at sea)
- **E**nvironmental – climatic change, holes in the ozone layer, pollution.

The sources of change are often interrelated. The move toward equal opportunities for women (a legal change), for example, was spurred on by social change (women's liberation). But for organisations, 'Change is inevitable – in a progressive organisation change is constant' (Peter Wickens). Managers must anticipate and respond to the effects that such changes have on their organisations, if the latter are to remain viable. Training is often an important response, so we shall look at these areas again in more detail in Chapter 9.

There are some serious implications arising from the changing environment for employees. Smaller organisations mean fewer opportunities for promotion from one level to another. But rapid growth in the size of an organisation may compensate for this, offering other opportunities. To be effective in this changing world, you as HR practitioners must keep in close touch with changes in the external environment, with employees, and with the community at large. Doing so will help you to anticipate and respond effectively to people issues. You will find that change is a recurring theme throughout this book. Reading the CIPD's magazine *People Management* and keeping in touch with current affairs is an important part of this process.

We will look more closely at how you might keep in touch with employees and the community in a later section on *Building bridges* (page 31). Here, though, we will first examine the corporate environment in which an HR function operates.

CHARACTERISTICS OF ORGANISATIONS

Organisations exist for different purposes and in a wide variety of sectors. Thus there exist organisations of very different types. The activities and functions to be seen in a manufacturing company differ markedly from those in a recruitment agency, for example.

An organisation of any size will be subdivided into different functions. In a traditional shoe manufacturing company, these might include groups of people responsible for purchasing, manufacturing, sales, finance, design and HR. Raw materials are purchased, shoes are manufactured and they are sold.

Manufacturing activities form a 'line' from supplier to customer. The people working in these functions are often referred to as being 'in the line' and their managers as 'line managers'. Costs associated with these functions are referred to as 'direct' costs.

People working in other functions such as finance, design and HR are not part of the line because the product does not pass through their responsibilities on the route from suppliers to customers. Often they are referred to as 'staff' functions. Costs associated with these functions are referred to as 'overheads'.

In a recruitment agency, however, some HR activities such as selection could be regarded as 'line' activities. Indeed, a large recruitment agency may have HR practitioners in both line and staff functions.

Staff functions are supportive to the main task or purpose of the business. One disadvantage for support staff is that they may be seen as less important because they are a cost and do not bring in business directly. An advantage is that they can often be nearer the heart of the business strategy and are impartial when it comes to conflict between line functions. For example, an HR practitioner (who is a staff rather than a line manager) should be involved in discussions about how to attract talented candidates. This is close to the business strategy because it can affect business decisions, such as where the organisation locates its operations geographically.

Not all organisations are commercial, and one way of distinguishing some characteristics that are important to the HR practitioner is to look and see to whom the organisation is accountable – for example, to shareholders, to a trust or to a government department. These characteristics will, in part, determine how practitioners should seek to influence others in the organisation.

It has been said that organisations do not have objectives – it is people who have objectives. Because of this it is also important for you to look at those people who have the greatest influence over the direction of your organisation. The circumstances surrounding them, their motivations and their accountability will exert a marked effect on what is regarded as important within any organisation.

We will look at some examples of different organisations and the accountability of their senior people.

The small private limited company

The owners of a small private company may well have much of their personal capital invested in the business. Although their liability is limited (to the capital they have invested in the business), they may find themselves in considerable financial difficulty if the business fails. In taking such risks they are usually seeking significant financial gain. Inevitably, this will affect how they view activities that may be desirable but which do not produce income. But it does not necessarily mean that wealth creation is the only or even the prime motivation. In such a company the chief executive is likely to have a clear 'vision' of where he or she wants the company to go and to be totally committed to the success of the enterprise.

You need to try to recognise this vision and relate your responsibilities towards achieving it. It will invariably help if you can also relate your activities to profit, productivity, risk reduction and the assistance of business growth.

The partnership

Partners who have equity in the business (who in effect have invested their own capital) may be of comparable standing with each other, especially in a small partnership. This often means that all the partners must be prepared to go along with proposals that you may make. However, in larger partnerships many matters will be delegated to a managing partner, a managing team or similar body. The influence that any individual partner has will be determined by the structure of each particular firm and his or her position in it.

Partnerships are common in the professions. Professional firms seek to maximise fee-earning activities and minimise activities that do not attract fees. It will be important to recognise this. Reducing the time that partners spend on problems associated with people management will be seen as a valuable contribution.

Many professional firms are limited liability partnerships (LLP), a form of partnership which protects the individual partners in the event that the partnership becomes bankrupt.

The public limited company – 'plc'

The shares in a public limited company are usually traded on the stock exchange. This can have a number of effects – for example, the senior members of the company may from time to time be heavily engrossed with how the shares are trading and with all the figures that influence how company performance is viewed. One knock-on effect of this is that you could be under pressure to keep very accurate figures about the numbers of employees. Public limited companies are hugely varied in their characteristics and range in size from small to multinational, but they are all strongly commercial because they have to provide a return for their investors.

You may work for a small subsidiary company of a large plc, or even for a small site within such a company. How much independence smaller units of that kind have depends on the approach of the parent company.

In some cases the chief executive may have his or her own vision and be able to manage the company with a fair level of independence, treating the parent company almost as if it were a banker. Such chief executives are not usually at as much financial risk as private owners. Although the chief executives may have shares in the organisation, they are unlikely to be rendered bankrupt personally if the business were to fail. Nevertheless, failure might bring serious consequences for their careers.

In other cases subsidiary companies may be subject to a strong corporate identity and firm control from the parent company. If this is the case, your chief executive is likely to be concerned with how his or her performance is viewed by the parent company, and this may influence how you or your senior managers relate to the chief executive.

Many factors influence the attitudes in any large commercial company: where the company's product might be in its life cycle, its position in its marketplace, the nature of its marketplace (whether it is growing or declining) and its edge, or otherwise, over competitors. In general, the more prosperous and secure the company, the more it is likely to invest in good employee relations. In companies that are less prosperous or suffering declining sales, you will have to work harder to get new ideas adopted and there may be a need to consider more difficult issues such as redundancy.

Public sector organisations

Organisations in the public sector can be very different from those described above. Public sector organisations are likely to have a hierarchical structure (see the next section) with more clearly defined jobs and positions than are generally found in the private sector.

The emphasis in the public sector is on service delivery and is underpinned by the public service ethos and the specific requirements placed on public servants. These organisations are significantly affected by government policy and changes in government at election time. For many organisations in the public sector, change and large-scale reorganisation prompted by political decisions has become a constant. In most public sector organisations there will be employed executives at a senior level in day-to-day control of the organisation, plus some 'lay' involvement through, for example, local councillors and non-executive directors. In some public sector organisations – for example, the NHS – a strong influence will also be exerted by professional bodies who regulate, register and train professional groups – for example, the medical Royal Colleges. Government organisations exist to implement government policies either locally or nationally. In addition, all spending is subject to the scrutiny of the Audit Office, which is independent of government and reports to Parliament directly on the effective use of public money.

Public sector organisations have to comply with European Directives, because failure to do so can render them liable to action in European courts. There are also various statutory duties placed on them by legislation. For example, within HR there are statutory duty codes of practice relating to equality issues. Private sector organisations have to comply with UK legislation and must be aware of the obligations of public organisations (such as employment tribunals). However, they do not have to comply directly with European Directives until they have been translated into UK law.

Government organisations therefore exist in a precise environment in which policies, procedures and actions are generally well documented.

It is important to be mindful of this as an HR practitioner. Those to whom you might report are likely to be very conscious of risks, accountability and compliance with legislation.

Some public sector organisations are centrally funded but relatively independent of direct accountability to an electorate, although there will still be accountability to government ministers and, increasingly, representatives of the local community, through such organisations as NHS Foundation Trusts. Universities, the NHS, local education authorities and various government agencies such as the Benefits Agency all account to the government and Parliament to a greater or lesser degree. Independence is provided by various funding arrangements, but when funds are granted, the grant is invariably subject to conditions that can restrict the level of independence.

Government control is also exercised in a variety of other ways. For example, league tables are used to monitor the performance of schools and universities, among others. Inspection authorities are used to assess standards, share best practice and assist continuous improvement – for example, the Office for Standards in Education (OFSTED) monitors performance in schools and colleges, while the Care Quality Commission inspects and reviews performance in the NHS, social services and the private care sector. The Audit Office monitors the organisation's activities, and tendering processes are used to ensure that services provided by public bodies and agencies are at a competitive level.

In such organisations it is inevitable that there will be a preoccupation with the measures used to determine performance and thus access to funds. Inspection processes require a focus on quality, good governance arrangements and good documentation. HR practitioners must familiarise themselves with the funding arrangements and control processes that exist in their own organisation if they are to contribute appropriately to meeting objectives.

The third sector

There is an increasing level of employment in what is often called 'the third sector'. This includes charities, employers of volunteers, and social enterprise organisations.

> Broadly, we define a social enterprise as a business with primarily social objectives. Surpluses are re-invested for the purpose in the business or in the community, rather than distributed as dividends to shareholders ... Social enterprises can encompass everything from mutuals, employee-owned businesses, private companies limited by guarantee or cooperatives.
>
> Douglas Alexander, *Social Enterprise* magazine, February 2002

Funding for these organisations can come from donations of various kinds but also from bodies in the public sector such as social services or primary care trusts. Charities can tap into public funds by providing services that might otherwise have been provided from within the public sector. The hospice movement is a good example.

Sometimes these organisations report to voluntary boards of trustees who appoint managers to administer day-to-day operations. There can be some important stakeholders in social enterprise companies (we expand on the term stakeholder later in the chapter) depending on the type of activity in which a company is engaged – for example, the public sector bodies already mentioned, the Charities Commission and various regulatory bodies such as the Care Quality Commission.

In many cases those in the third sector are motivated by altruistic rather than by hard commercial interests. Nonetheless, to have profits to re-invest they need to be reasonably astute and realistic about business.

Regulated organisations/sectors

Some organisations operating in certain parts of the private sector do so under significant regulatory control. An example of this is the care sector where residential homes (in England) are subject to the Health and Social Care Act. Homes can be inspected and there are specific expectations about such matters as induction, employment policies and procedures, health and safety, and many operational matters. Meeting inspection standards can be a major responsibility for managers in regulated sectors, in addition to the commercial pressures mentioned above.

Other organisations

It is important to realise that we have only scratched the surface here in terms of the types of organisations and the issues they may regard as important. We have not mentioned mutual societies (owned by their members), the armed forces, the police, nationalised industries or public-private partnerships – and even this list is not exhaustive.

ACTIVITY 2.1

Look carefully at your own organisation. What is specific to your organisation that distinguishes it from other organisations? To whom is it ultimately accountable? What is regarded as important? Are there regulations or inspections that affect how the business should operate? Discuss your conclusions with appropriate learning sources within and, for comparison, outside your organisation.

ORGANISATION STRUCTURES

Hierarchical

In a typical hierarchical structure each member of staff reports to an immediate superior and there are several 'layers' between the most junior and the most senior individuals. As a general rule each person has a relatively small 'span of control' with no more than five or six people reporting to him or her.

If the organisation is large, each job is likely to be specialised and may be closely defined. For example, within the HR function alone there may be separate departments for employee relations, apprentice training, staff training, management development, recruitment, and compensation and benefits. Such subdivisions will be reflected in other parts of the organisation.

Typically, each person reports to only one immediate superior to whom he or she is accountable for all job responsibilities. In practice, there can be some reporting to another person, often referred to as a 'dotted-line' responsibility because it may be shown by means of a dotted line on the organisation chart. For example, a factory HR manager might report to a head office HR director, but have a dotted-line relationship to the factory manager.

Hierarchies are characterised by protocol to varying degrees from the very informal to the strict. Conventions place restrictions on who talks to whom about what. Accountants do not often venture on to the shop floor, nor do sales people always talk to operatives. When one of the authors organised a Works Open Day, it was the first time most of the office staff (of whom some had been there decades) had seen the company's products being made. In a hierarchical organisation with very established protocols there can be little sideways communication between departments, all disagreements being reported upwards. These protocols arise for a variety of reasons – practical geography, communication channels, social interaction, personal background, professional pride and sometimes prejudices – but they can also help senior individuals maintain political power bases for security and reward.

It should be said that these very traditional approaches are under threat simply because they are ineffective. For example, in the NHS and associated bodies, great efforts are put into breaking down such barriers and getting people to work in multi-disciplinary/multi-agency ways.

For the purposes of looking more closely at organisation structures, we shall now use the example of a typical manufacturing company.

Figure 2.1 represents an illustration of this hierarchical structure. A salesperson may become aware of a customer need. In many cases he or she will have little or no contact with a product designer, perhaps partly due to geography but often because salespeople do not talk to designers. So the great idea has to travel up the organisation, through the regional manager to the sales director, who might talk to his or her colleague, the design and development director. When the idea finally reaches the designer, there may be an unforeseen problem.

Figure 2.1 A hierarchical organisation

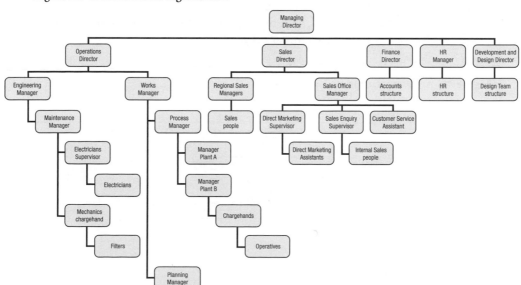

Does the designer then talk to the salesperson? The answer is 'It depends …' on many relationships, on protocol and on other organisational matters (such as geography). We touch on this in Chapter 4 when we describe the 'elevator structure' and the importance of inter-relationships across an organisation.

ACTIVITY 2.2

How many layers are there in your employer's organisation? Look for the most junior member and count the links between him/her and the chief executive officer (or other most senior post). You are likely to find that the number varies for different functions in your organisation. If you are familiar with another organisation (a partner's or relative's employer, for example), count the number of levels there. What does this information tell you about that organisation?

The need to reduce costs in order to meet international competition has led many companies to downsize their workforce, with consequential de-layering of the organisational structure. As well as reducing both costs and bureaucracy, downsizing and de-layering can often lead to much more effective internal communications. However, companies have to be careful to avoid downsizing to such an extent that the remaining staff only have time to deal with day-to-day operational activities and strategic thinking is driven out of the organisation altogether. The concept of 'shared services', which we shall explain later, often separates day-to-day activities from more strategic thinking.

Flatter organisations

This trend towards smaller organisations and flatter structures reduces the likelihood of protracted decision-making. With fewer organisational layers, individuals have easier access to senior decision-makers. However, each person is likely to be in greater demand, with many people reporting to him or her, and people at all levels need to have a wider range of skills.

Figure 2.2 A flatter structure

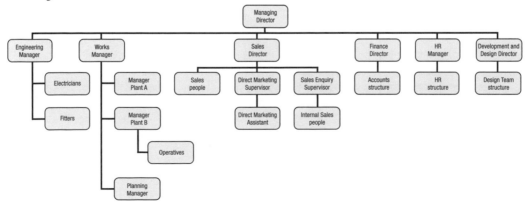

In a small company the HR practitioner may need to handle a range of HR activities. In larger but flat-structured companies, HR staff may still have a narrower responsibility (say, recruitment) but could find that they have to balance the needs of all the other functions in the organisation (sales and production, for example) rather than relying on one boss to set the priorities. This demands a greater understanding of the organisation's wider operations and its priorities.

In flat organisations individuals sometimes report to more than one boss, in what can be called a matrix structure. For example, the HR manager may be responsible to the factory manager, the sales manager, the distribution manager and the head office head of HR, all in approximately equal measures.

In this flatter type of organisation HR practitioners who want to introduce a new application form can talk to all their colleagues directly. When everyone is convinced of the benefits of the change, the practitioners can introduce the new form. By contrast, practitioners in a strict hierarchical structure would have to convince their immediate boss and (if they are lucky) the boss would then convince his or her own boss. Eventually a decision will be taken at a level sufficiently high for all the practitioners' colleagues to 'fall in line', and the new application form may be imposed from above.

Here we have looked at two important and relatively common forms of organisation structure. There are other forms – and even these two cannot be precisely defined, since they exist to varying degrees in different organisations.

If you want to influence decision-making, you need to understand how your organisation is structured and how decision-making takes place.

ACTIVITY 2.3

If you wanted to introduce a new recruitment application form (to reflect changes in legislation, perhaps), how would you go about getting a decision made? Which of the above scenarios most closely represents what ought to happen in your organisation? Is there another scenario that would apply? Discuss your conclusions with an appropriate learning source.

CORPORATE CULTURE

As we said earlier, HR activities take place within an organisation. This means that your role – what you do, and how you do it – is inevitably influenced, or even constrained, by the organisation's nature or corporate culture, not just by its formal structure.

It is valuable to understand your organisation: it will help you decide how to earn some 'brownie points'. It may be that you do not want to advance your career in terms of responsibility. But identifying and performing well in those activities that are valued will enhance the esteem in which you are held, your influence and, perhaps, your salary. If you are an employee of a shared services or an outsourced services provider, then knowing your client or clients may be important too, depending on your level of engagement with them. A drawback for companies that undertake outsourced activities is that they may be unfamiliar with the culture of their client organisation, especially if they are located on a separate site.

If you have changed employers during your working life, you will appreciate how they differ even within the same industrial sector. The differences between large and small organisations, between the various industrial sectors, and between public and private are even more marked.

Don't assume that the ways in which tasks are carried out in your organisation – say, the way in which job descriptions are prepared – is the only approach or, indeed, a necessary approach. Many companies, for example, survive profitably without job descriptions.

Within your organisation, observe the characteristics or 'culture' of different departments. In our experience, sales teams are often characterised by positive, outgoing attitudes and a preoccupation with status, targets, performance and reward (for example, the commission scheme).

Production teams are more likely to evince a 'no-nonsense' attitude, be driven by meeting deadlines, and reject what they see as 'time-wasting' activities (such as writing job descriptions, perhaps).

The predominant corporate culture will depend on the nature of the business. A trading company is likely to be driven by sales attitudes. A manufacturing company is more likely to be characterised by production attitudes. There are many ways of identifying and describing corporate culture. Table 2.1 gives examples of some other differences that characterise culture.

ACTIVITY 2.4

Think about other departments in your organisation, such as purchasing, finance, research and development, marketing, and data-processing, as well as the HR department. What characterises people in those departments in terms of attitudes to, and concern with, the following issues: deadlines, accuracy, documentation, cost, profit, status, ethics and personal financial reward?

ACTIVITY 2.5

Reflect on your employer and another employer with whom you are reasonably familiar – perhaps a friend's or your partner's employer. Make a list of the differences in attitude and concerns as outlined in Activity 2.4, and any other differences that are appropriate. How do you account for the differences?

Table 2.1 Cultural indicators

Business aspect	Indicators of corporate culture
The nature of reporting relationships	Does everyone have one established manager, or do managers change frequently in response to business needs?
The management style	Are employees managed by instruction and control, or by consultation and personal development?
Pay	Is it fixed or linked to performance, grading, or 'merit'?
Employees	Are they valued? If so, how is this obvious?
Customer care	Are customers valued? If so, how is it obvious?
Costs	Do they matter? How does their importance compare with potential income?
Profit	Are employees conscious of profit? Is it relevant or important?
Business objectives	Do employees identify with business objectives?
Status symbols	What role do they play? Are they a substitute for power or remuneration?
Ethics	Are ethics important? If so, how is it obvious?
Risks	What are the consequences of making a mistake?
Regulators	Is there a regulator for the sector? How does this affect the way operational and other tasks are valued and performed?

There is a series of indicators to show whether an organisation has a positive or negative culture (see Table 2.2 overleaf).

ACTIVITY 2.6

Look at the positive and negative indicators shown in Table 2.2 overleaf. How does your employer compare with the examples given? Is there a positive or negative culture prevailing? Look ahead at the section on *Building bridges* on page 31. Are there any actions you can take that would increase a positive perspective, particularly in the relationship between HR practitioners, employees, their representatives and the management team?

Table 2.2 Positive and negative indicators of corporate culture

Aspect	Positive indicators	Negative indicators
Organisational and personal pride	'Company problems are our only work problems'	'What do I care? – I only work here'
Performance/excellence	A success orientation	'It's good enough'
Teamwork/communication	Communication is open and two-way	Destructive conflict and unnecessary competition
Leadership and supervision	Leaders and supervisors are concerned with people and productivity	Leaders and supervisors see their role as checking and policing subordinates
Profitability and cost-effectiveness	People see a connection between profits and their well-being as employees	Opportunities for cost savings and increased sales are neglected or overlooked
Relationships with colleagues	People work hard to see that all colleagues are treated with dignity and respect	Company and employees tend to look at each other as having separate interests
Customer and consumer relations	Customer satisfaction is seen as vital to personal and organisational success	The customer and consumer tend to be looked upon as a kind of unavoidable burden
Honesty and safety	Safety regulations are taken seriously: people place a high value on integrity and support integrity in others	People are careless with company money or products, and neglectful in following or enforcing safety practices
Learning and development	Learning and development are looked upon as an integral part of all that occurs within the organisation	Learning is seen as unimportant and barely related to the day-to-day work
Motivation and change	People are eager to consider new and innovative approaches	People look at new ways of doing things with unwarranted suspicion or mistrust

Source: Based on work by Allen and Pilnick, and adapted from Edwards (1988)

WHAT SHOULD AN HR PRACTITIONER ACHIEVE?

That very much depends on your employer's expectations. Unless you work for a 'sole trader' (someone who is self-employed – see Chapter 3), your employer will be an organisation.

You may notice that in this book we refer to 'organisations' frequently, although we may from time to time use related terms such as 'employer', 'business' or 'company' where it might be more appropriate. 'Organisation', though, is a convenient term because the points being made will generally apply whether the 'organisation' is a small private enterprise or a multinational, a small charity or a government department.

We've looked at organisation structures above and given some general guidelines on the different types and some implications for practitioners.

Nevertheless, each organisation is unique and the models in this book will vary in their applicability to a greater or lesser extent with those different organisations. This is one of the reasons why we stress the importance of using learning sources in the first chapter.

It is therefore wise to think through the fundamental nature of the organisation for which you work in order to understand what your employer may expect of you.

It is time to look at what the members of an organisation expect of HR or personnel practitioners.

ACTIVITY 2.7

If you are an HR or training practitioner, prepare a 30-word statement describing the purpose of your job. (If you are not yet in the function, speculate on the purpose of someone who is in such a position in your organisation.) Ask yourself:

- Why do I have a job?
- What would happen if the tasks I do were not completed?
- How might my contribution be measured?

Human resources management in the United Kingdom can trace its origins back to the early part of the last century when welfare workers were appointed by organisations to exercise care towards employees. Personnel management, as a business function, assumed prominence in the latter half of the twentieth century. Over recent years there has been a substantial growth in use of the term 'human resources' or HR. Originally, a more strategic perception was associated with human resources – a view that it was a tougher, less people-sensitive function, and closer to the decision-makers. Today the terms are, arguably, indistinguishable and in practice they are often used interchangeably.

In 2008 Hall, Torrington and Taylor (2008: 10) offered an excellent description of personnel management as it had traditionally been seen.

> Personnel management is workforce-centred. Personnel specialists direct their efforts mainly at the organisation's employees: finding and training them, arranging for them to be paid, explaining management's expectations, justifying management's actions, satisfying employees' work-related needs, dealing with their problems and seeking to modify management action that could produce unwelcome employee response ... Although indisputably a

management function, personnel is not totally identified with management interests. Personnel managers seek to understand and articulate the aspirations and views of the workforce.

It is worth splitting Hall, Torrington and Taylor's explanation down into its component parts, because it provides a great deal of pertinent information, although our interpretations may not be exactly those made by Taylor, Torrington and Hall.

Finding employees

This is not just a question of advertising and recruiting, although that may be a major task. Effective practitioners build relationships with relevant local bodies such as schools, colleges, job centres, employment agencies, and the community at large. A good profile in the community helps to attract the best candidates. Finding employees is covered in detail in Chapter 5.

Training employees

Occasionally this is a separate, or sister, function, but HR and development are professionally linked. 'Training and development' does not mean only arranging training courses. As we shall see later, it can include diverse activities such as identifying needs, planning appropriate responses and evaluating the success of these activities. Training is important, for example, in the induction of employees to an organisation, in health and safety, and in helping an organisation to respond effectively to change. (See Chapter 11.)

Arranging payments

For many staff administrators in small organisations, administering the payroll is the entry route into HR practice. Paying employees regularly, properly and on time is a contractual obligation backed up by legislation (the Employment Rights Act 1996, for example). Proper authority, accuracy and absolute meeting of deadlines are vital issues for payroll staff. Because of this, a payroll officer should be allowed to work to a regular routine and not be interrupted by other priorities. The demands of working in an HR office can be slightly different – a point of which those making the transition from payroll to HR need to be aware.

HR aspects of paying employees can, at one extreme, involve clarification of entitlement to individual pay items and, at the other, negotiating pay rates.

It is good practice (to reduce the possibility of fraud) for those who authorise payments (such as HR practitioners) to have separate reporting relationships from those who pay employees (the payroll staff).

Explaining management expectations

While very much a traditional personnel role, HR is often the most appropriate organisational function to explain management decisions that affect staff to staff. The HR practitioners will need to develop necessary communication skills and may need to work closely with trade unions or workplace representatives. Examples of issues which HR practitioners have experience of explaining on behalf of management teams are productivity schemes, health and safety needs, and disciplinary policies and procedures.

A related area is collective agreements made between an organisation's management and a trade union (on behalf of members employed in that organisation). These agreements determine terms and conditions that apply to the employment contract and should therefore be explained by HR in co-operation with the trade union, and not left for shop stewards alone to explain.

Justifying management actions

Where you need to do this, we hope you will have been able to make a contribution to the decisions themselves. Justifying actions that you may not have chosen yourself is one of the greatest challenges for the HR practitioner. It is a central aspect of managerial responsibility that once you have put all your arguments, you accept and implement whatever is decided. That may be stressful, particularly if you have not been able to put those arguments at the right level. Typical actions that HR practitioners might be called on to justify are restructuring and redundancy, reductions in fringe benefits, changes within the place of work, and relocation. An example is provided in Case study 2.1 below.

CASE STUDY 2.1

A company providing services for the public carried out market research and found that it was losing valuable business by not opening on a Saturday. The board decided that it was in the interests of the company to move to Saturday opening – indeed, there was a risk, if it did not, of losing market share, with consequential risks to job security.

In this highly unionised company the trade union representatives were informed of the need to open on a Saturday and the HR manager took time to explain the reasons.

The objective, of opening on a Saturday, was defined and a consultation process was begun with the purpose of finding the most acceptable approach. The HR manager chaired several meetings with both line managers and representatives present.

The outcome was an agreed rota system, which meant that each staff member would work on alternate Saturdays for an agreed premium.

The union representatives felt unable to agree all aspects. Several employees did not wish to work on Saturdays and one in particular objected strongly. The HR manager then became involved in individual consultations. A conclusion was reached that if an exception was made (there was no good reason for one), the whole agreement would 'unravel'.

Together with the general manager, the HR manager held a meeting with all employees, re-emphasised the reasons and gave notice that Saturday opening would go ahead after the summer break (which was adequate notice for ending the contracts). The single employee realised he was on notice and, without compromise to the agreement, the HR manager continued to work with him to try to find a solution. Suitable alternative employment was not possible because Saturday working was a requirement for all jobs. When the notice expired, the employee left, claiming that he had been dismissed (which was correct, of course).

However, all other employees accepted the new terms and Saturday opening was achieved without further disruption.

The important good practice points here are the time taken to consult, a statement of the problem, consultation on a solution, a defensible agreement, proper notice to end one contract, consideration of reasonable alternatives, and the role played by the HR manager. Incidentally, the dismissal was judged to be fair.

Satisfying employees' work-related needs

These are issues such as health and safety, fringe benefits (company vehicles, for example), welfare matters and long-term protection such as life assurance and pensions. In large companies some of these matters may be dealt with by a separate department.

Dealing with employees' problems

Grievances are raised on a huge range of issues. Many of these will be settled by line managers. Those issues that are not will invariably require a relatively 'neutral' broker – an HR practitioner. We look at this in detail in the chapter on discipline and grievance-handling (Chapter 8).

Other employee problems for which you need to be prepared include early retirement, redundancy, debts and bereavement.

Seeking to modify management's actions

An example of a management action may be a move from weekly to monthly pay. The simple modification of providing an interest-free loan may generate acceptability from employees and enable a senior manager to achieve his or her objectives.

HR practitioners should be close to employees and be able to judge what will be acceptable to them. They should also recognise what may damage motivation and commitment, what may cause harmful stress, and what may lead to industrial action.

The very high levels of stress being experienced by employees today and the increasing likelihood of successful claims against employers in tribunals suggest there is a serious challenge here. Unfortunately, HR practitioners are not immune to stress themselves. They may be particularly vulnerable when they fail to modify those management actions that conflict with their own values.

A career in HR, as may have already been pointed out to you, is not a 'soft' option. Confidence, credibility, assertiveness, judgement and emotional resilience are qualities needed by effective practitioners. They are particularly important for those who take on the role of 'business partner', which we shall describe later. Given these qualities, practitioners are more likely to find that senior managers listen to HR practitioners.

We shall also look at how you can develop your personal skills in the chapter on personal effectiveness (Chapter 12).

Understanding and articulating employees' aspirations and views

HR practitioners' capacity to influence management actions depends on their ability to judge the outcomes of those actions. Judging outcomes means understanding the language of the employees; influencing managers means using the language managers understand. Understanding and communicating well with both employees and managers is an important skill for practitioners. You can foster both languages by spending time with each group.

Walking the floor is better than opening the door. Stay in your own office and you will meet only the more confident employees or those with specific issues to resolve, however wide your door may be open. Senior managers have their own language – that of the chief executive, for example, may be different from that of the board members. Management courses and finance or non financial managers courses provide some of the vocabulary. You may be able to learn from social opportunities – talking to senior managers at in-company award ceremonies, for example. There may be external opportunities to learn the decision-makers' language by taking on a responsible community role – for instance, by becoming a school governor or a magistrate.

Employees at your establishment may be represented by trade unions. If so, that is another group with which to develop a good relationship. Our experience has been that those who become involved in trade unions are genuine and articulate people. Their influence can be valuable in resolving differences between employees and management. It is usually easier to resolve a matter with a few representatives than with a whole workforce. Nonetheless, in our view managers must always reserve the right to communicate directly with their own employees.

As we stated earlier, human resources work is largely indistinguishable from personnel work, at least in many organisations. However, 'HR' can conveniently encompass training and development (HRD), health and safety, pensions and other major activities not regarded as pure 'personnel management' work.

Broad though this examination of personnel or HR work may be, it does not include every activity a HR practitioner may be asked to do. You will probably identify activities with which you are involved that are only touched upon here, or even omitted altogether. Managing the company car fleet, editing the company newsletter or carrying out health and safety audits are just three examples. Much of the work that falls to HR departments may not be viewed as strictly HR-related work. Indeed, a prominent twentieth-century management guru, the late Peter Drucker, described the HR department as the 'trash can' department that takes on almost any activity no one else wants!

It is important to find the balance between customer care activities, when you try to 'delight' customers, and taking on 'trash-can' activities, which will not earn any brownie points. The latter are activities that often don't add any value to the organisation, waste your time and do not gain any credit from the people who have influence over your career. Identifying which is which is not always easy; priorities have to be set. You may want to keep an eye on what activities influential people regard as being most important. It is easy to find yourself bogged down in marginal activities.

There is a view that many marginal HR activities should be done by line managers, leaving time for HR practitioners to concentrate on the medium- to long-term strategic issues. At one of our Certificate in HR Practice courses a guest speaker put it succinctly: 'We must avoid becoming embroiled in detailed reactive issues; in essence, more day-to-day HR activities must be the responsibility of line management.' Other approaches to dealing with activities associated with day-to-day issues is to outsource the work or to use a shared services centre.

But first we will look at the types of actions an HR practitioner can take in order to carry out the tasks that may be expected.

WHAT TYPE OF ACTIONS CAN PRACTITIONERS TAKE?

We describe several types of action below. In practice, the types of things that you can do arise from a complex mix of the authority vested in you, your persuasive abilities, your credibility with decision-makers, your responsibilities and the norms of your organisation. To these you should add your own capabilities, risk tolerance, emotional resilience and assertiveness.

Generally, you will have to discover for yourself most of the organisational factors in the mix, but we hope that the section on the characteristics and structure of organisations have given you some pointers. Observing and taking counsel from your boss, others in your department and others in the organisation is the way in which you should consolidate this. Personal effectiveness can be increased through self-development, as we outline later.

However, if you are a newly established 'HR person' within your organisation you will have less advice to draw upon. If you have grown to the position from within the organisation you will already have some idea of the authority you have and your own credibility. If newly appointed, then your manager will probably indicate the boundaries within which you can act. All being well, you will have a job description setting out your main responsibilities and accountabilities (we look at job descriptions in Chapter 5). This job description may indicate your 'authority' – perhaps it specifies a budget – but it is unlikely to be specific about every activity that you will undertake.

One approach is to examine each activity and in each case ask, 'Should I be taking administrative action, advisory action or executive action?' The answer will lie in the factors we discussed above. Let's have a look at each type of action.

Administrative action

This consists of maintaining procedures and operating systems. For example, an HR practitioner may be advised of the outcome of salary negotiations and then be expected to calculate new salaries and notify the payroll department. Other examples are the headcount (regularly establishing the number of employees), recruitment activities, maternity leave and issuing letters of appointment. In the case of administrative activities you will usually be given some specific instructions initially and, if supervised, details of how to carry out the task. This type of work is often assigned to a shared services centre because it it straight forward to delegate.

Advisory action

This assumes that you have some specialist knowledge or information and can provide guidelines for managerial decisions. Areas in which HR practitioners typically advise are disciplinary procedures and employment law. Clear knowledge and understanding here will enhance your credibility considerably. Keep in mind, though, that this is a difficult area – if in any doubt, seek advice from more senior colleagues or the Advisory, Conciliation and Arbitration Service (Acas).

In salary negotiations HR practitioners frequently brief the negotiating team on current remuneration packages or on market rates. They may also be members of the negotiating team.

Advisory actions can also be centralised as shared services utilising a central team to advise local line managers of disciplinary actions they can take. Advisory actions can sometimes be determined by 'expert systems' – essentially a computer providing a question-and-answer process. The questions and answers can be managed by an individual in a call centre or even provided as an e-HR resource for managers to access the advice for themselves. These processes are relatively new and no doubt some will work well and others prove to be unwise, at least initially. Incorporating 'experience' into a computer algorithm (decision-making process) takes time.

The development of policies and procedures may be seen as another form of advisory action. In creating these an HR department is partly providing documented advice and partly engaged with senior members of the organisation to arrive at decisions that will guide managers and others.

Executive action

This means taking full responsibility for certain tasks, making decisions and taking appropriate action. For example, in some organisations an HR practitioner may be sufficiently senior, and authorised, to take the decision to dismiss an employee. Similarly, some practitioners take full responsibility for salary negotiations – that is, for reaching an agreement and implementing it. You will not, of course, be taking such decisions unless you have been very clearly authorised to do so. These types of action are quite likely ones that will be taken by an HR business partner working, of course, in partnership with the line management.

Table 2.3 Activities and tasks of HR departments

Activity	Task	Executive	Advisory	Admin.
Recruitment and selection	Determining methods Defining requirements Advertising Processing applications Interviewing Taking part in decisions Organising programmes Offering jobs Taking up references			
Industrial relations	Attending meetings Applying agreements Acting as a specialist Advising on law Participating in procedures			
Direction and policy	Developing policy External relations			
Health, safety and welfare	Counselling Occupational health Pensions			
Pay administration	Instructions to pay Initiating transactions Dealing with complaints			
Manpower – planning and control	Maintaining records Controlling numbers			
Learning and development	Identifying needs Providing learning			
Employee communications	Planning Operating			
Organisation design	Job descriptions			
Information and records	Determining needs Providing information			

Source: Adapted from Farnham (1999: 114)

ACTIVITY 2.8

Study Table 2.3 above. Identify activities and tasks that take place in your HR department.

Now identify the types of action that your department takes, placing a tick in the appropriate column(s).

Circle those actions that you might take yourself.

Discuss the results with others in a similar position in different organisations.

How do the activities of your department differ from theirs?

This brings us to how you build good links between yourself, your management team, employees and the community. This is an important task, representing a whole group of actions that you can take. They will enable you to relate effectively to others in the organisation.

Building bridges

Spend some time considering the questions below and the discussion that follows each. They should give you some clues as to how you can develop the links we have just mentioned.

- What are your methods of communication?

  In face-to-face spoken communication only a small proportion of the communication is conveyed by the words used. Estimates vary, but it is somewhere in the region of 6 to 10%. The remainder depends on body language, eye contact, pitch, speed, volume, and tone of voice. So when we use the telephone, body language and eye contact are lost, and volume and tone can be altered by the telephone line to some extent. When we use email, what is left? We see this as a particular problem for shared services because emails can easily sound blunt. It is worth taking care in composing emails. We suggest that all employees need increasingly to develop keyboard skills so that they can respond using normal language. Responses abbreviated because a full grammatical sentence takes too long to type are too easily open to misinterpretation. Compose, read, amend, re-read, amend, re-read and send is one way of improving the written tone of emails.

- How do employees make contact with you?

  Interruptions are a major source of inefficiency, but at the same time you cannot afford to be remote. Is your department close to where most employees work? Is your department found easily? An open door encourages contact, whereas a formal appointment system may discourage it. For a larger department a 'front desk' helps avoid the whole department being interrupted by an enquiry. Intranets, perhaps with a Frequently Asked Questions page or a dedicated e-HR page, may be an effective way of reducing interruptions while also answering employees' questions. Placing HR policies and procedures on an intranet or online also enables employees to answer questions (such as about maternity leave) for themselves.

- How do you make contact with employees?

Making time to 'walk the floor' can ensure that employees know who you are, foster contact and help you to assess the general mood and spot any changes in mood. It takes time, of course, on your part and on that of employees. Furthermore, not all management teams will welcome direct contacts between you and (their) employees in this way. Another approach is to make a habit of going to see employees directly to deal with matters that arise, rather than telephoning, calling them to your office or issuing an email. You can inform the employee's manager first, if protocol requires it.

CASE STUDY 2.2

A successful 'walking the floor' strategy is demonstrated in this example. With the support of the managing director (who dealt with most protocol issues), the HR manager blocked out two hours each week to walk the shop floor. During the week he stored up suitable issues with which to approach particular individuals. These were not serious matters (they might otherwise have been handled by a memo or a telephone call) but he found it easier to discuss some relevant issue than simply to make small talk. He also made a note of where he had been each week so as to try to see everyone in the factory over the course of time. If stopped en route by an employee he made time to stop and talk.

He soon found it easier and easier to talk to individuals without having to have a particular purpose, and he began to look forward to the weekly exercise. When, at a later stage, major changes were required on the shop floor it was much easier for him to explain the need for the changes, and he could expect to be trusted.

- How good are your relationships with trade union representatives?

Keeping representatives in touch with issues that concern their members helps build good relationships. You need to be careful what you do discuss, consulting senior management members first if you have any doubts. Nevertheless, making time to talk with the representatives and taking an interest in their viewpoint can be revealing, and you may very probably see your organisation in a different light. Often you will pick up minor issues that you can remedy, or more serious ones in which you can still have an influence. We provide some background on trade unions in the section below.

- Are you in touch with your management team?

Using email is efficient and promotes good time management. On the other hand, using the telephone or visiting individuals may be more effective and, crucially, builds relationships. Face to face is even more effective in communication, as we discussed above. Be mindful of people's time and the pressures on them. Nonetheless, most managers enjoy discussing issues face to face. A useful tip is to stand up for informal meetings, thus encouraging contact to be short. The tip also works for telephone calls, because your voice changes when you stand up – it conveys more urgency. Attend relevant formal meetings. Some organisations have a 'meetings' culture, in which case you will probably want to attend as few as possible. Whatever the culture, try to be present at important meetings and go along prepared to make a positive contribution.

- Does the community regard your organisation as a good employer?

The manner in which you recruit, respond to unsolicited applications and reject unsuccessful job applicants is often commented upon, especially if you are in a small community. Contact between the community and a major local employer invariably increases the regard in which that employer is held. It may also provide you with valuable information – and liaison between HR practitioners and local bodies, such as schools or societies, is usually welcomed. If community activities interest you, you may be able to foster links in the community by being active in, for example, the Chambers of Commerce, or in the various clubs for executive, professional and business people.

- What is the department's profile?

The quality of communications can help set the scene. Here we are thinking of examples such as induction information and the staff handbook, notices on the noticeboards, clarity of payslips, notification of pay increases, web pages and contributions to the company newsletter. The tone of communications, even the tone in the staff handbook, sends messages. We see many such handbooks that refer to 'the employee' as if that is somebody completely different from the person who will be reading the handbook. How you deal with personal issues will go deeper. Learning good counselling skills helps here. Actions always speak louder than words.

- How will you react to a redundancy programme?

Redundancy-handling is one of the most emotive issues with which you are likely to come into contact. Whether you are involved in handling the issues directly or not, you will probably be identified with such programmes by other employees, and you should think through the implications of this. More information on handling redundancies is contained in Chapter 3.

- What else may you have to face?

Other personal issues such as bereavements, maternity, illness/disability, debts or bankruptcy may well demand your attention. The sympathetic, consistent and practical way in which you handle these will reflect strongly on your department's reputation. As with redundancy, it helps in these cases if you think through in advance how you will handle the issues. You will find help and guidance in Chapter 12 on developing the necessary skills.

We had a look at organisation structures earlier, and have examined the tasks required of an HR function and the types of action you as an HR practitioner may be able to take. But you will, in many cases, be working within an HR department. Organisations differ in how the role of HR is structured within an organisation.

ORGANISING THE HR FUNCTION

In a very small organisation – say, up to 50 employees – there is unlikely to be an HR department. Important HR activities are likely to be undertaken by the owner or managing director and the more administrative functions undertaken by a PA. Employment advice (which we look at in the next chapter) is often provided by insurance firms (who protect small employers from employment tribunal claims), law firms, accountants, employer associations or HR consultants. Unfortunately, when it comes to selection decisions, disciplinary hearings or attendance problems, the owner or managing director is often left to handle the difficult situation on their own.

Once an organisation employs more than this number it is typical for someone to be assigned to, or even appointed to, the HR role. It may be asigned to the PA who has been handling the administrative functions, or it might be assigned to the accountant or one of his/her staff. Ideally, a dedicated, qualified and experienced HR officer would be appointed – but this is more likely only as the number of employees increases beyond the 100 mark. But even organisations of 250 employees do not always have a dedicated HR person.

As the size of an organisation increases beyond this size, so it is increasingly likely that not only will there be a dedicated HR person but most probably an HR department. Such a department is likely to be 'generalist', handling a wide range of HR activities as we discussed earlier.

HR departments are structured in many different ways, often dependent on the role and size of HR and on the type of organisation. Some will encompass health and safety, training, facilities management and industrial relations. In other organisations these functions may be elsewhere in the organisation structure, outsourced or even not present at all. Job titles and terms vary too. The terms 'HR', 'personnel', 'director', 'executive officer', 'head of', 'manager', 'adviser', 'officer', 'assistant', 'secretary', 'trainer', and 'instructor' are just a sample of those you may come across. The significance of each title will also vary from one organisation to another. The term 'HR business partner' tends to have a particular meaning, which we address below.

Figure 2.3 shows an HR structure that might be found in a manufacturing organisation.

Of course, some organisations employ thousands of people, often with several sites, and most of our largest organisations operate internationally too. In these organisations there is likely to be significant differentiation even within the HR department. Further functions such as employee relations, recruitment, training, policy, strategic advice, and employment law may each have separate specialists or even separate departments.

In these latter circumstances the structure of the HR function itself becomes an important decision for the organisation. Should each location have its own team (decentralisation), should the main functions and particularly policy be centrally located at the head office, or should there be some combination with

Figure 2.3 An HR structure

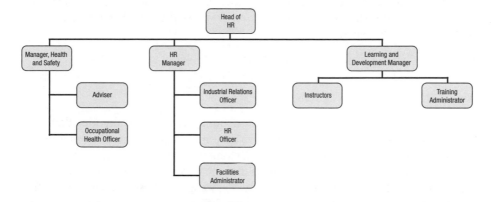

some aspects centralised and some distributed? Indeed, should the function be 'outsourced', in whole or in part, by using an external company to provide the service?

SHARED SERVICES, BUSINESS PARTNERS AND CENTRES OF EXPERTISE

Recent thinking, from David Ulrich in the USA, has led to a 'three-legged' organisation of the function in some of the larger organisations in the UK. One leg is a shared service centre. Many large companies, such as the BBC, Ford and Rolls-Royce, operate a shared services model. Rather than the roles in an HR department being duplicated at many individual sites, the services are centralised and then shared. So, for example, instead of separate databases of employees at each location, this data can be held and maintained on one central database. An internal call centre providing advice on employment legal matters would be a form of shared service. It is the day-to-day transactional and operational activities that are most likely to be shared.

The second leg is appointment of business partners. These HR practitioners will be located in the particular locations or business divisions of the organisation. The term indicates that they are to work in partnership with the business that they are assigned to in order to assist and develop the business itself. The role detaches itself from the daily administrative functions that can be handled by others. Instead, the HR business partners are more likely to be involved in solving problems with line managers and being more involved in strategic decision-making (at least in theory). In practice, the role is usually defined differently in different organisations, so if you apply for an advertised vacancy you should take care to understand the meaning of 'business partner' in the organisation to which you are applying. We have not used the term 'business partner' widely in this book because of the differing definitions.

The last leg corresponds to centres of expertise, comprising individuals or teams that supply a particular expertise. For example, trade union negotiations will often be handled by a team of industrial relations specialists; graduate recruitment similarly. Such teams may be located at the head office, or sometimes in different locations, but are likely to travel to where they are required on an 'as and when needed' basis.

Crucial to shared services is customer care.

THE CUSTOMER CARE CONCEPT

This concept originated outside the HR function. It is based on the idea that all functions have a responsibility to serve customers. Those functions that do not deal directly with the organisation's customers nevertheless have 'internal' customers. This concept applies a sound discipline to which it is easy to relate: we all experience the customer relationship when we are customers ourselves. In that position we expect to be treated with respect. Indeed, as we travel more, perhaps particularly to the USA and the Far East, we have developed an understanding of how good customer care can really be. In consequence, we increase our expectations.

In a shared services centre you are providing more than one part of your organisation, perhaps on different geographical sites, with HR services. Customer care concepts are particularly important because there is often some geographical distance between the service centre and the units served.

Activity 2.9 encourages you to look at what customer care might mean and how it might relate to the work you do.

ACTIVITY 2.9

Good customer service is most in evidence when things go wrong!

Think back over recent weeks and months when something did go wrong. Choose an occasion when you felt, despite the problem, that you had some excellent customer service. Make a list of what it was that led you to that feeling – how did the other person or organisation behave?

This activity works well in a small group because not all behaviours in excellent service occur on every occasion. *At the end of this chapter we have provided some thoughts of our own – but look at those only after you've made your own list and had at least an initial run through the rest of this exercise.*

Now, considering each experience in turn, review how much behaviour is in evidence in the department or central service where you work.

Finally, draw up an action plan of steps you could take to improve the customer service delivery of your department or service.

However HR is organised in your organisation you need to give thought to how you will be judged by your internal customers, and more often than not, that judgement will be on the service you are *perceived* to give to them.

Service-level agreements are an extension of the customer care concept so that it can operate within an organisation. A typical agreement might be one in which the HR department agrees to fill all staff vacancies within, say, 10 weeks of authorisation. As practitioners, we have found that setting some standards of service goes down well with other functions and motivates us strongly to achieve them. For HR departments (as with other functions and many professions) the question still arises: 'Who are our customers?' Are they other departments, prospective employees, current employees, senior managers, or all of these? Since the last option is essentially correct, how can we balance conflict between different customers? Who will have priority?

One way of understanding the dilemma this poses is to look at the notion of stakeholders.

THE STAKEHOLDER CONCEPT

In the stakeholder concept these other parties or customers are seen as having a stake in our department's time. Although balancing conflicting interests may be regarded as a managerial function, we all have to mediate between the various people who make demands on our time at and away from work.

As an example, consider others who have a stake in your personal time: your partner, your family, your source of income, any voluntary leisure commitments. You need continually to balance the demands of each of these on your time and energy and against each other.

Looking again at the work situation, the stakeholder concept is not restricted to internal departments. The organisation itself needs to consider a whole range of groups that have a stake in its activities. These are likely to include employees, shareholders, trade unions, the government and local communities, as well as customers and suppliers.

ACTIVITY 2.10

Taking your organisation, or the site within it where you work, identify the main stakeholders. Which groups or organisations benefit from the existence of your employer? Who would lose out if your organisation became less successful or reduced its presence? What implications do these stakeholders have for your work? (As an example, in a small community the local school may be a major supplier of new employees. The implications for you could be that you would wish to foster good relations with the school.)

Balancing the differing needs of stakeholders demands good communication, understanding, assertiveness and judgement. It is a major challenge for all managers.

Now have a look at Activity 2.11. *You will find feedback on this Activity at the end of the chapter.*

ACTIVITY 2.11

Think carefully of the service you or your HR department give to line managers or other internal customers in your organisation.

How might you measure the level of service that you provide?

Make a list of appropriate measures and appropriate levels of service that you might provide. At the end of this chapter we give some examples, but ones from your own experience are most valuable.

Up to now we have focused on organisations themselves, expectations of the HR function, how it might be organised and some underlying concepts behind service delivery. There is one particular stakeholder in most larger organisations: the relevant trade union or trade unions.

TRADE UNIONS

For many HR practitioners, trade unions are part of the organisational context within which they work. We will therefore provide some background to trade unions and the issues that surround working in a unionised environment.

WHAT IS A TRADE UNION?

A trade union is an association of members – in which respect it is different from, say, a private company, which has a distinct legal identity. To be a trade union an organisation has to be recognised by a Certification Officer (appointed by the government) and is usually a member of the Trades Union Congress (TUC).

Each trade union has its own rules for membership and its own administration and operation. However, there are significant restrictions on union activities brought in by legislation, much of it aimed at 'increasing democracy' within trade unions. For example, at one time trade unions were able to form 'closed shops' by which no one but members of particular unions were able to work in particular jobs or companies. This made it potentially difficult for employees to move jobs unless they carried the right union card. Legislation now outlaws discrimination in employment on the basis of membership or non-membership of a trade union, which effectively prevents closed shops. It also outlaws 'blacklists' that have been held by some less scrupulous employers' groups, even recently. These are where a list is kept of so-called 'troublemakers' who then find it difficult to get employment.

RECOGNITION AND COLLECTIVE AGREEMENTS

Not all employers, of course, welcome unions, and others pride themselves in having such good communications with employees that unionisation has not been desired by those employees. But the employers who recognise a trade union give that union the right to make collective agreements with them on behalf of its members. In order for a trade union to form and enter into collective bargaining, there are two requirements: the ability to organise, and recognition by an employer.

If groups of workers feel sufficient mutual interest for them to wish to negotiate jointly, they would normally join an appropriate existing trade union. 'Organisation' implies the ability of these workers to meet in one place and formulate some common objectives. This has always been easier in large establishments such as the NHS or BAE Systems. Industries in which workers are scattered in smaller groups (such as retail shops, hotels and farming) find organisation less practical, and they tend to be less unionised and therefore less likely to have collective agreements.

Where a union has a substantial number of members within a particular group of workers, it may apply to the employer for recognition. Employers may then draw up agreements with a union branch to 'recognise' the right of the trade union and its shop stewards to represent its members with the employer. Shop stewards are employees who are also representatives of the trade union at the place of work. Where recognised by the employer, they have legal rights to go about a variety of duties related to their trade union responsibilities.

Where employers do not reach agreement on recognition voluntarily, there is a legal procedure under which a trade union may apply to a Central Arbitration Committee (set up by the government) to have a ballot for recognition. Recognised trade unions have the right to negotiate on behalf of their members in relation to pay, hours and holidays as well as any other matter that may form part of the recognition agreement.

In addition, they have a statutory right to be consulted by the employers on a number of matters. This includes consultation on occupational pensions, on health and safety issues, on redundancy, on any transfer of ownership of the business, and on training policies and plans.

A key part of trade union philosophy, enshrined in the word 'union', is that by joining together employees can counter employers' powers to 'exploit' them. Traditionally, it was manual workers that most strongly felt this need, but in the latter part of the twentieth century, many white-collar workers became unionised in order to negotiate collectively. The process of negotiating is usually referred to as collective bargaining, and the outcomes of such bargaining as collective agreements.

In negotiating agreements, trade unions have a statutory right of access to the information necessary for the bargaining process. If they are denied access to particular information, they may apply to the Central Arbitration Committee for

CASE STUDY 2.3

A residential home for the elderly found it needed to respond to new employment legislation. The Employment Rights Act, Working Time Regulations and the Employment Relations Act (see Chapter 3), among others, had all created the need for more formal working relationships than had been the case in the past. Written particulars had been prepared and annual leave arrangements had been made. Employees were concerned about these changes and had joined a trade union that then sought and was granted recognition. Even so, members of staff were still concerned about the need for written particulars and the management team was uncertain how to deal with this new trade union relationship.

In consultation with an HR practitioner, the managers drew up an agreement that recognised appropriate rights for the trade union and confirmed the trade union's respect for the charitable status of the home and the aims of the management team. In particular it determined how collective bargaining would be conducted and how any disputes would be resolved.

The approval of the agreement at a meeting with the trade union has provided a framework for tackling employment matters jointly. In particular it has created a co-operative approach to the annual pay review. While other important changes have been taking place, nevertheless, it is acknowledged that a trade union environment has contributed to better working relationships.

adjudication on whether they are entitled to access the information. Collective agreements can cover almost any part of the employer-employee relationship. They may be divided into *substantive* and *procedural*.

Substantive agreements relate to aspects of the contract between employer and employee – for example, the terms and conditions of employment, the rate of pay or the hours of work. They are often subject to annual negotiation – the annual pay round.

Procedural agreements cover the procedures for regulating the relationship, including the method by which the parties will conduct collective bargaining. An overall procedural agreement is usually made in order to define the areas in which trade union representation is acknowledged. The procedures themselves provide a means of dealing with issues and resolving conflict in fair and consistent ways. Making procedures part of collective agreements effectively means that as long as the procedure is followed, unions and management will be in agreement on issues or have clear steps to follow in resolving them. Areas covered by procedures may include:

- how trade union representatives are appointed
- disputes, and the arbitration procedure if they are not resolved
- discipline and grievance-handling
- redundancy.

Procedures also enable the organisation to indicate the flexibility that it will allow individual managers in order to ensure that they do not make decisions that counter organisational objectives.

Procedures usually provide for disputes and disagreements to rise through levels of management if they cannot be resolved at a lower level. Generally, they would require matters to be raised at the lowest appropriate level first, and then at other levels later. So, for example, under a disciplinary procedure a supervisor may be empowered to warn an employee about his or her behaviour, but not to dismiss. Where such action is necessary, the supervisor will raise the matter to the next level.

Employers often see the principle of collective agreements as beneficial to them. It is necessary, for example, to consult workers at a factory that is closing. Where employees are unionised, employers can usually negotiate with a few representative individuals and form an agreement that covers all, or at least a whole category of, employees. Without a recognised trade union, an employer is dependent on workers' electing employee representatives or on information-and-consultation arrangements. Unless some arrangements are in place, the employer would have to consult every single employee on an individual basis. In our example that means all the workers at the factory. Those covered by collective agreements will have many, if not most, of their employment terms determined by such agreements. Where these terms are not to their liking, their first port of call is then their trade union shop steward – a practice which, in effect, filters out many minor issues.

Despite the advantages that collective agreements can offer, the consequences of industrial action lead the public, who are often inconvenienced by such action, to question collective bargaining. It is to such action that we now turn.

INDUSTRIAL ACTION

It can be argued that power implies the capacity to hurt another party (and the willingness to do so), even though exercising such power may involve a cost to both parties. The desire to avoid that cost means that much can be achieved by the knowledge that such power exists and the fact that it is in the interests of both parties to avoid the costs of a breakdown. Don't be deceived by media treatment that likes to emphasise the conflict between 'trade unions and management' just because it is more newsworthy – more often than not, the two parties work together very positively. Nevertheless, the fact that employees may decide to take industrial action is a source of power in coming to collective agreements. The power balance, of course, shifts continuously with many factors, such as the changing legal background, the level of unemployment and the market position of an individual employer.

Where employers and employees (represented, usually, by a union) cannot negotiate satisfactory agreements, either party may resort to industrial action. At the extreme, employers may use the 'lock-out' option (literally locking employees out of the workplace) or employees may strike. There are other options available, too. Employers may bring in a new contract and dismiss those who do not accept it. (Such dismissals may, or may not, be fair.) Employees may withdraw their goodwill and take all kinds of actions, of which 'working to rule' (interpreting rules so precisely that little practical work is accomplished) and overtime bans are typical. Significantly, it is possible for skilful manipulation to distort the picture of who is responsible for the breakdown of talks.

It therefore follows that great skill and care is required and that sensitive industrial relations issues will probably be handled by the most senior and the most experienced people in your organisation. You must be aware, too, that complex legislation regulates industrial action, that there is a need for a union to hold secret ballots, and that employees can exercise a right not to strike.

If circumstances mean that you cannot avoid involvement in a dispute, always seek appropriate advice. In a large organisation this will be from more senior members of the HR department. In a small organisation, Acas (see below) or a consultant practitioner may be your most important source.

ACTIVITY 2.12

Subject to consultation as appropriate with a senior member of your management team, initiate a discussion with a trade unionist, shop steward or convenor. Discover their views about the employment relationship, about trade unionism and about your organisation's corporate culture and objectives. Do they see themselves as partners seeking to work with management for the greater prosperity of the organisation, or as workforce representatives whose responsibilities are solely to represent the interests of their members?

THE ADVISORY, CONCILIATION AND ARBITRATION SERVICE (ACAS)

Acas is a body set up by the government but which is required to act impartially in seeking to promote good industrial relations. Its services are available both to employers and individuals, and it receives enquiries from both sources in comparable proportions. It can be called in by parties that are failing to agree on employment matters. It will endeavour to conciliate (essentially getting the parties to talk their problems through), appoint mediators (to suggest solutions to the parties) or appoint an arbitrator, who must have the full consent of both parties. In this latter case the parties agree in advance to accept the arbitrator's decision. The result is that Acas officials have a huge bank of experience in industrial conflict and are therefore excellently placed to assist in industrial relations.

Acas also has an important role in mediating disputes with individuals who have brought employment tribunal claims, of which more is said later in this book.

SUMMARY

- HR practice and management offer an interesting and exciting career. Potentially, the function encompasses any issue in which the employer, as a corporate body, relates to the employee. You should therefore have a good relationship both with employees (and their representatives – usually a trade union – where applicable) and with managers at all levels, as well as with relevant outside bodies.

- Practitioners must be mindful of the type of organisation within which they work so that they can direct their contribution and influence others appropriately.

- HR can be organised in different ways depending partly on the size and complexity of the organisation. Division of the function into a shared services centre with HR business partners and centres of expertise is tending to replace the traditional department in larger organisations in the UK.

- The HR function provides a service for the operational functions. It is not in itself profit-earning or a direct contributor to the operational purpose. What it does is to assist others in that role. To be effective it has to be mindful of caring for its 'customers' and of the various stakeholders, who may have conflicting interests.

- The actions that HR practitioners can take invariably include administrative actions, and frequently they include advisory actions. In many cases, particularly at senior levels, practitioners may have authority to take executive decisions as well. For practitioners to be well regarded, they must be in tune with the corporate culture in which they work: they need to identify what is valued.

- Practitioners cannot ignore the pace of change and the effects that that has on employers and employees. Anticipating these effects will greatly enhance your performance.

- To be well informed, practitioners must build and maintain good relationships with a variety of stakeholders, particularly managers, trade unions, employees and the community from which their employees come.

- Trade unions are relevant for many practitioners, and you will have seen that a union is a different entity from a private company, for example. You should now understand the concepts of recognition, collective agreements and industrial action.

EXPLORE FURTHER

REFERENCES AND FURTHER READING

CLARK, A. (2000) *Organisations, Competition and the Business Environment*. London: Pearson Education

CLAYDON, T. and BEARDWELL, J. (2007) *Human Resource Management: A contemporary approach*, 5th edition. London: Pearson Education

CURRIE, D. (2006) *Introduction to Human Resource Management: A guide to personnel in practice*. London: Chartered Institute of Personnel and Development

EDWARDS, E. (1988) 'Corporate culture', *Management Accounting*, May; p.19

FARNHAM, D. (1999) *Managing in a Business Context*. London: Institute of Personnel and Development

TORRINGTON, D., HALL, L. and TAYLOR, S. (2008) *Fundamentals of Human Resource Management: Managing people at work*. London: Prentice Hall

WEIGHTMAN, J. (2004) *Managing People*, 2nd edition. London: Chartered Institute of Personnel and Development

Useful information on human resource planning matters is available from:

INCOMES DATA SERVICES, Finsbury Tower, 103–105 Bunhill Row, London, EC1Y 8LZ. Tel: 0845 077 2911

WEBSITES

Advisory, Conciliation and Arbitration Service (Acas): www.acas.org.uk

Department for Business, Innovation and Skills: www.berr.gov.uk

Chartered Institute of Personnel and Development: www.cipd.co.uk

People Management: www.peoplemanagement.co.uk

Incomes Data Services: www.incomesdata.co.uk

Trades Union Congress: www.tuc.org.uk/

ACTIVITIES FEEDBACK

Activity 2.9

You may have points of your own that are not listed below – your points are still valid. Equally, you might not agree with everything on our list, but these points are valid for us.

- I was able to speak to someone quickly.
- My call was returned.
- When I explained the problem I knew I was understood because the problem was acknowledged by the other person (perhaps by them repeating it back to me in their own words).
- My complaint was treated as legitimate.
- The person spoke in language that I understood. For example, they did not use their jargon but understood and used mine.
- There were delays but I was kept informed.

- I was treated with respect.
- The person took responsibility for solving the problem. 'Responsible' is an interesting word – think of it as 'response-able', ie able to respond.
- The commitment to find out the answer was kept.
- The apology was genuine.
- The person was not able to help but I understood why.
- The person was not able to help but escalated it to his or her manager, without my having to explain the problem again.

Note how many of these behaviours are about communication and understanding.

What is on your list of actions that you can take?

Are there responses that you'd want to make but are not able to do so?

Are you changing the things that you can?

Can you accept and live with what you cannot change?

Do you know the difference?

Activity 2.11

Examples of service levels:

- response times to provide information on employees such as current salary or disciplinary record or attendance record
- response times for information on collective information, such as attendance levels for a department
- time to fill a vacancy
- time to resolve a job grading query
- number of disputes
- number of employment tribunal claims

CHAPTER 3

The legal background

LEARNING OUTCOMES

After reading this chapter you will:

- know which legislation is likely to apply in the main areas of HR activity
- be able to discuss the expectations of the law in employment matters with managers and legal specialists
- be able to respond to the fundamental legal expectations placed on employers
- recognise the limitations of your knowledge and know where to find further information
- have an understanding of the basic employment legislation affecting HR practice, including employment contracts, health and safety, and equal opportunities.

WHY IS LEGISLATION IMPORTANT?

Many practitioners in human resources (HR) and line managers feel that bringing the law into employment relationships creates rigidity and sometimes makes it difficult for the business to respond to opportunities. Employees, on the other hand, often feel that the law provides a degree of protection from poor management and exploitation. Many other feelings surround the question of law and employment. Some may arise from political beliefs, others from personal experience. The extent to which strong feelings exist, and their relevance to HR practice, varies from organisation to organisation. Government organisations necessarily attach great importance to legal matters, whereas some entrepreneurial business people may seek to minimise, or try to disregard, the impact of the law on their employment practices. Other employers adopt employment practices that are in excess of any minimum provided by the law. They aspire to practices that are the best that can be found, embracing the spirit as well as the letter of the law. One example, in the equal opportunities area, is the development of a truly diverse workforce in which every worker's dignity is genuinely respected.

Whatever an employer's intentions are, it is likely that there will be times when an employee feels that he or she has been unfairly treated. If that employee believes that the employer has acted unlawfully, then he or she may make a claim to an employment tribunal. If the tribunal upholds the claim it will, in most cases, award compensation. Such compensation may be thousands of pounds or, in some types of claim, an unlimited amount. Whether the claim is upheld or not, substantial preparation work is involved if the employer decides to fight the claim. Such work makes no direct contribution to business objectives, and adverse publicity may even damage achievement of those objectives.

In some cases, trade unions can challenge the employing organisation by taking actions that disrupt its activities, damage its relationship with customers and threaten its profitability. A knowledge of employment law is therefore a key requirement for HR practitioners.

However, employment law is not an area where issues are necessarily clear cut. Indeed, even at an employment tribunal with an employment judge, one party involved may not agree that the law has been correctly interpreted and may appeal against the decision reached. The matter will then be referred to a higher court for it to advise on interpretation of the law. In some cases it falls to the Supreme Court (and in the past, the House of Lords) or to the European Court of Justice to decide this. One consequence is that, quite frequently, the precise way in which the law is interpreted changes.

There is also a large body of legislation that is relevant in specific circumstances, and there is much detail in the various Acts and Regulations.

So although we shall explain the main principles that you need to know, you are likely also to need advice from more senior colleagues, the Advisory, Conciliation and Arbitration Service (Acas) (see later in this chapter), or legal and other specialists.

ACTIVITY 3.1

Think about your own organisation. How do managers and workers view the effect of law on employment? Do managers use it to control or manage people? If so, how? Do employment rights reassure employees? What do you think of the attitudes in your organisation? Write down your thoughts and discuss them with one of your learning sources, as described in Chapter 1 of this book.

A NOTE ON EMPLOYEES AND WORKERS

You will notice that we have already used the terms 'employees' and 'workers'. Legally, the term 'worker' includes employees. Much legislation is aimed at workers rather than employees (see *Contracts of employment* below). The intention of this legislation has been to include agency workers, freelance workers and other types of subcontractors in these rights. But the term 'worker' is sometimes used more narrowly to denote a manual, or blue-collar, worker. In this chapter we have tended towards the legal interpretation. So in our text, as an example, trade unions have generally represented employees (including white-collar employees) rather than workers (which in the legal sense could include self-employed people).

ACTS AND REGULATIONS

You will see these words quoted throughout this chapter and occasionally elsewhere in this book. Acts (Statutes) are major pieces of legislation debated and passed by Parliament. Regulations (Statutory Instruments) are prepared to regulate how the legislation operates in practice and invariably contain specific details. Also, in reading more widely, you will frequently see *cases* quoted. Case law indicates how courts and tribunals have interpreted the law in the past, and a decision by a court is binding on all lower courts and tribunals.

The purpose of this chapter is to give you background information. Reference to Acts and Regulations is sufficient to achieve this. However, the case studies in this chapter also indicate how the law might be interpreted in particular circumstances.

EMPLOYMENT LEGISLATION

It is useful to see employment legislation in three groups: civil law, employment protection rights, and other statutory legislation.

CIVIL LAW

This group deals with relations between two parties. Contracts are an example; breaches of them entitle one party to sue the other (litigation). Typically, in employment, this would be for failure to give proper notice (an example of wrongful dismissal). Most breach of employment contract claims are heard by employment tribunals.

Another example of civil law is the duty of care. This is implicit in all employment contracts. So an employee may sue his or her employers for damages if, for example, he or she is injured at work and believes the employer to be responsible. In doing so the employee may cite breaches of regulations – for example, not being informed of safety procedures. Personal injury claims are currently a matter for the County Court or High Court.

EMPLOYMENT PROTECTION RIGHTS

The major employee right is the right not to be unfairly dismissed, and this applies irrespective of the employee's contracted hours of work. The length of service an employee usually requires before acquiring this right is 12 months. The other main area of protection is the right not to be discriminated against. This comprises laws that protect equal opportunities, covering such areas as maternity rights and equal pay, reasonable adjustments for the disabled and the employment of ex-offenders. The right not to be discriminated against applies to applicants as well as employees and in some cases to past employees (as in giving a reference). Redress in employment protection matters is sought by a claim to an employment tribunal. The onus is on the aggrieved party to make this claim. This body of employment protection legislation is a major area for employers and one with which HR practitioners need to be familiar.

OTHER STATUTORY LEGISLATION

Many obligations are placed on the employer by other statutory legislation. In contrast to civil law and the employment protection legislation (where claims are made for damages or compensation), many breaches in this area leave employers (principally directors, but also managers and in some cases workers) open to criminal prosecution, fines and (in some extreme cases) imprisonment. For example, it is a criminal offence to employ an employee that does not have the required permission to work in the UK.

There are also legal requirements placed on the records that employers need to keep, and also on what they should not keep. Working Time Regulations 1998, the National Minimum Wage Act 1998 and the Data Protection Act 1998 are examples of Acts that place specific requirements on the records employers have to keep. The Health and Safety at Work Act 1974 (HASWA) and the Control of Substances Hazardous to Health Regulations 2002 (COSHH) are another two highly important pieces of legislation. Health and safety is a major area of legislation, especially for employers in the industrial sector, and one with which those who have health and safety responsibilities must obviously be familiar.

We shall look at the key issues in each area, starting with civil law.

CIVIL LAW

WHAT IS A LEGAL CONTRACT?

When one person agrees to do something for another, a contract exists. It may be binding in honour only, as for example when we offer to buy a drink for a friend (and he or she accepts our offer). In this example, if we suddenly discover we have left our money at home (and therefore cannot fulfil the contract), we do not expect to be sued! Nonetheless, an informal contract was made and, in failing to fulfil it, we would have broken that contract.

Legal contracts are more binding, and if we break them, the other party is entitled to damages. A failure to agree on what damages are due entitles the aggrieved party to seek redress in a civil court or, if it is an employment contract, in an employment tribunal. Legal contracts can be made by people or by 'legal entities' such as a limited company.

An employment contract is a particular type of legal contract. But let's first look at the conditions needed for a contract to be legally enforceable.

- Agreement
An offer has to be made and accepted. You might offer to buy someone's car for £5,000, but no agreement is reached until the offer is accepted. In employment, offers are often 'subject to' issues such as references, a medical or verification of qualifications. In such cases, agreement is not reached until all the 'subject to' issues have been resolved. In the case of the car, you might make your offer 'subject to' a satisfactory engineer's report.

- Consideration
There has to be an exchange of benefits – the car in return for your £5,000, for example. In employment it could be wages in return for work. 'Voluntary work' can be a grey area, but unless something tangible is given in return (genuine expenses, perhaps), there will be no legal contract. Incidentally, if work is not genuinely voluntary, the national minimum wage applies (see page 73).

- Intention
Both parties must intend to form a legally binding contract. This may be presumed, as in employment contracts, or should be recorded in writing, as in agreements between friends and relatives. Buying cars from friends can be problematic. If your friend gets a better offer while you are at the building society, it may be legally as well as practically difficult to enforce the contract. For self-employed people, employing friends and relatives can be problematic unless a specific legal contract is made.

- Certainty
It has to be clear what the parties have agreed so that the contract can be established with certainty. Oral agreements, though having the status of legal contracts if clearly made, can be difficult to enforce. If it proves difficult to establish with certainty what was agreed, then the contract may be void. For this reason it is good practice to put employment contracts into writing.

- Consent
The parties must come together freely and not under duress. In practice, unemployed people will often feel under pressure and can easily agree to terms they dislike. Unfortunately, such 'duress' is regarded as a normal fact of life. It does not invalidate the contract.

- Legality
Contracts can be formed for legal purposes only. This has implications for illegal activities, such as drug dealing. In instances where disputes cannot be resolved by recourse to law, they are often settled by use of violence.

- Capacity
The person making the contract on behalf of an organisation must be properly authorised to do so. This is very important for you as an HR practitioner. If you offer an employment contract without proper authority, your organisation could disown the decision. This would place you in a most invidious position and almost certainly leave you liable to disciplinary action. If the rejected

employee had already accepted your offer, and handed in notice in his or her current employment, he or she may seek damages.

Notice that contracts do not have to be in writing. Many offers are made and accepted over the telephone. If it can be established that the above conditions have been met, then an enforceable contract exists. Telephone offers are quicker and therefore reduce the danger of losing a good candidate while a written contract is being prepared. They can make negotiations easier so long as both parties are prepared for them and you have clear authority to reach an agreement. In the longer term, written offers and acceptance have the advantage that both parties know exactly what has been agreed. There is therefore less room for confusion (if references prove to be unsatisfactory, for example). Care has to be taken to be sure that an interview candidate is not led to believe an offer exists (by agreeing a pay rate, for example) when that is not the intention. Words such as 'If we were to offer you . . .' are important to help avoid confusion.

You need to find out whether your organisation has a policy on how offers should be made, or whether you are expected to use your best judgement.

Offers may be made and accepted by email. Offers can also be accepted by a person's behaviour: for example, arriving for work would indicate acceptance. It may be helpful to place a time limit on an offer, or formally to withdraw it if it is not accepted within a satisfactory time-scale.

EMPLOYMENT STATUS

It is important to understand whether someone who is doing work for you is an employee, a worker or a business. These are the main categories of employment status. But this is a very complicated area and we can look only at broad principles, which may be subject to change.

You may wish to offer work to a person who claims to be self-employed. One difficulty, if you reach an agreement on that basis, is that the Inland Revenue may not be willing to treat that person as self-employed. In that case you, the employer, will probably have to pay tax and National Insurance contributions to the Inland Revenue for the person (even if he or she has already been paid without deductions).

On the other hand, if a person is an employee, then he or she has a wide range of employment rights, including the right not to be unfairly dismissed. The claim to be an employee could come after a contract has ended, in order to assert employment rights. So let's have a look at the distinctions.

If you have your house decorated, you do not, usually, employ a decorator; what you do is make a contract for service. Your decorator is likely to be a business – it may possibly be the person's own business. The person you meet may be an employee of the business, but he or she will not be an employee of yours. However, if your organisation retains an individual person as a decorator to decorate its premises, then that person could be an employee or a worker.

Employees have a contract of employment. They will receive other benefits such as sick pay. Workers are people who do the work for you, or your organisation, personally (ie they cannot subcontract the work to others); usually they are supervised, and work specified hours. Employees are workers, but workers can also include freelance people and those from agencies. So all employees are workers, but workers are not necessarily employees. Workers are usually paid on a scale that is determined by the employer and may pay tax by PAYE. Workers have some employment rights, such as protection from discrimination. However, employees have additional rights, including entitlement to written particulars of employment and protection from unfair dismissal.

Whether or not agency workers have the status of an employee is a particularly fluid area and case law on this subject has served to complicate rather than to simplify matters. If the agency worker is an employee of the agency (with a contract of employment confirmed by written particulars), then that is a clear position. However, it is often not so clear-cut, and case law does not determine whose employee an agency worker might be, or indeed whether they are an employee at all. The Agency Workers Directive from the European Union should, when implemented, give temporary agency workers equal rights to permanent workers after 12 weeks' employment. This would mean comparable pay and conditions including, for example, sick pay and holiday leave, but not necessarily other employment rights such as the right to not be dismissed unfairly or the right to redundancy payments. So the Agency Workers Directive will not determine employment status. Unless it is quite clear who is employing an agency worker, this is an area where you should seek advice. Meanwhile, even if they are not employees of the organisation that provides the work, agency workers have certain worker rights – under the Working Time Regulations, for example (see page 73).

Genuinely self-employed people and businesses usually provide their own equipment (such as paint brushes in the case of decorators) and will almost certainly work for others as well as your organisation. They submit invoices and will probably be VAT-registered. They may contract to do a particular task (as opposed to working set daily hours), and any profit or loss in doing the work accrues to the business rather than your organisation. So as not to be held liable for any tax or National Insurance contributions, anyone contracting work from the self-employed may be wise to see a supporting letter from the Inland Revenue or a contractor's certificate.

If self-employed people do work for you and claim to be a business, make sure the set of conditions in the last paragraph is satisfied. If in doubt, you are usually safer to employ them on a contract of employment, deduct tax under PAYE, and accept that they will have employment rights. If you choose not to do so, you could find yourself liable for their tax and/or discover they are claiming employment rights nevertheless.

Genuine businesses would also be free to give the work to one of their own employees or workers for that person to carry out work on your behalf. Both self-employed workers and businesses have the right to turn work down if they

Table 3.1 The employment status of 'employees', 'workers' and others

The table below provides a broad guide to help you understand the employment status of different people. The genuinely self-employed are included in this table for completeness, but this group has no employment rights, unlike workers, who are protected by the National Minimum Wage Regulations, the Working Time Regulations, and equality rights.

Note that the table is drawn up from the viewpoint of an employer (who is therefore 'You').

Employee	Worker	Genuinely self-employed
S/he has a contract of service (ie to serve)	S/he does the work personally	S/he contracts for services – you are the customer
You pay by PAYE	You pay on invoice	You pay on invoice
S/he is not VAT registered	S/he may be VAT registered	S/he prepares business accounts
You set the working hours	Either may set the working hours	S/he sets hours of work
S/he can't decline work	S/he can decline work	S/he can assign work to others
You can expect work	You cannot expect work	S/he has no right to expect work
You provide written employment particulars	The contract may not be in writing	Contracts for each piece of work; could be written
S/he would be subject to disciplinary procedures	S/he may need to respond to complaints or may be subject to procedures in some cases	S/he must be prepared to respond to complaints but is not subject to disciplinary procedures
S/he uses company equipment	S/he may use own equipment	S/he uses own equipment
S/he is employed for an indefinite time	S/he works usually for a fixed time	The contract is by service, not time

Not included here specifically are agency workers because of the uncertainties surrounding their status. Indeed, in 2008 their employment status was described by one employment law specialist and adviser to government departments as a topic that was 'horrifically complicated'. He was also of the view that it was getting worse.

choose, and the organisation contracting with the business or worker is not obliged to offer work. Employer and employee do not have this freedom; there is instead what is called 'mutuality of obligation' by which one party is obliged to provide work and the other is obliged to do it.

Despite the differences explained here, it is very important to realise that the distinction is not always clear-cut and that you may need to seek advice. Courts and tribunals can come to differing conclusions on seemingly similar situations and are not bound by decisions made by other bodies such as the Inland Revenue. You will find frequently asked questions on employment status under that heading on the CIPD website. Remember that if a contract of employment is made, a statement of written particulars should be provided within two months.

ACTIVITY 3.2

Consider the people who help accomplish your organisation's objectives. Are they all employees? If not, how would you categorise them? Carry out some appropriate research into the nature of their relationship with the HR function. For example, you might want to investigate what records are kept for them and what employment rights they have, and reflect on how the responsibilities of the HR department differ for these people and your employees. Discuss the issues with your learning sources.

CONTRACTS OF EMPLOYMENT

The contract sets out the legal basis of the relationship. It should therefore include those matters on which you wish your employee to be legally bound and matters on which you, as an employer, will be legally bound. For example, you may want legally to bind an employee to your office hours. If there is a clear written agreement specifying this as part of the contract, then the hours become contractual.

Typically, disciplinary and grievance procedures are not part of the contract and it is advisable for only the minimum details required to be referred to in the written particulars. You may have good reason to use judgement in operating disciplinary and grievance procedures. If such procedures are contractual, a failure to follow them to the letter can result in a breach of contract claim. For example, if grievance procedures are part of the contract, and you refuse to use them when an employee raises a grievance, then the employee might claim that you have dismissed him or her by breaching the contract (known as constructive dismissal). In this case the employee could sue for damages such as entitlement to notice pay. He or she would be claiming wrongful dismissal – that is, dismissal in breach of the contract. The employee might also claim unfair dismissal, if he or she is entitled to do so. We will look at constructive and unfair dismissal again later. It is also important to remember that contracts cannot be changed unilaterally. To vary a contract, both parties have to agree to the change.

It is impossible to predict every possible employment situation that can arise. In areas where judgement or discretion is needed, some matters should as far as possible therefore not be contractual. Typical examples might be bonus scheme rules, job descriptions and procedures. For the employer, gauging the degree of flexibility that should exist in the employment relationship is an important decision and requires careful judgement, although the final decision as to whether a particular term is contractual or not may rest with the courts.

Just to clarify the issue further, let's take the example of job descriptions. If you include a job description in an employment contract, then every variation in the duties of the job can, potentially, become a legal issue. For this reason it is advisable to specify only the job title when making a contract. (Indeed, technically even this could be left for the written particulars – see below.) Similarly, there is no requirement to include a job description in the written particulars. There is actually no legal need to have a job description at all.

The degree of formality involved in job descriptions affects an employer's flexibility to a significant degree. At one extreme, a lot of formality (job descriptions signed, or included in the contract) tends to encourage disputes over duties. Such disputes can focus on wording rather than the purpose of the job or the interests of the parties concerned. At the other extreme, complete informality (no job descriptions) may aid early resolution but can make it much more difficult if relationships do eventually break down. In informal situations it is easy for the employer to have one expectation about the employee's responsibilities and for the employee to have another.

This brings us to the distinction between statutory, implied and express terms in employment contracts. Statutory matters are not usually written into the employment contract but override other terms. This also means that they apply whether the parties specifically agree to include them or not. They include the requirements of the Health and Safety at Work Act 1974 (HASWA), the right to maternity leave, to statutory sick pay, to itemised pay statements and a wide range of matters many of which are indicated elsewhere in this chapter and this book. Other matters that may be implied in the contract include:

- common law duties (such as the duty of care and co-operation with the employer)

- custom and practice (such as tea breaks, in cases where they are established).

Tribunals may imply terms into a contract where there is a dispute; they might consider the customs in the workplace and industry, or even the essential needs of the business, in reaching a decision. For example in the residential care sector, where 24-hour cover is needed, it might be implied that employees can be required to work on Christmas Day even if there is no express term to that effect.

What do we mean by 'express terms'? These are matters that are clearly agreed between the two parties, either verbally or in writing. They normally take precedence over implied terms. Typically, express terms include matters such as hours of work, pay and holidays, and a range of other employment details. If you want a matter to be contractual, then make it an express term – but you must be very careful in drawing up the contract, because it will not be easy to vary it later. For example, if you want the place of work to be part of the contract, then state it clearly and accurately.

However, you can put into the contract reasonable rights to vary aspects of the contract. So in the case of the place of work, you might include a mobility clause. Indeed, you can put into the contract (and written particulars) variation clauses for any right that you may wish to vary, so long as the variation is justifiable and reasonable; but if you are providing for something that might happen sometime in the future, you should still consult the employee(s) concerned when the variation is required.

It is important to include the notice period for termination of the contract by either party. Alternatively, the statutory minimum notice periods (based on length of service) may be stated.

Where a trade union is recognised, there may be collective terms included in the contract. These are terms that are agreed with a trade union and are applied to a 'collection' of employees. Employees need not be members of the trade union for collective terms to apply to them. This is because there should be no discrimination on the basis that an employee is, or is not, a trade union member.

In some circumstances employment procedures such as disciplinary and grievance procedures may be incorporated into the contract. This means that if such procedures are not followed (in carrying out a dismissal, for example), there may be additional compensation awarded at a tribunal because the contract has been breached. Many employers specifically exclude employment procedures from the contract to avoid this complication.

Both procedures and rules can be open to interpretation, and this may be a further case for not making them contractual. Nonetheless, contractual or not, they have significance because a tribunal will take their content, and the extent to which they may have been followed, into account when deciding whether an employer has acted fairly.

COMPONENTS OF THE CONTRACT

So a contract has many components and inevitably they interact. Their relative importance is summarised here, but the order should be taken as general guidance only.

Unwritten offers that may have been made and accepted form a contract, even though the fact may be difficult to prove in some circumstances. Matters discussed and agreed at a selection interview could be deemed part of the contract. Interviewers should be aware of this.

Statutory rights (and statutory terms such as the right to notice) apply to a contract once that contract has been made, even if that contract is only verbal. Furthermore, they apply even if the employee (or the employer) does not know about them! So, for example, if a worker agrees to work for a figure below the National Minimum Wage, because he does not know about it, he still has the right to that minimum wage.

Express contractual terms (made part of the contract, usually by the employer) do not override statutory terms but they can enhance such terms – by providing for more generous notice, for example. Express terms provide the opportunity for the employer (and, potentially at least, the employee) to determine how they wish the employment relationship to be structured.

Those terms that are determined by collective agreement must be specified in the contract (or written particulars, which we shall examine shortly), thus avoiding conflict between the main contractual terms and the collective terms.

Where there is no express contractual term, there could be terms implied into the contract if there are particular customs in an industry.

Lastly, rules, policies and procedures may be best kept out of the contract itself, but instead provided as guidance as to how the employer will act, what it expects of its employees and what it might regard as a breach of contract. Furthermore, they are invariably important in determining whether an organisation has acted fairly – a matter we return to in Chapter 8.

WRITTEN PARTICULARS

Written particulars are provided for information only and represent the employer's view of the terms of the relationship; where they conflict with contractual terms, the contract will prevail. New employees, employed to work for one month or more, have the right to receive written particulars of their employment within two months of starting employment. These rights are provided for in the Employment Rights Act 1996.

ACTIVITY 3.3

Look at the boxed text below that describes the required content of written particulars. Think through why the law provides these rights and what benefits they confer.

- Is it fair and reasonable for employees to know where they stand?

- Do written particulars protect employees from maltreatment? If so, how?

- Is a better understanding between employer and employee likely to arise as a result of putting particulars in writing?

- Why do you think many employers still do not provide written particulars? Is it:

  – through lack of knowledge of the law?

  – to save administration costs?

  – for power, gained by keeping employees ignorant of their rights?

WRITTEN PARTICULARS

The following are required in one document, termed 'The Principal Statement':

- names of employer and employee

- date when employment began

- date when continuous employment began

- scale or rate of remuneration or method of calculation

- intervals at which remuneration is paid

- terms and conditions relating to hours of work (including normal working hours)

- holiday entitlement (including entitlement to accrue holiday pay)
- job title or brief job description
- place of work.

The following may be provided in separate documents:

- terms relating to injury, sickness, and sick pay
- pensions and pension schemes
- period of notice each party must give to terminate the contract
- where the employment is temporary, how long it is likely to last, or the termination date for a fixed-term contract
- collective agreements which directly affect terms and conditions
- disciplinary rules and steps in the disciplinary and grievance procedures, specifying the people with whom, and how, an employee can raise a grievance or apply if dissatisfied with a disciplinary decision.

Certain additional details are also required for employees sent to work outside the UK for more than one month.

Compiling written particulars demands care. Simplicity can give rise to anomalies because simple solutions do not recognise different sets of circumstances. An example of this might be an employer who gives 30 days' holiday a year plus all public and bank holidays. This is a simple rule, but how do you interpret it for an employee who works only Monday and Tuesday each week? You could 'pro-rata' the 30 days to 12, but how do you handle public and bank holidays, which often fall on a Monday?

On the other hand, complex systems can lead to confusion and often mistrust. For example, a system could be devised in which we add up how many holidays have been taken and then pay the part-time employees for only some of them. Of the 30 days' holiday plus the 8 public and bank holidays we might pay 15.2 days (two-fifths of 38 days) as one and quarter days per month plus one extra every five years. Such a scheme might be precisely fair.

You may have found this latter explanation hard to follow and it might be quite difficult to administer. If employees find a process difficult to understand, it can create distrust or even lead to outright dispute in some particular instance. You have to learn how to strike a balance between the simple and the complex.

There are many guides available for preparing particulars – for example, the CIPD manuals on *Policies and Procedures for People Managers* and *Employment Law for People Managers* or the Business Link website (see *References and further reading* at the end of the chapter).

You might like to know what the consequences of not providing written particulars are likely to be. Bear in mind that government officials will not arrive to check their existence, and neither you nor your employer is going to be prosecuted for such failures. However, if you fail to provide written particulars within the time limit, an employee can apply to an employment tribunal, which may then determine particulars of employment as it sees fit.

More seriously, if a tribunal claim is made and you have failed to provide adequate written particulars, tribunals must award two or four weeks' pay to the employee as compensation. You may feel this is unlikely to happen. Although it is clearly not good practice to neglect written particulars, so long as relationships with employees remain fair, you might be right. However, redundancies, dismissals or even resignations increase the chances of aggrieved employees making employment tribunal claims. Furthermore, a complaint that you have failed to provide written particulars will substantially weaken your case at tribunal. So you would be wise to encourage the managers in your organisation to accept good practice. Indeed, most managers like to be thought of as 'good employers'.

ACTIVITY 3.4

Look into how contracts are made and written particulars are prepared in your organisation. Compare the written particulars for a typical appointment with the details here. Discuss any queries with a suitable learning source.

Let's look next at employment protection rights, starting with dismissal.

EMPLOYMENT PROTECTION RIGHTS – DISMISSAL

THE RIGHT NOT TO BE UNFAIRLY DISMISSED

As an employee you will be investing a good proportion of your life in the work of your employer. Most probably you will feel that you make a valuable contribution and represent a good investment, not least because of your ongoing desire to learn and improve your performance. All being well, your employer will be of the same opinion. Unfortunately, it is not always the case that employers and employees share the same views. What the employee may see as conscientiousness, the employer may see as being exceedingly pedantic. Single-mindedness may be praised or seen as tunnel vision. The list could continue. So employers and employees do not always measure performance in the same way.

Let's take another example. An employee may need to leave early for a doctor's appointment. If the employee forgets to clock out because of being preoccupied with concern over the appointment, he or she may see this as a simple oversight. The employer may see the same action as an attempt to defraud the company.

These conflicting views bring us to an important point: it is not acceptable, at least in the case of an employee who has been with the employer for some time, for the employee to be dismissed without some serious attempt to resolve conflict.

These are only two examples. There is a whole range of areas where employers and employees may have different perceptions of each other and of what is expected. Here are a few more:

- the reliability with which the employee attends work
- the quality of the work that is completed
- the language that is used at work
- the achievement of targets
- the attitude to authority
- what constitutes reasonable treatment of the sexes
- what constitutes reasonable treatment of minority groups.

There are other, more serious, areas where behaviour is totally unacceptable (gross misconduct) and where summary dismissal (ie dismissal without notice) may be justified:

- pilfering
- unauthorised absence
- violence
- fraud
- drunkenness.

The danger is that in any of these areas it could be that the employee is falsely accused. (Incidentally, dismissal without notice does not mean 'instant dismissal'. All cases of gross misconduct must be thoroughly investigated before a decision to dismiss is taken.)

Dismissals occur for other reasons, too. An employee may become ill and unable to work; a heavy goods vehicle driver could lose his licence; a job may no longer be required; or a reorganisation may lead to fewer jobs even though the same amount of work is being done.

As we have already mentioned, the qualifying period for the right not to be unfairly dismissed is now 12 months' service. For an employee to be dismissed fairly there must first be a fair reason for the dismissal and the employer must act reasonably in arriving at the decision to dismiss.

A fair reason

There are six potentially fair reasons for dismissal (although the fifth is quite broad):

- capability – the inability to perform the type of work for which the employee was employed. This can include health factors.

- conduct – failure to meet reasonable expectations. This can include failure to carry out reasonable instructions, bad time-keeping and attendance, as well as gross misconduct, such as theft from the employer.

- redundancy – the work for which the employee was employed has ceased or diminished. Here the selection of a particular individual has to be shown to be fair.

- legal restrictions – this may apply, for example, when the employee becomes disqualified from driving and the only work available requires the employee to drive.

- 'some other substantial reason' – this area is established by precedents in case law. An example might be a reorganisation, so long as there is a sound business reason for it. This reason may be used when an employer cannot afford to continue paying on current terms and conditions, dismisses employees for sound business reasons and offers them a new contract.

- retirement – here a process has to be followed that gives the employee the right to request to work beyond the organisation's retirement age (which has to be 65 or over). If the request is turned down on certain prescribed grounds, then retirement should be fair. This is a relatively new (and very complex) area of legislation and it may develop further during the life of this book.

Whenever a decision to dismiss is taken, it is wise to determine which of the above reasons is the true one. Dismissed employees (subject to one year's service) have the right to ask for a written statement giving particulars of the reasons for dismissal, and the reason, or reasons, chosen may have to be defended in a tribunal. Employees dismissed while pregnant or on maternity leave or adoption leave must be given a statement of the particulars of the reasons for dismissal irrespective of whether they request it.

Acting reasonably

Employers may also have to show that they act, or have acted, reasonably, and the best way to do this is to follow a fair procedure. There is a statutory code of practice for dismissals by reason of misconduct and performance, and more detail is given on this in Chapter 8. The code does not apply to redundancy dismissals or the non-renewal of fixed-term contracts Other requirements apply to dismissals by reason of redundancy. Even when the procedure has been followed, the employer has to show that he or she has acted reasonably in reaching the decision to dismiss. Various Acas publications cover these procedures in detail, and you should consult the Acas Code of Practice on Disciplinary and Grievance Procedures. (See the list of reference sources at the end of this chapter.)

William, a service manager, has employed Jason for four years mainly as an assistant in the car dealership, undertaking simple tasks such as valeting. He is well aware that Jason is not very committed. A conversation with Jason six months ago revealed that Jason felt undervalued because he had previously worked as a car mechanic for a small garage and felt he could accomplish much more. To address this, William persuaded the dealership owners to increase Jason's pay and re-title his job 'mechanic'.

One afternoon sometime later William discovered, quite by chance, that Jason had not tightened down a car's cylinder-head properly after some major engine work. On another occasion he discovered that Jason had gone home, apparently ill, leaving behind work that William thought he had completed.

Looking back now, William recalls several occasions on which Jason has left early for incidental reasons and failed to complete work in the expected time. The dealership is small and this lack of commitment must have impinged disproportionately on other mechanics who, William suspects, have been covering up for Jason. One Friday afternoon Jason again leaves early for a doctor's appointment – and this time the other employees are annoyed enough to speak out, providing a catalogue of hearsay evidence to the effect that Jason is careless and continually makes mistakes that others have to rectify.

The next day William gives Jason a note inviting him to a disciplinary hearing to discuss his lack of commitment. Jason attends the meeting and William tells him of the slow work (which Jason concedes), of the numerous mistakes (which Jason contends were rarely his fault), of the frequent time off (on which Jason is silent), and concludes by dismissing Jason for lack of commitment.

Jason appeals to the owner of the dealership, who holds a meeting, but backs William.

This is not likely to be a fair dismissal for a number of reasons, among them:

- Jason has never been previously warned formally about his commitment.

- Indeed, did William send the right message by increasing Jason's pay?

- After the promotion was he trained or even supervised?

- At the meeting Jason was not invited to bring a companion nor asked for an explanation, although he attempted to proffer some.

- Of the explanations offered ('not his fault'), there was no investigation.

- There has been no attempt to enquire after any mitigating circumstances. Why, for example, did Jason visit the doctor? Might the reason have some bearing on his pace of work, attendance, etc?

We look at procedures in more detail in Chapter 8. The purpose of this case study is to illustrate the need for them.

Different procedures are appropriate in different circumstances. Having disciplinary and grievance procedures makes sense for all employers because they provide a framework for resolving conflict fairly. Ill-health issues are more effectively tackled by a specific ill-health or capability procedure. What is a reasonable course of action when behaviour is within an employee's control may no longer be reasonable when illness is involved. (See Chapter 8 for more information.)

Reasonableness is the key to fairness. What may be seen as reasonable procedures for a small employer may be considered to be inadequate procedures for a larger employer. Case studies 3.2 and 3.3 below represent illustrations of this.

Workers also have the right to be accompanied by a fellow worker or trade union representative at disciplinary hearings. For the purpose of this right, any hearing at which you contemplate taking some action on behalf of the employer is a disciplinary hearing. So, for example, if you are discussing the employee's ill-health (and a demotion or transfer could be potential outcomes), the employee has the right to be accompanied – and you must tell him or her of that right.

It is worth noting that fairness will be judged in the light of information available at the time the decision is made. An employer must carry out a thorough investigation to gather as much relevant information as is reasonable. He or she needs to have grounds for his or her beliefs – eg for believing that an employee is stealing. However, in most cases employers may make the decision on the balance of probabilities; they do not need proof beyond reasonable doubt. Subsequent, more conclusive, evidence of guilt or innocence is not relevant to the fairness of the decision.

CASE STUDY 3.2

After establishing grounds for believing an employee to be guilty, a sole proprietor with 10 employees decides to dismiss the employee in question for fiddling his bonus. The proprietor may have been the only person to have investigated the allegation, may have been the only person to assess all the evidence, and may have taken the decision to dismiss without consulting anyone else. He might be expected to consider questions such as: Were other employees fiddling their bonuses too? Did the employee know, or was it reasonable to expect him to know, that bonus fraud was gross misconduct that could result in dismissal without warning? Although the employer can be expected to have asked and answered such questions, he may nonetheless have to make the final decision without being able to consult anyone else. He should, however, still have followed the Acas code of practice in arriving at the decision. He must also have allowed the employee to be accompanied at the disciplinary hearing, and at any appeal, having previously informed the employee of that right.

In an organisation of 2,000 employees, such a course of action could not rest with one person. More would be expected in terms of the degree of thoroughness. Were the questions posed above properly answered? Was the accusation thoroughly investigated by appropriate people? Was the decision to dismiss taken at a senior level in the organisation? Was the appeal heard by a more senior person who had not been involved in the original decision?

The guidelines contained in the Acas code of practice are crucial. The extent to which they are followed, or not followed, will not only be taken into account when a tribunal judges fairness but may affect any compensation.

DISMISSAL

Dismissal takes place when the employer terminates the contract with notice, without notice, or because of actions that effectively breach the contract. Fixed-term contracts that expire without renewal are also dismissals.

There are times when a dismissal is disputed. For example, a supervisor may 'blow up' at an employee, perhaps humiliating the employee in front of his or her colleagues. The employee decides 'enough is enough', goes home, and does not return to work. Has the employee been dismissed, or has he or she resigned?

On the face of it you might conclude that the employee has resigned. But these are circumstances in which the employee might be entitled to terminate his or her employment by reason of the employer's conduct. So let's look at some of the arguments that might be put either way.

The employer might argue that the supervisor carried out a reprimand, that it was justified, and that it was carried out respectfully – although it may be conceded that colleagues should not have witnessed it. The employer could maintain that the employee has simply resigned. There is therefore no question of dismissal, fair or unfair. Conversely, the ex-employee may produce evidence of previous mistreatment and seek to show that the reprimand was clearly humiliating and very public. It could have been 'the last straw'. He or she might contend that it would be quite intolerable to continue to work in such circumstances. Because of the actions taken, therefore, the employee may argue that the employer has dismissed him or her *constructively* – and unfairly at that. Before the employee can take the case to a tribunal, he or she should raise the grievance with the employer, and well-established and respected procedures facilitate this. But there is no guarantee that a grievance will be raised, and the employer may not get the chance to provide a resolution before an employment tribunal claim is made.

Were the case to come before an employment tribunal, the question of dismissal or resignation would be examined very thoroughly. For example, the words used in the reprimand (or emotional outburst), evidence of previous mistreatment and any protests the employee may have made in the past could all be taken into account. The employer's response to any grievance, or especially any lack of it, would be important. In some cases a tribunal may decide that the employee resigned. In others, it may feel that the employer's treatment of the employee meant that trust and confidence had broken down and that, in effect, the employment contract had been broken. This would be 'constructive dismissal', entitling the employee to presume, from the employer's actions, that he or she had been dismissed. That is, that the employer had broken the contract.

Whether such a dismissal would be unfair might depend on the reason for the reprimand, on whether there had been a thorough investigation, on whether the employee had been formally warned beforehand and on a range of other factors.

From the employer's viewpoint, sets of circumstances that could lead to an employee claiming constructive dismissal are to be avoided. A dismissal may be claimed even if it was not intended. The issue then becomes the employer's misconduct and the employer will have to listen carefully to any grievance. The employer will, in effect, have been 'wrong-footed' and will have given power to the employee. Rescuing the situation may require disciplining of the supervisor (not a very satisfactory situation), providing the supervisor with training or even changing reporting relationships.

Once again, the main relevant legislation here is the Employment Rights Act 1996. The Employment Relations Act 1999 has relevance to accompaniment at disciplinary hearings.

CASE STUDY 3.3

A distribution division of a large national clothing company employs 80 people either as drivers or on the warehouse floor. There are two drivers who work only locally, one of whom is Derek who has worked for them for 12 years. These drivers' responsibilities are to distribute smaller loads in the highly built-up area in the immediate vicinity of the warehouse. They are not HGV-licensed.

Derek was driving home from a private social function one night, was stopped by the police and subsequently lost his driving licence for 12 months. The distribution division should not dismiss him without first considering all the circumstances. For example, can Derek be employed in the warehouse? It is very likely that there will be some suitable unskilled work that he could do. Could someone else drive the van, perhaps someone from the warehouse, even though he or she might need some training? Has Derek any solutions to offer? Such options should be formally investigated, and if no solution is possible, the reasons carefully documented with evidence as to why they have been rejected. If Derek is dismissed and makes a claim, a tribunal will want to be satisfied that, taking into account the size and resources of the organisation, dismissal was the type of response that a reasonable employer might have made. If the employer cannot convince the tribunal of this, the dismissal will be unfair. Following procedures alone is not sufficient to establish fairness.

ACTIVITY 3.5

Many tribunal cases are reported in newspapers. Look through a better-quality daily paper for a report on a dismissal case. Review the case in conjunction with the text here. What was the reason for dismissal? Can you see, from the newspaper report, whether the employer acted fairly? While it is useful to complete this exercise, remember that newspaper reporting is not necessarily precise or particularly comprehensive – a whole week in a tribunal might be described in a few hundred words.

EMPLOYMENT PROTECTION RIGHTS – DISCRIMINATION

Here we shall be looking at a wide range of areas of potential discrimination; first we examine some broad principles.

Although it may be argued that it makes sound business sense to recruit people solely on their ability to do the job, that judgement is easily influenced by beliefs that are not, in truth, relevant. Even those committed to recruiting on ability can find themselves victims to prejudice that they did not realise they had. More disturbingly, there are still managers who will admit, privately, to unlawful discrimination. For example, they may have prejudices about what constitutes 'men's work' or feel unable to relate to people of a different culture from their own. Unfortunately, in bringing such prejudices to the workplace, they mistakenly believe they serve themselves and their employer better because of it.

As an HR practitioner you may need to examine your beliefs carefully. It is helpful to read relevant articles in *People Management* which show how HR practitioners are positively tackling equal opportunities issues. Make sure you understand your own organisation's policy and practices towards women, ethnic minorities and other groups. These policies should be designed to encourage equal opportunities by educating workers and decision-makers, and by positive actions to address inequality wherever it exists. The spirit or intention of equal opportunities legislation, as well as the letter of the law, is important.

Good management practices are well described by the principles of diversity (see Chapter 5). In any event, unlawful discrimination is an area of developing law. For example, the new Equality Act will have a profound effect on how organisations will need to respond to diversity principles.

Notwithstanding the merits of your employer's policies, men and women, ethnic minorities, disabled people and many ex-offenders (those with spent convictions) and others (see below) have protection against discrimination. So you must be aware of the legislation.

Keep in mind that applicants as well as workers can be discriminated against. Everyone who is applying for or undertaking work personally is eligible for these rights: there are no length of (employment) service requirements. So applicants as well as new workers can take a claim to an employment tribunal. Following an incidence of apparent discrimination, applicants, employees or ex-employees may submit a questionnaire to the employer. In this they set out why they believe they were discriminated against and the employer has to say whether it agrees with the claimant's version of events. Pertinent questions can also be asked. The responses can be used in employment tribunal claims – so if you receive such a questionnaire, answer it carefully. There are no limits to the amount of compensation that an employment tribunal can award in cases of discrimination.

If an employee makes a claim of discrimination to a tribunal and is then treated by the employer less favourably as a result, that is victimisation. Employees may seek further remedy at tribunal in that event.

You must also be aware of what harassment is, which can occur on the grounds of sex, race, disability, sexual orientation and others. As defined in the Employment Equality (Sex Discrimination) Regulations 2005, it is behaviour that violates the dignity of another person or creates an intimidating, hostile, degrading, humiliating or offensive environment. Harassment is specifically unlawful if perpetrated on the grounds of race, disability, religion, sex or sexual orientation.

The Equality and Human Rights Commission (EHRC) promotes equality and human rights. It provides advice and guidance, works to implement an effective legislative framework, and raises awareness of rights among employees.

As part of this work the Commission publishes statutory equality duty codes of practice. These codes of practice represent authoritative guidance on the requirements that must be met by public authorities to make sure they are complying with the law.

The EHRC has responsibilities in relation to racial equality, disability rights, sex discrimination and the more recently protected areas of sexual orientation, age, religion and belief, and human rights.

There are also in existence a number of codes of practice on the main areas of discrimination, created under previous statutory bodies. Failure to follow these codes may be taken into account by employment tribunals in deciding whether to accept claims of discrimination.

SEX DISCRIMINATION

The social unacceptability of sex discrimination has encouraged appropriate legislation, but much of it has been encouraged in particular by membership of the European Union, in which the Treaty of Rome 1957 provides for equal treatment of men and women.

Discrimination on the grounds of sex or on grounds of people's married status is unlawful, except in certain special circumstances. However, employers and designated (ie by the Secretary of State) training bodies can take positive action to promote equality. For example, they can set up management courses for existing women workers only, if women are underrepresented at managerial levels. Another positive action would be to encourage applications from one sex. The Equal Opportunites Code of Practice provides guidance in these matters. The new Equality Act makes relevant changes in this area.

Both direct and indirect discrimination are illegal. Direct discrimination means allowing gender to influence employment decisions – eg in passing a woman over for promotion in favour of a less-qualified man. Indirect discrimination occurs if conditions that effectively create discrimination are applied. These could be certain criteria on job specifications or advertisements if they tend to preclude women or men. For example, a job specification that determines a minimum height would be indirectly discriminatory and unlawful unless objectively justified. Since men tend to be taller than women this would discriminate indirectly against women. An objective justification would be if there were safety implications to being below the minimum height.

ACTIVITY 3.6

In your capacity as an HR practitioner, assume you are invited to assist a manager at an interview. You fear that the manager has no intention of accepting a woman for the vacancy although two of the five interviewees are women. Write down what you would do. Discuss your intentions with one of your learning sources.

There are a number of genuine occupational qualifications (GOQs) that do allow some sex discrimination. Such GOQs cover reasons of privacy, decency, welfare and authenticity (eg modelling clothes), certain accommodation circumstances, certain single-sex establishments (eg prisons) and, to some extent, work in private homes.

MATERNITY RIGHTS

Since the 1970s women have had maternity rights. That is, they have the right not to be unfairly dismissed because of pregnancy, the right to maternity pay, and the right to return to work following maternity leave. Over the years, legislation and case law have strengthened and enhanced these rights. Dismissal on maternity-related grounds is now automatically unfair, irrespective of length of service or hours of work. All women employees have the right to 52 weeks' maternity leave and 39 weeks' maternity pay. It is also important to recognise that the contract of employment now continues through the maternity leave period. This has a number of effects. For example, annual leave accumulates during the period of maternity leave and may have to be paid in lieu if the woman does not return to work.

OTHER PARENTAL RIGHTS

In addition to maternity leave and pay there are a number of other parental rights including paternity pay and leave, parental leave and adoption leave, as well as time off for emergencies involving dependants.

If you are called on, as well you might be, to administer these rights and the corresponding pay, there are government publications and other sources, such as updated reference books, which you can use for guidance. See *References and further reading* at the end of this chapter.

EQUAL PAY

Men and women are entitled to claim equal treatment in respect of pay and conditions.

In practice, the operation of equal pay is complicated by measurements. Equal treatment requires determination of like work, of work rated as equivalent, and of work of equal value. And of course, what constitutes equal treatment itself is not easy to measure. Tribunal cases arising under the Equal Pay Act 1970 have frequently led to appeals, proving very expensive for employers. Despite the complications, therefore, every endeavour should be made to ensure equal treatment of men and women. There is now an Equal Pay Code and employers are being encouraged to adopt equal pay policies and carry out equal pay audits (see Chapter 7 for more information). Legislation is now forcing more transparency in pay policies so that inequalities are brought into the open.

THE BURDEN OF PROOF

In the event that an applicant or employee can provide evidence of probable discrimination, it is the employer's responsibility to prove it has treated men and women equally. This means that you need to keep good records of all employment decisions so you can show that such decisions did not discriminate on unlawful sexual grounds. See Case study 3.4.

CASE STUDY 3.4

John is a small businessman employing five people. Emma returned from maternity leave recently, having been his administrator prior to that.

While Emma was away John employed Joan as a temporary replacement. It was at this point that he realised how inefficient Emma had been in the three years she had worked for him. Joan introduced new computer software, reorganised the filing system and took on a range of valuable duties in the resulting free time that she herself had created.

On Emma's return John decided to make Emma redundant, maintaining that the work she was employed to do no longer existed, and to retain Joan. He now faces an employment tribunal claim for unfair dismissal and sex discrimination. If the tribunal concludes (as it seems it must) that the work is suitable and appropriate for Emma or that Emma has been dismissed for a reason related to her pregnancy or maternity, then John will lose this case.

The right to return from maternity leave is heavily protected in law and employers cannot safely 'construct' situations that suit their ends.

The main legislation relating to sex discrimination of which you should be aware is:

- the Sex Discrimination Acts 1975 and 1986
- the Equal Pay Act 1970
- the Employment Rights Act 1996
- the Employment Relations Act 1999
- the Employment Act 2002
- the Equality Act 2010.

PART-TIME WORKERS

During the 1990s, rulings by the European Court of Justice (ECJ) about what constitutes 'pay' effectively gave part-timers the right to equal treatment with full-timers. This meant they acquired unfair dismissal and redundancy pay rights after the same periods of service as full-timers. Equal treatment covers a range of pay elements such as pensions, severance pay, access to promotion and training opportunities and sickness benefits. This equal treatment is now provided for in statutory legislation, and failure to recognise the right to equal treatment can give rise, at an employment tribunal, to claims of discrimination or to claims for equal pay. The relevant legislation is in the Part-time Workers (Prevention of Less Favourable Treatment) Regulations 2000.

RACIAL EQUALITY

Many larger and progressive organisations in both the public and private sectors provide good examples of best practice in equal opportunities.

Cultural diversity has often developed more slowly in other sectors. Ethnic minorities and immigrant workers still tend to be over-represented in low-pay occupations.

Whether diversity is driven by a desire to be morally right, by commercial pragmatism, or by the law, there exists legislation to underpin racial equality in employment and other areas. The legislation is similar to that provided to eliminate sex discrimination. Direct and indirect race discrimination are both outlawed. There are legislative exceptions for genuine occupational qualifications, but in this case only reasons of authenticity and welfare qualify as genuine occupational qualifications. Positive action, such as the provision of training, to redress an imbalance of particular racial groups is permitted. There is also a code of practice; this encourages ethnic monitoring to help identify and eliminate race discrimination. You should obtain a copy of the code. The relevant legislation in this area is the Race Relations Act 1976.

THE RIGHT TO WORK IN THE UNITED KINGDOM

Not everyone has the right to work in the United Kingdom, and it is the employers' responsibility to check that individuals that they employ do have that right. The Home Office website publishes details of who has the right to work here and specifies the documents that the employer must be provided with to be checked. The same process of checking eligibility should be applied to everyone whom you employ. To apply one process to applicants who appear to be British and another process to those who are apparently East European would be a form of unlawful discrimination.

DISABLED PEOPLE

It may be difficult to come to terms with the fact that a disability has no practical implications for job performance, and yet in many circumstances that is precisely the case. Accomplished blind and deaf musicians are one reminder that disability need not be a barrier to achievement. We have to be very wary of mind-sets that lead us to make unjustified assumptions about others.

In Britain comprehensive anti-discrimination legislation protects disabled people. It is unlawful to treat a disabled person less favourably, on account of their disability, than you would treat someone in a similar position who does not have that disability. Employers are also required to make reasonable adjustments to premises, interview arrangements or work stations, etc, so that disabled applicants or workers are not put at any substantial disadvantage. The employment provisions of the Act apply to all employers.

There is a code of practice and, again, you should obtain a copy of it. It is very helpful in explaining what you may or may not be expected to do in a variety of situations. Relevant legislation is in:

- the Disability Discrimination Act 1995
- the Disability Rights Commission Act 1999.

EMPLOYING EX-OFFENDERS

Unless people who have served prison terms can be rehabilitated into employment, it logically follows that they are likely to resort to crime again. So there is some legal protection for those who have received sentences of not more than 30 months. They have the chance to 'wipe the slate clean' after a certain time. The time required varies according to the original sentence. 'Spent' convictions do not have to be disclosed, and even if disclosed, cannot be taken into account in employment decisions. There are, however, exemptions where the work involves access to vulnerable groups such as young people or those with disabilities. The relevant legislation is the Rehabilitation of Offenders Act 1974 and Rehabilitation of Offenders Act 1974 (Exceptions) Order 1975. If you employ people in an exempted occupation, you will need to familiarise yourself with the services provided by the Criminal Records Bureau.

SEXUAL ORIENTATION, RELIGION OR BELIEF, GENDER REASSIGNMENT

Direct or indirect discrimination on the grounds of sexual orientation, religion or belief is unlawful. In the case of religion or belief Acas have issued guidance to deal with putting appropriate practices in place. There is some limited exemption to allow discrimination on sexual orientation for religious reasons, and also limited possibilities of genuine occupational requirements where the nature of the employment requires membership of a particular religion. What amounts to a religion or a belief is not specified in statutory legislation but is interpreted by tribunals. In some cases, therefore, you may need to take further advice.

There is also protection against unfavourable treatment for people who intend to undergo, have undergone or are undergoing gender reassignment.

The relevant legislation is:

- the Employment Equality (Sexual Orientation) Regulations 2003
- the Employment Equality (Religion or Belief) Regulations 2003.

AGE DISCRIMINATION

Legislation making age discrimination unlawful is relatively new in the United Kingdom, coming into force with the Employment Equality (Age) Regulations 2006.

Broadly, it is unlawful to make an employment decision using a person's age either as the reason or as a factor in the decision. But there are a few exceptions at both ends of the scale. Young people, for example, have a lower minimum wage, and older people from 65 onwards can still be retired – even if they would prefer to work on.

Making decisions on a basis that could be age-related (such as on a person's length of service) or providing service-related benefits could be discriminatory. Nonetheless, there are circumstances in which it may be justified. Case law is developing in this area and will have to be considered in specific instances.

Although the minimum age at which you can retire an employee is 65, you need to follow a procedure of giving over six months' but less than 12 months' notice of your intention to retire the person. At the same time you must give them details of their right to request the opportunity work on. But even if an employee makes a request, an organisation can still refuse the request fairly easily. The important point for the organisation is to have a process in place so that the relevant advice is given at the right time.

The Equality Act may create changes in age discrimination, so you should refer to this Act once it is in force.

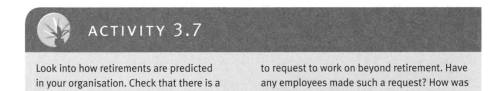

ACTIVITY 3.7

Look into how retirements are predicted in your organisation. Check that there is a process for informing employees of their right to request to work on beyond retirement. Have any employees made such a request? How was it handled, and what was the outcome?

OTHER STATUTORY LEGISLATION

First we take a brief glance at Northern Ireland, where legislation particular to the province outlaws religious discrimination. Then we look at the Working Time Regulations, the national minimum wage and human rights, before we consider the philosophy behind the health and safety legislation introduced over the past few decades and we refer to the legislation on trade unions.

RELIGIOUS DISCRIMINATION — NORTHERN IRELAND

Fair employment legislation is further-reaching than any other anti-discrimination law. It demands that employers strictly monitor their workforce and applicants. It may require employers to take affirmative action to redress imbalances. Several aspects of the legislation are backed by criminal law. The Fair Employment Commission publishes a code of practice that, if your responsibilities cover Northern Ireland workers, you should obtain.

The relevant legislation is the Fair Employment (Northern Ireland) Act 1989.

THE WORKING TIME REGULATIONS

These introduced a maximum working week of 48 hours as averaged over one of three possible periods: 17 weeks, 26 weeks (certain special cases), or 52 weeks by workforce agreement. They provide restrictions on the maximum length of night shifts, and provide for rest periods, work breaks and statutory annual leave of 5.6 weeks.

Workers can opt out of the 48 hours voluntarily, but leave must be taken: it cannot be paid in lieu.

The Regulations place specific requirements on records that are kept in relation to the 48-hour week and night shifts, and records will, of course, be needed if there are disputes over any of the other provisions.

The Working Time Regulations are complicated, so you would be wise to take advice if they have implications for decisions you have to make.

The legislation is the Working Time Regulations 1998 and the Health and Safety (Young Persons) Regulations 1997 providing additional protection for young workers.

THE NATIONAL MINIMUM WAGE

The way in which the wage has to be calculated (with particular pay and hours elements) is quite specific, and employers have to be able to show that they are complying.

It is necessary to calculate a wage for all workers and to be able to provide the necessary information for the Inland Revenue. Individuals are also entitled to statements on request. Failing to keep records is a criminal offence.

The relevant legislation is the National Minimum Wage Act 1998.

HUMAN RIGHTS

The abuse of human rights by state agents during World War II led in 1950 to the development of a European Convention of Human Rights. This is an agreed set of fundamental human rights. The intention was to restrain governments from abusing the rights of their citizens in the future. Government employees are also citizens, and this is one reason for its relevance to HR work. Such employees can take action against the government for infringement of their rights.

Before the Human Rights Act citizens who considered that their government was abusing their rights were obliged to pursue their case in the European courts. However, most of these rights (defined by Articles in the Convention) can now be taken up in the UK courts. Courts and tribunals are also agents of the government. They therefore have to take account of human rights in considering the issues brought before them.

Privacy is an important area. This could be invaded if an organisation monitors the use of the telephone, the Internet or email for personal (private) purposes. Similarly, the use of drug, alcohol and medical tests in selection or employment could intrude upon privacy, as could locker or body searches. However, some of these activities are inevitable for a variety of sound reasons. So that such activities avoid compromising rights, it is crucial to have clear and well-communicated policies as to what will be done in the name of the organisation and what employees can and cannot do.

Freedom of expression also impacts on employee relations. For example, can you specify what your employees wear? There can be good reasons for doing so. Image is an important part of business and it is reasonable, in customer-facing jobs particularly, to insist on standards. Again the answer is carefully developed policies on dress code, appropriate language (in some cases) and on other matters of personal expression that could impact on the business.

Finally, citizens should enjoy freedom from discrimination on a wider range of grounds than current UK law. What practical effect this will have still remains to be seen.

All the above are areas where the law is still developing through case law, so it would be wise to keep up to date with the latest developments.

The relevant statutory legislation is the Human Rights Act 1998.

ACTIVITY 3.8

Choose a piece of legislation that has been enacted in the last few years. Investigate what practices have changed as a result. You could look at application forms, staff handbooks, induction and other training documents, disciplinary procedures and other staff records. Is there anything that should have changed in response to the legislation but still needs attention?

DATA PROTECTION

This has implications for HR information systems, and details are provided in Chapter 4.

PUBLIC INTEREST DISCLOSURE

This has implications in relation to grievance procedures and is covered in Chapter 8.

HEALTH AND SAFETY

At the (then) IPD's Harrogate Conference in 1995, a speaker – Henry Olejnik of Motorola – told how his father lost two fingers in an employment accident in the 1950s. He related how, at that time, such an incident was almost regarded as acceptable. It was seen as 'just the way things are'. The point he went on to make is that we tend to accept the psychological damage (ie stress) that we do to people today as 'just one of those things'. He questioned what judgement future HR practitioners might make of our then current attitudes.

The principal issues here are that, first, we no longer found it acceptable that workers should receive physical injuries at work; and second, we still tended to accept emotional and psychological injuries as not being the direct responsibility of the employer. Has much changed?

There is continuous progress in attitudes because a mature society, and a caring employer, will look after its people with great care physically and emotionally. In Britain we have seen an increasing legal underpinning of physical and emotional welfare since the early 1960s. The responsibility of the employer to take reasonable steps to manage stress is increasing as a factor in civil court and employment tribunal cases and settlements. See Case study 3.5.

CASE STUDY 3.5

Mr Walker worked for Northumberland County Council as a social services officer from 1970 to 1988. Throughout that time the workload placed on him increased dramatically. He told his superiors on several occasions that his department was understaffed. He threatened to leave unless he was given support. He suffered a first nervous breakdown in November 1986 (then aged 49) and he went on sick leave. By February 1987 he had recovered sufficiently to contemplate a return to work. His doctor had informed him that he should only consider this if he was provided with more staff to relieve his work burden. His employers agreed to supply him with an assistant. On his return to work he was not given any extra assistance and he suffered a second nervous breakdown in September 1987. In February 1988 he was dismissed by the Council on the grounds of ill-health. The Court decided that the Council was in breach of its duty of care when they failed to provide support when he returned to work. This was the first time that the High Court recognised that an employee could sue for work-related stress.

Walker v Northumberland County Council [1995] IRLR 35, Copyright material taken from Jordans Employment Law Service reproduced with permission of Jordan Publishing Ltd.

Early health and safety legislation related chiefly to premises and concerned working conditions, toilets, first-aid boxes, record-keeping, and fire precautions – the need for fire escapes and for employee training so that people knew what to do if there was a fire. These provisions are now contained within more recent statutes.

Health and safety legislation introduced in the 1970s

The main relevant Acts were related to factories and then to 'offices, shops and railway premises'. Hazards, though, are different in different industries. Since 1974 legislation has required employers to produce health and safety policies for their organisations. Because hazards vary from organisation to organisation, the policy is expected to reflect the circumstances of each. This provision is contained in the Health and Safety at Work Act 1974 (HASWA), which requires employers to safeguard the health and safety of workers 'as far as reasonably practical'. It covers all workers, as well as members of the public who may be exposed to hazards from the employer.

Written health and safety policies are a statutory requirement for all employers with five or more employees. A central part of the policy is the General Statement. This must identify responsibilities for health and safety both at different levels and for specific matters. It has to explain how workers are involved and their acceptance gained. The main policy requirements are summarised in the box below.

Health and safety policies should:

- reflect the plant, equipment and substances used in the organisation
- address particular hazards
- indicate arrangements for emergencies
- clarify how safety is communicated to employees and visitors on site
- indicate training, safety provision for new workers, etc
- register the regular checks and inspections that are needed.

ACTIVITY 3.9

Look at your organisation's health and safety policy. Is it readily available? Compare it to the guidelines provided above – does it address each area? Is it up to date? Make a list of any matters that you think should be addressed.

As well as the requirement for a written health and safety policy, HASWA made managers personally responsible for safety. It also placed a legal obligation on employees to comply with their employer's safety policies. Trade unions were given the right to appoint safety representatives and employers obliged to consult them. Factory inspectors were given powers of enforcement, enabling them to issue improvement and prohibition notices.

An improvement notice means that a safety aspect has to be improved within a set time. A typical improvement notice might be to reduce the level of dust in the working atmosphere. Prohibition notices mean that equipment or premises cannot be used until changes have been made. A typical prohibition notice may prohibit use of a cutting machine until a guard has been placed on it.

Health and safety at work is overseen by the the Health and Safety Executive (HSE), which has wide powers to enforce health and safety and investigate industrial accidents. It issues a code of practice which, again, you should obtain. The HSE enforces the law where responsibilities are not covered by other bodies such as local authorities. All enforcing bodies can appoint inspectors. As well as being able to issue improvement and prohibition notices, inspectors can enter premises without notice and can prosecute employers and workers.

The relevant legislation is the Health and Safety at Work Act 1974.

Health and safety legislation introduced in the 1980s and 1990s

To improve enforcement, new reporting requirements were introduced in 1985. These required employers to report 'injuries, diseases and dangerous occurrences' to the HSE or, where appropriate, to the local authority. They also required the keeping of records and an accident book. Factories and all employers with 10 or more people must ensure that all accidents, however minor, are recorded in an accident book.

It had been known for many years that substances encountered at work (eg coal dust and asbestos) caused illness. Research has continually been adding other substances known to cause cancer. So in 1988 and again in 1994 new Acts required employers to assess health risks that arise from hazardous substances in their work activities. Employers must provide controls that will be effective in protecting workers and anyone else who may be affected by such work. The main obligations on employers are shown in the box below. The relevant legislation is the Reporting of Injuries, Diseases and Dangerous Occurrences Regulations 1995 (RIDDOR) and the Control of Substances Hazardous to Health Regulations 2002 (COSHH), which were originally introduced in this period.

CONTROLLING SUBSTANCES HAZARDOUS TO HEALTH
The main obligations on employers are to:

- assess the risks and the measures necessary for control of exposure
- prevent or adequately control exposure to hazardous substances
- ensure that control methods are used and maintained in efficient working order
- monitor the work environment
- carry out health surveillance on employees where appropriate
- provide information, instruction, and training on risks and precautions.

The European Commission is now a major force in British health and safety legislation. Such issues are decided by majority voting in which no nation can exercise a veto. Member nations are obliged to bring domestic legislation into line. The result is a strengthening of existing legislation. The main features of health and safety at work regulations are summarised in the box below.

HEALTH AND SAFETY AT WORK REGULATIONS
The following areas require attention by the employer:

- managing health and safety (eg assessing risks)
- workplace health, safety and welfare (eg working environment, housekeeping)
- provision and use of work equipment (eg tools to be suitable for their purpose)
- manual handling (eg avoiding or assessing needs and methods)
- protective equipment (eg ensuring that it is properly used)
- display screen equipment (eg satisfying certain minimum requirements).

Health and safety should be managed like other functions, with clear reporting relationships, planning, control and monitoring. Workers need comprehensive and relevant information and proper training. The Regulations require an assessment of the risks to health and safety that arise from the employer's activities. This is to guide the employer as to measures that may have to be taken to comply with statutory requirements. Anyone employing five or more employees is required to record the findings of the assessment.

New minimum standards for the workplace have been set covering such issues as maintenance of equipment, ventilation, temperature, cleanliness, traffic routes, the potential for falling objects, washing and changing and rest facilities.

Work equipment must be suitable, properly maintained and its operatives trained. Controls for starting and stopping machinery have minimum requirements, as do isolation procedures to prevent, for example, equipment starting up while maintenance is being undertaken.

More than a quarter of reported accidents are associated with manual handling, so regulations provide for a particular procedure to assess such risks. There is an obligation to avoid activities where there is a risk of injury, perhaps by automation or mechanisation. Where avoidance is not completely achieved, measures have to be implemented to minimise risks so far as is reasonably practical.

Personal protective equipment should be seen as a last resort after all other methods of improving safety have been considered. Regulations cover its quality, suitability, use, and the requirement for proper training.

Display screen equipment stipulations cover not only computer screens but other forms of display, such as microfiche readers. A variety of risks must be assessed, including positioning, posture and the work environment. Those who use such equipment are entitled to free eye tests and to basic costs of glasses to correct vision defects associated with using the equipment.

You can find risk assessment forms in a variety of publications such as *Employment Law for People Managers* (see *References and further reading* at the end of this chapter).

Extensive guidance and codes of practice are contained in a series of brochures issued by the HSE. They are important to obtain if you have responsibilities in the areas covered. Pertinent legislation includes the Management of Health and Safety at Work Regulations 1999; the Health and Safety (Display Screen Equipment) Regulations 1992; the Manual Handling Operations Regulations 1992; the Health and Safety (Young Persons) Regulations 1997; and the Provision and Use of Work Equipment Regulations 1998. There is also a variety of other regulations specific to particular work or industry sectors.

ACTIVITY 3.10

Pick a topical health and safety issue in your department or organisation – for example, the use of computer screens. Research the appropriate legislation and good practice.

Compare the legislation and good practice with what actually happens. Make a note of suitable improvements.

TRADE UNIONS

The legislation that regulates the activities of trade unions is complex. But understanding how trade unions fit into the employment framework is important for HR practitioners. They have to know what a trade union is, what shop stewards do, the significance of trade union recognition and of collective agreements, the importance, particularly in the public sector, of partnership working, and the power of trade unions as manifested in the threat of industrial action. Awareness of Acas and the services it offers is also important. All these matters are covered in Chapter 2.

The legislation that regulates trade unions and their activities is the Trade Union and Labour Relations (Consolidation) Act 1992 as amended, and the Employment Relations Act 1999.

REDUNDANCY

When an organisation has more employees than it needs for its activities, it invariably has to look to reducing the total number. Employees are a major cost and an organisation whose income is depleted (by the loss of a major order, for example) may not be able to continue to afford to pay all its employees. The process of reducing the number of employees when they are dismissed for this reason is known as redundancy. In legal terms there are two slightly different definitions of redundancy. The Employment Rights Act 1996 s139 refers to:

- a reduction or cessation of work of a particular kind, or
- a reduction or cessation of work of a particular kind at the place where the employee is employed.

The Trade Union and Labour Relations (Consolidation) Act 1992 (TULR(C)A) s195 refers to redundancy as being dismissals where the reason(s) for dismissal are not related to the people being dismissed. Although it may seem inconvenient to have two meanings, in practice one refers to the employees' rights and the other to the need to consult.

There is a duty under TULR(C)A s193 to give 30 days' notice to the Secretary of State (a form is available from the Employment Service) where there are 20 or more employees who may be made redundant at one establishment. If 100 or more may be made redundant, the notice period is 90 days.

The law protects redundant employees in a number of ways.

Consultation

Firstly, there has to be consultation, and there are precise rules on the length of consultation required according to the numbers to be made redundant (for more detail see one of the online manuals such as the CIPD's *Policies and Procedures for People Managers* or *Employment Law for People Managers*; see also *References and further reading* at the end of this chapter). Consultation has to be with a trade union or with employee representatives (if there is no recognised trade union) and with the individuals themselves. The consultation has to seek to avoid redundancies. We will therefore discuss some of the alternatives to redundancy.

Where the reduction in work could be temporary, it should be possible to reduce the labour cost by means of reductions in overtime, by short-time working (working less than normal hours) or by lay-offs (periods of time in which employees do not work and might not be paid).

In circumstances where the reduction is not expected to be temporary, one of the most popular alternatives to declaring redundancies is to use 'natural wastage'. This refers to the fact that in any organisation people tend to leave 'naturally'. They may retire, find other jobs or leave for personal reasons such as a partner moving his or her job location. Indeed, organisations facing redundancies may seek to encourage wastage by offering voluntary early retirement packages, reduced promotions or steady wage levels. During the consultation process there may be requests to allow natural wastage to take its course or for early retirement packages to be enhanced.

Allied to natural wastage is a 'recruitment freeze'. In these circumstances the organisation places a ban on recruiting more employees. Trade unions may call for a recruitment freeze partly because it puts pressure on the organisation.

This pressure encourages consideration of other alternatives such as redeployment (to alternative work) and re-training. It is not unusual for an organisation to be recruiting in one area of its activities and making redundancies in another. Organisations have a high level of investment in employees in terms of their experience of the organisation's culture. Redundancy is also expensive in terms of payments to individuals as well as the disruption it causes to the day-to-day activities and the senior management time that is invariably involved, so redeployment and re-training may be a cost-effective option.

Other options include offering employees sabbaticals, seconding them to other organisations, or asking for voluntary reductions in hours or even pay.

Relocation to another place of work, a form of redeployment, can also be an option in some cases. While redundancy may be a cessation at a place of work, it may be reasonable to offer alternative work some short distance away. How far is reasonable is best based on advice. There are several past cases that give guidance.

Retaining specialist skills and experience is important so that an organisation is better placed when its economic situation improves. But this is not always possible.

Voluntary redundancy may be an alternative to compulsory redundancy. Here employees who might have been considering leaving or retiring are offered a financial package (usually a favourable one) to encourage them to leave voluntarily. During a consultation process there may be requests to improve the package to encourage volunteers.

Outplacement, career assistance or other means of assisting employees to find other work is often provided. Because the employer is seen as a party with a vested interest, these services are often provided, at the employer's expense, by outside consultancies. They may be provided before an employee has been declared redundant, to assist natural wastage, or afterwards.

Because demand for employees can fluctuate, some employers keep employees on after they no longer need them – ie they keep a surplus pool of employees. An opportunity may arise later and the employee is there, ready to take the position. In addition, natural wastage can take effect over a longer period. Surplus employees are sometimes seconded to charities. This can keep their skills up to speed, give the charity some benefit and avoid a demotivated employee remaining on site. It is an expensive option, though, generally taken up by large employers with substantial resources only.

When all else fails, an organisation will be forced to declare 'compulsory redundancies'.

Fair redundancy

For the employees, their next line of protection is that their selection for redundancy has to be shown to be fair. One of the most popular means of establishing fairness is a simple rule such as 'last in, first out'. Here the employees most recently recruited are the first ones on the list if redundancies are declared. This does not always serve the employer's interests. For example, recent recruiting may have been a response to a skills shortage. Employers therefore often use alternative procedures to determine who is to go first.

Furthermore, the 'last in, first out' selection process can be considered indirectly discriminatory on age grounds. This is because it is more likely that those recruited most recently will be younger than those who have been employed for some time. As a last resort, however, it is generally considered acceptable (although that may change).

The essential point of any procedure is that it must be demonstrably fair. Dismissing those who lack essential skills may be fair. Dismissing on the basis of a performance rating may also be fair. However, if the rating is a subjective one, perhaps involving ratings where different employees have been rated by different people, that would be very questionable.

Ideally, the rules for determining fairness will have been laid down at an earlier (less emotional) time – ie a redundancy policy and procedure will have been agreed. Consultation is therefore likely to centre on application of the rules ensuring that they are indeed applied fairly.

Unfortunately, this is not always the case. The rules, formulated at an earlier time, may no longer be appropriate. Or there may be no rules at all. In these circumstances there is little option but for the determination of the rules to form part of the consultation process.

Redundancy pay

Finally, a redundant employee aged over 18 with two years' service or more has a statutory right to redundancy pay. The precise details of this are in reference books, but the amount ranges from one week's pay to 30 weeks' pay depending on the employee's age and length of service.

The main relevant legislation is the Trade Union and Labour Relations (Consolidation) Act 1992 and Employment Rights Act 1996.

INFORMATION AND CONSULTATION

Employees, whether trade union members or not, have the right to be informed and consulted about matters that affect their employment. The right applies to employees in organisations of 50 or more employees. Where employers do not provide for this right, employees have the right to request it.

There will be different arrangements for this process in different organisations but there has to be an agreed method of informing and consulting employees. That method must include all employees and have been formally approved by the employees.

Particular issues have to be included in the information and consultation, such as the development of the organisation, of employment within the organisation and any matter that is likely to result in substantial change. More detail is provided in the CIPD publications listed in *References and further reading* at the end of this chapter – see particularly the Information and Consultation document.

The legislation is the Information and Consultation of Employees Regulations 2004.

THE ROLE OF HR PRACTITIONERS

In employing you in the HR function, your organisation will be looking to you and your colleagues to help keep its activities in line with legislative requirements, if not to go further and help it to adopt best practices. But don't be surprised if, from time to time, colleagues outside the function do not seem as committed to such premises as you might expect. Let's have a look at your likely roles.

AN ADVISORY ROLE TO LINE MANAGERS

To be effective, you need to know and understand the basics of employment law and to know where to go to find more detailed information in specific instances. This chapter has outlined the main aspects of employment law but it can only provide general guidance. Minor details of law can become very important in specific instances, so always check the detail if you have decisions to make. Follow the law, not your intuition. Remember that the legal situation changes continually both in response to legislation and in the way in which it is interpreted. To help you, there is a wide range of reference books available; those that are regularly updated are particularly valuable. Such books are available on CD-ROM and with online support, which makes it easy to access particular topics or information.

You will also find Acts and Regulations available on the Internet at the OPSI website (see page 86). However, it is crucially important that you do not overestimate your understanding of the law, so if you are in any doubt, always seek further advice. This would normally be from senior colleagues or from bodies such as Acas. Acas has offices in all regions of the United Kingdom except Northern Ireland, where similar services are available from the Labour Relations Agency.

A DECISION-MAKING ROLE

From time to time you may be called on to make decisions that require an understanding of employment law. As an example, you might be involved in the decision to move employees from one place of work to another. While you must act within a legally defensible position, be wary of invoking the law with employees in a direct fashion. It would be inappropriate, for example, simply to demand that an employee moved his place of work just because, five years ago, he signed a contract which included such a clause. However, much can be achieved by consultation and negotiation. Remember that you are expected to act fairly and reasonably, and in this context that would mean consulting with the employee about the issue. So acting fairly and reasonably is not just a moral requirement but also a legal necessity. As an HR practitioner, therefore, you may often find the law supporting you in your desire to 'do the right thing'.

AN OVERSEEING ROLE

If you maintain regular contact with your colleagues by 'walking the floor' in workshops and offices or through other network activities, you will often become aware of potential legal problems or potential disputes that can be 'nipped in the bud'. Some overseeing roles may have to be more formalised, such as equal opportunities monitoring, which is essential for public sector employers. Health and safety audits must also be formal, although if you have specific responsibilities in this area you should seek further appropriate training.

AN ADMINISTRATIVE ROLE

This may be your key role, ensuring good accessible records of contracts, and keeping equal opportunities records, health and safety records and disciplinary records. Your diligence in this area may attract scant attention, and even a little resistance. But when problems arise, these good records can afford real protection for employers and managers who may need to defend their actions at a tribunal or in other courts.

A TRAINING OR EDUCATIONAL ROLE

If line managers are to take true responsibility for HR matters – a direction in which many organisations are progressing – then they too will need an understanding of employment law. The very process of passing on your own understanding will force you to become more familiar with the subject and should reinforce your own role as 'the expert' in your organisation.

SUMMARY

- In this chapter we have outlined the main areas of legislation that have relevance to HR activity. We have explained the difference between civil law, employment protection legislation and other statutory legislation, discussed the essential components of contracts and described the main characteristics of contracts of employment, written particulars, employees as opposed to workers and the nature of business relationships.

- In looking at employment protection rights, we examined the question of unfair dismissal and looked at the need for a fair reason and a fair procedure and the requirement to establish dismissal in alleged constructive dismissal cases. We indicated the main areas of protection against discrimination so that you will know where to take care in decision-making. When looking at legislation we included some of the most recent additions to the legislature – the Employment Equality (Sex Discrimination) Regulations 2005, the Employment Equality (Age) Regulations 2006 and the Equality Act 2010.

- Finally, we considered redundancy and the HR practitioners' main responsibilities in this area.

You will by now be familiar with the terms used and know which legislation is likely to apply in the main areas of HR activity. References, further reading and website addresses are provided at the end of this chapter for your information, and Activities have been suggested throughout. You are encouraged to complete some, if not all, of these Activities in order to reinforce and apply your learning.

ACTIVITY 3.11

Visit an employment tribunal as an observer. You will find observing a tribunal case puts much of the practice discussed in this book into a real context.

EXPLORE FURTHER

REFERENCES AND FURTHER READING

AIKIN, A. (1999) 'Working titles', *People Management*, 3 June, p.25

DANIELS, K. (2008) *Employment Law: An introduction for HR and business students*, 2nd edition. London: CIPD

GENNARD, J. and JUDGE, G. (2005) *Employee Relations*. London: Chartered Institute of Personnel and Development.

LEWIS, D. and SARGEANT, M. (2009) *Essentials of Employment Law*. London: Charatered Institude of Personnel and Development.

MARTIN, M. and JACKSON, T. (2009) *Employment Law Pocketbook*, 3rd edition. Alresford: Management Pocketbooks

TORRINGTON, D., HALL, L. and TAYLOR, S. (2005) *Human Resource Management*. Hemel Hempstead: Prentice Hall

WILLEY, B. (2003) *Employment Law in Context: An introduction for HR professionals*, 2nd edition. Harlow: *Financial Times*/Prentice Hall

CODES OF PRACTICE AND OTHER GUIDES

The following and other advisory handbooks and booklets are available online, or by telephone, fax or email from ACAS Publications: tel.: 08702 42 90 90, fax: 020 8867 3225, email: acas@eclogistics.co.uk

Acas Code of Practice Acas – Disciplinary and grievances at work (2009). Leicester: Acas

Discipline and grievances at work: The Acas guide (2009). Leicester: Acas

The following codes of practice are available for online download from the Equality and Human Rights Commission: www.equalityhumanrights.com. There are also other codes of practice on the website including statutory duty codes of practice that place specific duties on employers in the public sector.

Code of Practice – Sex Discrimination

Code of Practice on Equal Pay

Statutory Code of Practice on Racial Equality in Employment

Code of Practice: Employment and Occupation

Fair Employment (Northern Ireland): details from the enquiry line of the Equality Commission for Northern Ireland: 028 90 890 890

The CIPD publication *Employment Law for People Managers* is an employment law subscription that provides a manual, online access, updates and newsletters. Tel.: 0870 442 1022

The CIPD publication *Policies and Procedures for People Managers* is a subscription service that provides a manual, online access, updates and additional materials. Tel.: 0870 442 1022

Similar services are available from other sources including:

XpertHR: tel.: 020 8652 4653, email: marketing@xperthr.co.uk

Croner Publications Ltd, Croner House, London Road, Kingston on Thames, Surrey, KT2 6SR; tel.: 020 8547 3333, email: info@croner.co.uk

For members of the CIPD, there is a vast library of information in many different formats, fact sheets, research papers, books, podcasts, etc on the CIPD website.

WEBSITES

Arbitration, Conciliation and Advisory Service (Acas): www.acas.org.uk

Business Link: www.businesslink.gov.uk

Business in the Community (Opportunity Now): www.bitc.org.uk/

Chartered Institute of Personnel and Development: www.cipd.co.uk

Department for Business, Innovation and Skills: www.berr.gov.uk (at time of writing, new website being created)

Health and Safety Executive: www.hse.gov.uk

Incomes Data Services: www.incomesdata.co.uk

The Office of Public Sector Information: www.opsi.gov.uk

People Management: www.peoplemanagement.co.uk

The Stationery Office: www.tso-online.co.uk

TUC: www.tuc.org.uk

UK Government site: www.direct.gov.uk

Working Famiilies: www.workingfamilies.org.uk/

CHAPTER 4

Job analysis

LEARNING OUTCOMES

After reading this chapter you will:

- be aware of the relevance of job analysis and design to HR responsibilities
- be alert to opportunities to design jobs that have both meaning and efficiency
- have an outline of approaches to job analysis that you can develop for your own use
- recognise that there can be a number of obstacles in implementing job design
- know the main techniques for job evaluation and be able to discuss the practicalities.

INTRODUCTION

Job analysis should determine what a job-holder is expected to do and how the job should best be performed. It will also help decide what skills and qualities are required of the person who is to perform the job. Questions of how the task and work should be organised, how the job inter-relates with other jobs, how many people are required to meet the demand of the workload and how the work itself might flow from one job to the next are all among those answered by job analysis.

HOW IS SUCH INFORMATION USED?

Job analysis and design plays a major role in organisations – indeed, you could say that organisations are made up of jobs rather than people since many 'jobs' are performed by machines, both mechanically and electronically. In small organisations the analysis and design may be very informal, perhaps only in the mind of the business owner. Even in medium-sized enterprises there is often no formal process.

But in looking at a job we should be able to assess for that job, for example:

- day-to-day tasks that will be involved
- the skills or competencies required

- the qualifications or the body of knowledge required
- physical requirements
- specific interpersonal skills, such as the ability to sell
- the degree of interpersonal skill required – say, in balancing conflicting interests
- key performance indicators (KPIs).

A knowledge of the content, demands, and authority to use discretion in jobs impacts on all aspects of an organisation, from recruitment to redundancy selection. These include:

- staffing levels
- recruitment
- selection
- productivity and performance
- performance appraisal
- job evaluation
- reasonable adjustments (for disability)
- business process engineering
- redundancy selection pools.

Staffing levels are determined using information from job analysis, even if that is only a manager recognising that there is a job to be done that could add value, or needs to be done to fulfil another criterion such as absence cover. When you queue at a supermarket checkout, you might reflect that the number of till operators has to be determined by job analysis. Without analysing how long it takes to carry out the transactions (and the arrival rate of customers), determining the required number of checkout operators would be a guess, at best.

Recruitment, as we shall see in the next chapter, should be done to a person specification, which flows from a job description which in turn flows from job analysis and design. Even if these documents are not created formally, this process takes place even if only in the head of the person carrying out the recruitment.

Selection decisions also rest heavily on the quality of the job analysis. Unless we know clearly what the job requires, we are not going to be able to make an informed judgement as to whether the person in front of us can do the job. Where assessment centres and/or psychometric testing are used (Chapter 5), the design of the job is crucial to deciding for what you will be testing. Selection tests and processes need to stand up to scrutiny and be based on an accurate analysis of the job requirements. Where the process of selection is automated – for example, using psychometric tests – you may need to demonstrate the logic of the selection process to an applicant. It is your responsibility to do this (not that of the test agency), so it is important to know that this information would be available if you use an agency. Job analysis is important so as to be able to demonstrate that the selection criteria are related to the job (and not unlawfully discriminatory).

Job design can help the organisation to improve its *productivity and performance*. The speed and efficiency with which tasks can be performed directly affects an organisation's competitive edge or the cost of providing its services. This is particularly so in repetitive work such as assembling products, checking out groceries or data entry.

Table 4.1 Analysing by splitting into component parts

Where a job is analysed by splitting it into its component parts, many opportunities for productivity improvements come to light.	
Eliminating repeated actions	If you iron a shirt, how many times do you run the iron over each area: once – or several times? If once is enough, you save time by not doing it again.
Identifying the critical path – the sequence of actions that will take the least time to complete a task	In making a cup of tea, the critical path would be: filling the kettle, boiling the water, brewing the tea, pouring it out. Other tasks – such as getting the cups out, putting milk into cups or even warming the pot – can be carried out in parallel and so are not critical. Reducing the time means that you need to address critical path actions – such as boiling no more water than is needed, so that the kettle boils more quickly.
Symmetrical actions	Often two or more actions can be made at the same time. These work better if they are symmetrical – for example, lifting a clean pan onto the draining board with the right hand while picking up a dirty pan with the left and putting it in the sink.
Eliminating unnecessary steps in an operation	Next time you make breakfast, study how many times you walk around the kitchen. With a little planning, could you reduce back-tracking? Some people eat breakfast standing up: that may be unwise, but it eliminates one step – ie sitting down!
Save four minutes a day on routine chores, and you have another day in the year – in every year.	

Performance appraisal should not be done in isolation but against a job description, performance targets and skill needs.

The demands of the job, the experience required, qualifications and other aspects of the job design are crucial to effective *job evaluation*, which we shall look at later in this chapter. Again, even when job evaluation is not done formally, a subjective assessment of these factors is usually carried out, perhaps in conjunction with a knowledge of labour market rates, before determining a salary.

Job evaluation also has an important role to play in equal opportunities by helping to ensure that work of equal value is determined as such without any gender or disability bias. In the latter case job analysis can help identify 'reasonable adjustments' – although these cannot be determined generically. Reasonable adjustments must relate to the disability in question.

Businesses consist of processes. If you think of a supermarket, there are ordering processes, supplier payment processes, stock control processes, point-of-sale processes – to name just a few. It is part of the effectiveness of a supermarket to have efficient processes. For example, when you buy a product, the point-of-sale equipment can update the stock list, and as the stock list falls, more stock can be ordered from the supplier and the cost put into the cash flow for future payment. In businesses these processes are carried out by people to a greater or lesser degree.

Designing the workflow round the organisation is known as *business process engineering*. As a business develops and grows, more and more of these processes become standard and need to be 're-engineered', often to integrate them with computer processes. Job analysis assists integration of work with new processes. Although not necessarily the case, business process *re*-engineering usually leads to a reduced need for staff and, often, redundancies. It does not, therefore, have a very popular name.

And so, finally, job analysis can be relevant to redundancy in a wider context. *Redundancy selection* must be made from a pool of employees, and these should be ones who are doing similar types of work – work that has either ceased or diminished perhaps because of a recession or on account of business process re-engineering. Determining the pool on a basis that can be defended is crucial to fair selection in redundancy situations, and job descriptions can be helpful in determining the pool.

In moving on it is useful to see three very broad categories: jobs with repetitive activities, technical/administrative positions, and managerial/professional posts.

JOBS WITH REPETITIVE ACTIVITIES

Many jobs require measurable, determinable activities that are repetitive. Examples are:

- assembling parts on a production line
- checking out groceries at a supermarket
- checking in luggage at an airport.

These activities may be repeated many times, perhaps hundreds of times, a day. The length of time therefore that each task takes is critical to the level of staffing required to make a car, collect cash or to avoid queues at check-in. And shaving a few seconds of each repetition saves labour costs for an organisation and increases its competitiveness.

Table 4.2 The method study approach

I keep six honest serving men
(They taught me all I knew);
Their names are What and Why and When
And How and Where and Who.

Rudyard Kipling, *Just So Stories*: 'The Elephant's Child'

Kipling's six honest men provide the basis for the method study approach to analysing jobs and improving productivity. The following table presents examples of how they may be used. We are going to consider evaluating a job as the task in question. We've picked this because it is relevant to the chapter, but you could test the process out yourself with any activity with which you might be familiar, such as making breakfast or a work activity.

WHAT	The job is being evaluated to assess the value of the work to the organisation.
WHY	There are many reasons, the most common of which is to determine a salary level for the organisation. This answer can be tested by asking if other, alternative approaches could satisfy the reason why this activity is being carried out. Questioning the reason for an activity opens up other options and alternatives.
WHEN	This activity has to be performed after a job analysis has been carried out and a job description has been prepared – but before the job is assigned to a salary band or level. In asking this question we can consider whether this is the best time in the sequence of events. For example, job analysis and job evaluation might be combined in one operation, saving significant work. The purpose of method study is to examine alternatives such as this – to challenge the status quo.
HOW	We've already looked at some approaches to job evaluation, but we might broaden this question in many ways. For example, could the evaluation be carried out by a software application or even by the job-holder themselves completing an online questionnaire? Again, the purpose of method study is to learn to 'think outside the box'. Many supermarkets trust customers to check out their own grocery purchases, so by comparison this idea might have some mileage.
WHERE	It may be best to carry out this activity on site or in a remote office. Asking the question encourages consideration of the pros and cons. On site may make it easier to check out any queries. Conversely, a remote office removes the evaluator from pressure that could arise from individuals on site who may wish to influence the evaluator. The key point of a question like this is to discourage assumptions.
WHO	We can assume we want an 'honest broker' to carry out the activity. That could be someone in HR, but then their knowledge of the jobs may be biased. In some cases they may be familiar with the job while in other cases they will rely on paper. Perhaps the task could be carried out by an external consultant or a computer program.

Analysis of these jobs is founded on scientific management, which originated in the early twentieth century. Its principle is that by applying scientific methods to managing work, productivity can be improved. It led to a range of techniques to improve productivity of which the most famous (or infamous) is 'time and motion', in which each component of a task is timed with a stopwatch. More formally, this is known as work measurement, and it forms the basis on which work can be examined and on which improved methods can be developed.

Aligned, therefore, to work measurement is method study, where the work itself is examined and methods evaluated using the questions shown in Table 4.2.

APPLYING WORK MEASUREMENT TO STAFFING LEVELS

Using information from work measurement and method study it is practical to build up a database of times for tasks and therefore assess the staffing levels required for any new operation.

In an assembly line each operation along the line is carefully planned so that the step can be completed in a specified time, before the product moves to the next operation. In a motor vehicle assembly line the planning is detailed and complex, and just watching the process is impressive.

At a supermarket checkout the number of checkout operators is determined by both the time taken to serve a customer and the rate at which customers arrive. Statistical methodology (known as operational research) is applied to ensure that staffing does not allow over-lengthy queues to build up. Such methodology is routinely applied to call centres, in hamburger outlets and in cleaning firms to determine optimal staffing levels.

ASSESSING JOBS WITH MULTIPLE ACTIVITIES

Often it is more relevant to know how a job is made up – that is, how much time is spent on the various activities involved in performing the job. Continuous observation of a job is very time-consuming and for much of the time a job-holder will be engaged on one activity before moving to another. To render observation cost-effective, 'activity sampling' is employed. This involves observing the job at regular intervals and noting what activity is being undertaken at that time. In this way several jobs can be observed in the same time period.

An example would be carrying out a sampling observation in a steel stockholding warehouse and noting regularly the crane-driver's activity, the slinger's activity, the forklift truck driver's activity, and the activities of the warehouse operative. This enables a job profile to be completed for each employee over a period of a few shifts. Statistical techniques are used to determine how frequently to make observations and over how many shifts.

Observation whether by work measurement or activity sampling can distort the true picture of a job because job-holders may alter their behaviour when they are being observed. Many employees find it intrusive and some find it stressful to be observed at work.

IMPROVING JOB CONTENT AND MEANING

Often the design of repetitive jobs is very prescriptive and detailed instructions for carrying out each repetitive task are provided. Quality assurance processes and standard operating practices seek to eliminate discretion on the part of individual operators who may be trained to follow these practices precisely. This approach has been widely criticised for designing jobs that are devoid of meaning. To address this issue three concepts evolved in the twentieth century:

- job rotation
- job enrichment
- job enlargement.

In *job rotation* the workers move from one job to another on a periodic basis. For a worker in a shoe factory, for instance, this might mean cutting leather in one period, skiving (shaving the edges of the leather so it can overlap) in the next period, and glueing components in the third period.

In *job enlargement* workers still work at the same level but do a wider variety of tasks at that same level. For example, instead of each worker carrying out one task in making a shoe, he or she might make a whole shoe.

In *job enrichment* the work should include tasks at different levels. So the worker may be asked to plan his or her workload, take responsibility for recording his or her work and deal with contingent problems arising, such as components not arriving when they should – as well as making a shoe.

The cynics describe rotation as combining one boring task with another, enlargement as doing more boring tasks, and enrichment as doing someone else's boring tasks as well! Overall, this creates lack of commitment on the part of workers

---

CASE STUDY 4.1

In 1974 Volvo pioneered a revolutionary approach to job design in the whole construction of its automotive plant at Kalmar in Sweden. The concept was that a whole team of workers carried out an entire assembly, such as a dashboard, rather than individual workers carrying out small steps. Volvo's objectives were outlined by the head of Volvo at the time, Pehr Gyllenhammar, and were to create a plant that, without sacrifice of efficiency or the company's financial objectives, will give employees the opportunity to work in groups, communicate freely among themselves, to switch from one job assignment to another, vary their work pace, to identify with the product, to be conscious of a responsibility for quality and to influence their own work environment. When a product is made by people who find meaning in their work, it must inevitably be a product of high quality.

Quoted from C. Berggren (1992) *Alternatives to Lean Production: Work organisation in the Swedish auto industry*. Ithaca, NY: ILR Press/ London: Macmillan

– understandably. So other approaches have developed, of which Volvo's Kalmar plant – a trailblazer at the time – is one (see case study 4.1), and *kaizen* is another.

KAIZEN

This is a philosophy imported from Japan and applied in their manufacturing industries, notably at Toyota, before spreading much more widely. It seeks to harness the collective knowledge and experience of the whole workforce to create more effective processes and ultimately better products and services. It is associated with quality circles, continuous improvement and lean manufacturing.

In job design terms it seeks to create links from the individuals who carry out tasks (and therefore know how they can be improved) to senior management who can take the necessary action, but it often also empowers workers themselves to take actions. In this approach workers at all levels take a major role in the analysis and design of their own jobs and even the product. It used to be said that many workers needed more brain power in driving to work than they needed at work. *Kaizen* seeks to capitalise on the huge mental capacity represented by the workforce as a whole unit.

While *kaizen* is primarily a philosophy, its impact on job design is substantial. Two examples serve to illustrate this.

Inspection

Traditional manufacturing industry had inspectors of quality at every stage. In the steel industry rejected product would find its way into the electric arc furnace where it could be rescued, admittedly at some cost, and still form saleable steel. In other industries – pottery, for example – rejected product finds its way into factory shops and other outlets as 'seconds' or sub-standard goods. Worst of all, many industries have no such oulets or opportunities and rejected product forms landfill.

There is a strong argument that you cannot *inspect* quality into a product or service. The quality has to come from the people who carry out the operations to make the product. Today, there are far fewer inspection or quality control departments in manufacturing than there were in the twentieth century.

CASE STUDY 4.2

The story is apocryphal but illustrates a point. A manufacturer placed an order for 10,000 components with a Japanese manufacturer. In the contract was a clause specifying that they would be inspected on receipt of the delivery and only 2% faulty components would be acceptable.

The components were duly delivered on time: 9,800 perfect components and 200 faulty components provided in separate packaging. The supplier used no inspection process – the faulty parts were made to order!

ACTIVITY 4.1

Investigate how quality is managed in your organisation. Does your organisation use inspection techniques? If so, are the inspectors employees of the organisation or from external regulators? How effective are these processes, in your view? Forming a view will help you understand the processes better. You may agree with them or not, but it would be useful, also, to discuss your views in a 'safe' environment – perhaps with others on a CIPD or management course.

If your organisation does not use inspection techniques, how does it control the quality of the product or the service provided? Are there processes of traceability? These latter processes enable the final product to be traced back to and along the production line so as to be able to troubleshoot quality problems. Is the quality of service assessed by other criteria, such as customer feedback? Again it would be useful to discuss this with others and to form a view – are the processes effective, for example?

Improving processes

Another traditional favourite is the suggestion scheme. Sometimes administered by the HR department, such schemes provide awards for employees who come forward with good ideas for improving the product or processes. They have mixed success. Ideas are not the problem – it is the process of changing even minor details that too often leads to failure.

Quality circles are a concept by which groups of workers come together to analyse problems and present solutions to managers. Often they are empowered to make changes to the process, within boundaries but without reference. In theory it is possible to turn the organisation on its head and have it effectively run by those who make the product, who have direct access to the customer and understand the customers' needs.

While these techniques – work measurement, method study and *kaizen* – are primarily of value in repetitive activities, many jobs include repetitive components and are carried out to fixed methods. So these techniques have a wider application in administrative and technical jobs, as well as in some professional and managerial jobs.

ADMINISTRATIVE AND TECHNICAL WORK

This type of work necessarily requires more in terms of mental processes, and the concept of discretion in performing the job becomes more important. Analysis of these jobs involves considering such concepts as the numerical and written content of the job, the need to communicate with others and the amount of technical knowledge required for the tasks in the job. It may also involve considering pressures such as the level of potential conflict with other functions, the severity of deadlines and the need for accuracy.

In situations where there is a variety of tasks, activity sampling can therefore be particularly relevant.

There are other approaches to the analysis of these types of jobs.

INTERVIEWING THE JOB INCUMBENT(S)

Apart from the benefit of obtaining valuable and relevant information, this approach involves individuals in the process. It is therefore more likely to bring about acceptance of any future outcomes, such as a job grade that determines the individual's salary. Of course, this latter possibility will inevitably lead to individuals' seeking to represent their job as being demanding, important and adding value, perhaps to the point of exaggeration.

Interviews therefore need to be carefully structured and conducted similarly from job to job. That said, there is also a need to establish a rapport with each person and to explore aspects that may be crucial to a particular job. Interviewing – as we will see in Chapter 5 – is an imprecise art. As well as the incumbent, the interviewer is necessarily a factor in the information gathered and in the importance that might be attached to particular aspects of the job. For example, an interviewer from an engineering background may have difficulty relating to the work of someone in a creative role.

Notes should be taken of the interview either during the interview (which can inhibit good listening) or immediately afterwards. If you share your notes with the job-holder, any misapprehensions can be corrected. These processes should be open and transparent in any event.

QUESTIONNAIRES

In questionnaires the information-seeker becomes remote and is therefore less a factor in the outcome.

Like interviews, these should be structured so as to bring out the importance of the various potential aspects of the job – the concepts such as interpersonal skills that we listed at the beginning of this chapter. A difficulty with questionnaire design is that the person answering the question may not interpret the question in the same way as the person who asked it. If the question is 'What is the most important activity you undertake?', the people answering may interpret both 'important' and 'activity' in different ways. In an interview that can be clarified, but a questionnaire rarely provides such an opportunity.

Furthermore, the answers themselves will be subject to interpretation when they are analysed, so the overall picture of the job could be distorted.

Bias in interpretation may be overcome to a degree by means of a multiple-choice style of questionnaire. But the questionnaire designer has to be very careful to ensure that the questions are answerable, or provide an additional box for 'Other' responses. The latter means interpreting each response again. So designing a questionnaire is a very skilled task and not to be undertaken lightly.

To answer these reservations, there are a number of proprietary questionnaires available, such as McCormick's Position Analysis Questionnaire and Saville and

Holdsworth's Work Profiling System. The great advantage of these systems is that question design has been carefully addressed, responses may be cross-validated and the systems themselves are checked for their validity (do they measure what they claim to measure?) and their reliability (are they valid in a wide variety of different circumstances?).

WORK LOGS

Asking job-holders to record on a regular basis the tasks that they do can reveal valuable information about how they spend time. The resultant work logs are often used to improve time management and the two purposes can often be combined into one task. Again, a structure is required so that tasks and time taken are revealed in a consistent way. Where many jobs are to be analysed, the way in which a work log is completed may vary from individual to individual, making analysis more difficult.

DO THE JOB YOURSELF

This can be useful in getting some insight into the job and perhaps building the respect of the job-holder – but it needs caution. If you are not a technician, you will probably not have the knowledge required. If you are not skilled, you may be unable to perform the job effectively.

PROFESSIONAL AND MANAGERIAL JOBS

These three distinctions – jobs with repetitive activities, administrative and technical work, and professional and managerial jobs – are to some extent artificial. Many technical and administrative jobs include professional and managerial aspects, and vice versa. Indeed, some aspects of professional and managerial jobs can also include repetitive elements, such as responding to emails or filling teeth. And we have already seen how *kaizen* introduces a measure of managerial responsibility into otherwise repetitive jobs.

But the importance of building relationships, relating to others, communicating effectively with different people, exercising judgement, thinking on one's feet and a range of other job requirements become more important in this category.

Analysis of professional and managerial jobs lends itself to the addition of further techniques which are still, to some degree, applicable to other categories too.

DOCUMENTATION

Managerial jobs are often characterised by responsibilities, performance targets and objectives. Minutes of meetings may therefore be relevant as may also be documentation surrounding the creation of the job in the first place. Indeed, in all categories we have considered there may be existing job descriptions, operating standards, service level agreements, training manuals, etc.

CRITICAL INCIDENTS

Examining these would commonly be done during an interview. The technique is essentially a method of enquiry into particular events that have been seminal in achieving success in reaching targets or fulfilling objectives. Additionally, mistakes are also critical incidents and important to analyse too. Gladstone's words 'No man ever became great or good except through many and great mistakes' may seem a little daunting for us lesser mortals in corporate life, but they emphasise the fact that mistakes are excellent learning experiences and good for insight into job analysis. The culture of the organisation will influence how willing a job-holder might be to discuss mistakes.

In the critical incidents approach the analysis explores what skills are needed to respond effectively to those incidents, and it helps to define the requirements of the job.

REPERTORY GRID

This is a specialist technique which has its origins in clinical psychology. Typically, in job analysis it consists of asking a manager to distinguish three individuals who report to them by saying how two are similar to each other but different from a third. So a manager might say that reports A and B are very focused, whereas report C 'thinks outside the box'. By asking the manager to distinguish individuals along a variety of lines or 'constructs' it becomes clear what is important in the job. In practice this works well if a significant number of constructs are identified and compared to success in the job. But this rapidly becomes complex, and for this reason computer programs are generally used to manage repertory grids. Additional levels of sophistication can be added, such as statistical analysis, and a very clear picture of what is needed to be successful in the job emerges.

Jobs do not exist in isolation and so it is important to consider a job not only in terms of its own role and demands but in the context of its inter-relationship with others in the organisation.

THE ORGANISATION CHART

This shows the formal inter-relationship between the various jobs in an organisation. Typically, it shows who reports to whom and provides a reference point to discover who has responsibility for main aspects of the organisation's function. It can also help show where the power lies within an organisation – who has a seat on the board, for example. As we discussed in Chapter 2, there are different organisation structures and a chart is useful for giving a pictorial representation. Often the responsibility for preparing it falls to the HR department. In all but the smallest of organisations computer software is valuable in making the task manageable.

THE INFORMAL ORGANISATION

Not charted is the informal organisation, which can be as important. Who actually has access to whom, individual personalities, past history and personal relationships are all part of the informal organisation.

Notwithstanding these parallel structures, you may think that the aims of the organisation are determined and then the main functions follow from these. Within each function the tasks are split up into departments and departments into jobs. Thus each job has a relationship to the main aim of the organisation and is somehow a subdivision of that main aim.

This would be very hierarchical – described by Rosabeth Moss Kanter of Harvard as an 'elevator structure'. Thus to get a decision, the question for resolution has to go up in an elevator to the top floor (where the senior management reside) and then the decision goes down in another elevator to the relevant department for action. But even within a hierarchical organisation it does not usually work quite that way.

The various functions need to interact with each other. For example, a sales department needs to work with a production department without every decision being referred to the managing director. The processes by which the various departments and functions interact, how they make decisions together, and the business process itself are important factors in the competitiveness of that organisation.

So the inter-relationship between jobs is an important factor in job design. A typical graduate training scheme, and good induction processes for managers, place heavy emphasis on the needs of these people to form relationships with key people in other departments and functions. This is why graduate training schemes place graduates in a variety of departments over, say, a year.

ACTIVITY 4.2

Examine the informal 'structures' that exist in your organisation. Look for people who have relationships that somehow do not fit with the formal structure. Who talks to or socialises with whom? Does anyone wield power or authority that appears out of line with their apparent position? Why is this?

CHANGE AND JOB DESIGN

Although job analysis is an important part of job design it is not the only factor. For example, in 2003 PricewaterhouseCoopers performed job analysis on schoolteacher workloads and identified 25 administrative tasks (such as photocopying) which they said should be performed by support staff rather than by teachers. Opinions vary as to how effectively that job analysis had been transformed into the job design of a schoolteacher. In particular, the main aim of the study was to reduce teacher workloads by removing these tasks from the teaching job. Seven years later, most would argue that this has not been achieved. Many factors – such as local politics, industrial relations, insecurity, management training, and the availability of resources – have impacted on the practical reality of implementation.

Job analysis is valuable, and it does impact on an organisation. But there are many factors in the reality of designing a job, and job analysis is only one – even if arguably the most important one.

A job that is designed using these techniques should be documented. This may be in the form of an operating procedure, a job description or simply a set of agreed performance objectives. A person specification, defining the qualities, experience, and qualifications sought in the job-holder, is also a valuable document.

Job descriptions typically define the person to whom the job-holder is accountable, the duties (the tasks the job-holder will probably carry out himself or herself), the responsibilities (the tasks delegated to others but for which the job-holder is accountable) and potentially the job-holder's level of authority and sometimes performance criteria.

CASE STUDY 4.3

Some years ago a board of trustees appointed two employees – one entitled 'manager' and the other 'supervisor' – to run a small residential home on behalf of a charity. Although the manager was nominally the more senior, both employees reported to the board. Personal circumstances led to the manager working fewer hours and eventually being granted extended leave, although he ensured continuity of his essential responsibilities remotely from his home.

During his period of leave, serious problems arose with the management of staff. Three left, two went on sick leave citing anxiety-related conditions, and a further staff member raised a complaint under the home's bullying and harassment policy. Agency staff were being employed to run a home that had previously been run by employees alone, and costs were mounting. Whose responsibility was this?

By examining the job descriptions of each, the board was able to answer the question. The manager's responsibility was to manage the home and make sure that supplies were ordered, accounts were kept, and the overall needs of care standards were met. All staff matters were with the supervisor, including the relevant part of care standards. The words 'day-to-day management of staff' were written in her job description. The responsibility for problems that were arising from human relationships (not resources) was hers, and the board of trustees was able to investigate and make decisions accordingly.

These details together with other details arising from the job analysis are frequently used to determine a salary, and often via a process of job evaluation – to which we now turn.

JOB EVALUATION

Job evaluation has the advantage of providing an objective platform on which to determine the earnings of an individual job. The emphasis is on the job. However, the job content, role and authority of the job is sometimes determined more by the person who holds the job than by the paper description – so job evaluation is an inexact science.

It also rests heavily on job descriptions, which are themselves inexact – as we hope you will realise if you carry out Activity 4.3. One factor that you may uncover in your discussion during this Activity is that some managers and job-holders are more articulate than others in describing their duties and responsibilities. Furthermore, any prior knowledge of what will advantage them most may cause them to slant the job description accordingly.

ACTIVITY 4.3

Who should write the job descriptions? There are several options. The job-holders themselves can do so – after all, no one should know the job better than they do. But then, their manager knows far better what it is that needs to be done, doesn't he or she? Yet if we allow either of these parties to write the description, there will be no consistency with job descriptions written across the organisation – and that would pose serious questions for job evaluation. So a job analyst or HR practitioner may be best, perhaps. But then the analyst or practitioner will need to rely on the techniques we outline in this chapter.

Discuss the feasibility and merits of these three different approaches with a learning source in the context of your organisation.

There are a number of proprietary job evaluation systems, some consultants specialise in using such systems, and many organisations develop their own systems to meet their particular needs. Some of the proprietary systems have the added advantage that they link into regional and national pay surveys, enabling easy comparison of jobs with the external market.

There are also a number of approaches to the process, of which we will discuss three:

- ranking
- paired comparisons
- points profiling.

RANKING

This is the simplest, and essentially consists of putting jobs in rank order of their importance to the organisation, and additionally assigning a rank to each different level within each function. Formally or informally, it is very common in smaller organisations (where the task of ranking is smaller) and in larger organisations when there is no formal job evaluation. Ranking can be related to different salary grades, as discussed in Chapter 5. There is no real examination of the demands of the job, the skills needed or necessarily the qualifications required. The ranking can be subjective, and there is little basis for resisting an average performer who feels strongly that he or she deserves a higher ranking. Then there are cross-department comparisons. Should an HR practitioner be ranked higher or lower than a qualified technician in the research department? There is little basis for deciding.

PAIRED COMPARISONS

As an approach this is designed to deliver acceptance by involving a wide range of evaluators and working on their perceived valuations of a job. A computer program presents pairs of jobs to those participating. They then have to say which of the two jobs is more valuable in their opinion, and select it, and then the program presents another pair. The individual's own job is not included, but a wide selection is provided on a broad basis. Because many participants are involved, the program developers claim high levels of acceptance. While the authors find this an interesting approach, none has used it in earnest.

POINTS PROFILING

This well-proven approach to job evaluation is more thorough, complex and expensive than most. Our outline here is just that, an outline. Proprietory and other schemes may be constructed slightly differently.

The first task is to develop a points scheme that is appropriate to the organisation, that mirrors what the organisation regards as important, and that is equal-pay-proof. Consultants and other sources can provide a typical scheme that an organisation adapts. Points are ordinarily awarded for factors such as the discretion allowed to the job-holder, the level of knowledge or experience, the qualifications required, accountability for the work of others, pressures of the job such as regular deadlines or critical decision-making, accountability to others outside the organisation (such as HMRC), etc. Care has to be taken that none of the factors chosen is discriminatory in any unlawful sense and, especially for equal pay considerations, discriminatory against women.

Sometimes there are two points systems. For example, a system for salaried staff and one for hourly-paid may be appropriate. Using two or more points systems is problematic and can be difficult to defend in equal pay claims. This would be particularly so if one system applies mainly to jobs occupied by women and one to jobs mainly occupied by men.

Given that the points profiling system is a prominent method, we shall look at the actual job evaluation process based on this system.

The evaluation process

The points profiling system in private sector organisations is sometimes kept confidential so that employees cannot write job descriptions designed to maximise their own points. In practice this does not necessarily work, because such information has a habit of leaking out. Sometimes it is disclosed to an independent party to demonstrate its fairness. It may have to be disclosed if there is an equal pay claim made to a tribunal. In the public sector, job evaluation schemes (many of which are points-based) are usually open and transparent, and often designed and agreed in partnership with trade union representatives so that all affected are clear how decisions will be reached and what factors go to make up the particular job evaluation system.

Points can be allocated for various job characteristics, of which the list below contains only examples. Many of these characteristics may have a rating scale. For example, points added would be different if a specific qualification was required and may also be different according to the level of the qualification. So the need for a professional qualification such as a Certified and Chartered Accountant (ACCA) would carry more points than the need for an Associate of Accounting Technicians (AAT) qualification. Experience might be allocated points according to years of experience in a particular field, etc:

- qualifications
- experience
- a need to be proactive
- interpersonal skills
- analytical skills
- critical thinking ability
- supervisory/managerial skills.

Then a number of benchmark jobs must be selected across the organisation. These should cover the range of functions and the various levels of jobs performed in the organisation. The number of benchmark jobs must be sufficient to give a representative cross-section of the organisation.

A panel of people within the organisation is selected and trained to evaluate the jobs. The panel would include some senior people – ones with wide experience and minimal bias (HR, for example) and, where recognised, usually trade union representatives. Indeed, in the public sector there is often a requirement for job evaluation to be conducted in partnership.

The benchmark jobs are evaluated against the points system by the panel, ideally making decisions by consensus. It can be a daunting task.

Benchmark jobs are then assigned to appropriate salary (or wage) levels to reflect the points that they have been allocated. As a general principle the aim is that the average salaries as determined by the evaluation system will match the current average salaries paid. Inevitably, some jobs' salaries will go up and some down.

Then other jobs are slotted in to the structure that has been provided by the benchmarked jobs, and thus to appropriate salaries.

Some drawbacks

A problematic aspect of job evaluation in general, and the points system in particular, is market demand and supply. There are always some skills shortages. An organisation which needs scarce specialist computer skills (or any other scarce specialist skill) cannot ignore the need to pay higher salaries to attract and retain such staff. But market forces fluctuate and it may be unwise to include them in a points system.

One of the reasons that job evaluation is so expensive is that those who are already being paid more than the salary determined by the job evalution scheme will have their earnings 'red-ringed'. That is, their salaries will remain the same and be held there whenever there is a general increase, until such a time as their salaries match those of their jobs, as evaluated. Whereas those who are earning less than the job evaluation determines will receive an increase. For the organisation there is therefore invariably a net increase in salary cost.

Most schemes allow employees to appeal against their job evaluation rating. Market forces are a common reason for employees to appeal a job-evaluated salary grade. Employees have little to lose, especially if they have been red-ringed, so appeals are common. They have to be heard by another small panel, at least. This can be time-consuming and adds to the cost.

In a world of rapid change a typical job evaluation scheme has a life of only a few years simply because tasks and technology change and the relative importance of skills and knowledge fluctuates over time. This can create 'drift' in evaluated levels, and eventually inequalities. Then the process will have to commence all over again.

There are those who believe it is simply not worth it, and prefer subjectivity, negotiating and bargaining with individuals. Although this may work in a small to medium-sized private company, the larger and more complex an organisation is, or becomes, generally, the more likely it is to have job analysis, job design and job evaluation.

THE ROLE OF THE HR PRACTITIONER

The role expected of you will vary considerably from one organisation to another. It is very likely that job descriptions, person specifications and job evaluation will involve you to a greater or lesser degree. Work measurement, method study, productivity improvement, and job analysis may well be part of a specialist function and, in any event, be aligned more closely with the operational functions than with HR. But there are no set rules. Should it be your role, you may be challenging line managers as much as serving them. The status of one's job and that of one's subordinates is very close to one's personal image, so having it examined, or analysed, is a very sensitive matter. Managers will usually seek to use what political power they have to create the best outcome for themselves. This can hinder the objectivity of the processes.

AN ANALYTICAL ROLE

If analysis is expected of you, you will need to become familiar with appropriate techniques that have been outlined in this chapter. You may be able to take advantage of one or more of the proprietary systems on the market, which provide both training and support.

AN EVALUATIVE ROLE

As 'honest broker' you may be called on to evaluate jobs. You are unlikely to be doing it on your own. Evaluation is usually carried out by a small, confidential group with a cross-section of experience related to the jobs to be evaluated. If you get the opportunity, it is an interesting role which will give you insight into the wider organisation.

DOCUMENTING JOB AND PERSON SPECIFICATIONS

Elsewhere we have asked you to consider who should prepare job descriptions where no specific job analysis is being undertaken. In our view you should be very wary of taking on too much responsibility for determining job descriptions. A more appropriate role for HR is to take responsibility for ensuring consistency between descriptions that may have been prepared by different managers. In relation to person specifications you may be able to make a valuable contribution with respect to the qualifications and attributes required, taking particular care that no unlawful discrimination is enshrined in the specification (or indeed in the job description).

FACILITATING CHANGE

Change management is an area of expertise in its own right, and an ability to drive change is an invaluable skill. On the whole, HR practitioners are less likely to be drivers of change and more likely to facilitate change initiated at senior levels of the organisation. Indeed, without support at the most senior level in an organisation any change programme is likely to flounder.

So if job analysis and design produces the need for serious change, you may be involved in re-training activities, redundancies, industrial relations issues and even some serious internal politics. Many of these matters will be the province of experienced practitioners, but that may depend on the resources of the organisation. Many of our colleagues have been through a 'baptism of fire' at some point in their HR careers.

AN ADMINISTATIVE ROLE

Apart from job descriptions there is often a significant administrative role in simply keeping the whole process fully documented, arranging meetings, recording outcomes and ensuring the steady progress of a complex project. Because these can be sensitive areas, these tasks may well fall to the HR department and invariably require some involvement on your part.

ACTIVITY 4.4

Square pegs – should the round hole be redesigned?

There is an assumption in this chapter – and, indeed, in this book – that jobs are designed and people fit them, or are recruited and selected to fit them. This is not always the case. Often, particularly at more senior levels, jobs are restructured to fit the particular qualities brought by a promising candidate. Discuss this with a learning source. Is this a sensible approach, and if it is, in what circumstances? What implications does it have for job analysis? Does it have implications for equal opportunities?

If you want to consider the implications of this activity in more detail, Google the words *job sculpting*, read some of the entries there and revisit the Activity.

SUMMARY

- In this chapter we have examined the value of job analysis by looking at the main areas where it can have impact on HR activities such as recruitment, performance appraisal and redundancy pool selection. It has both a wide and deep application in HR and in the operation of the business generally.

- We've seen how jobs may be categorised as repetitive, technical and administrative, and managerial and professional. There is a wide range of analytical tools that can be used across these categories although some are more applicable to one category than another. This should give you a reasonable number of tools to use in any analysis, although some would require specific training.

- You've been alerted to some established approaches to job design in the form of *kaizen* and the evolution of the Volvo plant at Kalmar in the 1970s.

- Fitting jobs into the organisation is important and you will now have some awareness of the issues created by how this is done.

- Finally, job evaluation has been described in some detail, providing you with three approaches, and looking at one of these – points profiling – to understand the process and also considering some of the potential drawbacks.

It's a fascinating area and addresses the question that many who are first leaving full-time education ask: 'The company employs one thousand people. *What do they all do?*'

REFERENCES AND FURTHER READING

BERGGREN, C. (1992) *Alternatives to Lean Production: Work organisation in the Swedish auto industry*. Ithaca, NY: ILR Press/London: Macmillan

BOBKO, P. (2008) 'A systematic approach for assessing the currency ("up-to-dateness") of job-analytic information', *Public Personnel Management*, Vol.37, Issue 3, Fall: 261–77

CHANG, I.-W. and KLEINER, B. (2002) 'How to conduct job analysis effectively', *Management Research News*, Vol.25, No.3: 73–81

PEARN, M. and KANDOLA, R. (1993) *Job Analysis: A manager's guide (developing skills)*, 2nd edition. London: Chartered Institute of Personnel and Development

TAYLOR, S. (2008) *People Resourcing*. London: Chartered Institute of Personnel and Development

Guidelines for Best Practice in the use of Job Analysis Techniques available on request from SHL Group Ltd, The Pavilion, 1 Atwell Place, Thames Ditton, Surrey KT7 oNE – or at http://www.shl.com/ OurScience/BestPractice/Pages/AssessmentPractice.aspx

WEBSITES

www.cipd.co.uk/subjects/pay/general/jobeval.htm

www.job-analysis.net

ACTIVITIES FEEDBACK

Activity 4.2

Power and authority can be founded on a number of different bases. The ability to reward or carry out sanctions against another gives power. Denying access is an example of a sanction, whereas promotion would be a reward if it is a promotion that the individual would want.

Knowledge, personal confidence (or conversely, insecurity), personal relationships, stereotyping and prejudices all have an impact on who can influence whom and hence on the informal structure.

Activity 4.4

A candidate may bring opportunities for business development, processes or oganisation that have not been considered by the job designer, perhaps because the candidate has brought special experience that would be valuable. A candidate who has a disability may be able to carry out the main part of the job to an excellent level but not be able to carry out other parts. It may well be justified to redesign the job around him or her.

Job analysis would still contribute because it allows redesign of the jobs on a structured basis – not losing sight of critical aspects of the job that may need to be reassigned.

An *ad hoc* approach to designing the job around the person does have implications for equal opportunities. It will become more difficult to meet a challenge from an unsuccessful candidate who might have been a better match for the original job description. So care must be taken to be able to objectively justify amending the job to the candidate, because changes 'on a whim' could lead to accusations of discrimination and these could be difficult to defend. You can, though, make reasonable adjustments for a candidate with a disability without facing a legitimate claim from a person without a disability.

CHAPTER 5

Recruitment and selection

LEARNING OUTCOMES

After reading this chapter you will:

- understand why it is important to adopt sound recruitment and selection practices

- be able to identify the constraints and opportunities presented by legislation in this area and be prepared to keep up to date with forthcoming changes

- appreciate the need for rigorous HR planning and job analysis as a starting point for the whole recruitment and selection process

- be able to choose appropriate sources of recruitment and methods of selection, depending on the nature of a vacancy, and be willing to evaluate the outcome of your decisions

- be able to identify the factors needed to ensure an effective induction process that meets organisational and individual needs.

- be more able to anticipate and plan for the demand for new employees

- be better placed to find suitable sources of employees in the labour market.

INTRODUCTION

Many human resources practitioners spend a great deal of their time engaged in activities associated with the recruitment and selection of staff. This can range from one-off recruitment episodes to major recruitment campaigns carried out to recruit and select replacement staff, staff with specialist skills, trainees, graduates, etc. HR practitioners often thus gain a great deal of experience in the range of administrative, interviewing and other selection activities associated with staffing the organisation. In larger organisations specialist recruitment officers may be appointed within the HR team or recruitment services may be delivered from a recruitment service centre, whose main role is to ensure that (to borrow a time-honoured expression) 'the right people with the right skills are employed at the right time' by the organisation. Other HR practitioners have little involvement in recruitment and selection, however, because these activities have been devolved to line managers or outsourced to specialist agencies and the in-house practitioners may only get involved in limited activities or in overseeing the process.

Although recruitment and selection are core activities for many HR practitioners, they are activities that are affected by the organisation's policy and the external environment – such things as business expansion or contraction, developments in employment legislation, the general economic climate and skills shortages. Whatever the economic climate, the workforce planning process is by no means simple. Organisations need to predict their workforce requirements (eg numbers, skills and levels of responsibility) in accordance with future corporate objectives. In times of business contraction, even if it is obvious that fewer staff will be required in the future than currently, it is highly unlikely that a recruitment freeze would deliver the changes in workforce make-up where they are required or could be effective for an extended period of time if the organisation is to remain viable. There are many factors to be taken into consideration (eg existing skills, training and development provision, retention, career progression and labour turnover), and it would be an unusual – and fortunate – employer that did not need to look to the external labour market to 'buy in' new skills and abilities for key posts.

The employment situation over the years shifts from a seller's to a buyer's market and back again and the approach of HR practitioners and the amount of time spent on recruitment and selection activities must reflect and anticipate this. However, this effect is not always evenly balanced across different employment sectors. In some sectors, downsizing of operations or removing hierarchical tiers leads to losses of jobs through redundancy exercises. In others, relocation of manufacturing and/or service facilities to areas, often outside the UK, where labour costs are cheaper (and employment legislation may be less restrictive) leads to more radical approaches to recruitment and selection. While in certain sectors, growth and the development of new business, new technology or changing markets can mean real skills shortages in the face of which recruitment and selection become of prime importance.

In this section we will consider the context within which recruitment happens and the factors impacting upon recruitment, the place and impact of employment legislation and the importance of equality and diversity in recruitment and selection practice. We will also provide an overview and detailed information on the recruitment and selection processes, considering both activities and skills, and will look at the transition to becoming an employee.

THE CHANGING NATURE OF THE WORKFORCE

Two significant factors can be seen to be having a continuing impact on the nature of the workforce in the UK, both with implications for recruitment and selection activities: demographic change, and the use of more flexible less traditional working patterns, including the growth in outsourcing.

DEMOGRAPHICS

Over coming years the workforce is set to become more diverse in terms of gender, age and ethnic balance, building on changes that have already happened:

- In relation to gender, there is a continuing trend for more women to enter the workforce, raising issues such as equal pay and the provision of childcare.

- In relation to age, falling birth rates and greater longevity mean that by 2030 46% of the UK population will be over 50 – compared with 33% in 2002. Pension changes will also impact in this area, leading to many people working for longer.

- In relation to ethnicity, government predictions indicate that by 2020 net migration will account for more than 40% of the growth in the working age population.

All of these matters are important and complex and will take serious consideration by organisations during recruitment as well as other employment activities. Employers will need to do more to both attract and retain a more diverse workforce. The complexity of these issues can be seen by considering further just one of these elements – age – in more detail.

To maximise the participation of different age groups within an organisation's workforce and encourage age/generational diversity, the particular needs and expectations of each age group will have to be taken into account in designing jobs, in recruitment activities and in induction into the workplace. Although not homogenous in their expectations, there are some common themes that are apparent in the different generations at work.

Generation Y

The younger age group (up to 30), often referred to as Generation Y, have been the subject of much recent research because they are perceived by many to be very different from previous generations in their approach to work. Research has shown that even within Generation Y, what people are looking for from work is not homogenous, but that there is some common ground. The dominant expectation of this group about work is for fulfilling roles and career development. Other things found to be of importance are work–life balance, opportunities for longer periods of time off, the working environment and organisational values, a need for challenge, stretch and change, the organisation's approach to social responsibility, having motivating and inspirational managers, and having opportunities to work from home. Pay and location of work, although important, were not high on the list. Research has also shown that boundaries (of place and time) between work and life outside work for many in this generation are breaking down. Also, many have high expectations (and skill) around the use of technology at work, particularly the 'participatory' web – forums, blogs, networking, webcasting, etc. For this generation, being able to be yourself, feeling highly valued and being in a supportive and inspiring workplace drive satisfaction and happiness at work. They are excited by career development, particularly the opportunity to gain transferable skills and knowledge through professional and academic qualifications.

Generation X

Workers within the middle age group (Generation X) are the most likely to have the dual responsibilities of dependant children and dependant parents. Characteristics of this group include not wanting to work long hours, being keen to learn new skills and stay employable, a lack of trust in institutions, feeling increasingly uncomfortable in corporate or large organisation life, a desire to see fairness in approaches to promotion based on performance not tenure, and a preference for an entrepreneurial or independent style of working. Perceived difficulties at work include not being as comfortable with technology as the younger generation (but being less willing to admit to it than the older generation) and having to manage the younger generation with their different approach.

Baby boomers

The older, 50+, generation (baby boomers) are approaching retirement much more flexibly than previous generations. They are most likely to have the dual pressures of very elderly parents and supporting children through early adulthood. There is no longer an absolute cut-off retirement age, and many work – and want to work – into retirement: so-called 'retirement jobs'. The reasons for this include financial security, enjoying work, an ongoing need for the friendship and companionship found at work and a fear of full retirement as an unknown experience. At work they value personal growth, want to be involved, believe in team orientation and value organisation commitment and loyalty. They are motivated by teamwork and responsibility and seek reward for long hours and their work ethic.

Generation Z

When Generation Z (those currently still in education) are added in, the complexity all of this adds to the activities of recruitment is clear to see. Organisations will need to find new and improved ways of widening the groups from which they recruit. Even in organisations that are anticipating reductions in the workforce, it will still be critical to future success to be able to attract and retain staff with the right skills and experience. Indeed, with a workforce reduced in size, it will be even more important to ensure that recruitment processes are selecting staff with the right skills and competences and that retention is focused on keeping talented staff and managing out those whose performance is not at the required level. To ensure the necessary level of creativity within a smaller workforce, diversity will become ever more important.

Now see Activity 5.1 and consider the age diversity in your organisation.

ACTIVITY 5.1

Consider the age/generational diversity in your own team/department/organisation. Do the issues outlined above seem familiar to you? Have you interviewed people of different ages recently? Did any of these differences come across during the recruitment process? Talk to some people of different ages. What things are most important to them in relation to their job and work situation? What things are most important to you?

FLEXIBILITY

The trend away from a reliance on 'permanent' full-time contracts of employment to the increasing use of more flexible and atypical working arrangements – eg homeworking, compressed hours working, term-time contracts and part-time arrangements, as well as outsourced services and contracts for services – can be seen to be a continuing one. The reasons for this include:

- legislation – ie the unfair dismissal rights of employees, agency workers' rights

- employee expectations about work–life balance

- changes in career paths as knowledge workers move to self-employment

- organisations' utilising a range of options to resource their non-core functions

- organisations' requiring increased flexibility in terms of hours of work, location, skills development and the duration of the employment relationship in order to respond quickly to market demands

- government policy on outsourcing and efficiency in the public sector

- business gurus' – notably Tom Peters' – encouraging companies to concentrate on what they are good at and to outsource the remainder.

We have thus seen many organisations move towards the 'flexible firm' model proposed by Atkinson (1984). Essentially, this means that employers retain a core group of primary workers who are likely to be permanent employees (although increasingly this group includes key part-time and other flexible working posts as well as full-time posts). Numerical and functional flexibility is then provided by employing a range of temporary, casual, fixed-term and agency workers as well as outsourcing activities to other companies and self-employed individuals.

Please note that whatever the make-up of your workforce, the same level of care and attention has to be paid to the recruitment and selection process (of employees and other 'workers') in order to ensure that the organisation's workforce requirements are satisfied in as cost-effective a manner as possible. See Case study 5.1 for further verification of this point.

A company director in a FTSE-100 company learned his lesson the hard way about the dangers of compromising good practice with regard to recruitment and selection. After the resignation of his PA/secretary, he used a secretary supplied by a local recruitment agency as a temporary measure while seeking to recruit a permanent replacement. It was a particularly busy time of year and the 'temp' coped well in the circumstances. She put in a lot of effort and worked long hours because she was keen to impress. As the weeks passed, the director decided not to bother with a proper recruitment and selection process but to offer the permanent position to the temp. She gratefully accepted – and that was when the situation took a turn for the worse. As the workload of the department settled back to normal, it became apparent to the director that the secretary did not possess the full range of skills that were expected of a PA. A capability procedure was adopted as a late measure but the situation was irredeemable. Eventually, they reached a mutual decision to part company – but in the meantime there had been months of disruption and soured relationships. The secretary felt that she had been misled and badly treated, and was conscious that this experience would be viewed as a black mark on her previously good employment record.

As can be seen from the sections above, it is important for organisations to know what type of posts they need in their business and to know something about the labour market they are operating in. We shall now look at human resource planning as a means of obtaining this knowledge.

HUMAN RESOURCE PLANNING

There are two components to the process of human resource planning (HRP): managing the demand for human resources, and managing the supply. An effective plan keeps the two in balance.

DEMAND

One source of demand arises from the organisation's activities requiring more resources. As a general rule managers like to increase their staff. The fact of having more subordinates signifies an increase in power and influence, boosts self-esteem and, quite possibly, leads to a higher salary level or increased prospects. 'Empire-building' is a mark of success in both public and private sectors, although a reputation for the activity can be damaging. However, an increase in employment costs invariably leads to an increase in overhead costs. There is a downward effect on overhead costs from shareholders (who expect the organisation to make a profit) in the private sector, and from the Treasury, and ultimately the electors, in the public sector. From time to time there can be pressure to reduce overheads, and this is particularly likely to arise if there is a reduction in demand for the organisation's products or services. When it comes to cutting overhead costs, the number of options can be limited and a reduction in staff (usually the greater part of these costs) is the inevitable outcome. HR practitioners should keep the long term in mind and seek to curb unwise or unnecessary increases (or decreases) in employment. You might reflect on whether, in your organisation, it would be easier to gain approval to employ another member of staff at £25,000 per year or easier to get an increase of £25,000 in the training budget. The potential benefits of each should be considered in your deliberations.

Another source of demand arises from the organisation's strategy. If it is expanding, opening more branches or services, opening new hospitals, serving new markets, for example, then it will require more people to staff those activities. There is of course a converse to this – namely, downsizing, where it may be closing branches, or services, or relinquishing markets. The longer the time horizon on which these actions are planned, the better the HR practitioner will be placed to respond effectively. This applies just as much whether it is a recruitment drive or a redundancy programme. The key for HR practitioners is gaining the confidence of the decision-makers so that the HR function can be involved at an early stage in the decision-making. Often it is necessary to prove your mettle in other areas of HR activity before you can gain the trust of the strategists.

An easier source of demand to manage is that resulting from the routine turnover of employees, or the 'attrition rate'. If this is steady, it provides a guide as to how much recruiting is likely to be required in a year. You need to keep an eye on changes in the rate that might be anticipated, such as the activities of competitors in your labour markets (see the discussion on *Supply*, below) or a glut of retirements.

The labour turnover rate is a useful figure to calculate for this purpose. This is calculated thus:

$$\text{Labour turnover} = \frac{\text{Number of employees leaving in a year}}{\text{Average number of employees in a year}} \times 100$$

Labour turnover rates are also a good measure of the 'health' of an organisation. The best way to make a judgement is by benchmarking organisations in the same sector, industry and locality. You may be able to find the information you require from networking or from industry sources, or from publications such as those from Incomes Data Services.

Very low turnover rates (especially if they reflect the recruitment rate) may be a cause for concern. It is important for organisations to get 'new blood' from time to time as part of a process of keeping up to date with skills and experience available in the labour marketplace.

High turnover rates are invariably bad news. Recruitment costs vary but are, typically, 10–20% of the first year's salary for each person recruited. On top of this, the leaver may have left a position vacant while the new employee is recruited. The new employee is likely to need training and time to establish relationships. He or she will not be performing at maximum capacity during this period.

If your organisation is experiencing high turnover rates, it is important to establish whether this arises from new recruits leaving the organisation in the first few weeks of employment (the induction crisis) or whether employees with longer service are leaving. The most valuable statistic in deciding this will be the labour stability rate:

$$\text{Labour stablility} = \frac{\text{Number of those employees still in employment today}}{\text{Number of employees in employment a year ago}} \times 100$$

A high labour stability rate (combined with a high turnover rate) means that most employees stay for many years but that in some job roles or functions there must be, nonetheless, a high turnover rate. This may suggest an induction crisis, and attention should therefore be paid to recruitment and induction. (See later in this chapter for further information on both of these subjects.) Another possible explanation is that in some job roles or functions employees simply do not stay because of poor management practices. If the turnover is several times a year, the effect will not show up fully in the stability rate. Apparent inconsistencies are always worth investigating.

However, the figures must be viewed in the context of the industry. In the hotel and catering industry, high turnover and low stability is not unusual. In a specialist research unit, on the other hand, it could mean that valuable skills and knowledge – the lifeblood of the organisation – are draining away.

Both these figures are difficult to calculate because finding and interpreting the raw data on which they are compiled requires persistence, judgement and significant resources on the part of the HR department. Consequently, they are often not calculated. But the critical point is that they enable the HR practitioner to assign costs to certain organisational shortcomings. By doing this, the practitioner can raise the perceived value of an effective HR function.

SUPPLY

Although the level of control over demand may be problematic at times, it is more difficult to exert much control over the supply of employees. The external environment has a major influence here, and anticipating changes can be valuable.

What practitioners can do is to increase their knowledge and understanding of their labour markets. Most organisations operate in a variety of labour markets and you should identify and research the ones that are relevant to you. These can be defined using the following factors, which must be considered in conjunction with each other.

Skills shortages

Skills shortages arise because the demand for particular skills exceeds the numbers of people trained in those skills. Periodically, national shortages are reported in the press and this raises the profile politically. Consequently, the government has sought to address these problems over the years through a variety of initiatives. Current at the time of writing this chapter is the 'train to gain' initiative, which helps to finance approved relevant training in organisations. An HR practitioner can make a significant contribution by keeping in touch with such initiatives. But not everyone believes that skills shortages are serious. Indeed, there is an ongoing debate about the importance of such shortages.

Nonetheless, in particular sectors, at particular times, skills shortages do arise. Training existing staff can do much to avert skills shortages, but it takes time. For example, it takes years to train an engineering apprentice and unexpected shortages can therefore not be rectified quickly. So HR planning needs, in part, to consider, and where possible to address, shortages that can be anticipated arising from retirement, changes in technology or from the social perception of certain types of work, for example.

Be aware, though, that shortages can be very specific and relatively transient. Searching for skills shortages on the Internet can produce current information about skills and occupational types in which there may be shortages.

Geography

Here you need to clarify where your employees travel from in order to work for you. Manual workers and junior staff may be very locally based, and this is where you would seek them. Some of the skills you seek may also be local, and this can be an issue if your organisation is considering relocating its activities. Managers and directors may travel from much further, especially if you are in a metropolitan area. In addition, when you come to seek senior or well-qualified people, the market can be national or international. Your strategy for finding employees will depend in part on where you believe they are living now.

Economic situations

You should keep in touch with the unemployment rate within the markets in which you are interested. This is particularly necessary if you envisage a recruitment drive in which you are seeking a significant number of employees.

Occupational types

The UK labour market is very diverse when it comes to occupational types. By thinking widely you may be able to identify sources of employees that others miss. When solving supply problems remember to include possibilities such as part-timers, job-shares, shift-workers, students, new graduates, outsourcing, homeworkers, teleworkers, self-employed workers, agency workers and workers from abroad. As mentioned above, an Internet search can provide information of occupational types and their current availablility.

Competitive positions of organisations

You compete with other organisations not just for sales but also for employees. Some organisations take this so seriously as to create employer brands, just as there are product brands. Your organisation may have a monopoly in its product marketplace or its labour marketplace. Its main product may be new and rising in success, or you may be in a 'sunset' industry. These factors influence your ability to find and attract employees and emphasise the importance of understanding your organisation in relation to its potential or actual labour markets. If you don't keep in touch, you could find your employees leaving, even for marginally higher rates, very rapidly. Valuable information on labour market competitors can come from local sources, such as Chambers of Commerce, HR discussion groups and networking. Desk research from sources such as Incomes Data Services can also be very helpful for the wider market. Your local library may be well worth a visit; discuss your research needs with the librarian.

Having considered HR planning, we shall now explain why the interlinked activities of recruitment and selection are so important, before outlining the relevant legislation and the practical issues involved in the recruitment and selection of staff. We shall be covering the key recruitment stages of job analysis and advertising, selection (candidate data collection, interviewing and other selection methods), assessment and comparison. Finally, the induction and evaluation processes and the various roles played by HR practitioners will be considered.

WHY ARE RECRUITMENT AND SELECTION IMPORTANT?

As we saw above, it is crucial that selection choices result from a thorough and systematic process. As HR practitioners you will need to be knowledgeable about the wider issues involving recruitment and selection decisions, such as legislation and good practice, and the range of recruitment sources and selection methods, as well as being skilled in interviewing and assessing potential employees.

Examples of poor practice in recruitment and selection decisions and their possible outcomes are listed below:

- When a job becomes vacant, failure to question whether it ought to be redesigned by making changes to, say, the level of responsibility, remuneration package, hours of work, working methods and reporting lines – or even whether it should be filled at all (ie where the work could be absorbed by existing members of staff) – will have cost implications, because the job has not been designed to suit current needs and the possibility of potential savings has been ignored.

- A hurried attempt to meet an advertising deadline in the local paper may result in inaccurate copy which, at the very least, misleads potential applicants and, at worst, discourages them from applying.

- Failure to carry out effective research into advertising media for a specialist post may well result in a lower standard of applicants than envisaged, and the necessity then to re-advertise in, say, a specialist journal will lead to additional expense.

- Untrained interviewers projecting a poor public relations image of the organisation to prospective employees and the use of inadvisable lines of questioning (eg family circumstances) may lead to claims of sex discrimination.

- Untrained and inexperienced observers used to assess too many candidates against too many criteria in a lengthy group exercise during an assessment centre may lead to invalid results.

- A decision to offer posts to candidates who performed best on the day even though they fell short of the requirements defined as essential for performing the job satisfactorily (see the person specification section on page 125) may result in their leaving or being dismissed in the short term or requiring more training than was envisaged in the long term.

We could go on! The important factor to note is that all of the above examples of poor practice result in unnecessary costs to the organisation. Advertising alone is expensive, but once you move beyond a wasted advertising opportunity to the salary costs of an unsuitable employee or the potential cost of a lost employment tribunal case, then you may be facing the loss of thousands of pounds (and the wrath of higher management).

THE LEGISLATION

Before moving on to look at the mechanisms of recruitment and selection, we are going to outline the relevant legislation before considering the important issue of good practice. The legislation is referred to and commented on throughout this chapter as well as being specifically referred to in Chapter 3. You should be aware of the impact of the following main pieces of legislation:

- the Sex Discrimination Acts 1975 and 1986

- the Race Relations Act 1976 (Amended 2000)

- the Disability Discrimination Act 2005

- the Equal Pay Act 1970

- the Part-time Workers (Prevention of Less Favourable Treatment) Regulations 2000

- the Equality Act 2006

- the Employment Equality (Age) Regulations 2006

- the Employment Equality (Sexual Orientation) (Religion or Belief) (Amendment) Regulations 2007

- the Immigration, Asylum and Nationality Act 2006

- the Data Protection Act 1998

- the Freedom of Information Act 2000.

Other relevant legislation concerns amendments to the above legislation, fixed-term contract workers and flexible working arrangements. The legislation listed also includes specific public sector equality duties, which those of you working in the public sector should be aware of. Much of this legislation will be amended by the Equality Bill currently going through Parliament and due to be enacted in 2010. The intention is to harmonise and simplify much of what currently exists. In simple terms, the equality legislation makes it unlawful for organisations to take into account a person's gender, marriage, colour, race, nationality, ethnic or national origin, disability, hours of work, sexual orientation, religion or belief in making employment decisions. Here we are specifically concerned with decisions at the point of access to the organisation. Thus you should ensure that you take account of equality and diversity at all stages of the recruitment and selection process, from job analysis and advertising, the choice of selection methods and the making of selection decisions through to induction into the organisation. You should note that this protection from discrimination applies before, during and after employment, so training, promotion and termination decisions are also covered.

The advisory and enforcement agency associated with the promotion of equality and diversity in the workplace is the Equality and Human Rights Commission. The role of the Commission is to promote equality and human rights, which it does through providing advice and guidance, working to implement an effective legislative framework and raising awareness of rights and responsibilities. Codes of practice giving guidance to employers on how to comply with the legislation are available from the Commission. For instance, it is recommended that employers have written equal opportunities policies, procedures for making complaints and monitoring arrangements, and that they take positive action to redress any imbalances in the make-up (eg gender or race profile) of their employees by, for example, wider advertising, flexible working hours arrangements and help with child care.

The immigration, asylum and nationality legislation creates a legal requirement for employers to check the entitlement to work in the UK of all prospective employees in advance of their start date. Failure to do so is a criminal offence.

Finally, in Chapter 3 we covered the Rehabilitation of Offenders Act 1974 which provides protection from discrimination for ex-offenders with spent convictions. However, certain sectors where employees work with children and vulnerable adults are exempt, notably the health and care sectors and education. The Criminal Records Bureau helps employers to obtain information on job applicants in order to screen out unsuitable candidates. See the website references at the end of the chapter for further information.

And for more information on both freedom of information and data protection, see Chapter 10.

Now consider Activity 5.2.

ACTIVITY 5.2

Have a look at your organisation's equality and diversity policy. Is it readily available? What impact does it have on recruitment activities in your organisation? How are new employees made aware of it and their responsibilities under it? How are the responsibilities within the policy monitored in relation to recruitment activity?

Find out more about the new Equalities Bill. Consider how your equality and diversity policy and recruitment practices might have to change to reflect the new legislation. Discuss with colleagues whether the new legislation will simplify and harmonise the previous legislation.

EQUALITY VERSUS DIVERSITY

So far we have considered only those groups of employees who are covered by legislative provisions. Many leading organisations in the equal opportunities field have policies that include reference to groups not specifically protected by legislation. Recruitment and selection decisions are thus based on objective criteria only. For instance, factors such as background, appearance, social class and regional accents are not taken into consideration unless they impact on the ability to do the job. Here we are moving towards a distinction between an 'equal opportunities' employer and an organisation which embraces diversity.

You are strongly advised to read the CIPD Infosource documents referred to at the end of this chapter under *References and further reading* for more guidance on best practice in the fields of recruitment and selection, equal opportunities and managing diversity.

We will now take a few minutes to examine a case study on this subject and an associated Activity.

CASE STUDY 5.2

An organisation in the environmental field publicises itself as an equal opportunities employer on all of its job vacancy notices. Last year the equal opportunities policy was replaced with a Diversity Statement, which reads as follows:

> To fulfil our vision of a better environment for present and future generations, we will develop an organisation where all employees are actively supported in giving their best contribution to corporate aims and objectives. This means attracting people from all parts of the community, valuing the differing skills and abilities of all our employees and responding flexibly to the needs of individuals in achieving organisational goals.

The organisation recently lost an employment tribunal claim in which the applicant claimed race discrimination. The tribunal chair commented that there was little evidence that the organisation was an equal opportunities employer or embraced diversity in its workforce.

OVERVIEW

Continuing on the theme of good practice, we are now at the stage of considering the practical issues relevant to recruitment and selection. We shall, for simplicity's sake, be considering these processes separately – the recruitment process, selection, making the appointment, and induction – but it is obvious they are closely interlinked, as demonstrated by the simple flowchart in Figure 5.1.

THE RECRUITMENT PROCESS

There are two major stages involved here: job analysis and attracting applicants. We have already looked at examples of the potential pitfalls of inactivity, hurry or sheer carelessness at these and other stages in the section above on why recruitment and selection are important. With regard to job analysis, it is generally preferable that line managers retain responsibility and ownership for this activity for their own staff, and do not view this purely as an HR function, although HR will often be involved in an advisory capacity. Regarding advertising, the design and placing of advertisements is often handled centrally – ie by HR practitioners – to maximise control (to ensure consistency and management of organisation image) and minimise costs.

Job analysis is looked at in detail in Chapter 4. In this chapter we provide just an overview/reminder of job analysis and look at attracting applicants in detail.

JOB ANALYSIS

We will be concentrating here on the role of job analysis in recruitment and selection, but – as seen in Chapter 4 – it is also relevant to work design, organisation structures, job evaluation, the identification of training needs and performance management issues, especially the setting of objectives.

There are three elements in job analysis important in the recruitment process:

- research
- job descriptions
- person specifications.

We shall take each in turn.

Figure 5.1 Recruitment and selection flowchart

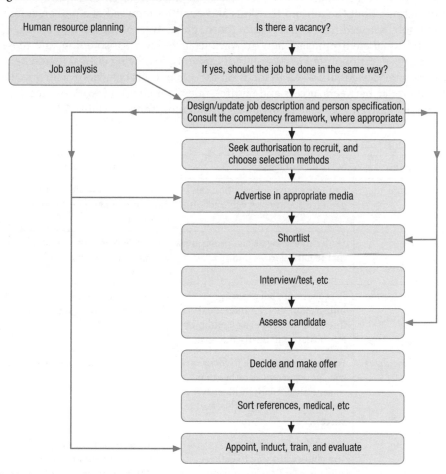

The black arrows indicate the sequence of events, and the grey arrows indicate where information from one stage is fed into another. For instance, the scrutinising of the job application for shortlisting purposes should not be carried out as a separate event but should be based on the information provided by the person specification on the characteristics and qualities that are being sought. In fact, application forms, if well designed, can help you make a judgement as to whether applicants possess the characteristics or qualities that are deemed to be essential.

NB: It is important to examine at each stage areas where discrimination could occur, and take preventative action.

Research

The first stage is to determine whether the post you want to recruit to is a genuine vacancy – because a new post has been created or an existing post-holder is leaving/has left. You need to define accurately and clearly the nature and purpose of the job and whether you need to fill it. Thinking about the job and asking yourself some questions allows you to weigh up the alternatives – such as redesigning the job, subcontracting it or using technology to do parts of the job. This stage also allows you to challenge some of the assumptions you may have about the job – for example, about the way the job should be done or about the kind of person who should do it.

Having decided that there is a genuine job to be filled, in order to acquire information about the job and the skills and qualities required of a person suited to that job, we need first to carry out a thorough analysis of the job and its organisational environment. There are various techniques for so doing, and these include observation, interviews, group discussions, reviewing critical incidents (where interviewees are asked to focus on aspects of their behaviour which make the difference between success and failure), questionnaires and work diaries. Each has its own advantages and disadvantages, as demonstrated in Table 5.1.

Table 5.1 Job analysis techniques

Technique	Main advantages	Main disadvantages
Observation	Comprehensive information can be gathered about observable activities.	Very time-consuming. Those observed may act differently from the norm.
Interview	Skilled interviewers can probe areas that require clarification.	Interviewees may seek to impress the interviewer by 'talking up' the job.
Group discussion	Provides more balanced information than an individual interview because exaggeration by job-holders will be discouraged.	Time-consuming and logistically complicated to arrange.
Critical incidents	Forces an interviewee to focus on specific occurrences rather than to generalise. Helps to identify the types of behaviour that lead to success.	A complex and time-consuming process.
Questionnaire	Objective, efficient and straightforward way to gather a wealth of information. Less opportunity for interviewer bias.	If questions are not carefully designed, the information gathered may be difficult to analyse.
Work diary	A systematic way of gathering comprehensive information. Most suitable for higher-level jobs.	Very time-consuming for the individual, and if not structured, may be difficult to analyse.

Please note that although the techniques listed above can be used on their own, the outcome of the job analysis will be more reliable if a combination of techniques is used.

The aim of job analysis is to answer the following questions:

- What is the job-holder expected to do?
- How is the job performed?
- What skills are required, and what is the level of those skills?
- Should the job be reorganised (eg change hours or level of responsibility, incorporate duties into other posts)?

The research stage should provide information that can then be formulated into 'user-friendly' documents – ie the job description and the person specification.

Job description

In simple terms, this describes the job. Organisations usually have their own standardised formats for job descriptions and although they vary enormously, they generally include the following sections:

- identification data: job title, department, pay grade, main location
- organisational data: responsible to and for, other working relationships (this could be visually presented as an extract from the organisation chart)
- job summary: a brief statement of why the job exists
- job content: an explanation of the principal duties or key result areas with brief summarised descriptions
- miscellaneous: unusual arrangements such as shift-working, a need to be mobile, casual car-user allowance plus a reference to any other documents – eg collective agreements – which provide further details.

Recent years have seen a move away from this traditional approach to job descriptions in some organisations. Some have questioned whether they are necessary at all in that increased flexibility and empowerment mean it is difficult to summarise many jobs. Further, some organisations now use generic job descriptions for job groupings rather than drafting job descriptions for each job type. There is, however, a strong argument that detailed job descriptions are still necessary for effective recruitment, job evaluation, training and performance management purposes (to name but a few). It is essential that the unique features of the job – particularly shift patterns and the need for mobility – are spelled out to job-holders and potential recruits in written particulars, if not in a job description.

We are also seeing the use of terms such as 'key accountabilities' and 'role profiles' in place of job descriptions. Both documents cover the information listed above, but the former also emphasises performance measures for each job (admittedly, performance standards have been included by some organisations for their more senior posts for many years). The latter tends to combine the information required for job descriptions and person specifications, and often makes use of competencies (see below).

Person specification

Alternative commonly used terms are the 'personnel specification' or 'job specification'. All three are used to describe 'the ideal person for the job'. (We would recommend that you use the term 'person specification' or 'personnel specification' but avoid the term 'job specification' because this has different meanings across organisations.)

Once again, person specifications vary in content and format depending on the 'house style'. We see, in examples of person specifications, the terms 'skills', 'experience', 'qualifications', 'knowledge', 'personal qualities' and, increasingly, 'competencies' used, but basically their purpose is the same: to set down the minimum requirements that an applicant must possess before being considered for a vacancy.

Further, most person specifications go beyond stating the minimum (essential) requirements and also state other (desirable) requirements, as demonstrated in Table 5.2. (In this example, you will see that the methods of assessment are also suggested. Please note that these are not the only choices, and – as a note of caution – the application form would have to be very well designed to ensure that sufficient information was available for assessment against all these criteria. References too have their limitations.)

Table 5.2 Example person specification form

Company name			
Job title:	HR Manager		
Department:	HR		
	Essential requirement	*Desirable requirement*	*Method of assessment*
Qualifications	Graduate calibre (ie at least two good A-levels). CIPD-qualified.	Graduate in relevant subject. MCIPD.	Application form and certificate check.
Experience	Minimum of three years' experience in generalist HR work at HR officer level.	Significant relevant experience in a unionised environment.	Application form, interview, and references.
Knowledge and skills	Up-to-date knowledge of employment legislation. Organisational skills. Financial awareness. Computer-literate.	Knowledge and skills in employee relations and negotiating. Experience of working with XYZ HR information system.	Application form, interview and role-play, plus references.
Personal qualities	Good communicator – written and oral skills, good judgement, confident, persuasive, approachable, dependable, uses initiative, average numeracy.		Application form, interview, group exercises, tests, and references.
Motivation and expectations	Desire to develop HR function. High expectations of self and others.		Application form, interview, and references.

Thus a successful candidate will be expected already to possess all the essential requirements and to be capable of, or have the potential to be trained to, an acceptable standard in the desirable ones. You should take note that all the requirements must be realistic, justifiable and non-discriminatory. An example where this would not be so is as follows:

- A stipulation that candidates for a supervisory position be fluent in Urdu, Bengali, Welsh and English and be physically strong enough to handle sheets of lead for sustained periods of time would be unrealistic: there are simply not enough people meeting those requirements out there in the labour market (particularly for the salary on offer!).

- The above requirements would also be unjustifiable if in reality the job did not involve communications in all the specified languages or did not entail the need to lift heavy items for sustained periods. (It would also undoubtedly be safer to provide special lifting equipment.)

In any event, care must be taken to ensure that person specification requirements do not discriminate either directly or indirectly on the grounds outlined in the *Legislation* section above.

ACTIVITY 5.4

Taking into account best practice, study your own job description and person specification (if they exist) and draft out accurate, up-to-date and comprehensive versions after carrying out a systematic analysis. Discuss their contents with one or more of your learning sources. You will be surprised at how much you do!

We shall now consider the role of competencies in this area.

COMPETENCIES

Competencies are used in many organisations and provide an outline of the skills and abilities an employee must have (or acquire) to do a job and achieve the required standard of performance. They provide an individual with an indication of the skills and abilities that are expected and that will be valued and recognised within an organisation. Competencies are often expressed in competency frameworks, which may contain both the behavioural and technical competencies required. Such frameworks are common in most organisations but less so in small private sector organisations. Competency frameworks provide a common set of criteria (which must be measurable) across a range of HR activities. They are multi-purpose and can assist managers in:

- recruitment and selection decisions
- performance appraisal discussions
- career development planning
- the distribution of rewards.

The deficiencies of person specifications, such as the example provided in Table 5.2, have resulted in a growth in the number of organisations using competency frameworks for recruitment and selection (including job analysis) purposes. So what are the deficiencies of traditional person specifications? It's quite simple – we tend to use expressions such as 'good communicator' and 'effective leader' and expect everyone to know exactly what is meant. It is obvious that this is not the case, and these terms must be precisely defined so that interviewers and assessors, in particular, have a common understanding and will be able to assess candidates accordingly. Thus competencies are used to describe the typical behaviours that we would expect to see when we observe a good performer – eg a good communicator or an effective leader. This area is a complicated one and you will

Table 5.3 Typical content of a competency framework

Competency cluster: SHOWS THE WAY
COMPETENCIES with levels

- DIRECTION

  Level 1: develops strategies that account for the short-, medium- and long-term needs of the business

  Level 2: keeps others informed of business goals and inspires buy-in to them

  Level 3: supports business goals by addressing issues likely to affect achieving them.

- LEADERSHIP

  Level 1: is consistent in expectations of others and provides clear leadership

  Level 2: operates openly, is accessible and approachable to others.

- PLANNING

  Level 1: ensures that business plans are achievable and integrated with business goals

  Level 2: ensures that plans meet local needs and that they account for the needs of other teams

  Level 3: uses appropriate planning to succeed in own role.

BEHAVIOURAL INDICATORS (for Direction)

Level 1: Develops strategies that account for the short-, medium- and long-term needs of the business	Level 2: Keeps others informed of business goals and inspires buy-in to them	Level 3: Supports business goals by addressing issues likely to affect achieving them
• Produces and regularly communicates three- to five-year plans to ensure that strategies remain relevant • Balances long-term goals with short-term deliverables to achieve business goals • Ensures that business goals are communicated and understood across the business.	• Develops local goals to support wider business goals • Inspires buy-in to business goals by showing how individual efforts contribute to them • Provides timely and appropriate information to support achievement of business goals.	• Focuses and encourages others to focus on delivering the business goals • Regularly reviews and communicates progress on business goals • Uses the business goals to prioritise work.

Source: Whiddett and Hollyforde (2003) *A Practical Guide to Competencies*. London: CIPD. Reproduced by permission.

find some excellent reading in Whiddett and Hollyforde (2003). They provide the example in Table 5.3 of a competency framework, showing the various levels of competency applicable to different jobs.

In summary, assuming that we have decided there is a vacancy to be filled and we have permission to do so, we must ensure that:

- we carry out a thorough job analysis and design working documents (job descriptions and person specifications)

- we consult the competency framework, where this is available, to determine exactly what sort of behaviour signifies good performance in the job.

Armed with this information, we must choose appropriate methods to attract candidates before we are ready to advertise the vacancy.

ATTRACTING APPLICANTS

Attracting applicants can be a very expensive activity – especially if we get it wrong. It can be tempting to sit back and congratulate ourselves on a thorough job analysis that has resulted in workable and user-friendly documents – ie the job description and the person specification. We need, however, to be just as systematic and methodical in our approach to attracting applicants to the vacancy and in managing their contact with the organisation for the duration of the process. The key is to aim at attracting a suitable pool of candidates, promoting the job in a way that attracts a small number of suitable candidates rather than a large number of less suitable ones – particularly in an economic climate where unemployment levels are high. The prime method of attracting applicants is through advertising – although this can include a wide range of activities, not just the traditional (and often high-cost) advert in a newspaper/journal.

Being systematic and methodical in advertising means considering the content and design of the advert, the timing of the advert and our choice of media/advert location.

In commencing the advertising process you need first to be aware of the sources of possible recruits:

- existing employees – ie internal recruitment
- job centres
- employment agencies or recruitment consultants
- advertising
  - shop windows or factory gates
  - local and national newspapers
  - the ethnic press, publications and meeting venues
  - professional, specialist or technical journals
  - local radio
  - television
  - the Internet
  - social networking sites

- the graduate 'milk round'
- outplacement agencies
- armed forces (and police/fire service) resettlement programmes
- word of mouth (personal recommendations)
- networking
- headhunters
- 'waiting lists' or speculative queries
- open days
- liaison with schools and colleges.

Different sources are appropriate depending on the group of potential applicants that you wish to target. For instance, you may decide to use the free facilities of the job centre for semi-skilled positions, especially when you expect to find a wealth of unemployed talent in the immediate locality. However, if you wish to attract managerial, specialist or technical personnel, you will probably need to spread the net further and make use of national newspapers, appropriate journals and/or the Internet. This will obviously be more expensive, but there is also a cost attached to not filling a key post – eg in overtime payments and missed opportunities. We do assert that an advertisement is cost-effective only when it is concisely worded, well designed and attracts a sufficient number of suitably qualified candidates.

You should note that in order to comply with equal opportunities legislation vacancies should be advertised as widely as possible. Relying entirely on internal recruitment, 'on file' applications or personal recommendations may leave the organisation open to criticism, and is highly unlikely to redress gender, race or other imbalances in its workforce profile. Adverts themselves should not contain any discriminatory language or requirements. It should also be noted that where imbalances exist in the current workforce, advertising can be targeted towards under-represented groups.

The timing of the advertisement is also of crucial importance, especially when advertising in newspapers and journals. You must ensure that:

- for the local press, you choose the day job-seekers know that jobs will appear
- you avoid advertising just before a holiday or shutdown period, because you may miss potential applicants who are on holiday or disillusion others who cannot contact the organisation for further information
- you check the dates for final copy and meet them in order to avoid unnecessary delays in recruitment (this can be protracted if using monthly publications).

Another important tip is that you must be very specific regarding the section of the publication in which you wish to place your advertisement. Odd-numbered pages are generally more widely read than even-numbered ones, but also you do not want your advertisement for a new chief executive to be lost among the double-glazing sales pitches or the lonely hearts column!

An organisation in the NHS was experiencing difficulties attracting candidates for housekeeping assistant vacancies. It had tried advertising the vacant posts in a variety of ways and was spending increasing amounts of money on adverts in the local paper without any success.

An HR adviser decided to try a slightly different approach. All adverts placed by the hospital in the local paper (including the housekeeping assistant vacancies) went into the 'display' section of the jobs pages – where adverts are larger, include artwork, contain organisation logos, etc. The HR adviser noticed that many smaller organisations advertising for similar posts put very small adverts in the 'lineage' section of the jobs pages – no artwork/logos, just a couple of sentences about the job. The hospital decided to give this a try with their housekeeping vacancies.

When the adverts appeared in the lineage section of the jobs pages, the hospital received a 20% increase in applicants to these posts and managed to fill nearly all the vacancies.

Now we shall concentrate on the design and content of the advertisements themselves. One of the most popular mnemonics used by HR practitioners is AIDA. This provides a guide to successful advertising by highlighting the four steps:

- **A**ttention
- **I**nterest
- **D**esire
- **A**ction.

To work, an advertisement must catch the attention of the target audience and spark the reader's interest by establishing the relevance of the job to the individual so that the whole message is read. Further, it should arouse a desire to pursue the opportunity offered and should stimulate action in the form of applications from the target audience.

This may be easier said than done, but studying examples of advertisements is very useful for highlighting good and bad practices. An example of an advertisement that fails to comply with AIDA is provided in Case study 5.4. It was found in the General Appointments section of the *Daily Telegraph* on a Monday, and is reproduced without reference to the real organisation in order to avoid embarrassment.

So what should we do to avoid making mistakes in advertising? There are no golden rules, but generally an advertisement, drawing on and summarising the job description and the person specification, should be composed as follows:

- job title/location/salary (these are of key interest to job-seekers)
- brief description of the job
- brief description of the nature of the organisation (unless very well known)
- brief description of the 'ideal person' (highlighting, as a minimum, the essential requirements)
- organisational benefits and facilities (if attractive)

FINANCIAL CONTROLLER

This is an exciting opportunity to join one of England's top football clubs. The successful candidate will be a qualified, experienced accountant used to working in a commercial environment who understands the importance of 'bottom line' and has a flair for evaluating systems and ideas for their business potential and cost-effectiveness.

Reporting to the Company Secretary, you will be responsible for the financial control of all Club operations.

Age is not important – a dynamic, enthusiastic attitude is. A competitive salary will be offered together with a full executive benefits package. Please send your CV to:

G. Taylor
Neversaydie Football Club
Green Lane
Neverton

As you can see, the advertisement is poorly located (how many potential financial controllers will be reading this section of the *Daily Telegraph* on a Monday?), is not designed to grab your attention or hold your interest (the fact that the job would entail working for a football club is not capitalised upon at all), gives vague and limited information about the job and the person sought, and so fails to arouse desire (further, there is no indication of the salary banding), and it is unclear about the application procedure – ie the action that should follow – because there is no contact number for further information and no closing date.

- unique features (such as hours of work, need for mobility, accommodation provision)
- application procedure and closing date
- reference number (if used)
- equal opportunities statement
- reference to the organisation's web pages, where applicable.

In essence, you must give enough information about the job (to target the right people) and the person required (to attract only suitable candidates to apply). The image portrayed should be inviting but also reflective of the style and culture of the organisation. For instance, an eye-catching headline seeking an 'Action Man or Wonder Woman' would probably not be appropriate for a filing clerk's post in a local authority, but has been successfully used for a security officer's role in a large toy store.

INTERNET RECRUITMENT

We mentioned Internet recruitment (or online or e-recruitment) above. This can be advertising on your own company website, on sector-wide websites such as 'NHS jobs', using specialist online recruitment websites, or, increasingly, using social networking websites such as Facebook and Twitter as part of a recruitment campaign. The former can be very useful in that the company retains total control over the process, but will be less successful if your organisation is not well known or if insufficient attention is paid to maintaining the website. It is still important to consider the factors outlined above about advertising wherever your organisation opts to advertise vacancies, and it is likely that an approach to advertising that appropriately uses different routes and different media will bring best results. There are both advantages and disadvantages to using online advertising, although it can look very attractive because of the relatively lower cost. We will be concentrating on the use of the wider Internet rather than company websites in the Activity that follows.

ACTIVITY 5.5

What factors would you take into account when deciding whether to advertise a technical post:

a) in a specialist journal?

b) via an established online recruitment

website such as www.netjobs.co.uk or www.monster.co.uk?

Compare your responses with the feedback provided at the end of this chapter.

Assuming that your advertisement has attracted a manageable number of suitably qualified and experienced candidates, we shall now move on to the important stage of selecting the right candidate. Please note that as we indicated earlier, the processes of recruitment and selection are not discrete, so you should by now have made the decision on which selection methods you wish to use (see Figure 5.1, page 123).

THE SELECTION PROCESS

You should make your decision on the successful candidate as a result of:

- candidate data collection
- candidate assessment
- comparison.

You should always avoid making a simple comparison of candidates with each other, because this is likely to be highly subjective and will lead to an offer of the position to the candidate who was deemed to be 'the best on the day'. Instead, you should use the person specification and, at each stage, compare the candidates with the essential and desirable requirements listed. Bad selection decisions can be very costly, and it is always better to make no appointment than the wrong appointment.

CANDIDATE DATA COLLECTION

Information can be gathered about candidates through:

- application forms
- curricula vitae (CVs)
- interview performances
- tests (ranging from physical, intelligence and aptitude tests through to personality profiles)
- appraisals (for internal candidates)
- references
- online questionnaires
- assessment centre performances.

In order for this process to be directed at achieving your aim – ie to recruit the person who most closely fits your person specification profile – you should ensure that you collect only relevant information about the candidates. For example, an applicant's bizarre taste in music or socks is unlikely to be relevant and can lead, like discussions of which football team he or she supports, to unfounded prejudices.

The first stage of the selection process – shortlisting (or deciding who to invite for interview/further assessment) – generally takes place using information provided on the application form or CV. Assessment of the information provided by candidates in this way should be done in line with the requirements of the post as outlined on the job description and person specification, and should be as objective and consistent as possible. Shortlisting should take place as soon as possible after the closing date, many larger organisations specifying that at least two people should be involved in the shortlisting process. Some organisations use a two-stage shortlisting process, particularly where large numbers of applicants are involved or the post is a very senior one. These two stages are often referred to as longlisting and shortlisting. The first stage is where a larger number of applicants are invited to take part in an initial selection process (for example, a first interview or an online assessment). Longlisting is often a tool used to 'screen out' or disqualify applicants from involvement in later stages of selection. Many organisations find it helpful to aim for between four and six candidates on the final shortlist. Shortlisting also gives the first real indication of the success (or not) of the recruitment and advertising stages of the process.

Later stages of the selection process involve gathering data about candidates using some of the other methods outlined above.

We are now going to consider three of the above methods in more detail. We will start with interviews and then move on to provide summaries of the latest thinking about tests and assessment centres. These latter two methods have increased in popularity and are designed to provide more information about the candidate than can be obtained by exclusive use of the much-maligned interview. Tests and assessment centres have also usually been validated to see whether the tests and exercises used adequately measure relevant characteristics and abilities in order to predict job success. There is a wealth of reading and commentary on this area for your further enlightenment. Articles in the CIPD's *People Management* magazine would be a useful starting-place; see also the CIPD publications listed under *References and further reading* at the end of this chapter.

The interview

Unlike tests and assessment centres, the interview, as a selection tool, has been much criticised for its lack of validity. (The results of unstructured interviewing have been found to be only slightly higher than random selection at predicting future success in the job!) Nevertheless, any coverage of recruitment and selection would be incomplete without reference to 'the interview'. Although we can see the pitfalls of its use, few appointments are made without the interview playing some role. You should note that the effectiveness of interviews can be improved by thorough preparation and by ensuring that all the questions asked are relevant (and seen to be relevant) to the job. The majority of employing organisations still use interviews as a crucial stage before deciding on new appointments because they see that interviews can be useful for:

- verifying information
- exploring omissions
- checking assumptions
- providing the candidate with information.

In fact, candidates themselves seem equally loath to dispense entirely with interviews. Many feel that the interview provides the only opportunity for them to reveal their personalities and to 'sell' themselves to the employer.

So how do we get the best out of an interview? The structure of the interview should, in simple terms, follow the mnemonic WASP:

- **W**elcome
- **A**cquire – What information do you have?
  - What else do you need?
  - What should you check?
- **S**upply – What information should you impart?
  - What will happen next?
- **P**art.

Thus you should bear WASP in mind when drawing up your list of questions for interviewees. If you are involved in a panel interview, each member of the panel can lead a different section of questions while still maintaining a logical structure overall. A checklist for successful interviewing practice and an examination of the types of questions to be used and avoided are reproduced in Tables 5.4 and 5.5. Note, however, that the checklist in Table 5.4 is likely, with some adaptation, to be applicable to a large number of interviewing situations, not just those designed for staff selection purposes.

Table 5.4 Interviewing checklist

BEFORE
- Familiarise yourself with the job description and person specification.
- Read the application form and/or CV.
- Meet the rest of the interview panel to agree the division of question areas and roles to be played – eg chair, scribe, timekeeper.
- Arrange the interview at an appropriate time and place.
- Book the venue.
- Inform the applicant well in advance, providing details of location, time, expected duration, need for preparation, travel expense provisions, number of stages in the selection process, etc.
- Ask if particular arrangements need to be made – eg a personal loop system for a candidate who is hard of hearing.
- Confirm the arrangements with the panel members.
- Notify security and reception of the arrangements.
- Ensure that the venue is private and that interruptions will not occur.
- Allow enough time between interviews for breaks, discussions, and completion of assessment forms and, at the end of all the interviews, for a full review.

DURING
- Start on time.
- Start with a welcome.
- Seek to establish rapport.
- Explain the purpose of the interview, the stage in the selection process and that notes will be taken to provide a record of the interview.
- Ask relevant questions (see Table 5.5).
- Allow the applicant to do the majority of the talking.
- Listen actively.
- Do not seek to fill silences (or you may discourage the candidate from providing more information).
- Observe non-verbal behaviour (and check anomalies between this and the verbal messages).
- Check gaps, omissions, or contradictions.
- Check claims re level and type of experience.
- Use a logical sequence of questions and provide links between sections.
- Provide brief information on the job and organisation.
- Allow sufficient time for the applicant's questions.
- Ensure that the candidate's responses are noted by relevant panel members.
- Keep control of the content and timing.
- Summarise.
- Close on a positive note – thank the candidate and reiterate the next stage of the process.

AFTERWARDS
- Compare the information gained about the applicant with the person specification requirements.
- Complete the assessment form after reaching agreement with the panel members.
- Follow up the interview with the appropriate documentation – eg an invitation to the next stage, a rejection letter.

Table 5.5 Types of interview questions

Generally questions should be:

open   to encourage full responses
   eg 'Tell me about. . .'

probing   to check information provided in the application or interview
   eg What?, Why?, How?, Explain . . .

Probing questions include situational or behaviour-based questions to elicit practical experience or judgement; and 'contrary evidence' questions to check an assumption made about the candidate by seeking evidence to the contrary.

Closed questions – ie those demanding a yes or no response – should be used only for clarification or control – eg bringing a line of questioning to its conclusion.

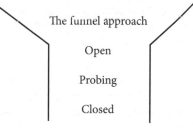

The funnel approach

Open

Probing

Closed

We recommend a *funnelling* approach, as indicated above. You should start with an open question – eg 'Tell me about your current responsibilities' – followed by progressively narrower probing questions – eg 'What experience have you had of formal negotiating situations?' At the end of this section of questioning you should use a closed question such as 'So would it be accurate to say that you have had limited experience in formal negotiating situations, and if you are successful in being offered this vacancy, you would welcome specialist training in this area?' The candidate is very likely to say yes, effectively bringing about a 'full-stop' to this section. You should then provide a link to the next section of questioning – eg 'Thank you for your responses to those questions; we will now move on to discuss . . .'

The following types of questions should generally be avoided:

leading   eg 'You are fully trained in the use of an XYZ HR Information System, aren't you?'
   (The candidate knows exactly what answer you are looking for here!)

multiple   eg 'Tell us about your educational background, your career history to date, and your strengths and development needs.'
   (By the time the candidate has finished telling you about his or her educational qualifications, you will probably both have forgotten what else you asked. Further, a clever candidate will undoubtedly tell you about his or her strengths but ignore the issue of development needs!)

If you do fall into either of the above traps, it is relatively easy to rectify your mistake by asking additional probing questions. Keeping brief notes, both of the candidate's responses and the further questions that you feel it necessary to ask, will help you here.

The above guidelines apply to a range of approaches to interviews – eg behaviour-based, situational and telephone interviews.

Competence or behaviour-based interviewing

Competence or behaviour-based interviewing has developed in line with the use of competency frameworks (see Table 5.3 on page 128 for an example). It is grounded on the premise that the best way to predict future job performance is to understand a candidate's past performance and behaviour in job-related situations. It allows candidates with limited job experience to compete on equal terms with more experienced candidates. (See *References and further reading* at the end of the chapter for more information on this subject.)

Let us take the example of a vacancy for a bar attendant in a hotel. There are three steps to follow:

- developing a competency profile based on the behaviour necessary to be a successful bar attendant – eg adherence to health and safety, hygiene and quality standards, customer service, knowledge of the hotel's products and services, selling ability and cash-handling

- developing appropriate 'benchmark' behaviour-based interview questions against which the interviewers measure each candidate's response to a specific situation: these are open-ended questions which focus on the candidates' describing critical incidents in their current and previous jobs as well as in their life experiences

- scoring the responses by measuring each candidate's answer against each of the respective profile statements.

Advocates of this approach say that their organisations have achieved financial benefits due to reductions in recruitment and training costs, improvements in productivity of newly appointed workers and reductions in staff turnover.

ACTIVITY 5.6

Draft competency/behaviour-based questions which seek to determine whether a candidate possesses the following competencies:

- effective leadership skills
- the ability to handle conflict
- problem-solving ability
- project management skills.

Compare your responses with the feedback provided at the end of this chapter.

Situational interviewing

Situational interviewing is similar to behaviour-based interviewing in that it centres on critical incidents, but instead of focusing on past behaviour, it is future-oriented. Thus questions tend to be hypothetical and are related to dilemmas that job-holders might encounter. It is based on the assumption that intentions predict behaviour. Candidates are presented with 'What if . . .?' job-related scenarios and asked 'What would you do in this situation?' The responses are then assessed against a pre-prepared scoring guide covering the possible range of responses, indicative of poor, average or good performance.

Proponents of this approach point to its high predictive validity, reliability and freedom from bias, and there is research evidence that backs up this contention. There are, however, many dissenters who have concerns that candidates may not actually behave in the real world in the same way that they say they will in the interview. We would conclude that this approach can be useful, especially when applicants do not have experience in your industry or sector, but would suggest that it is used alongside a variety of other questioning approaches, some of which look at past performance and behaviour as indicated above.

Telephone interviewing

Telephone interviews are increasingly being used by recruiting organisations for two main reasons:

- As an initial short-listing device it is more cost-effective than a face-to-face interview, especially if candidates live outside the locality.
- Many employees now spend a large proportion of their time communicating with customers by telephone – eg call centre staff – and the telephone interview provides an opportunity to start to assess skill and approach in this area.

There are drawbacks to telephone interviews, especially when candidates have not been notified that they may receive a call and that it is a crucial part of the selection process. It is possible, however, to capitalise on their use by following the rules of thumb below:

- Thoroughly prepare your questions beforehand and have at hand an easy-to-complete interview assessment form.
- Telephone the candidate at the agreed time and explain the nature, purpose and structure of the telephone interview.
- First ask screening questions such that candidates must answer these satisfactorily before progressing on to the remainder of the interview.
- Next ask a range of probing questions, such as behavioural or hypothetical questions, so that you are able to assess as many skills or competencies as possible.
- 'Sell' the job opportunity and provide information on the company, as required.
- Check the candidate's understanding and continuing interest in the post.
- Provide details of the next steps in the selection process and tell the candidate when he or she will be notified about progression (or not) to the next stage.
- Make a preliminary decision on the candidate's suitability and complete the paperwork while the interview is fresh in your mind.

Those in favour of this approach point to the advantages to both parties in that neither has to travel. More importantly, they say that people are less inhibited than in face-to-face interviews and so the quality of information provided can be higher.

We now move on to consider the use of tests in selection decisions.

Tests

The use of psychometric tests is certainly on the increase, although they tend to be used more extensively by larger organisations with established HR departments. The main applications of such tests in the recruitment and selection field are that they can be used to measure individual differences in personality and ability, and make predictions about future behaviour.

The CIPD's factsheet on psychological testing broadly supports the concept of testing but recognises the many concerns about their use. It answers these by setting out six key criteria for their use:

1 Everyone responsible for the application of tests including administration, evaluation, interpretation and feedback should be trained to at least the level of competence recommended by the British Psychological Society.

2 Potential test users should satisfy themselves that it is appropriate to use tests at all before incorporating tests into their decision-making processes.

3 Users should satisfy themselves that any tests they decide to use actually measure factors that are directly relevant to the employment situation.

4 Users must satisfy themselves that all tests they use have been rigorously developed and that claims about their reliability, validity and effectiveness are supported by statistical evidence. (The Data Protection Act 1998 is relevant here. If candidates are selected by an automated process, they have the right to know the logic used in the selection decision.)

5 Care must be taken to ensure equality of opportunity among all those individuals required to take tests.

6 The results of single tests should not be used as the sole basis of decision-making; this is particularly relevant with regard to personality tests.

We next consider assessment centres (ACs).

Assessment centres (ACs)

Nowadays ACs are used not only for large-scale recruitment, graduates and senior positions but across a large number of appointments to specialist, technical, customer service and other positions within organisations. The use of assessment centres – and development centres – is undoubtedly on the increase but many organisations fail to adopt good practices.

What are ACs? There is no typical AC but a good AC should include the following:

● a variety of selection methods or assessment techniques – ie a combination of any of the following: interviews, psychometric tests, in-tray exercises, job sampling or simulations, questionnaires, team-building activities, structured discussions, presentations, report-writing, role-playing exercises

- assessment of several candidates together
- assessment by several trained and experienced assessors/observers
- assessments against a number of clearly defined job-relevant competencies.

ACs thus answer some of the criticisms of the use of sole techniques such as interviews and tests. This is because they enable assessors to observe and assess candidates' behaviour in a number of different situations that provide a more comprehensive and rounded picture of the individuals concerned, as demonstrated by the example AC matrix in Table 5.6.

Table 5.6 Example matrix – project manager

Competency	Selection technique				
	Interview	Group exercises	In-tray exercise	Presentation	Written report
Leadership	✕	✕			
Problem-solving	✕	✕			✕
Verbal communication	✕			✕	
Written communication			✕		✕
Time management			✕	✕	✕
Decision-making		✕	✕		✕
Negotiating and influencing skills	✕	✕		✕	
Analytical ability		✕	✕		✕

We have seen that we need to gather a range of data about our candidates via various methods such as the application form, the interview and the use of tests and assessment centres. We now consider the second key stage of the selection process: candidate assessment.

CANDIDATE ASSESSMENT

In assessing our candidates, we need to evaluate each candidate against the job-relevant criteria detailed in the person specification and reach a considered and objective judgement in every case. Here your skills in defining those criteria in very specific and measurable terms should stand you in good stead. Referring to the example person specification form shown in Table 5.2 (see page 126), as we have already stated, the requirements should really be defined further. In the absence of a competency framework, it is necessary to define what you mean by terms such as 'good verbal communicator'. For instance, should our successful candidate be an articulate, experienced and polished presenter or simply have a reasonably good vocabulary?

At the shortlisting stage you are likely to have only the information contained on the application form. If this has been well designed, it should be relatively easy to filter out those candidates who do not meet the minimum (essential) requirements. Curricula vitae (CVs) are often used at this initial shortlisting stage, but because they are not standardised and often contain incomplete information, they may be much less useful here. Actually, you can help this process by giving clear instructions to candidates regarding the type of information that you want them to provide in submitting their application forms and CVs.

If you still have a large number of potentially suitable candidates after considering the essential requirements, you may shortlist further by producing a list of candidates who appear to possess a number of the desirable requirements also. Interviews, tests and exercises can then be used to gain more information on your shortlisted candidates. Depending on the number of suitable applicants and the seniority of the post, the selection process may consist of one, two, or even three stages (with a different combination of selection methods and HR involvement at each stage).

COMPARISON

Here you are comparing the candidate assessment with the person specification and looking for the closest 'fit'. The candidate who most closely matches the 'ideal person' described in your person specification should be offered the vacancy. You should not select the person who performs 'best' overall, because this is likely to result in the recruitment of an overqualified person (ie in excess of your requirements) or an underqualified person (ie all the candidates fell short of your requirements). If you are confident that you have carried out a systematic job analysis, you should realise that those candidates who appear to be overqualified for your needs may be equally as 'unsuitable' as those who clearly fall short of your requirements. Thus you are aiming to achieve:

the right person for the job

and

the right job for the person.

ACTIVITY 5.7

Look back at a recent vacancy within your organisation and analyse the process of recruiting and selecting the successful candidate by answering the following questions:

- Was an appropriate choice of advertising media made?

- Was good documentation (job description, person specification) available?

- Was an appropriate choice of selection methods made?

- What lessons have been learned, and what suggestions do you have for improvements in the event of similar vacancies arising in the future?

Discuss your recommendations with an appropriate learning source.

MAKING THE APPOINTMENT

Once you have decided on your preferred candidate, you are in a position to make an appointment. In many organisations this involves two stages – undertaking any necessary employment checks, and making a job offer.

EMPLOYMENT CHECKS

Although some employment checks may be made at earlier stages of the recruitment and selection process, it is likely that most will be made as the process nears its conclusion – either for all shortlisted candidates or just for the successful candidate. There is a range of different checks that may be undertaken. These may include health checks, references, qualifications and professional registration, identity and right to work in the UK and criminal records. In larger organisations there may well be established procedures for undertaking such checks, and the associated tasks often sit with the HR department. It is likely that most organisations large or small will want to take up references from previous employers to monitor a candidate's employment history and to undertake some form of health check to ensure that there are no factors that would prevent the candidate from doing the job effectively. Please note, though, that the requirements of disability legislation to make reasonable adjustments in the case of a candidate with a disability still apply. Where particular qualifications (for example, GCSEs or an HGV licence) or professional registration (for example, as a teacher or nurse) are required, the organisation will want to check that the candidate possesses these by inspecting certificates or contacting the relevant registration body. There is a legal requirement for employers to check an individual's right to work in the UK. This is contained within the Immigration, Asylum and Nationality Act 2006, which sets out the requirements and possible penalties for non-compliance. Criminal record checks are currently undertaken through the Criminal Records Bureau and apply to posts that are exempt from the Rehabilitation of Offenders Act. Many such posts are found in the health, care or education sectors, although not exclusively. Full details of the types of checks required and workers for which they are necessary can be found in the

Safeguarding Vulnerable Adults legislation. Further details can be found on the Independent Safeguarding Authority website, the address of which is in the *References and further reading* list at the end of the chapter.

JOB OFFERS

It is likely that you will initially make a verbal offer, if you are authorised to do so, but you must be careful to emphasise any 'subject to' conditions. Conditional offers most commonly refer to some of the checks outlined above.

A probationary period may also be stipulated.

All these areas are fraught with difficulties and it is not our intention to cover them all here, but you should note the following:

- It is advisable to make job offers conditional on receipt of references which are 'satisfactory to the company'. If the references you subsequently obtain are unsatisfactory, the offer of employment can then be withdrawn without the employer being in breach of contract.

- Evidence of health problems should not be used for withdrawing an offer unless it can be justified on material and substantial grounds. For example, a food factory may be justified in not employing someone with a serious nut allergy if they could not make reasonable adjustments for the applicant to avoid contact with nuts. Medical information can help the employer to ensure compliance with the Disability Discrimination Act 1995 (see Chapter 3 for more information).

- Despite requests by line managers to bring new recruits on board as soon as possible, you would be advised to await references and medical information before confirming start dates. (See Case study 5.5.)

CASE STUDY 5.5

You have probably read over the years a number of stories in the press about employees – particularly in the medical, educational and caring professions – who have lied about their backgrounds and qualifications in order to obtain work. Some of these stories have had alarming outcomes; hence the press coverage. It would appear that due to the competitive nature of today's job market, there is more temptation for some applicants to embellish the contents of their CVs.

One medium-sized organisation found themselves in difficulties recently when they appointed a finance director. His CV indicated that he had an impressive array of qualifications and was experienced in the industry sector. It quickly became apparent, however, that he was not up to the job. The HR manager was notified and was concerned to learn, four weeks after he commenced employment, that a reference request to his former employer had been returned as 'not known at this address'. Further investigations showed that the finance director did not have the qualifications that he claimed, and that he had been dismissed by one of his previous employers for alleged fraud, although he had not been prosecuted. The finance director remained unaware of the HR manager's investigation until it had been completed and the decision was taken to dismiss him. This 'damage limitation' strategy was successful in that the company was not financially exposed, but the experience did cost the company time and money, and they then had to start the recruitment and selection process all over again.

Turning back momentarily to employment contracts – fuller detail of which is provided in Chapter 3 – do contracts have to be written to be enforceable? The technical differences (and overlaps) between contracts of employment and written particulars of employment were covered in Chapter 3. In essence, a contract comes into being once a verbal offer has been made and accepted. Good practice suggests that you should ensure that the following occurs:

- Once a successful candidate has been chosen, you make a verbal offer promptly, if your company policy allows this, and state any conditions.

- You follow this up with a written conditional offer accompanied by a written statement of particulars or, as a minimum, the main terms and conditions of employment – eg salary, hours, location, benefits.

- You keep in touch with the chosen candidate during the time he or she takes to make the decision, providing additional information as necessary.

- If he or she does accept, you continue to keep in touch with the successful candidate, notifying him or her when the conditions of the offer have been satisfied, when they can start their new job with you, and the arrangements for induction and any necessary job training.

- Unsuccessful candidates are treated with respect and notified promptly of your decision.

- If not sent with the offer, a written statement of particulars is provided for the successful candidate as early as possible in the process (but no later than two months after the commencement of employment).

We now move on to consider the induction and evaluation processes for our new employee before summing up the role of the HR practitioner.

INDUCTION

Successful organisations will ensure that this process is treated as an important activity and has sufficient resources devoted to it. The main reason is that new employees who have undergone an effective induction programme are likely to be competent performers at their jobs more quickly than those whose induction was scanty or non-existent. Also, the former group are less likely to leave the organisation at an early stage than the latter group (in respect of whom this phenomenon is commonly known as the 'induction crisis' and signifies a dissatisfaction with the job or the organisation or both).

Different employees have different requirements, but they are all likely to need:

- to learn new tasks and procedures
- initial direction
- to make contacts and begin to develop relationships
- to understand the organisational culture
- to feel accepted.

There are, however, certain groups of employees who may need particular consideration, such as:

- school- and college-leavers
- people returning to work after a break in employment
- employees with disabilities
- management/professional trainees
- people from minority groups
- employees who have undergone internal transfer or promotion.

The Acas Advisory Booklet *Recruitment and Induction* provides guidance on these needs and how they can be accommodated.

The commencement of the induction process is difficult to pinpoint because for employees new to the organisation, the imparting of information begins with the job advertisement. We could therefore argue that the process starts at this early stage and plan accordingly. Usually, however, when designing an induction programme, we start with the first day of employment and then timetable activities to be included over the first few weeks and months.

Induction programmes vary between two extremes – from the simple 'tick box' approach (covering the essential organisational information that an employee must be told) to comprehensive induction packages (which include, for example, video messages from the chief executive, guest speakers, 'getting to know you' exercises, and group activities). Some induction processes, particularly in larger organisations, may combine the two approaches with a simple induction carried out in the relevant department and a more comprehensive induction carried out on an organisation-wide basis.

The former approach is likely to be brief, take place at the workstation, and involve the new employee and his or her line manager only. The latter, more sophisticated (and more costly) approach is likely to take place away from the workplace and involve more people at a senior level in the organisation. Also, in accordance with economies of scale, organisations are inclined to provide this programme only periodically (usually monthly or quarterly) – ie when there are sufficient numbers of new employees who can attend.

Neither of these approaches is preferable to the other: their worth is gauged by how successful they are in helping the new employee to settle down quickly and become effective in the job. Often employers combine these approaches with other methods of delivery in providing a comprehensive induction programme for new appointees. See Table 5.7.

Table 5.7 Example methods of delivery and their key applications in the induction process

Method	Key applications
Welcome pack containing information on the organisation, main terms and conditions, joining instructions, etc	Generally provided pre-employment to aid the gathering of essential employment information and promote good first impressions of the organisation
Face-to-face meetings between the new appointee and people who are key to the role in question, both from within and external to the organisation	Usually arranged in the first few days of employment to facilitate good working relationships and impart formal information about the job and informal information on the organisational culture
Formal sessions aimed at groups of new appointees	Held periodically, as a cost-effective means of instilling organisational values, providing consistent core information and allowing for networking opportunities across functions
Information provided on the organisation's intranet	A useful backup to the information provided elsewhere. Should be an up-to-date and detailed source of reference
Interactive e-learning activities	Enable individuals to learn at their own pace, place and time, and provide an evaluation mechanism to ensure that the learning cycle has been completed

Finally, let's consider the information that should be provided. As a minimum, employees should be informed about:

- the organisation's background and structure
- the organisation's products, services, markets and values
- the terms and conditions of employment – eg pay, the hours of work, holidays, sick pay, the pension scheme
- the organisation's rules and procedures – eg how to report in sick, disciplinary rules
- the physical layout of the organisation
- health and safety issues (NB it is crucial that these are covered in the very early stages of employment)
- first aid arrangements
- data protection policies and practices
- equal opportunities policies and practices
- employee involvement and communication arrangements
- trade union and/or employee representative arrangements
- welfare and employee benefits and facilities
- access to the organisation's computer facilities and its security processes.

Please note that we have concentrated on general induction above – ie core induction programmes applicable to all new recruits. We must not forget that this should be combined with induction that meets the individual's needs as well. During the recruitment and selection process you will have gathered a lot of information about the candidate's skills, abilities and development needs. Instead of filing this information, use it to agree a personal development plan with the individual, which will involve planning on-the-job and specialist skills training as well as other development activities. Finally, activities aimed at integrating the new appointee into the team should also not be forgotten.

ACTIVITY 5.8

Look back at a recent appointment made within your organisation and analyse the induction programme carried out when the successful candidate took up his or her post. (This exercise can still be applicable if the successful candidate was an internal one.) What suggestions do you have for improvements in the induction process for the future? Discuss your recommendations with an appropriate learning source.

EVALUATION

As with the majority of activities that HR practitioners become involved with, there is a strong argument for evaluating the success of your recruitment and selection procedures. This is, however, not just a simple matter of concluding that, for instance, an advertisement for a clerical officer's post was successful because 250 applications were received. In fact, it is likely that the reverse is true, because sifting through 250 application forms will have been a time-consuming and costly exercise. Every stage of the recruitment and selection process should be reviewed to see whether mistakes were made, whether a repetition of them can be avoided in the future, and what can be learned.

It would be good practice to consider the following questions – but note that some may be more appropriately addressed or re-addressed in three, six or 12 months' time:

- Did you get the job analysis stage right? That is:
  - Did you carry out a thorough field study?
  - Is the job description an accurate reflection of the range and type of activities and the level of responsibility involved?
  - Are the person specification requirements defined in specific and measurable terms?
  - Are there any important omissions or unnecessary inclusions in the person specification?
  - Was a new recruit justified or should the work have been organised differently?
  - Are the selection criteria too restrictive or potentially discriminatory – eg are age limits stated or is an unnecessarily high level of qualifications called for?

- Have you considered flexible working arrangements to encourage applications from people who are unable to work conventional office hours?
- Is the total employment package sufficiently competitive?

- Did you get the recruitment stage right? That is:
  - Is recruitment being targeted too narrowly – eg have you concentrated only on those sources that you have used in the past?
  - Did the advert give sufficient information about the job and the person required to encourage suitable applicants only?
  - Was the advert eye-catching?
  - Did you choose the most appropriate media?
  - Did you get the timing right?
  - Have you carried out an analysis to see which media produced the most cost-effective results?

- Did you get the selection stage right? That is:
  - Did you choose the most appropriate methods for selection?
  - Did you ensure that the information generated by each method was cross-checked for validity?
  - Did you ensure that only relevant information was considered in decision-making?
  - Have you carried out an analysis to see which of the methods used were the most fruitful and cost-effective?

- Did you get the induction stage right? That is:
  - Did the induction programme run smoothly?
  - Was the employee properly assisted to settle in and quickly learn the job?
  - How much did the induction process cost?

- Did you select the right person? That is:
  - Did the employee become effective as quickly as expected?
  - Did the employee require more assistance, training or support than expected?
  - Is the employee still in the post and performing at a satisfactory level?
  - Has the employee made satisfactory progress regarding salary reviews or career progression?

- Did you ensure compliance at all stages with equal opportunities legislation?

- What would you do differently next time?

Let's return to our example at the beginning of this section, of the advertisement for a clerical officer's post. It may be tempting to blame a high level of unemployment in the locality for the overwhelming response, but it is quite likely that the job advertisement was too vague in stipulating the essential requirements. Potential candidates were thus not encouraged to deselect themselves from the process and it was necessary to plough through all 250 application forms to see which candidates were really suitable for shortlisting. So the person responsible for the poor drafting of the advertisement has not only wasted the time of all those involved in the recruitment and selection process (and organisational money) but has also falsely raised the hopes of a large number of unsuitable candidates.

ACTIVITY 5.9

After studying the section above on evaluation, consider which methods are currently employed by your organisation to evaluate the success or otherwise of the recruitment and selection process. Suggest two or three major improvements. Put these down in the form of an action plan with, if possible, time-scales and the names of persons responsible. Discuss your recommendations with one of your learning sources.

Having considered this important but often forgotten issue of evaluation, we now summarise the many roles played by HR practitioners in carrying out the activities associated with the recruitment and selection of staff.

THE ROLE OF HR PRACTITIONERS

In considering the activities above we have touched on a number of the roles performed by HR practitioners at various stages of the recruitment and selection process.

AN ADVISORY ROLE TO LINE MANAGERS

It is rare – and, indeed, would be inappropriate – for all of the above activities to be performed solely by HR practitioners. In any event, it is generally wise for line managers to lead the job analysis stage because of their specialist knowledge, and be very involved at the selection stage so that they play an integral part in selecting their own member of staff and are therefore more likely to be committed to the new employee's success. Following on from this, it is worth noting that interview panels commonly consist of the line manager and an HR practitioner. This may involve you in an influencing role when, say, the line manager is tempted to offer the post to a candidate for subjective reasons (eg the manager and the candidate attended the same school) rather than objective reasons (ie ones linked to the person specification).

AN ADMINISTRATIVE ROLE

This is to ensure that information is sought, chased and checked; that appropriate records are kept; and that all interested parties remain in touch with the timetable of events.

A TRAINING ROLE

This may cover the design, organisation and delivery of skills training for interviewers/assessors or coaching for inexperienced managers during the recruitment and selection process. There will also be an educational or possibly a compliance role to ensure that equal opportunities principles and policies are adhered to at all stages of the process.

A PUBLIC RELATIONS ROLE

This arises owing to the need to attract suitable candidates, and involves conveying information about the job, the person required and the organisation itself. Also, the way in which candidates are dealt with in making enquiries, pursuing applications and attending interviews may confirm or contradict their first impressions of the organisation.

AN ASSESSMENT ROLE

HR practitioners play a role in assessing candidates by interviewing, observing, testing and evaluating them using a range of selection methods.

AN EVALUATION ROLE

Finally, HR practitioners are likely to be responsible for ensuring that the process of recruitment and selection is periodically evaluated against its objectives – ie did you employ the 'right people in the right jobs at the right time'? (See the section above.)

SUMMARY

- You should by now be familiar with the key issues involved in the recruitment and selection of staff. We have looked at why recruitment and selection are important (regardless of the economic climate), the relevant legislation, the various stages involved and the importance of a thorough job analysis. We pointed out the importance of a robust and systematic process for all appointments – ie not just those concerning your core group of employees. We also considered the keys to effective induction and evaluation processes and the various roles played by HR practitioners.

- You should note that even if your experience of recruitment and selection is limited, it is likely that you will have applied for at least one position for which you were granted an interview or were invited to attend an AC. Thus, if you are unfamiliar with the whole process from the viewpoint of the interviewer or assessor, you will be familiar with it from the candidate's perspective. Nothing can replace the experience of actually conducting your first interview, administering a test or being involved in running an AC, but you are likely to have an opinion on the good and bad practices that you observed. Reflect on such experiences to ensure that you do not make the same mistakes that others may have made. Continue this learning process by, if you have not already done so, attempting some of the activities provided above before moving on to the next chapter.

EXPLORE FURTHER

REFERENCES AND FURTHER READING

ACAS (revised 2003) *Advisory Booklet on Recruitment and Induction*. Leicester: Advisory, Conciliation and Arbitration Service (ACAS Publications, PO Box 235, Hayes, Middlesex, UB3 1HF; tel. 08702 429090)

ATKINSON, J. (1984) 'Manpower strategies for the flexible organisation', *Personnel Management*, August: 28–31

CMI (2008) *Generation Y: Unlocking the talent of young managers*. London: Chartered Management Institute

ERICKSON, T. (2008) *Ten Reasons Generation Xers Are Unhappy at Work*. Boston, MA: Harvard Business Publishing

HACKETT, P. (1998) *The Selection Interview*. London: Institute of Personnel and Development

PROCTOR, G. and LEIGHTON, P. (2003) *Recruiting Within the Law*. London: Chartered Institute of Personnel and Development

TALENTSMOOTHIE (2008) *Generation Y: What they want from work*, Survey report. London/Newbury: Talentsmoothie

TAYLOR, S. (2002) *People Resourcing*. London: Chartered Institute of Personnel and Development

WHIDDETT, S. and HOLLYFORDE, S. (2003) *A Practical Guide to Competencies*. London: Chartered Institute of Personnel and Development

WOODRUFFE, C. (2000) *Development and Assessment Centres*, 3rd edition. London: Chartered Institute of Personnel and Development

Also available from the Chartered Institute of Personnel and Development (CIPD), 151 The Broadway, London SW19 1JQ; tel. 020 8612 6201, are:

CIPD *Policies and Procedures for People Managers* manual

Annual CIPD Recruitment surveys.

WEBSITES

ACAS: www.acas.org.uk

Chartered Institute of Personnel and Development: www.cipd.co.uk

Criminal Records Bureau: www.crb.gov.uk

Equality and Human Rights Commission: www.equalityhumanrights.com

Independent Safeguarding Authority: www.isa-gov.org.uk

Legislation: www.legislation.hmso.gov.uk

See also on the website of the Chartered Institute of Personnel and Development (CIPD), www.cipd.co.uk/Infosource:

> *Assessment Centres for Recruitment and Selection*
>
> *Discriminatory Questions at Selection Interviews*
>
> *Psychological Testing*
>
> *Recruitment*
>
> *Recruitment on the Internet*
>
> *References*
>
> *Telephone Interviewing*

ACTIVITIES FEEDBACK

Activity 5.3

The differences between equal opportunities and managing diversity are summed up in Table 5.8:

Table 5.8 Equal opportunities *v* managing diversity

Equal opportunities	Managing diversity
• entails removing discrimination against specific groups • is primarily an issue for HR specialists • relies on positive action • has a moral/legislative focus • is driven by domestic and EU discrimination legislation • can be adapted to the existing organisation	• entails maximising employee potential through an appreciation and utilisation of people's differences • involves all managers • is unlikely to rely on positive action because this will not be inclusive • has a business focus • has a global application in that it supports a variety of cultures • challenges the nature, values and structure of the existing organisation

The tribunal would have looked at areas such as:

- the demographic make-up of the workforce in terms of gender, race, disability, age, etc, across the various functions and levels, and whether this reflected the outside population

- signs of support from top management – eg diversity champions, value statements which incorporate diversity principles, publicity for policies and practices

- attitudes within the workplace as evidenced by witnesses' responses to questions at the tribunal hearing

- recruitment sources, to see whether positive steps were taken to encourage applications from under-represented groups – eg advertising in ethnic minority publications

- selection methods, to ensure that they were not tainted with discrimination and that selection decisions were based on fair and objective criteria

- working arrangements – ie are part-time, term-time, homeworking and other flexible working arrangements available?

- training provision – ie have managers received appropriate skills training and has awareness training been provided for all employees?

- the handling of complaints about discriminatory matters – ie are grievances dealt with appropriately, and are offenders disciplined?

- the provision of equal access to training and promotion opportunities for all employees – eg are adjustments made to the timing of training events in order to include part-timers?

- an integration of relevant policies with each other, backed up by company practices – eg employee involvement in establishing a dress code that respects differing cultures and needs, a policy on religious observance that is actively promoted rather than tolerated by line managers.

Activity 5.5

In Table 5.9, there are a number of factors listed, and a tick indicates, in general terms, where one avenue has the advantage over the other.

Table 5.9 Factors to take into account when advertising a technical post

Factors	a)	b)
Speed in placing an advertisement		✓
Speed in receiving and processing applications		✓
Size of target population		✓
Access to international labour market		✓
Ease of access to additional company information		✓
Security of information, eg CVs	✓	
Less likely to attract poor-quality applicants/time-wasters	✓	
Ability to correct and update information in the advert		✓
Less costly		✓
Facility to use an online selection questionnaire		✓
Established source for this type of vacancy	✓	
Increasing trend to use this medium		✓

Activity 5.6

Your questions should be on similar lines to those listed below. Please note that supplementary questions can then be asked, depending on the responses received.

Table 5.10 Behaviour-based questions

Competencies	Questions
Effective leadership skills	Give me an example of a situation in which you were responsible for helping others to complete a task or project . . . What steps did you take to motivate the team members?
The ability to handle conflict	Describe a situation where you were faced with views that differed from your own . . . How did you deal with this conflict?
Problem-solving ability	Give me an example of a problem you had to solve recently . . . What was the outcome, and what steps did you take in solving the problem?
Customer focus	Tell me about a difficult situation which involved you in dealing with an internal or external customer . . . How did you ensure that you understood the customer's needs and that they were met?

Performance management

INTRODUCTION

The CIPD survey of performance management (2004) shows that many organisations claim to operate a formal performance management process, although the mix of the activities involved varies greatly from one organisation to the next. Further, there was little agreement on what successful performance management looks like. Thus the impact of performance management on the achievement of organisational goals is debatable: some organisations fail to evaluate it in either quantitative or qualitative terms. As with most HR and development activities, experiences vary greatly and in addition to success stories there are also accounts of poorly designed and implemented performance management systems.

In the next section we consider what performance management is, why performance management is important for HR practitioners and the organisations they work for, and note the reasons for some of the difficulties that arise, before looking at the differences between performance appraisal and performance management. We then go on to look at performance appraisal in more detail: its purposes, history and trends; the move towards competence-based performance review; the various components of schemes, including the issue of objective-setting; good practice considerations; and some of the skills involved in undertaking performance apprasials. We thereafter provide sections on good practice in giving and receiving feedback, motivation, dealing with poor performance, and the legal considerations. Finally, we examine the differing roles played by the HR practitioner and the skills necessary for effective appraisal interviewing.

Before doing this we would draw your attention to another distinction in terms: 'performance management' as against 'managing performance'. The first term tends to be used in reference to activities designed to motivate and encourage employees to work towards objectives that are in line with organisational goals. The second term includes managing good and poor performance, and therefore encompasses activities such as disciplinary procedures and absence control. In this chapter we provide an overview of dealing with poor performance while concentrating on performance management, and would refer you to Chapter 8 for reference to managing poor performers via disciplinary or capability routes. (Chapter 8 also provides guidance on absence management tools.) Please note that the processes of disciplinary or capability procedures and performance appraisal should complement each other in these circumstances. (See the information on the *Legal considerations* on page 179.)

WHAT IS PERFORMANCE MANAGEMENT?

In broad terms, at its best, performance management is an all-encompassing process comprising many elements of what makes up good practice in people management. It operates as a continuous cycle rather than a one-off event. Commentators on the subject use a number of different definitions. In the words of Armstrong and Baron (2004), it is

> a process which contributes to the effective management of individuals and teams in order to achieve high levels of organisational performance. As such it establishes shared understanding about what is to be achieved and an approach to leading and developing people which will ensure that it is achieved.

Because it can cover so many aspects of people management practice, it is useful – indeed, some may say vital – to have a structure and framework in place to support the process. However, any such structure and framework must be flexible to allow for individual and managerial freedom and discretion, and to avoid performance management being seen as just a bureaucratic form-filling exercise.

As a critical part of an integrated approach to managing people, performance management is a key role and activity for line managers and one in which they frequently look to HR departments for support and help. An effective performance management process enables line managers to undertake their people management responsibilities well and get the best from the people they manage.

Features of a performance management process may include:

- appraisal
- assessment of competence
- objective-setting and review
- learning and development activities
- performance-related pay
- coaching and mentoring
- succession planning
- personal development planning.

WHY IS PERFORMANCE MANAGEMENT IMPORTANT?

Performance management is important for a number of reasons, both at an individual employee level and at an organisational level. In relation to the organisation, suffice it to say here that without performance management, individual and team work may not be organised to achieve the optimum results. For instance:

- Salespeople may be achieving their sales targets, but the discounts and special incentives that they offer customers in order to do so have a detrimental effect on the profit margins – profit being the driving force of the company they are working for.

- A university lecturer whose brief is to recruit a certain number of students to a full-time course of study may find that in the current economic climate there is less money available for individual student grants and other means of finance. Thus there is a smaller pool of potential candidates with the requisite qualifications than in previous years. The college tutor decides that rather than failing to reach the target, he or she will have to lower the entry requirements to the course. This will satisfy the immediate intake need but is likely to lead to problems at the 'output' stage, because a larger percentage of students may fail to get the qualification under study. The university's finances (and business goals) will be dependent on the overall intake and output targets being reached.

- Computer helpline staff may point to the numbers of users they have helped over a period of time as an indication of their hard work and efficiency. However, this figure does not take account of those users who failed to get through to the busy switchboard system and had to seek assistance elsewhere. If the main aims of the computer company are to increase market share and maintain customer loyalty, then this aspect of 'after sales' service would have to be re-evaluated. The dissatisfied group of customers will be less inclined to buy from the same supplier again and will also not recommend friends and colleagues to do so.

Thus we can see, in the above examples, that the employees concerned were all seeking to do what they had been told to do – ie they were probably being efficient – but were they being effective?

Efficient: doing things right

Effective: doing the right things.

The answer is no – in each case, insufficient thought had been given to ensuring that employees' individual targets were geared towards the overall business goals. The key is to ensure that there is a clear link between the tasks and activities that employees are involved in and the achievement of organisational goals. It is also crucial that evaluation methods are set up to judge whether this happens. We shall return to this question in a later section.

In relation to individual employees, performance management is a key aspect of being managed well. For an employee, amongst other things, effective performance management leads to clarity about their role and where it fits and contributes to the organisation, helps build a positive relationship with their manager, ensures they get feedback on how they are performing, and highlights learning and development needs. All of this contibutes to an employee who is more likely to be motivated, engaged, productive and committed to the organisation.

It is a fact, however, that many organisations do not adopt performance management processes, and even where they do, the process may come in for criticism or be counterproductive. Next, therefore, we examine why this might be the case.

WHY IS PERFORMANCE MANAGEMENT NOT ALWAYS SUCCESSFUL?

There are many reasons – for instance:

- Employees recognise that there is a lack of management commitment to the process and become cynical about its intentions.
- Managers lack the skills necessary to carry out effective appraisal interviews.
- Individual objectives are not reviewed often enough. For example, a six-month objective to recruit a specific number of people can quickly become inappropriate if there is a downturn in the organisation's market.
- Performance management favours what can be measured and there is always the danger of leaning towards efficiency rather than effectiveness, as in the examples above.
- Even within those performance indicators that can be measured, individual performance in a large organisation is often outside the control of individuals. For instance, if the main employer in a small town makes its workforce

redundant, the effect on retail sales in retail organisations in the town is outside the control of individual store managers.

- Success often rests on qualitative, intangible matters such as the quality of relationships built up by an employee, an understanding of commercial realities or the ability to motivate others. Purely quantitative measures that focus on shorter-term results can compromise long-term benefits.

- When performance management is linked to reward, such as salary increases, the process can be problematic. In these circumstances individuals may tend to deny their weaknesses, may bury mistakes and may even blame others for any perceived shortfall in performance.

PERFORMANCE MANAGEMENT V PERFORMANCE APPRAISAL

In very simple terms, performance appraisal is the 'tail that wags the dog' in its relationship with performance management. The exercise of appraising performance is necessarily retrospective because it concerns making a judgement about the past performance of employees. Appraisals can be used to improve current performance by providing feedback on strengths and weaknesses. (NB 'weaknesses' are probably better labelled 'areas for improvement' or 'developmental needs' if we wish to emphasise the positive and constructive nature of this feedback.) Appraisals can therefore be effective in increasing employee motivation and, ultimately, organisational performance. Performance appraisal can, and should, be linked to a performance-improvement process, and can then also be used to identify training needs and potential, agree future objectives, focus on career development and solve problems. One such performance improvement process would be a performance management system (PMS).

Building on the overview and introduction to performance management given above, we can see that performance management is a vehicle for the continuous and evolutionary improvement of business performance via a co-ordinated programme of people management activities. Most commentators agree that these activities include:

- strategic planning
- the definition of organisational goals, priorities and values
- the translation of organisational goals into department, team and individual goals, targets or objectives
- the development and application of a performance measurement process based on the achievement of the above
- an appraisal process
- personal development planning
- learning and development activities
- various forms of contingent pay.

The company sells and hires cars as well as running a garage to sell petrol and other goods. Several staff are employed, each specialising in one of the above areas or in accounting or clerical positions. The majority of staff enjoy their jobs and feel that they are reasonably well rewarded in terms of financial and other benefits. There is no formal means of appraising staff, but the owner-manager does see all staff on a regular basis to inform them of their progress and to discuss any problems. He adopts a well-used 'open-door' policy. In the main, the employees are highly motivated and industrious, and achieve high efficiencies in the work that they do.

With such a favourable environment, you might assume that the overall business performance of the company would be optimised. But you would be wrong, because the owner-manager recently discovered that the profits for the last tax year were not as high as he had expected. To cut a long story short, he employed a placement student studying a CIPD qualification to investigate the reasons for this enigma. The answer, when it was discovered, was a simple one: the employees were hard-working but because there was no link between their personal objectives and the organisational goal (in this case, profit), the result was that although they might be deemed to be efficient, they were not effective.

After a period of research, which consisted mostly of interviews with staff, the student produced a comprehensive report for the owner-manager. This covered her research findings as well as providing a lot of information on performance management in general. The owner-manager saw that there were some systems already in place but that there was a lack of co-ordination between them all. For instance, the car sales staff were expected to provide relief cover when the person employed on the car-hire counter was at lunch. The sales staff resented this because they felt that they might miss sales opportunities through being 'tied up' at the car-hire desk. Their individual and team performance sales targets were naturally seen as a much higher priority than the need to provide a high-quality service for potential car-hire customers. Further, the former activities were rewarded by the payment of commission, whereas the latter 'customer care' activities were not formally assessed by their manager and did not attract any sort of reward, financial or otherwise. The hiring of cars, however, did contribute substantially to the overall profit level of the company and, unlike car sales, provided a steadier flow of income, because car hire is less subject to seasonal trends. To the owner-manager, who set the business goals, it was equally important to maintain a good reputation for selling high-quality cars as it was to provide a reliable and competitive car-hire service.

With the help of the student, the owner-manager decided to clarify the business strategy, to review the existing interventions and to scrap, modify or replace them (as appropriate) in line with the company's goals. However, he also learned that a balance must be struck between reward-driven and development-driven approaches. This is because performance management systems can fail when their implementation becomes dominated by the link to financial reward. Schemes designed to improve employee performance – eg incentive, bonus, profit-sharing and commission approaches – can thus have the opposite effect when employee expectations are not realised. In fact, the owner-manager had experienced this in the past when there was an unexpected rise in the price of petrol. In order to preserve his profits he was forced to reduce the pot of money available for a discretionary bonus paid to the shop staff. They therefore received much less than had been anticipated, based on their past experiences. Although the reasons were fully explained at the time, it took quite a while for the shop staff to regain their normal levels of motivation: they felt that although they had been working hard, they had been punished for something that was outside their control.

As we have already stated, there is no universally accepted definition of performance management, but we can safely say that it is a much broader concept than that of performance appraisal. To demonstrate some of these points, consider the example of a small owner-managed garage in Case study 6.1.

The main lesson that the owner-manager learned in Case study 6.1 was that there should be clear and co-ordinated two-way links in all the stages between the strategic plan and individual objectives (see Figure 6.1).

Figure 6.1 The two-way links model

This model does not mean that individuals cannot seek to satisfy their own personal objectives, but it does help to focus them on their own roles and contribution to the overall business performance. The result will hopefully be a motivational one because their efforts are directed at those activities which best serve organisational goals. (Further consideration of this motivational aspect is provided below.)

The issues are the same regardless of the size of organisation; the key is to ensure that there are feedback mechanisms in place, as demonstrated in Figure 6.1.

To return to the case study, the owner-manager was able – with the help of the student – to begin the process of ensuring that the new and revamped PMS was fully co-ordinated and geared towards the achievement of business objectives. This was not a trouble-free process, but the result was an encouraging improvement in the level of profits in the following year. One example of a new intervention was the one set up to reward the achievement of a monthly car-hire target, based on maximising the use of the hire cars. The car-hire employee was sent on a selling course in order to improve her skills at getting new business (she had previously viewed her job as simply an administrative one). The system involved accumulating points towards the team target and included all those staff who provided cover on the car-hire desk. This may not have been a perfect solution but did ensure that all the staff involved were 'rowing in the same direction'.

PERFORMANCE APPRAISAL

Performance appraisal (or performance review, as it is also referred to) is one tool for managing individual performance and is more frequently used by line managers than HR professionals. It can help in reinforcing the values of the organisation and in maintaining employee loyalty and commitment. The appraisal process is about providing an opportunity for a manager and member of staff to get together and have a conversation about the member of staff's performance, development and the sort of support they need from their manager. Done well, it should be a constructive and positive two-way process.

PURPOSES

Performance appraisal often serves three different purposes (and most schemes incorporate at least two of these):

- *performance reviews* – With employees, managers discuss progress in their current posts, their strengths, and the areas requiring further development, in order to improve current performance. This purpose focuses on past performance.

- *potential reviews* – With employees, managers discuss opportunities for progression, the type of work they may be interested in and capable of in the future, and how this can be achieved, by identifying their developmental needs and career aspirations. This purpose is future-focused.

- *reward reviews* – These are usually separate from the appraisal system but the decisions on rewards such as pay, benefits, promotion and self-fulfilment are fed by the information provided by performance appraisal. This purpose will only apply where reward in the organisation has a performance contingent element. (Further information on reward, including performance-related reward, can be found in Chapter 7.)

Well-conducted performance appraisal interviews therefore usually involve a manager and an employee in a constructive discussion concerning the employee's recent performance (say, over the previous 12 months), plans for improved performance – which will probably involve agreeing future objectives or targets (see below) – and plans for meeting the developmental needs of the employee. At a later stage, a reward review interview may be arranged if appropriate so that the manager and employee can openly discuss, for instance, the level of performance-related pay (PRP) that has been awarded.

However, it is ranked by many managers as the most disliked managerial activity, and is often viewed by employees as the least effective HR policy – often due to the way it is carried out by managers. This indicates the need to pay attention to appraisal and strive for the most effective approach for the organisation's culture.

As HR practitioners, you are likely to know already that appraisals do not always go according to plan. For instance:

- Work pressures or a lack of skills or training may result in managers' seeking to avoid the regular performance appraisal interview, thereby leaving interviews to the last minute when they are poorly prepared, and they then rush the process.

- Not all managers are good at people management activities and as a result may be inconsistent or subjective in their approach and base the appraisal on their relationship with the individual employee rather than on performance.

- Not all employees are good performers, and managers may not be as constructive as they should be in their delivery of feedback.

- In an organisation in which there are few promotion opportunities, employees (and their managers) may view learning and development activities as somewhat pointless.

- If a high-performing individual's expectation of PRP is not realised (often through factors outside his or her own control), he or she may decide not to try so hard to achieve targets or objectives in the future.

- Not all employees seek personal development. They may favour limited change and view talk of 'continual improvement' as a means of increasing their targets or workload with no additional financial reward.

The motivational effect of performance appraisal is thus often debatable. On a positive note, Hale and Whitlam (1998: 2) provide an interesting model – see Table 6.1 – of how performance appraisal can be used to satisfy employees' basic motivational needs (based on the now famous research of Peters and Waterman, 1982, into successful organisations).

Table 6.1 Performance appraisal and employee motivation

Peters and Waterman factors	How performance appraisal can satisfy these needs
Need for meaning	Clear linking of individual jobs with the objectives of the organisation
Need for control	Joint discussion between subordinate and manager regarding future job priorities and targets
Need for positive reinforcement	Provision of effective feedback from manager to subordinate
Actions shape attitudes and beliefs	Performance appraisal as the starting-point for deciding future action, which entails senior-level commitment to help the individual develop

We shall discuss the skills of performance appraisal interviewing, applicable in both good and poor performer situations, and provide more detail about motivation in a later section.

HISTORY AND TRENDS

As we have already said, with the emergence of performance management the main change in performance appraisal schemes has been the establishment of clearer links between individual objectives and organisational goals. In recent years there have been other changes, many of which have complemented this principle. Hale and Whitlam (1998: 19–22) provide the following breakdown of recent trends.

From traits to results-based assessment

In the 1960s a 'management by objectives' (MbO) approach evolved, based on a more scientific approach and on more forward-focused performance appraisal. Thus there was a move from schemes that made judgements on employees' traits and behaviours such as leadership, teamwork and diligence, to those where the emphasis was placed on the achievement of results and outputs linked to targets. MbO schemes are still in existence today, but many have foundered because they failed to establish the link between individual and organisational objectives.

From effort to results focus

In line with the MbO approach, the method of assessment has shifted away from effort measures such as concentration, enthusiasm and self-organisation to results measures such as quality of work, sound decision-making and financial performance.

From judgemental to joint problem-solving

The closed type of appraisal scheme in which the manager told the employee what judgement had been made on his or her performance has given way to a more open, joint identification of strengths and development needs, as well as joint planning for improved future performance. (In line with this we have seen self-appraisal play a much more important role in the whole process – indeed, it may form the basis for the appraisal interview in some schemes.)

From managerial to all jobs

Whereas many organisations still operate separate schemes for appraising managerial and non-managerial posts, there has been a move towards incorporating employees at all levels within the performance appraisal system. In some organisations the net has been cast even wider to encompass appraisal for workers rather than employees only. (The distinction between worker and employee is discussed in Chapter 3.)

We can add two further trends to this list.

From top-down to 360-degree appraisals

Appraisals have moved on from a fairly simple manager-subordinate (or top-down) relationship (possibly including self-appraisal) to 360-degree appraisals, involving stakeholders who provide feedback on an individual's performance.

Figure 6.2 Stakeholders in 360-degree appraisal

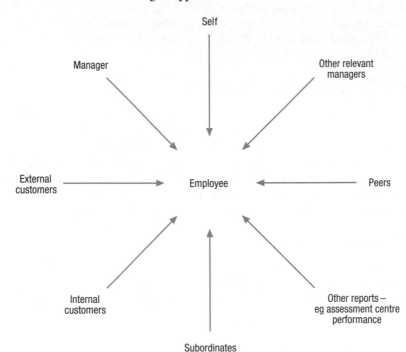

Figure 6.2 shows an example of the stakeholders that might be involved in an individual's appraisal. There is great variety in the way in which 360-degree appraisal is implemented in organisations. On the one hand, the appraisal interview may include all the stakeholders giving face-to-face feedback to the appraisee (who may well feel that the term 'victim' is more appropriate here!). On the other hand, some organisations operate systems whereby the collection of feedback from the chosen stakeholders is done via formally constructed questionnaires. This information is then collated and fed back to the individual by a neutral third party (possibly an HR practitioner). Larger organisations have even invested in computer packages to cut down on the administrative burden attached to collecting and collating this information on a large scale. To appreciate the potential benefits of 360-degree appraisal, see Case study 6.2.

An HR director in a large public sector organisation was concerned about the level of staff turnover in his own department. He was satisfied that the department was well resourced, had clear objectives, and was, on the whole, well regarded by others in the organisation. He had a very effective deputy who managed the HR team on a day-to-day basis. As part of a wider development programme he participated in a 360-degree appraisal process, using a number of staff in his department as stakeholders. The results were collated and fed back to him by an independent third party. The feedback he received through this process indicated that his team members had a fairly negative view of their relationship with him. He was seen as distant, very externally focused, not accessible and disinterested in the day-to-day activities of his department and team. As a result team members felt their contributions weren't valued by the senior managers in the organisation, and this was a major factor in decisions to leave. The 360-degree appraisal gave the director a perspective and some feedback he had not received through any other source, and enabled him to start building stronger, more personal relationships with members of his team.

From achievements to competencies

Following on from the shift in focus from 'effort' to 'results' above, we have seen a move from just concentrating on *what* a job-holder achieves to also assessing *how* the job is carried out. Thus many organisations now review the achievement of objectives and targets as well as the behaviour exhibited by the job-holder. Not only does this take a wider view of the role the individual employee is undertaking, but it also considers the impact of behaviour on colleagues and customers. This competency-based approach can be applied across the full range of HR and development processes, but is particularly relevant to job evaluation, recruitment and selection, training and development, performance review and reward.

THE PERFORMANCE REVIEW CYCLE

As a result of the above trends, most performance appraisal schemes nowadays follow the stages of the performance review cycle, as set out in Figure 6.3.

According to Whiddett and Hollyforde (2003: 75), competencies can make significant contributions to all stages of the performance review process – ie by:

- identifying factors relevant to performance in the job
- collecting information on performance
- organising the information
- discussing or reviewing the information (eg for solo reviews)
- agreeing outcomes.

We shall discuss the much-debated issue of objective-setting shortly, but first let's look at the various components of performance appraisal schemes.

Figure 6.3 The performance review cycle

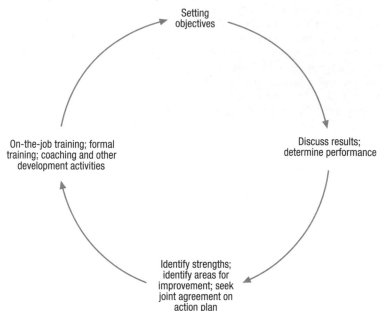

THE COMPONENTS OF PERFORMANCE APPRAISAL SCHEMES

If you are designing a performance appraisal scheme, you need first to determine its purpose (or purposes) and seek to integrate the new scheme into your PMS, if one exists. Against this backdrop you must then make the following decisions, depending on the organisational circumstances:

1 Who is to be appraised? That is, you must decide what levels or functions of employees are to be involved.

2 Who appraises? This could be the employee, the manager only, the manager and subordinates, or other stakeholders (see the previous section regarding 360-degree appraisal).

3 What is to be appraised, and what criteria will be used? The options include traits *v* results *v* competency-based assessment, and achievement of objectives.

4 What assessment methods will you employ? You could opt for a descriptive or narrative report, a checklist, ratings or gradings, comparison with objectives, comparison with others (ranking individuals in order of performance), critical incidents (recorded incidents of positive and negative behaviours), or competence-based assessment (assessment against the achievement of set standards). An example of this last method is provided in Table 6.2.

Table 6.2 Competence-based assessment

Competency: Meeting customer needs	
Anticipates, responds to and seeks to exceed the expectations of existing and potential customers	
Competent	**Needs developing**
Strives to provide the best customer service	Unhelpful to customers, not taking time to understand what they need, and then jumping in with any solution
Adopts a positive and professional approach to meet the needs of customers	Sees customers as 'not part of my job' – focuses instead on internal or administrative requirements
Provides advice that is beneficial to both customers and the bank	Does not combine products to meet customer needs
Always ready to help by anticipating and responding to customers' needs in the most appropriate way	Is target-driven, ignoring customers' real needs

Competency: Self-control	
Performs effectively by keeping emotions under control, particularly in stressful and difficult situations	
Competent	**Needs developing**
Is patient and even-tempered	Is easily flustered – runs around panicking
Remains calm; does not appear to become irritable or anxious	Takes the reactions of other people very personally
Does not panic under pressure	Appears childish, petulant
Does not react to provocation – maintains poise and professionalism when challenged	Loses cool; becomes aggressive or defensive
Accepts refusals and rebuffs; does not take things personally	Bottles up stress and then explodes – takes out frustrations on others

Source: Extracted from the Barclays Bank plc *Performance Attributes Directory* and reproduced by kind permission

Please note that you may need to define different levels or standards for each competency, according to the level and responsibilities of the job under consideration.

5 Will you incorporate assessment of promotion potential? A link to reward or a salary review? A means of appeal against a (perceived) unfair assessment?

6 How often is the formal appraisal interview to be carried out – eg once every three, six or 12 months? Will you include interim reviews to accommodate the pace of change?

7   How will you ensure that the action points are implemented (eg the meeting of development needs)?

8   How will you evaluate success (ie the achievement of the purpose(s) of the scheme)?

ACTIVITY 6.1

Find out as much as you can about the appraisal scheme(s) used by your organisation (or another organisation with which you are familiar). Investigate the paperwork, talk to your manager and other line managers, talk to other employees, and use other learning sources to compare your practices with those of outside organisations. Then answer the eight questions above.

The Acas advisory booklet *Employee Appraisal* (2008: 5) lists the following key points for successful appraisal schemes:

- Make sure that senior managers are fully committed to the idea of appraisals.

- Consult with managers, employees and trade union representatives about the design and implementation of appraisals before they are introduced.

- Monitor schemes regularly.

- Give appraisers adequate training to enable them to make fair and objective assessments and to carry out effective appraisal interviews.

- Keep the scheme as simple and straightforward as possible.

We add the following suggestions:

- Before implementing the scheme across the whole organisation, carry out a pilot run in, say, one department in order to gain invaluable feedback on possible teething problems that can then be solved before the main launch. Start with the most senior people in your pilot area, so that you gain their commitment, and encourage them to lead by example and to cascade their learning downwards.

- Ensure that appraisers and appraisees jointly identify strengths and areas for improvement, and that appraisers provide constructive feedback on performance and support the appraisee in meeting his or her development needs in line with business goals.

- Provide familiarisation training for appraisees so that they understand the purpose of the scheme and are able to gain the maximum advantage from their participation.

ACTIVITY 6.2

Following on from Activity 6.1, suggest some improvements that could be made to the scheme(s) you have chosen for your analysis.

Present them in the form of a written report to senior management, making sure that you justify your proposals.

We have mentioned the place of objective-setting several times within the context of performance appraisal and performance management. We now seek to examine this concept further.

OBJECTIVE-SETTING

The trend from a focus on traits or behaviours to a results-oriented approach has seen the emergence of objective-setting as a key issue. Objectives are about improvement, and there are a number of levels:

- business objectives
- team/division/departmental objectives linking with the above
- individual objectives linking with all of the above

as well as

- individual objectives resulting from developmental needs
- project objectives
- training and development objectives.

However, rather than trying to set objectives, managers would be better advised to seek to agree objectives with their staff. Thus, during the course of the appraisal process the manager and employee should jointly agree objectives for the forthcoming period which comply with the mnemonic SMARTS:

- **S**pecific
- **M**easurable
- **A**greed
- **R**ealistic
- **T**ime-bound
- **S**tretching.

Which of the following two objectives is SMARTS?

- To improve supervisory skills by taking responsibility for the training and development of a new trainee over the coming year
- To research, design and implement a new sickness absence monitoring system that differentiates between certified and uncertified absences and that records frequency, duration and reasons for absence. (This new system would be linked into a company-wide initiative to reduce costs by appropriate absence

management techniques.) The budget for this exercise is x, the ongoing maintenance costs should be limited to two clerical labour hours a month, and the time-scale for implementation is y months.

The first example is not SMARTS because it is not specific and its outcomes would be difficult to measure. However, the second example provides a specific task with several measurable outcomes for the evaluation of success. The objective is presumably (barring disasters) realistic for the employee working with available resources, and is clearly time-bound. It would also be stretching if it involved the employee in areas of work that he or she would not normally encounter in day-to-day activities. Thus he or she would be able to build on new experiences and develop new skills and would be more likely to agree to it. This individual objective is also clearly linked to an organisational goal: cutting costs.

Obviously, not all objectives can be defined in this way because many lean more to qualitative rather than quantitative measurement, which is necessarily more subjective. Nevertheless, the mnemonic SMARTS provides an ideal to which you should aspire as far as possible.

ACTIVITY 6.3

Think about your own job role and what you would like to achieve over the next 12 months. Write down three to six key objectives for this period. Make sure that the majority of them tie in with business goals and that they all comply with the SMARTS guidelines. Discuss them with one of your learning sources.

We shall now return to considering performance appraisal in general terms by looking at the benefits of a well-designed and implemented scheme before we summarise best-practice issues.

THE BENEFITS OF PERFORMANCE APPRAISAL

Employees are often suspicious of new or revised appraisal schemes, particularly during times of rapid change or rationalisation. If you are faced with the task of introducing a new or updated scheme, you should pick your timing carefully, because many employees (sometimes rightly) view such innovations as a cynical way of selecting candidates for redundancy. As a consequence, many employers (eg in the educational field) have sought to shift the emphasis from an appraisal approach (current performance) to a developmental approach (future needs).

In any event, if the design incorporates the list of key points provided in the section above on the components of performance appraisal schemes, the benefits for both the organisation and the individual should include the items listed in Table 6.3.

Table 6.3 The benefits of performance appraisal

For the organisation	For the individual
Improved communication of business goals	Increased understanding of strategic aims and own role in organisational success
Improvements in work performance and therefore overall business performance via, for example, increased productivity or customer service	Increased motivation
	Increased job satisfaction
	Development of potential
Identification of potential to aid succession planning	Better informed career planning
Training provision or development activities targeted at identified needs rather than provided on an ad hoc or 'first come, first served' basis	Increased ability to meet own individual objectives as well as wider department or business objectives
	Opportunity to publicise ambition
Evaluation of effectiveness of selection criteria for new or newly promoted employees	Better understanding of the link between effort, performance and reward
	Employability security
More objective distribution of rewards	
Improved retention of employees	

The benefits listed in the table demonstrate why organisations should seriously consider the value of introducing performance appraisal – but they should also bear in mind the many potential pitfalls. A half-hearted attempt to introduce formal performance appraisal may be more damaging in the long run than no attempt at all.

In order to help you to avoid the pitfalls suffered by some performance appraisal schemes, we have summarised a list of best-practice features.

GOOD PRACTICE IN PERFORMANCE APPRAISAL

There is no right or wrong in relation to appraisal and how it is established or conducted, but effective schemes and approaches will generally incorporate the following:

- support from top management
- systems that are open and participative
- agreement at all levels about the purpose(s) of the scheme
- separation of reward reviews from the appraisal interviews
- clear, specific and well-communicated (SMARTS) objectives that are jointly agreed
- line managers' recognition of their critical role in this process – ie it is not seen as an HR function
- clear links to the disciplinary and/or capability procedure when handling conduct or poor performance issues so that the messages to the employee are the same

- training for appraisers and appraisees, including giving and receiving feedback
- a 'maintenance' programme to ensure that follow-up action is taken – eg training or development programmes are arranged as agreed
- a flexible approach to cater for individual and organisational needs
- simple administrative procedures
- consistency in managers' reporting standards
- formal regular appraisals and interim informal reviews between managers and their staff regarding performance and progress.

Finally, you should ensure that there is vertical and horizontal integration of the performance appraisal scheme within the business. Vertical integration means that there must be a link between the purposes of performance appraisal and the business strategy. Horizontal integration means there has to be a 'fit' between performance appraisal and other HR and development activities.

In relation to conducting a performance appraisal meeting, good practice would indicate that the person being appraised should do most of the talking, with the appraiser being an active listener – this will be a good starting point for a system to be participative. There should be opportunities for reflection, clarification and summarising to ensure shared understanding. The whole period under review should be covered, not just recent or 'big' events, with a focus on performance in the job rather than on the personality of the appraisee. Feedback should be both positive and constructive, with achievement being recognised as well as agreement on areas for further development. Agreement should be sought at the end of the meeting about next steps and actions needed. Additionally, all the logistical matters relating to any type of interview – quiet location, no interruptions, good preparation, etc – should be fulfilled.

In the list above we pointed out that appraisal training should include development in giving and receiving feedback. We now consider this important issue.

GIVING AND RECEIVING FEEDBACK

Here we are referring not only to the giving and receiving of feedback in formal performance reviews, but also to the regular and informal feedback that employees should be able to expect throughout the year. Obviously, not all feedback will be positive although anecdotal evidence unfortunately suggests that managers are reluctant to give negative feedback and employees are poor at receiving it. But poorly handled feedback can have a detrimental effect on future performance and working relationships, so we must work hard to try to get it right.

In Table 6.4 we seek to identify how feedback, whether negative or positive, can be given in a constructive way.

Table 6.4 The dos and don'ts of giving constructive feedback

Do ensure that your comments are:

- objective and based on facts or observations
- specific
- focused on behaviour, not personality (what people do, not what they are)
- based on behaviour that can be controlled by the recipient of the feedback
- timely
- given in an adult-to-adult, respectful, non-judgemental way
- regular and informal, not only given as part of the appraisal process
- an appropriate balance of positive and negative
- non-prescriptive, leaving the recipient with the choice of whether or not to change
- in amounts from which people can learn
- two-way.

Don't:

- start by asking questions – for example: 'How do you think you're doing?'
- make a statement, and then soften it by going round the houses with ifs, buts and maybes
- go straight to suggestions of how things might be put right
- talk down to people, tell them off or adopt an 'I know best' attitude.

Source: P. Swinburne (2001) 'How to use feedback to improve performance', *People Management*, 31 May; p.46

Following this advice can be very powerful in terms of getting your message across in the right way and in helping the recipient to understand and accept what you are saying. This is demonstrated in Case study 6.3.

CASE STUDY 6.3

The manager of the soft furnishings department of a large store in Oxford Street, central London, was not known for his tact and diplomacy. He was regarded as a workaholic and expected his staff to meet his own high standards of commitment and loyalty. He particularly detested poor timekeeping and any behaviours he considered amounted to less than 100 per cent attention to customer service. Last week he bawled out one of his retail assistants when she returned late from her lunch break. He called her 'a lazy, idle good-for-nothing' in front of two of her colleagues. The assistant was very upset about this incident and is thinking of handing in her resignation rather than carry on working for this man.

ACTIVITY 6.4

In Case study 6.3,

- What 'sins' did the manager commit?

- How should he have tackled this situation?

Compare your responses with the feedback provided at the end of this chapter.

In Case study 6.3 we saw how destructive feedback can be, and how, in such a situation, it would be difficult for the recipient to react in a constructive way. In any event, employees often lack the skills to receive feedback effectively, even positive feedback. For instance, when someone unexpectedly praises or thanks you, you may be inclined to reply with such statements as 'It was nothing,' or 'It's just part of my job.' What's the result? That person may be less inclined to praise or thank you next time!

So how *should* we receive feedback?

TIPS FOR RECEIVING FEEDBACK

- Listen to the message.

- Do not defend or argue.

- Clarify if you are unsure.

- Accept praise – don't write it off.

- Focus on what is being said – don't feel that you have to agree or disagree.

- Ensure that you understand what is being said; show that you understand.

- Consider asking what he or she would like to see done differently.

- Thank the giver – he or she has just taken a risk for you.

Source: P. Swinburne (2001) 'How to use feedback to improve performance', *People Management*, 31 May; p.47

DEALING WITH POOR PERFORMANCE

As noted throughout this chapter, performance management is a positive process aimed at improving individual and thereby organisational performance. However, in all organisations there will be instances of poor performance. This can result from a whole range of factors – for example, lack of skill or knowledge, problems with attitude and behaviour, poor management, lack of resources, poor systems or processes of work or external factors. As is evident, not all of these relate to or are within the control or influence of the individual employee, and it is very important to be clear why the poor performance is occurring. An effective performance management system can help to identify the causes of poor performance, and ensure that an appropriately broad view is taken of how performance might be improved. This might range from interventions in learning and development to changing systems of work, ongoing discussion and supervision with managers, etc. Where the reason for the poor performance does lie with the employee – perhaps related to conduct, performance or health – then, in most organisations, there are separate procedures for dealing with it. Further information on this is contained in Chapter 8 on *Employee relations*.

MOTIVATION

We saw in Table 6.1 above some of the links that can be made between performance appraisal and motivation. Individual performance depends on a number of factors – skill, knowledge, competence, aptitude, attitude and behaviour, amongst others. Underpinning the application of these factors by an individual employee in the workplace is the level of motivation, which itself is affected by a range of variables. Motivation is a very complex and individual issue – what motivates one person won't necessarily motivate another, and for each individual, motivating factors fluctuate in their importance according to the changing circumstances of his or her life. Motivation is important because it directs, energises and sustains behaviour in the workplace. Many studies have been carried out into motivation and many theories have been developed as a result. There is a variety of ways to classify these theories, but here we shall look at just three broad categories – reinforcement theories, need theories and cognitive theories.

REINFORCEMENT THEORIES

These theories propose that behaviour is shaped by its consequences – that positive reinforcement (for example, praise, approval, promotion or bonuses) increases the likelihood of that behaviour's being repeated, whereas negative reinforcement (for example, punishment or reprimand) motivates behaviour by leading to the avoidance of the undesired behaviour. The proponents of these theories believe that positive reinforcement is a more effective motivator than negative reinforcement. In principle this theory is fairly simple, but in the real world it doesn't usually operate so smoothly because reinforcement at work (for example, praise for a job done well) is often inconsistently applied or not forthcoming at all. There is also the question of which reinforcements are appropriate for which workers. One example of a reinforcement theory is Herzberg's motivation-hygiene theory, which looked at a range of factors and concluded that satisfaction and dissatisfaction arise from different factors – motivators (for example, achievement and the work itself) providing positive reinforcement, and 'hygiene' factors (for example, pay and work conditions), if not handled well, having a negative effect.

NEEDS THEORIES

A number of theories of motivation suggest that people have needs that are satisfied (or not) by working. These needs might be tangible, such as the need for food and housing, or less tangible, such as the need for respect from others.

Some people suggest that individuals usually have a preference or bias towards particular needs, the motivational impact varying for each individual, while others have suggested that needs occur at different levels and individuals move through these levels as lower-order needs are satisfied. One example of a needs-based theory is Maslow's 'hierachy of needs', in which he identified five levels of need, from physiological needs (eg hunger, thirst) at the bottom to the need for self-actualisation (eg realising your potential) at the top. As needs at the bottom are satisfied, they cease being primary motivators and an individual becomes motivated to satisfy higher-level needs. The different levels and associated needs can be seen in Table 6.5 below.

Table 6.5 Maslow's hierarchy of needs

self-fulfilment	realising potential, creativity and self-development
ego needs	autonomy, esteem, self-respect, confidence, sense of achievement, recognition/status, appreciation
social needs	sense of belonging, association, being accepted, giving and receiving, love and affection
safety needs	protection from danger and deprivation, physical and psychological security
physical needs	food, drink, shelter, rest

The theory acknowledges that people don't necessarily move in a continuous direction through the different levels of need, and also may be at a different place in different aspects of their lives – at work and outside work. As with everything, there may also be exceptions to this theory and some people may be happy to remain at a level below the top.

COGNITIVE THEORIES

These theories recognise individuals as rational thinking beings with differing views about reward, which therefore puts motivation on a much more individual basis. Such theories suggest that workers bring inputs to a job – for example, experience, qualifications, energy and effort – and expect to receive outcomes in return – for example, pay, recognition, benefits and interesting work. The inputs and outcomes are weighed up and perceived as either fair or unfair by the individual both at his or her own level and in comparison with others. One example of a cognitive theory is Adams' equity theory, which states that workers are motivated by a desire to be treated equitably or fairly. If workers perceive that they are being treated fairly, the motivation to work will be sustained and effective performance can be expected.

Now consider Activity 6.5.

ACTIVITY 6.5

Think about what motivates you at work. Try to write down a number of different factors and their impact on you – do they motivate you or demotivate you? Try to arrange these factors in order of how important you think they are in motivating you.

Now talk to a couple of colleagues – see what motivates them and what priority order they come up with. How does that compare with yours?

Now think about the factors that you and your colleagues have come up with. How good is your organisation at addressing these factors

LEGAL CONSIDERATIONS

The two main pieces of legislation relevant to the area of employee reward are the Equal Pay Act 1970 and the National Minimum Wage Act 1998. Both are summarised in Chapter 3 of this book.

With regard to performance appraisal, it would appear at first sight that there is no specific legislation. Yet Appendix 1 of the Acas advisory booklet *Employee Appraisal*, summarised (and updated) below, leaves little room for doubt concerning the relevance of certain legal considerations.

APPRAISAL – THE LEGAL CONSIDERATIONS

Trade unions

Employers who recognise one or more trade unions are required (if requested by a union) to disclose information for the purposes of collective bargaining. In these circumstances, particularly where merit pay schemes are in operation, they may be requested to explain how appraisal systems operate and to describe the criteria against which employees are rated. Further, recent changes to the Employment Relations Act 1999 have extended the rights of recognised trade unions. They now have a statutory right to be informed and consulted on training policies and plans.

Data protection

The Data Protection Act 1998 (supplemented in the public sector by the Freedom of Information Act 2000) gives individual employees a legal right of access to personal data (such as appraisal details). 'Personal data' includes not just factual information but also opinions expressed about employees. Employees could therefore have access to opinions recorded about their performance or attitude at an appraisal. However, any indication of intentions – such as an intention to promote – is outside the scope of the Act. Employers must, moreover, respect the confidentiality of any information relating to third parties.

Equal opportunities

Under the Race Relations and Sex Discrimination Acts, employees who feel that they have been refused promotion or access to training on grounds of their race or sex have the right to make a complaint to an employment tribunal. The Disability Discrimination Act 1995 introduced a similar right for disabled people treated less favourably because of a reason related to their disability, and/or without a justifiable reason. Recent years have seen an expansion in the grounds upon which discrimination complaints can be made to include age, part-time working, fixed-term contract working, sexual orientation and transgender, religion, belief, etc.

In discrimination cases appraisal forms and procedures may be used by employees to support their complaints. It is important for employers regularly to monitor their appraisal systems and promotion policies to ensure that criteria used to assess performance are non-discriminatory in terms of race, sex and disability.

Poor performance

Employees dismissed on the grounds of inadequate performance and who subsequently complain of unfair dismissal sometimes indicate in their applications that they have received little or no indication of alleged poor performance while in employment. Appraisal schemes should not be used as a disciplinary mechanism to deal with poor performers, but it is important to establish a procedure for informing employees in writing of unsatisfactory ratings. The consequences of failure to meet the required standards should be explained to the employee and confirmed in writing. The appraisal form is not, however, the place to record details of verbal or written disciplinary procedure. There should be space on the appraisal form to record unsatisfactory performance together with the notes of action to be taken, both by the individual and by management, to remedy these deficiencies. See Case study 6.4 below. (Many organisations now choose to have separate capability procedures to cover this eventuality – see Chapter 8 for more guidance on this.)

Equal pay

The main tenet of the Equal Pay Act 1970 is that men and women are entitled to equal treatment in respect of pay and conditions of employment. Recent legislative changes have introduced the concept of equal pay questionnaires, issued by employees to employers for them to justify any perceived disparities in reward. This process is intended as a precursor to employment tribunal proceedings, which are notoriously long-winded in equal pay claims. Proactive employers are wise to consider carrying out equal pay audits which examine all aspects of their reward policies and practices with a view to eradicating bias. For instance, the basis upon which managers have reached decisions on the awarding of contingent pay to their teams would be closely scrutinised. (See Case study 6.4 below.)

CASE STUDY 6.4

In our experience managers are often loath to tackle poor performance. They turn a blind eye when sub-standard work is produced by a team member, and do not communicate their discontent. Although the appraisal process should not be the starting point for tackling poor performance issues, it does provide an opportunity to discuss examples of where an individual's performance must be improved. For some managers, however, there may be a temptation to duck the issue entirely and, for example, rate the employee concerned as 'good'.

This is exactly what happened in one City-based securities organisation. The manager was then surprised to receive a grievance claim and equal pay questionnaire from his female member of staff. She had taken exception to the fact that her annual bonus, supposedly based on individual performance measures, was considerably lower than that received by her male colleagues. Although there were grounds for arguing that her performance was inferior in terms of outcomes, the legal advice was that this was not a claim that could be defended because of:

- the complete lack of objectivity in

awarding bonuses throughout the organisation

- the fact that no action, formal or informal, had been taken to notify the employee that her performance was unacceptable and plan a course of corrective action

- the disparity between her performance appraisal rating and the level of bonus paid.

The manager learnt his lesson the hard way as protracted negotiations then took place, and a compromise agreement (a legal agreement that can be entered into when a member of staff leaves employment in certain circumstances) was the eventual outcome. The organisation also realised that a more open and transparent approach to rewarding staff was required in the future. They decided to carry out an equal pay audit.

This area is a complex one, but the Acas advisory handbook on *Discipline and Grievances at Work* provides excellent guidance on how to handle problems concerning poor performance; it is essential reading in this area.

We next consider the role of HR practitioners in designing, administering, maintaining and evaluating performance appraisal within their organisations.

THE ROLE OF HR PRACTITIONERS

HR practitioners adopt a multifaceted role in the area of performance appraisal and within the wider remit of performance management in their organisations. Those of you in generalist roles are likely to get involved, with varying degrees of support from more senior and experienced staff or even outside consultants, in a number of the following stages:

- identifying the need for a new or revised scheme

- designing the scheme

- implementing and communicating the scheme

- designing and organising training for appraisers and appraisees

- administering the scheme

- monitoring the scheme

- maintaining the scheme (ie is it working efficiently?)

- evaluating the scheme (ie is it working effectively and does it meet its objectives?).

You will thus carry out all or some of the following roles (or possibly assist outside consultants in undertaking their roles).

A RESEARCH ROLE

This covers finding out about current thinking and good practice in performance management, the various types of scheme in other organisations, their purposes and links to the achievement of business objectives, and their effectiveness, etc. (See the section on *The components of performance appraisal schemes* earlier in this chapter.)

A CREATIVE ROLE

The aim here is to design a scheme that is tailored to your organisational circumstances and culture and the needs of your employees.

AN INFLUENCING ROLE

The purpose of this role is to 'sell' the benefits of the scheme to senior managers, to the line managers who will be operating it, and to each and every employee who will be appraised.

A TRAINING ROLE

This may cover the design, organisation and delivery of training for both appraisers and appraisees in relation to their familiarisation with the scheme and the skills of appraisal interviewing.

AN ADMINISTRATIVE ROLE

This involves implementing the scheme, communicating with all those affected at each stage and ensuring that all the paperwork flows through the system according to the requisite time-scales, and that action points are followed up.

AN ADVISORY ROLE

Advice has to be given to managers regarding, for example, developmental opportunities for their staff.

A MONITORING ROLE

You need to oversee consistency in applying standards, allocating rewards and ensuring that appeals are handled fairly and constructively.

MAINTENANCE AND EVALUATION ROLES

These ensure that the scheme continues to enjoy a high priority and that feedback on the success of the scheme (in reaching its objectives) is acted upon in amending, updating and enhancing it.

AN APPRAISAL ROLE

This is both as an appraiser for your own staff and as an appraisee in your own right. Further, if your organisation operates a 360-degree appraisal scheme, you may be involved as the neutral third party to provide feedback for a number of employees on the collated information provided by all the stakeholders involved in the process. (See Figure 6.2, page 166.)

INTERVIEWING SKILLS

Chapter 5 provides general guidance on interviewing techniques and skills. The majority of these are also applicable in an appraisal situation, although the purposes of appraisal interviews are of course different from those of selection interviews. Here we are concentrating on the skills necessary to be an effective appraiser.

We tackle appraiser skills by referring to the 'Dos and Don'ts' of appraisal interviewing: see Table 6.6.

Table 6.6 Appraisal interviewing – the appraiser

	Do	**Don't**
Before	<ul><li>give the appraisee notice of the meeting and any preparation necessary</li><li>book a suitable venue (checking whether any particular arrangements need to be made for disabled appraisees)</li><li>allow sufficient time</li><li>read the job description</li><li>identify suitable competencies if you intend to use these as the basis for discussion, and provide the appraisee with details of the competencies</li><li>review past appraisals and achievement of objectives</li><li>review performance over the whole period</li><li>check on development opportunities</li><li>collect facts and examples, perhaps using any chosen competencies as a framework</li><li>reflect on what you are trying to achieve</li><li>consider future objectives</li><li>plan the agenda</li></ul>	<ul><li>wait for the formal appraisal interview to tackle performance issues (good or bad)</li><li>be swayed by the 'halo or horns' effect (ie when one feature exhibited by the appraisee governs your perception of his or her overall abilities. An example of the 'halo' effect would be a belief that because an employee has a business studies degree she is highly numerate. On the other hand, the 'horns' effect would apply when you assume that an employee who is persistently untidy lacks commitment and is unproductive. The beliefs may be correct but need to be verified by more objective methods)</li><li>be overly influenced in your assessment by recent events</li></ul>

	Do	Don't
During	• seek to establish rapport • state the purpose and structure of the interview • check whether the appraisee wishes to add any other relevant items to the agenda • invite the appraisee's views on his or her own performance • keep notes • praise strengths and discuss areas for improvement • listen actively and maintain eye contact • ask open and probing questions • jointly seek solutions • invite the appraisee to summarise first • agree an action plan and future objectives • end on a positive note	• be afraid to tackle difficult issues • be bullied • be afraid to use silence • concentrate on weaknesses at the expense of strengths • concentrate on personality issues at the expense of results • make assumptions – eg about ambitions • argue • give vague responses to questions • make false promises • impose future objectives
Afterwards	• complete and return paperwork • ensure that the appraisee and other authorised parties receive copies of the form • ensure follow-up to action points • carry out regular reviews • hold frequent discussions re progress.	• file the papers and give the matter no more thought until the next review!

ACTIVITY 6.6

If you are inexperienced in appraisal interviewing – either as an appraiser or as an appraisee – set up a role-play with a like-minded individual so that you can both practise and receive feedback on your skills in appraisal interview situations. (See Table 6.4, the *Tips for receiving feedback* box, and Table 6.6 for guidance.)

SUMMARY

- In order to achieve the learning objectives of this chapter we have sought to distinguish between the broad concept of performance management and the part played by performance appraisal within this framework. We have also explored the importance of the link between individual objectives and business goals, and have concluded that a lack of integration is a major stumbling-block towards a truly effective PMS for many organisations.

- Performance appraisal has been examined in detail – its purposes, motivational effect, history and trends. The differing components of performance appraisal schemes have been highlighted, such as the setting of objectives, and the major benefits and best-practice issues, including those concerning feedback, have been detailed.

- The legal considerations, the role of HR practitioners and the skills necessary to be an effective appraiser have been identified.

You will by now be familiar with the terms used and will be able to relate your learning to the scheme or schemes with which you are familiar. References and further reading are provided immediately below for your information, and Activities have been suggested throughout. You are encouraged to complete some, if not all, of these Activities in order to reinforce and apply your learning.

EXPLORE FURTHER

REFERENCES AND FURTHER READING

ACAS (2009) Advisory Handbook on *Discipline and Grievances at Work*. Leicester: ACAS

ACAS (2008) Advisory Booklet on *Employee Appraisal*. Leicester: ACAS

ACAS (2005) Advisory Booklet on *Appraisal-Related Pay*. Leicester: ACAS

ARMSTRONG, M. (2002) *Employee Reward*, 3rd edition. London: Chartered Institute of Personnel and Development

ARMSTRONG, M. and BARON, A. (2004) *Managing Performance: Performance management in action*. London: Chartered Institute of Personnel and Development

ARMSTRONG, M. and MURLIS, H. (1991) *Reward Management: A handbook of remuneration strategy and practice*, 2nd edition. London: IPM and Kogan Page

CIPD (2004) *Survey of Performance Management*. London: Chartered Institute of Personnel and Development

FLETCHER, C. (1997) *Appraisal: Routes to improved performance*, 2nd edition. London: Institute of Personnel and Development

HALE, R. and WHITLAM, P. (1998) *Target Setting and Goal Achievement*. London: Kogan Page

HOLLYFORDE, S. and WHIDDETT, S. (2002) *The Motivation Handbook*. London: Chartered Institute of Personnel and Development

MARCHINGTON, M. and WILKINSON, A. (2002) *People Management and Development*, 2nd edition. London: Chartered Institute of Personnel and Development

PETERS, T. J. and WATERMAN, R. H. (1982) *In Search of Excellence*. London: Harper & Row

SWINBURNE, P. (2001) 'How to use feedback to improve performance', *People Management*, 31 May; pp.46–7

WHIDDETT, S. and HOLLYFORDE, S. (2003) *A Practical Guide to Competencies*. London: CIPD

WRIGHT, A. (2004) *Reward Management in Context*. London: CIPD

ACTIVITIES FEEDBACK

Activity 6.4

What 'sins' did the manager commit?

It's difficult to find anything that this manager did get right, so you will probably have highlighted the facts below:

- He was not objective.
- The feedback was not two-way in that he did not check the reasons for the lateness.
- He focused on personality traits, not behaviours.
- The feedback was not timely and was made in public.
- He was not respectful and adopted a parent-to-child role rather than adult-to-adult.

How should he have tackled this situation?

He should have:

- held the discussion at an appropriate time and in an appropriate venue
- remained unemotional
- related what he observed – ie that the assistant returned late from her lunch break
- stated how that made him feel – eg that it had been inconvenient because the department was short-staffed during a busy period
- asked for an explanation
- sought clarification, if necessary
- discussed with the assistant how to avoid a recurrence
- jointly agreed with her a plan of action.

Reward

INTRODUCTION

Reward is a broad concept and one in which there has been a lot of change in recent years. Traditionally, reward is thought of as pay (including performance-related pay) and other contractual-type benefits, such as holidays, sick pay and pensions, the aim of these being to attract, motivate and retain employees. The purpose of each element of reward was thought to be clear – for example, performance-related pay was considered to be about motivating people. More recently, these very clear distinctions about purpose – and, in fact, the definition of what elements are considered to make up reward – have changed. For very many people reward is one of the most important aspects of working life: it is certainly one in which many HR practitioners will be involved. In this chapter we aim to provide an overview of reward, considering what is meant by the term 'reward', giving an introduction to different reward systems and structures, and looking at the links between reward, motivation and performance management. We then look at some of the legal issues connected with reward, and consider how pay decisions are made and the different roles that HR practitioners can play in reward.

The reward system in an organisation is about rewarding people fairly and consistently for their individual contribution and value to the organisation and for their skill and performance. A good reward system will ensure that individual employees' efforts are directed to those activities that will help the organisation to achieve its goals and objectives. It can be a very sensitive subject – the way in which reward is handled can have a big impact on morale, motivation and productivity.

A useful definition of reward is provided by Michael Armstrong.

Armstrong (2002: 4) says that:

> a reward system consists of financial rewards (fixed and variable pay) and employee benefits, which together comprise total remuneration. The system also incorporates non-financial rewards (recognition, praise, achievement, responsibility and personal growth) and, in many cases, performance management processes. The combination of financial rewards, employee benefits and non-financial compensation comprises the total reward system.

This introduces the concept of a 'total reward package' which many organisations consider when thinking about their reward policy and strategy, and shows a broader, more inclusive approach to reward than that indicated by the more traditional approach outlined above. In effect it means the combination of financial and non-financial rewards available to employees, and covers a much wider range of issues than just pay and other contractual-type benefits such as holidays and pensions.

WHAT DO WE MEAN BY 'REWARD'?

As noted above, reward is a broad concept covering both pay and non-pay items. The increasing number of organisations taking a total reward approach reflects a growing evidence base and understanding that performance, productivity and motivation are influenced by a much wider range of factors than those addressed in the past. Looking at total reward requires consideration of such elements as basic pay, any 'contingent' pay (ie any element of pay based on individual factors such as performance, skill, competence, etc), non-pay benefits and wider non-financial rewards, such as the work environment, job security, company culture, employee recognition practices, opportunities for personal development and growth, and factors intrinsic to the job. A survey of 520 employers covering about 1 million employees conducted by the CIPD in 2009 showed that around one-fifth of employers had adopted such a total rewards approach, while a further 22% were planning on taking that approach. Table 7.1 features the most commonly used pay incentives and non-pay benefits in the survey.

Table 7.1 Commonly used pay incentives and non-pay benefits

Most commonly used pay incentives	Most commonly used non-pay benefits
Individual-based pay rate	Pension plan
Scheme driven by business results	Training and development
Combination	25 days' or more paid leave
Executive share option schemes	Tea/coffee/cold drinks
Share incentive plan	Christmas party/lunch
Company share option plan	On-site car parking
Save As You Earn (SAYE)	Childcare vouchers

Source: CIPD (2009) *Reward Management Survey*, survey report

The place of reward in the employment relationship is too important to be left to chance. It is advisable for organisations to adopt a managed approach to reward, which, if done well, will ensure:

- that people are rewarded in line with what the organisation wants to pay for
- that rewards are linked to business objectives
- that messages about organisation culture, values and desired behaviours can be communicated, and desired outcomes rewarded
- the development of a performance culture
- that the right people with the right skills are attracted and retained
- that employees are motivated and engaged
- the development of a positive employment relationship and psychological contract (see Chapter 8).

ACTIVITY 7.1

Consider your own organisation. How is reward dealt with – does your organisation take a total reward package view or not? Is there a reward strategy or policy? What elements currently make up the total reward package? What information is collected about how successful these elements are in attracting, retaining and motivating employees? Discuss your thoughts with one of your learning sources.

Clearly, reward is about far more than just pay. However, pay is a critical component of reward. In the next section we go on to consider the different ways in which pay is organised through a consideration of pay systems and structures.

PAY SYSTEMS AND STRUCTURES

There are many different types of pay system and structure in place in different organisations – which are used will depend very much on the organisational context, size and sector. 'Pay systems' tends to refer to the way in which individual employees are rewarded for their contribution, whereas 'pay structures' refers to the way in which different levels or groupings of pay are organised linking related jobs and providing a framework for making payments.

PAY SYSTEMS

There are two main categories of pay system: basic rate schemes and variable or incentive schemes. The systems in use in some organisations include a combination of the two, whereas in others only one of these systems is used. In basic rate schemes the pay does not vary according to achievement or performance, whereas in variable or incentive schemes, either all or part of the pay of an individual will vary depending on things such as team or individual performance, company profits, level of skill or competence. Some of the most commonly used incentive schemes are listed in Table 7.1 above. Within public sector organisations basic pay schemes are more common, whereas incentive schemes are more common in the private sector.

Basic rate systems

Here an employee will have a fixed rate of basic pay set in reference to a particular time period – for example, per hour, per week or per year. There may be other payments in addition to basic pay, such as overtime or additional pay for working shifts or nights, for example, but the basic pay rate will not vary according to individual contribution or performance.

CASE STUDY 7.1

A basic pay system can be illustrated by looking at the example of a nurse working in the NHS. An individual nurse's job is allocated to a pay band with a number of pay points by undertaking job evaluation. Each pay band attracts a basic annual salary on an incremental scale. Individual nurses progress up the pay band and receive an incremental increase in their basic salary each year until they reach the top of their pay band. In addition, they also receive an annual cost-of-living pay increase, negotiated nationally, to reflect increases in inflation, etc. All nurses on the same pay band are treated in the same way, and any differences in their effort or performance are not reflected in their basic pay. Although there is no performance or contingent pay, nurses can add to their basic pay in a number of ways:

- Those working in the London area will receive a high-cost area supplement.

- Those who are on call outside their normal working hours will receive an additional percentage of their basic pay depending on the frequency of the on-call commitment.

- Those who work additional hours over and above full-time hours may be eligible for overtime pay at time-and-a-half.

- Those who work nights, weekends or on bank holidays will receive percentage enhancements to basic pay of between 30% and 60% for the 'unsocial hours' element.

Basic rate systems apply to many employees in the UK and are used in a large number of different organisations. There are both pros and cons of using a basic rate system.

Basic rate schemes relate to the job rather than the individual doing the job, and are frequently determined using reference to the 'going rate' for that type of job in that locality, sometimes supported by job evaluation. Further information on job evaluation can be found in Chapter 4 on *Job analysis* and design.

Variable or incentive pay systems

Here an employee's pay – or, more usually, part of their pay – will vary dependent on their individual performance, the performance of the team they are in or the whole company's performance. The most common types of scheme relate to individual performance and apply only to part of the employee's wage or salary. Examples of variable or incentive pay systems include sales commission, appraisal-/performance-related pay, payment by results (for instance, piecework) and skills-based pay. Again, there are both pros and cons associated with variable or incentive pay systems.

CASE STUDY 7.2

A variable-rate pay system can be illustrated by looking at the example of a financial adviser. Posts such as these may be found in either large financial institutions, such as banks, or in smaller companies dedicated to providing financial advice. The financial adviser will generally receive a basic salary, expressed as a 'per annum' figure, from the company they work for. In smaller companies, any increases to the basic salary tend to be negotiated on an individual basis, whereas in the larger companies, financial advisers may get an annual salary increase in line with the national average earnings index. In addition, financial advisers earn income for their companies by providing advice and selling financial products to customers. If an individual financial adviser achieves a predetermined level of income earned over a given time period (each month/quarter/year, for example), he or she will receive a bonus, which is usually a percentage of the amount of income earned. Thus the more income that individuals earn for their company, the higher the level of bonus they will receive. Such bonuses may be paid to each individual on a monthly, quarterly or annual basis. In addition to the basic salary and the performance-related bonus, the financial adviser will often also receive other benefits, such as a company car or car allowance.

Many organisations use a combination of both types of pay system in order to increase the degree of flexibility they have to respond to changing circumstances. In this way a lot of employees will have both a basic pay rate and some element of variable pay (such as a bonus scheme).

PAY STRUCTURES

Pay structures provide a framework for defining different levels of pay for jobs or groups of jobs. This is often done in relation to both the external job market and the internal value placed on different types of jobs. Childs and Suff (2005) define pay structures as being

> all about valuing jobs and understanding how jobs relate to one another and the external market. Employees and their individual competence, experience, and standards of performance should fit into, and be valued by, the structure.

In smaller organisations (fewer than 200 people) formal pay structures may not exist, but they are generally found in larger organisations across all sectors. Pay structures often consist of grades or pay bands, individual jobs being allocated to a particular grade/band depending on the responsibilities of the job. The purpose of using pay structures is:

- to create a framework for pay that is transparent and easily understood
- to make sure that payment reflects what the organisation is trying to achieve
- to help ensure fairness and lawfulness.

Pay structures can be multiple, so that there are different pay structures for different categories of workers within one organisation (for example, one structure for manual workers and a different one for non-manual workers), or, increasingly, single structures where the same structure applies to all employees. Many larger organisations and public sector bodies, such as local authorities, have been implementing 'single-status' schemes that are equally applicable to all employees. However, even where single status has been introduced, you will still often see separate arrangements for senior executives. An e-reward survey in 2007 found that 56% of organisations used single pay structures.

The different types of pay structures in use include:

- graded structures
- broadbanding
- individual pay rates/spot salaries
- job families
- pay spines.

We shall now look at each of these in turn.

Graded structures

These structures involve a sequence of job grades in which the pay for each grade is identified and in which jobs of equivalent value are placed in each grade. Such grading structures can be narrow-graded, usually involving 10 or more grades, or broad-graded, usually involving between six and nine grades. Narrow-graded structures typically have either narrow pay ranges or a single salary point, whereas broad-graded structures have a single salary point or slightly wider pay ranges – although progression through these wider pay ranges is sometimes controlled so that not everyone in the grade can reach the top of the pay range. In both graded structures, progression through the pay range is generally linked to performance, competence or length of service. With graded structures, employees can often reach the top of the pay range quite quickly, which can lead to pressure for upgrading or grade drift. The 2009 CIPD survey on reward showed that 13% of organisations use narrow-grading structures.

Broadbanding

This involves the use of a smaller number of pay bands or grades than in traditional graded structures – typically, four or five pay bands. Within these bands pay can be managed more flexibly: they can be more responsive to things such as changes in market rates for particular jobs. The pay range within a broad band will necessarily be quite wide, and the band can sometimes incorporate a number of different grades. The effect of broadbanding is to flatten the pay and grade hierarchy. Because of the wide pay ranges associated with broad bands, some organisations have introduced 'zones' or 'bars' so that not all employees in a particular band can expect to move right through the band to the top. The 2009 CIPD survey on reward showed that 24% of organisations use broadbanding.

Spot salaries/individual pay rates

This involves the setting of one fixed rate of pay for one job, which allows for no progression in basic pay, although there will often be incentive payments (eg bonuses) in addition to the spot salary basic pay rate. In practice, spot rates might be amended from time to time in line with such things as inflation or changes in the job market for a particular type of job. Spot rates are seen most often in relation to low-skill/low-pay occupations, perhaps where the minimum wage is used as the spot rate, and at the opposite end of the job spectrum in executive pay, where the total reward package might be made up of a spot rate salary and a range of other benefits.

Job families

In this structure, similar types of jobs (eg sales, finance, etc) are grouped together and have a pay structure with a number of different levels (similar to a graded structure). The basic skills and knowledge required of jobs within the family are the same but there are different levels of responsibility that attach to individual jobs. Such a structure can be appropriate when there are distinct job markets for certain types of jobs (eg IT specialists). This makes it easier for the organisation to respond to market forces in the labour market. For example, it may be necessary to pay a higher salary to attract scarce skills than might have to be paid for an equivalent level of skill in another job family. Progression within a level in a job family is often linked to contribution or competence.

Pay spines

This structure exists where a pay spine with a wide range covers all jobs from the lowest- to the highest-paid. Different grades or pay bands are often superimposed over the pay spine, in effect meaning that no one moves from the bottom to the top of the whole spine. Progression within a pay spine is frequently linked to length of service. Pay spines allow greater certainty and control over pay than some of the other structures, and are common in the public sector.

FLEXIBLE BENEFITS

In some organisations, regardless of the type of pay system or structure used, there is flexibility in the total reward package that an individual can receive. In flexible systems employees can exchange certain elements for others – for example, exchanging an amount of pay in return for childcare vouchers. In this way reward packages can be tailored and individualised to suit the circumstances of the employee. Common considerations for employees in opting for flexibility and exchanging benefits are personal circumstances (for example, in the case of childcare vouchers) and the tax implications (for example, in the case of company cars). This is sometimes referred to as the 'cafeteria system' by analogy with an employee being able to choose the elements of a meal according to their own preferences. Common flexible benefits are:

- buying and selling holidays
- childcare vouchers
- advances and loans
- company cars
- mileage expenses
- company shares
- private health schemes
- medical insurance
- gym membership.

ACTIVITY 7.4

Consider what sort of issues must be thought about when an organisation is considering introducing flexible benefits.

Compare your response with the feedback given at the end of this chapter.

LINKING PAY WITH PERFORMANCE

Performance is not always linked with pay – far from it. Indeed, there is ongoing debate about how effective pay is as a motivator of performance. However, if pay is linked with performance, then – as seen in Chapter 6 on *Performance management* – for a performance management scheme (PMS) to be successful, each and every aspect of it must be clearly linked and work towards the overall aim of continually improving business performance. This can be achieved only through your employees, who will expect to be rewarded for their loyalty, hard work and contribution both extrinsically (factors generated by others) via promotions, salary, fringe benefits, bonuses, stock options, etc, and intrinsically (self-generated factors) via feelings of achievement, responsibility, personal growth, competence, etc. The satisfactory integration of reward into the PMS is undoubtedly a difficult thing to achieve – not least because the factors that motivate employees vary from individual to individual. Further, for each individual, motivating factors fluctuate in their importance according to the changing circumstances of their lives – for example, at the start of an individual's working life the level of pay might be the most important factor, whereas for someone with childcare responsibilities work–life balance might be the most important factor. There is even disagreement about whether some extrinsic rewards have any motivational impact at all, but here we shall proceed on the assumption that they do have a short-term effect in increasing effort and, therefore, productivity.

DEFINITIONS

In this section we are specifically concentrating on those rewards which are most closely linked to performance management – ie performance-related pay (PRP) and competence-related pay.

Armstrong (2002: 261) states that PRP:

> provides individuals with financial rewards in the form of increases to basic pay or cash bonuses which are linked to an assessment of performance, usually in relation to agreed objectives.

In contrast, Armstrong (2002: 289) defines competence-related pay as

> a method of rewarding people wholly or partly by reference to the level of competence they demonstrate in carrying out their roles. It is a method of paying people for the ability to perform.

(In answer to criticisms of both of the above, some organisations have sought to combine performance- and competence-related pay by rewarding for both performance (outcomes) and competence (inputs). This is known as a contribution-related pay scheme.)

THE LINK TO MOTIVATION

In linking pay to performance, we are concerned with the types of reward system available to organisations to encourage their employees to make worthwhile contributions towards the achievement of business goals. Armstrong and Murlis (1991: 282) state that for reward systems to act as real incentives to employees they must satisfy three basic requirements:

- that the reward should bear a direct relation to the effort
- that the payment should follow immediately or soon after the effort
- that the method of calculation should be simple and easily understood.

Thus rewards such as salaries, fixed hourly rates and profit-sharing do not satisfy all of the above requirements. However, many contingent reward schemes are designed to succeed on all three counts. For instance, merit pay schemes may provide salary or wage increases in recognition of excellent job performances during the review period, and incentive or bonus schemes may provide payments in addition to base salary or wages related to the satisfactory completion of a project or the achievement of an individual or group target.

But PRP, for example, is not without its problems, mainly because of the difficulties encountered in trying to measure individual or team performance objectively and in establishing the most appropriate pay-out levels. For instance, working hard all year to be eligible for a maximum merit award of 4% would probably be less motivating than seeking to achieve, say, three specific targets and a bonus payment of 10% to 20%. Competence-based pay can also be problematic – not least in the skills and time demanded of line managers in operating such schemes. With careful thought, contingent reward can be introduced as an effective strategic tool linked to business needs, but it should not be relied upon as the sole motivator for employees.

ACTIVITY 7.5

Think about the key components of your organisation's reward system – eg hourly rates of pay, incremental rises, shift premiums, competence-related pay, PRP, recognition schemes. List three financial and three non-financial rewards that you feel help to motivate individuals to improve their performance.

Compare your response with the feedback provided at the end of this chapter.

Performance-related pay schemes are not the only motivators and, as we have seen, it is debatable whether they are motivators at all in some instances. There is a wide range of other financial and non-financial rewards at the disposal of employers when they are seeking to motivate staff, and generally, a mix of both is to be recommended.

We shall now consider non-pay rewards.

NON-PAY REWARDS

We have addressed the topic of a total reward package above, and have outlined a variety of pay systems and structures. To ensure a full consideration of reward requires us to look at non-pay rewards. 'Non-pay rewards' usually refers to those items that are not pay or benefits but still have a role to play in recruiting, retaining and motivating employees and generating loyalty and commitment. Such forms of remuneration are often intrinsic to the job itself and reward employees by giving them opportunities for growth and development and by recognising contribution. The online guide to reward, *e-reward*, in its factsheet about non-financial rewards, identifies the main non-pay rewards as:

- achievement
- recognition
- responsibility/autonomy
- influence
- personal growth.

There is a significant amount of agreement that non-pay rewards are often the most important to individual employees, and this is particularly true in the public sector. A 2002 Audit Commission study of public sector workers looked at the factors influencing individuals' decisions to join, remain in or leave a public sector organisation. The five most common reasons for joining a public sector organisation were:

- making a positive difference
- working with people
- a career people had always wanted to do
- interesting work
- career progression.

Pay was not indicated as an important factor in decisions to join the public sector jobs, although it was important to employees in making a decision to stay in or leave a job. From this we can see the importance of the non-pay aspects of the reward package, and the fact that different rewards are important not only to different people but also to the same people at different points in their life/career.

What we have outlined above about both pay and benefits and non-pay rewards shows just what a complex area reward is, individual choice and differing views about what is important at different stages just adding to this complexity. Case study 7.3 gives a picture of this in one public sector organisation.

CASE STUDY 7.3

A survey was carried out in an NHS trust looking at how important different benefits were to employees, and how satisfied employees were with these benefits. A range of 15 different benefits which existed within the trust were included in the survey. The most important benefits to employees were support from managers and open and honest communication. Opportunities for career development and for training came 6th and 7th respectively, while having a competitive salary was ranked as the 9th most important benefit, and a good pension scheme was ranked as 10th. When reporting how satisfied these employees were with these benefits, the pension scheme was ranked as the benefit employees were most satisfied with, training and career development opportunities came 4th and 10th respectively, support from managers came 8th, open and honest communication came 12th while salary came 13th.

Employees were also given the opportunity to respond to an open question about what additional benefits they would like to see introduced. The largest percentage of comments was made about pay – 24% of all comments made – comments such as:

> Benefits and services can be nice, but proper pay and suitable working conditions are what is important.

and

> Increasing pay to recognise the growing problems for lower-paid staff dealing with the rising cost of living. We are losing bright young staff in whom we have invested time and money who are forced to leave to (a) work in agencies or (b) move to jobs in cheaper areas of the UK.

These comments were made despite 'having a competitive salary' being relatively far down the list of which benefits were important.

This shows the complexity for organisations in understanding what to include in their benefits package and also delivering on what matters to their employees.

We will now move on to consider the law as it applies to reward.

THE LEGAL ASPECTS OF PAYING EMPLOYEES

NATIONAL MINIMUM WAGE

The National Minimum Wage Act (NMW) provides a minimum wage for all workers – and this includes employees, many apprentices, employees of subcontractors, agency staff and homeworkers.

Only a few workers are excluded, and these include those who are genuinely self-employed, certain students and trainees on particular government-funded training schemes. Because the exact categories of who is included and who is not change from time to time, it is important to check with authoritative sources such as the Department for Business, Innovation and Skills (BIS) website.

In many cases it will be simple for you to assess whether your workers are being paid the NMW, but in some cases you will need to check carefully to see that you are complying with a minimum wage. Circumstances such as piecework, commission-only payments, on-call or stand-by elements, or project work may demand careful attention because the rules and calculations of pay and hours differ depending on the type of work.

Individuals have the right to apply to a court or tribunal for non-payment of the national minimum wage. So you must keep sufficient records to show that you are paying your workers this minimum wage for all the activities they are engaged in on your behalf. There are a number of criminal offences under the Act, including refusing to pay the minimum wage – so be careful!

MATERNITY AND PATERNITY, STATUTORY SICK AND REDUNDANCY PAY

Here minimum rates are determined by legislation. The rates themselves are reviewed annually. Each also has qualifying conditions and periods for which payments are due. These change from time to time as new legislation is enacted.

A WEEK'S PAY

For the purpose of some statutory requirements, such as notice pay and redundancy pay, there are precise rules for calculating a week's pay. While broadly this is an employee's normal pay for their normal hours, without overtime, it is important to follow the rules that are current at the time. Consult the BIS website. Incidentally, for redundancy purposes there is a maximum amount, reviewed annually.

THE RIGHT TO BE PAID

An employee must be paid a wage per hour, a salary per annum, or some variation (per week, for example). Piecework – once common in some UK industries – must be related back to an hourly rate to demonstrate that it complies with the national minimum wage. Although there is no longer the right to be paid in cash – as applied many years ago – the minimum payment (at least) must be in monetary value: it cannot be made up of the company's products. For example, relatively recently, desperate Russian workers were shown on UK television selling candelabras on the platform at a railway station. Their employer could no longer afford to pay them and so gave them the factory's output – candelabras – instead. So the right to be paid in currency is very important and is enshrined in the contract of employment.

An employee's remuneration must be stated in writing in the written particulars, as we have seen. The written statement is valuable to an employee because it prevents the employer from making unilateral changes to the amount an employee is paid. Pay is part of the contract, and it cannot be unilaterally varied. That means an employer cannot reduce an employee's pay without the employee's agreement. To do so would be a breach of the contract. It would give the employee the right to claim constructive dismissal, and very likely it would be found to be unfair (but see below).

RIGHTS ON THE TRANSFER OF AN EMPLOYEE'S EMPLOYER

In some sectors employees transfer from employer to employer quite frequently. For example, a cleaner may work for a school on a full-time basis. The school then contracts the work to a cleaning company and the cleaner has the right to 'follow the work' and become an employee of the cleaning company. Later on, the school becomes dissatisfied with the cleaning company and so engages another. Once again the employee follows the work and becomes an employee of the new company. These are transfers under the Transfer of Undertakings (Protection of Employment) Regulations 2006 (TUPE).

The definition of a transfer of an undertaking is quite technical, and the interpretation has changed from time to time under case law anyway. There other technical aspects concerned with transfers, such as the need for consultation. Because it is a complex area, we should let others decide whether the legislation applies in any particular case – or if you need to decide, take advice. For this reason we have not examined the concept in the legal background to HR. But when it comes to pay, there are important considerations that you must not ignore.

Employees' pay and terms and conditions are protected after a transfer. They can be improved by the new employer but no aspect can be reduced – even if there is compensation provided elsewhere. Furthermore, employees lose the right to agree any detrimental change to their pay. The protection applies indefinitely.

An employee's pay can, nevertheless, come under threat from several other very real possibilities.

SHORT-TIME WORKING

Employers can put employees on 'short time' – that is, they can reduce the hours that the employees work and reduce their pay accordingly. The right to put an employee on short-time working is sometimes put into the contract of employment as a right to vary hours. Without this variation, short-time working would be likely to enable the employee to claim constructive dismissal and, again, this would very likely be unfair dismissal.

However, overtime hours can be cut or stopped altogether without breaching the contract of employment, and this is often a first step in periods of austerity.

LAY-OFFS

As with short-time working, the right to lay employees off (ie tell them to go home or stay at home) without paying them is sometimes put into the contract of employment.

REDUCING PAY RATES

It is not unusual for employers in hard times to ask employees to take a pay cut. The prospect of a 10% cut is more attractive than a 100% cut! Employees often agree, especially if there is a reasonable hope of saving their employment by doing so. The important word here is 'agree'. Employers should not put employees under duress to obtain such agreement. Additionally, note that employees cannot agree to be paid less than the national minimum wage, and they may not be free to agree if their employment is protected by transfer from a previous employer, as we explained above.

AGREEING PAY REDUCTIONS

In some industries – particularly some manufacturing industries – lay-offs, short-time working and even short-term pay cuts are part of the culture. In those circumstances the employees' 'agreement' might be implied into the contract. If there have been such events in the past, you may be able to consider them options in the future.

Collective agreements can also provide an avenue where these determine the employees' terms and conditions of employment. An agreement with the recognised trade union may therefore provide the opportunity for pay reductions to be agreed.

As we have said, employees may agree to any of these austere measures in order to protect their employment. If an overwhelming number of employees do agree, you may be able to impose the change on the remainder. If they leave and claim constructive dismissal, it is reasonably likely that such a dismissal will be held to be fair on the grounds of sound business reasons (that is, 'some other substantial reason'). It is good to be aware of this, but unless you are very experienced, it is wise to take further advice about how to handle this first.

UNLAWFUL DEDUCTIONS

There are a few purposes for which you can deduct money from an employee's wage or salary without their permission – tax and National Insurance (where due) being examples. But to make a deduction for other purposes – say, to deduct parking fines – you must have the employee's explicit permission to make the deduction *before* the incident occurs – not just before the deduction. If you do not have the permission, ask the employee to write you a cheque. Advance permission for this type of deduction and others, such as union dues, can be put into the written particulars (or a separate document), but these must be signed so that there is no question over the explicitness of the permission. If you deduct an amount in contravention of the employee's rights, you will have to pay the amount back and it will no longer be lawful to obtain it in any other way.

As you will have seen, the law relating to pay can be quite complicated and is very detailed, so we would always advise you to seek further advice because getting pay wrong is a serious problem.

EQUAL PAY LEGISLATION

Employers are obliged to pay men and women equally where they are doing the same work. If the rates are different, the employer has to show there is a genuine reason that is not related to their gender.

On the face of it this seems very simple, but if disputes arise, it does become extremely complicated. An aggrieved woman (or, in principle, a man) has to establish 'a comparator' – that is, someone of the opposite gender who is in the same employment as they are. Usually this is someone working at the same establishment as they are working in, but in some circumstances a person can select someone at a different establishment.

The next question to arise is whether the work is equivalent, and this would generally require determination by a job evaluation scheme. The work could be of equivalent value even if it is different work – for example, enabling a cook to compare herself with a warehouseman.

CASE STUDY 7.4

The landmark case in equal pay was *Hayward v Cammell Laird Shipbuilders*. Ms Hayward was a canteen cook and she observed that she earned less than a warehouseman. She felt what she did was of equal value to her employer and so challenged this at the Liverpool industrial tribunal (the forerunner of employment tribunals). The tribunal found that she could compare her pay with another employee who was doing a job of equal value to the employer, irrespective of whether it was the same job. At the time (the 1980s) this caused a stir – could any woman compare her job with any job? Where would this end? Cammell Laird appealed. Accepting that the work was of equal value, they appealed on the grounds that when the overall package was taken into account Ms Hayward was treated as favourably as the men. However, while this was accepted by a higher court, the House of Lords (the highest court in the UK) overruled the decision. They determined that Ms Hayward was entitled to equal pay without evaluation of the total package. Equal pay claims are now considered contract clause by contract clause.

If there is no job evaluation scheme, or if there is more than one, the employee has to compare herself with another and show that the work is of 'equal value', in effect carrying out a job evaluation exercise on her job and that of the comparator.

For this purpose the tribunal may require a report from an independent specialist.

As we have already seen, pay may be made up of many different components and it is not unusual for the woman's pay package to be made up differently from that of her male comparator. The law allows the woman to compare herself on every term in the contracts of employment. It is not the 'package' as a whole that counts.

Workers (not just employees) who feel they are not paid equally can complete and send a questionnaire to their employer asking questions about equal pay. The employer's answers can be used in tribunal proceedings – so if you receive one, the response is a task for an employment solicitor, company legal department or experienced specialist.

The employer has one major line of defence and that is to show that there is a genuine material factor to explain the reason for any difference in pay. Examples might be the different skills, qualifications and experience of the people being compared.

This is a complex and increasingly important area. In the year 2007 to 2008 there were 40,000 unfair dismissal claims and 60,000 equal pay claims made to employment tribunals. Because these claims are expensive to defend and, as we have seen, complicated, equal pay principles cannot be ignored.

EQUAL PAY AUDITS

There are complex reasons why pay can be unequal. Market forces and historical trends are not necessarily sound as a defence but are often a reality. There is a tendency for part-time work to be low paid, especially where there is no full-time comparator (which would render the difference unlawful), and to attract women

Figure 7.1 An equal pay audit: the five-step process

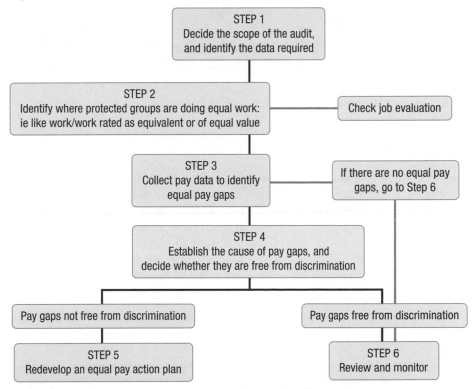

Source: http://www.equalityhumanrights.com/advice-and-guidance/information-for-employers/equal-pay-resources-and-audit-toolkit/carrying-out-an-equal-pay-audit/about-the-toolkit/

with families, rather than men. Breaks to bring up a family interrupt a career and damage salary prospects as well as leading to the need to 'catch up' on skills and experience in a rapidly changing world.

One of the most effective ways of establishing whether your organisation is providing equal pay is to undertake an equal pay audit. The Equality and Human Rights Commission recommends that every organisation should conduct such an audit. The purpose of conducting an audit is:

- to compare the pay of men and women doing equal work

- to identify any gender pay gaps

- to eliminate any such pay gaps that are based purely on gender.

At the time this book was under preparation, an Equality Act was envisaged for 2010. One of the proposed provisions was to make equal pay audits compulsory for all employers with more than 250 employees. You would be advised to check if this is in fact now the case.

The Equality and Human Rights Commission publishes a code of practice on equal pay and suggests a policy for employers. It also provides an equal pay toolkit to assist in creating an equal pay environment. See Figure 7.1.

ACTIVITY 7.6

Should sleeping dogs be left to lie?

Discuss in a group the pros and cons of initiating an equal pay code of practice and an equal pay audit your organisation.

Compare your response on the pros and cons with the feedback provided at the end of this chapter.

TRANSPARENCY IN EARNINGS

The Equality Act mentioned above was also set to address transparency in earnings. If the substance of the Act has not yet become statutory at the time you are reading this, we suggest that there is nevertheless pressure for greater transparency in earnings so that apparent gender inequalities can be challenged. Some employers use pay secrecy clauses that stop employees discussing their pay with their colleagues. We question how effective these are, but they may become illegal. However, employees will not be compelled to discuss their pay with others!

We now go on to consider the different factors that influence decisions about pay.

MAKING PAY DECISIONS

Employees' wages and salaries are not determined in isolation. Individuals themselves make comparisons of their benefits packages with those they perceive as being their peers (inside and outside the organisation, with jobs they see advertised and with numerous other sources). In some labour markets employees will leave quite quickly if there is a better offer near by, whereas in other markets they may accept poor rates relative to the market because of other compensatory factors in the total reward package.

The appropriate rate is important, not just to retain employees – although that is important in itself – but to have motivated employees. Dissatisfaction arising from a feeling of being underpaid or undervalued can be a major demotivator whether the low pay is real or imagined. It is for the latter reason that many organisations provide a total pay statement. In such a statement the organisation puts a value on each aspect of the reward package and totals it up. This helps reassure individuals who may see better salaries elsewhere. For example, the true value of a good pension scheme, usually with life assurance included, can be hard to grasp in our early twenties. But an organisation can show employees how much they would have to earn to obtain such benefits if they bought them personally. Adding such figures into a total pay statement helps employees think carefully about what may, at first sight, seem a more attractive employment proposition in another company. It also helps to curb dissatisfaction.

Many wage rates are locally determined to ensure that they are competitive in the local labour market. Others – for example, many rates in the public sector – are determined nationally to reflect the national job market and national job evaluation schemes. Pay rates for many senior jobs are more regionally, nationally or even internationally determined.

INFORMATION TO DETERMINE PAY DECISIONS

The labour turnover rates and the labour stability rates that we looked at in Chapter 5 are good indicators of how your pay and salary rates fare in the marketplace. Indeed, high labour stability and low turnover may indicate that you are paying too much!

In considering salary rates, the contribution that an employee is making becomes an important factor. Performance management (which we looked at in Chapter 6) and job evaluation (which we looked at in Chapter 4) assist us in making internal relative comparisons. Job evaluation in particular can also help in external comparisons too. There are proprietary systems, such as Hay, that have their own job evaluation system so that jobs can be related to local, national and regional rates directly. Other salary survey systems can nevertheless give good comparisons based on the job function, level of responsibility and location. It is best to acquire a little understanding of some basic terms such as 'median', 'upper quartile' and 'percentiles' to get the most from such data.

Incomes Data Services provide invaluable reports on pay rates in different industries and job functions, the 'going rate' in pay settlements, and valuable data such as the annual increase in earnings that is relevant to pay reviews.

These sources of information are available for a fee or subscription (see Case study 7.5). Discussion groups are free in that they require only time. Data such as the Retail Prices Index and the Consumer Prices Index is widely available. Local CIPD groups, Chambers of Commerce and newspaper articles can be valuable as well as, increasingly, the Internet and discussion forums.

Recruitment agencies should be treated with caution, since they have a vested interest, but they do have a shrewd idea of the salary levels that are necessary to attract good candidates. Indeed, advertisements themselves can give you an idea of how much others are prepared to pay to attract your employees away!

CASE STUDY 7.5

The position of shipping manager is a complex and critical role. The term 'missing the boat' has real and serious implications for anyone in such a position. There can be great stress in making sure that everything goes together, the container arrives on time, the product fits into the container and the container arrives with all the necessary documentation completed at the port on time. If you are exporting to remote parts of the world, the next boat may be weeks or even months hence. You can understand that anyone with that responsibility needs to feel they are getting the salary they deserve. So when our shipping manager felt the job evaluation was not leading to the salary he thought he deserved, he complained. We looked carefully at our purchased salary survey data (which contained salary levels for that very position) and considered the level of the job and our location in the UK. He was comfortably above the median salary for the position. Of course he would have liked to be paid more, but we were able to satisfy him that he was being fairly rewarded.

PENSIONS

THE STATE PENSION

The basic state pension is minimal. There is an additional state pension paid from National Insurance contributions. The actual additional state pension paid will depend on the person's own individual contribution record. State benefits are paid out of current contributions; there is no pool of investments to provide this income. Thus those in employment now are paying the pensions of those who are currently drawing their pension.

Employers who offer an alternative to the state scheme provide a 'contracted-out' scheme. Employees can choose to join the scheme if they qualify on the basis of the scheme rules. If they choose to not join, the employer refers to them as 'contracted-in' to the state scheme. In a contracted-out scheme both employer and employee pay lower-rate National Insurance contributions.

Schemes offered by employers must meet stringent contracting-out conditions. Employees must be told if there is a scheme available to them that is contracted-out of the additional state pension. This should be done in the written particulars given to employees on joining.

FINAL SALARY SCHEMES

These are becoming much less common because most members of such schemes entered employment some years ago and the schemes are often now being closed to new employees. In final salary schemes the employees' pension is based on their salary (usually their final salary when they retire or leave the scheme) and their length of service. They may also receive a lump sum within Inland Revenue limits and the restrictions of the scheme.

In the past inflation has eroded the benefit of a fixed pension. Thus final salary schemes often provide for increases either in line with inflation or according to a simple formula.

These pensions are paid out of funds accumulated from past contributions that have been invested by fund managers, and it is partly their responsibility to ensure that the return on the money invested is sufficient to meet the fund's liabilities for paying pensions. Employers have to pay in sufficient amounts to ensure that the benefits employees (members) are entitled to can be met when an employee retires. A shortfall will have to be met by the company, and the value of the pension fund has to be shown on the Annual Report of a private company – which can affect the share price of that company. This is one reason why many employers are ceasing to offer final salary schemes to new employees.

MONEY-PURCHASE SCHEMES

In a money-purchase scheme, the employee's contributions (together with those of the employer) are invested. The pension the employee gets is based on the total payments into the pension fund, and how well these investments have done. In general, the longer the funds have been invested, the larger the pension the employee gets when he or she retires.

The difficulty here is that the performance of the fund largely determines the final pension that the employee receives at the time an employee retires.

The employee uses the money built up in a money-purchase scheme to buy an *annuity* from an insurance company – an agreement to pay him a pension for life – when he retires. Annuity rates vary, so the final pension can be very dependent on the financial environment over the lifetime of the contributions and at the time the pension has to be taken.

With money-purchase schemes it is the employee, rather than the employer, who takes the risks, but who could, on the other hand, gain if there are fortunate improvements in the financial world.

An employer of five or more people has to offer a *stakeholder pension scheme* unless it is of sufficient size that it can offer an occupational scheme. *Personal pension plans* are set up by or for an employee, whereas stakeholder pensions are offered by the employer. Both are money-purchase-type schemes.

COMMUNICATING WITH THE EMPLOYEE

The Financial Services Act 1986 and subsequent legislation restricts those who can advise on investment matters to *independent financial advisers* who have been trained appropriately.

This means that as an HR practitioner you can advise employees of the options that exist, but you cannot advise them as to which option to take. You cannot advise them to take an employer's scheme, for example, although you can describe the financial benefits, how the scheme works and factual differences such as who pays the administration charges for the scheme.

The same applies to any decisions about a lump sum, their options if they leave your employment or other benefits where the employee has a choice. You should advise that they see an independent financial adviser and never advise them yourself. These are listed in Yellow Pages under 'Financial Advisers'.

ACTIVITY 7.7

This applies if you are in a pension scheme. Look at your latest pensions statement or ask your pension provider for a statement. Take time to understand every aspect of it. It is quite possible that there will be figures that you do not quite understand. So ask questions of your provider if you are unsure. If you are early in your career, it may not seem important now – but it is likely to be so in time. In any event, as an HR practitioner you should understand the essentials of your organisation's pension scheme.

THE ROLE OF HR PRACTITIONERS

Reward can be a complex and specialist area of HR work. Indeed, many very large organisations have individuals or whole teams of reward specialists ensuring that their reward strategy, systems and approaches are at the leading edge of reward practice. In contrast, many smaller organisations rely on general HR practitioners to provide the necessary advice about reward. In some organisations there are salary and wages departments (or, indeed, paying staff may be an outsourced function) to do the administrative work associated with paying people. The different roles HR practitioners are likely to play in reward are as follows.

AN ADVISORY ROLE

You may need to provide both managers and employees with advice about the reward package in your organisation – how it works, what it includes, how decisions are made, etc. This role might be one you need to fulfil on a face-to-face basis, in meetings or by developing written materials (for example, for a staff handbook) to explain the reward system.

A RESEARCH ROLE

This covers finding out about pay rates and reward packages in competitor organisations and the labour market you are operating in. It may involve researching different pay systems and structures and making decisions about which will be appropriate in your organisation.

AN ADMINISTRATIVE ROLE

This could mean implementing your organisation's chosen pay system, some involvement in paying wages and salaries, and administering other aspects of the total reward package, such as holidays or gymnasium memberships.

A MONITORING ROLE

There will be different aspects of the reward system in your organisation that need monitoring. You may have to make sure that the way in which your pay system operates is fair and equitable, and you may have a role in monitoring how competitive your reward package is in your local labour market.

A TRAINING ROLE

You may be called upon from time to time to train others (HR colleagues, line managers, trade union representatives) in how various aspects of the reward system work. You may also have some involvement in raising awareness about the reward package at events such as induction training programmes for new employees.

SUMMARY

- In this chapter we have sought to address the objectives by outlining the key components of reward within an organisation. The various different reward systems and structures available to organisations have been outlined, and some of the pros and cons of each addressed. We have introduced the concept of total reward, which shows that reward is about much more than just pay, and that how reward is dealt with has many links to other aspects of HR work, such as performance and motivation. The law as it relates to pay, including equal pay legislation, has been considered along with the need for specialist advice in this area. We have also provided an overview of one very important aspect of the reward package – ie pensions, an area in which there has been a lot of recent media interest and significant change.

- You will by now be familiar with some of the terminology used in the field of reward and be able to make links with what happens in your organisation. We have suggested a number of different roles for HR practitioners and you will be able to use this as a means of assessing the role that you play in reward in your organisation.

References and further reading are provided immediately below for your information, and Activities have been suggested throughout. You are encouraged to complete some, if not all, of these Activities in order to reinforce and apply your learning.

EXPLORE FURTHER

REFERENCES AND FURTHER READING

ACAS (2006) Advisory Booklet on *Pay Systems*. Leicester: ACAS

ARMSTRONG, M. (2007) *A Handbook of Employee Reward Management and Practice*, 2nd edition. London: Kogan Page

ARMSTRONG, M. (2002) *Employee Reward*, 3rd edition. London: Chartered Institute of Personnel and Development

ARMSTRONG, M. and MURLIS, H. (1991) *Reward Management: A handbook of remuneration strategy and practice*, 2nd edition. London: IPM and Kogan Page

AUDIT COMMISSION (2002) *Recruitment and Retention: A public service workforce for the twenty-first century*

CHILDS, M. and SUFF, P. (2005) *CIPD Reward Management*. London: Chartered Institute of Personnel and Development. (loose-leaf; kept up to date with amendments)

E-reward (2008) *The e-reward grade and pay structure survey* 2007 (online) www.e-reward.co.uk

PERKINS, S. and WHITE, G. (2008) *Employee Reward: Alternatives, consequences and contexts*. London: Chartered Institute of Personnel and Development

SCRIMSHAW, A (2001) *Pensions*. London: Chartered Institute of Personnel and Development

WRIGHT, A. (2004) *Reward Management in Context*. London: Chartered Institute of Personnel and Development

The following are available from the Chartered Institute of Personnel and Development (CIPD), 151 The Broadway, London, SW19 1JQ; tel.: 020 8612 6201:

CIPD (2009) *Reward Management Survey*. Survey Report.

CIPD Factsheets on: *Total Reward* (2009), *Pay and Reward: An overview* (2009), *Pay Structures* (2008), *Pay Progression* (2008)

WEBSITES

Acas: www.acas.org.uk

Chartered Institute of Personnel and Development: www.cipd.co.uk

E-reward: www.e-reward.co.uk

ACTIVITIES FEEDBACK

Activity 7.2

The table below provides some of the pros and cons of basic rate pay systems.

Table 7.2 Basic rate pay systems

Pros	Cons
Relatively cheap and simple to administer and operate	No incentive for improved performance or quality
Certainty and stability in pay for the employee	Individual employees may feel aggrieved if they perceive themselves to work harder or perform better than others
Relative simplicity in how pay progression happens	Can be rigid and hierarchical
Costs of the workforce can be more easily forecast	
Potentially fewer grounds for disagreement and dispute at an individual level	

Activity 7.3

The table below provides some of the pros and cons of variable rate pay systems.

Table 7.3 Variable rate pay systems

Pros	Cons
Rewards individual contribution and performance more directly	Potential subjectivity and perceived bias and unfairness
Can be more flexible and responsive to changing business priorities	Can be damaging to long-term business success in the achievement of short-term results
Can be self-financing and linked to productivity	Can work against effective teamworking
Easier to control increasing pay costs by managing the variable element	

Activity 7.4

Before introducing flexible benefits, an organisation would be well advised to consider:

- how employees feel about the current reward package, and whether they are open to change
- whether the benefits under consideration will be attractive to the employees in that organisation
- whether the resources are available to design, introduce and maintain a flexible benefits package
- whether external expert help should be sought in designing the flexible benefits
- the level of senior management support for the concept.

Activity 7.5

You are unlikely to have listed financial rewards such as hourly rates of pay, service-related benefits, profit-sharing and other team- or company-based rewards where the links between individual effort and the reward are difficult to establish. The list below indicates some of the financial and non-financial rewards that would be more likely to have a motivational impact:

- individual PRP
- bonuses
- incentives
- commission
- accelerated service-related pay
- skill-based pay
- competence-related pay
- praise
- employee of the month title
- feedback
- prizes/awards
- training and development opportunities
- responsibility
- autonomy
- self-development.

Activity 7.6

Some pros:

- If you know what is wrong, you can address it.
- Better to be driving change than be driven by it.
- It gives a chance to negotiate proper remedies rather than being forced into them by an adversarial process.
- In the event of a claim it may help your defence if a policy is in place.
- In the event of a claim it may help your defence if you have done a review.

The following pros are put forward by the Equality and Human Rights Commission:

- Complying with the law and good practice.
- Identifying, explaining and eliminating unjustifiable pay gaps.
- Having rational, fair, transparent pay arrangements.
- Demonstrating to employees and to potential employees a commitment to fairness and equality.

- Demonstrating your values to those you do business with.

You may think of more, equally valid, pros.

Some cons:

- Organisations have more important things to do – like survive.
- You immediately alert workers to the possibility that they may have a claim.
- You may be giving workers ammunition that they could use in a claim.
- Once a claim is made, you lose control.
- Claims are very expensive to defend.
- Remedies can be very expensive too – potentially six years' back pay with interest.
- A code of practice and/or a pay review that is then ignored will be used against the organisation – you could be hoisted by your own petard!
- It is important for you – if badly handled, it could be a career-breaker.

You may think of more, equally valid, cons.

CHAPTER 8

Employee relations

LEARNING OUTCOMES

After reading this chapter you will:

- understand the changing nature and continuing importance of employee relations

- be able to define the differences in the purposes, content and operation of disciplinary, capability and grievance procedures

- understand the good practice steps and statutory requirements that ensure the effective handling of conduct or capability cases

- be able to assess the suitability of a range of tools for managing long- and short-term absences

- realise the importance of responding appropriately to employee grievances concerning individual and collective matters

- appreciate the part played by employee involvement initiatives, including employee communications and consultation, in unionised and non-unionised environments, in seeking to introduce change and maintain harmonious employee relations

- be able to analyse which employee involvement approaches are likely to be suitable for your own organisation.

INTRODUCTION

In this chapter we will be considering employee relations within organisations. David Farnham (2000: xxiii) defined employee relations as:

> that part of managing people that enables competent managers to balance, within acceptable limits, the interests of employers as buyers of labour services and those of employees as suppliers of labour services in the labour market and workplace. Within this framework, the main task of those responsible for managing the employment relationship is to develop appropriate institutions, policies and rules to promote 'good' working relationships with those whom they employ. This means preventing unnecessary conflict between management and employees over those matters in which both parties have mutual, though sometimes diverging, interests.

However, it is a field of HR practice and an approach that has changed much over recent years, and it is worth considering other views of what employee relations is. In the CIPD Change agenda survey (2005) into 'What is Employee Relations?', interviews with HR executives, leading organisations and a review of academic research indicated that employee relations is still an important aspect of HR work, but gave no single definition. It was seen as a field of work that comprises:

- managing the employment contract and relationships
- ensuring compliance with employment law
- communication with employees
- promoting retention, involvement and engagement
- collective processes of negotiation and consultation.

Thus employee relations involves managing conflict situations and seeking to gain the commitment of employees to organisational goals. Both these aspects will be addressed in this chapter.

Conflict, potential or actual, may be of an individual or collective nature. In this chapter our emphasis will be on individual conflict situations, because these are the ones most likely to be faced by the majority of the readers of this book. Such individual conflict is likely to be born out of differences between employers and employees on matters such as conduct, performance, absence, working relationships, individual employment rights and contractual matters and communication. Formal procedures will exist in most organisations for dealing with discipline and grievance matters that arise. Procedures may also exist, particularly in larger organisations, on issues such as capability, bullying and harassment, absence and whistle-blowing. It should be noted, however, that employee relations does not just operate at a formal level, and that much of the interaction between managers and staff can be construed as employee relations. There has also been a growth in the use of less formal and less procedural approaches to dealing with conflict – for example, workplace mediation.

Later in the chapter we will be referring to strategies aimed at averting collective conflict – ie situations that involve groups of individuals or the whole workforce. Our contention is that collective conflict is often triggered by organisational changes such as restructuring, changes in ownership or working arrangements and relocation. Managers must take care to ensure that they comply with their legal obligations in their communications, consultations and other means of involving employees as well as adopting good practices.

In the opening sections of this chapter we set out to explain what we mean by disciplinary rules and disciplinary, capability and grievance procedures. We highlight the importance of the revised Acas Code of Practice 2009 and the Acas Guide. We consider good practices in disciplinary, capability and grievance-handling as well as exploring bullying and harassment, whistle-blowing and a number of absence management tools. We then move on to consider effective strategies for employee involvement, including those involving trade unions. We also briefly cover the impact of the psychological contract on the management of employee relations. All of the above is set against the backdrop of relevant legislation, much of which has been covered in Chapter 3.

Finally, we look at the complex nature of the role of HR practitioners in employee relations. Suggested activities to develop your knowledge and skills in this important area can be found throughout the chapter. More information on the associated skills can be found in Chapter 12.

First, we shall consider how employee relations has been changing and why it is so important that potential individual conflicts, such as disciplinary incidents and employee grievances, and potential collective conflicts, such as plans to introduce new technology, are handled with skill and according to laid-down procedures.

THE CHANGING NATURE AND FOCUS OF EMPLOYEE RELATIONS

The term 'employee relations' has gradually come to replace the term 'industrial relations', and in doing so, reflects a change in the nature and focus of relationships in the workplace. As the CIPD outlines in its survey, 'industrial relations' is generally used and understood to mean relationships in the workplace that are collective – ie between the employer and groups of employees. 'Employee relations' tends to be used more in connection with matters to do with individual employment. In recent years there has been a decline in the number of matters dealt with on a collective basis and an increasing focus on relationships with individual employees. A number of different factors indicate this shift:

- a significant decline in trade union membership
- a significant decline in the number of employees covered by collective agreements
- a significant decline in the range of matters addressed by collective bargaining
- a shift in what union officials spend their time on – from negotiating pay and conditions to individual representation and support
- a reduction in industrial action
- the increasing importance attached to the employee 'voice' and employee involvement
- growing interest in the use of mediation to resolve disputes.

This individual employee relations activity is a key aspect of managing people in all organisations and will be something both managers and HR professionals spend a significant amount of time on. Additionally, in certain sectors and types of organisation – for example, the public sector, some larger private sector organisations and former public sector bodies – collective employee relations still plays a major role. Further information on the collective aspects of employee relations is included later in this chapter.

WHY IS IT IMPORTANT TO MANAGE EMPLOYEE RELATIONS?

It is important to have a focus on and positive approach to employee relations for a number of reasons, including creating a climate for productive relationships at work and to fulfil legal obligations. We consider here a couple of the formal mechanisms for managing employee relations. Concentrating on discipline first, rules and procedures exist to help employees to improve their performance. They should not be regarded as just a means by which managers can dismiss employees legally. There are several outcomes of poor practice in addressing disciplinary matters:

- A lax approach to potential disciplinary incidents will lead to an ill-disciplined workforce who do not respect management's authority and are likely to 'play the system' to their own advantage – eg by making their own decisions about working methods and break times. When managers do want to assert their authority by, say, enforcing break times, employees will rightly point to the fact that established custom and practice have overridden written policy and procedure.

- An overenthusiastic or inconsistent use of the disciplinary rules and procedures will lead to employee discontent and is unlikely to be beneficial in realising employee potential and thus maximising productivity.

- Ultimately, management may be faced with a decision to dismiss an employee. If their reason is insufficient (eg they have overreacted to the incident), or if they act unreasonably in dismissing that employee (eg by failing to follow the procedure correctly), the chance of the employee's making a successful claim of unfair dismissal to an employment tribunal is increased. Fighting such claims will be costly and time-consuming and, regardless of the outcome, does little to enhance the reputation of the organisation in the eyes of its employees and outside parties.

Turning now to grievance-handling, procedures exist to enable employees to have a formal means of complaint about their terms and conditions, working environment and related issues. Failure to encourage use of this provision or to respond appropriately to grievances will result in:

- discontent among the workforce because they feel that management are not interested in and do not value their views. This may lead to poor motivation and low productivity

- missed opportunities to tackle problems at an early stage to ensure that they do not continue, thus creating difficulties for other employees. For example, claims of harassment, discrimination and bullying should be handled carefully and be fully investigated to avoid accusations of unreasonable delay or indecision. Failure to do this could lead to constructive dismissal claims

- the threat of industrial action when complaints about issues which affect several employees – such as health and safety matters – are perceived by the workforce to have been handled badly.

Similarly, with regard to collective conflict situations, failure actively to involve employees, listen to their requests or concerns and/or seek their buy-in to proposals can result in a range of responses from apathy and lack of commitment to employment tribunal claims, strikes and other forms of industrial action.

We will now look at these matters in more detail.

DISCIPLINE

The legislation relevant to the handling of disciplinary matters (and grievances) is referred to and commented on throughout this chapter. The major piece of relevant legislation is the Employment Rights Act 1996 (ERA). This Act contains most of the legislation applicable to the individual rights of employees, including the right not to be unfairly dismissed for employees who have one year's continuous service, regardless of the number of hours worked.

Obviously, not every disciplinary situation will result in a dismissal, fair or unfair, but HR practitioners and line managers would be well advised to bear in mind the provisions of ERA and the guidelines provided by Acas (see below). This is because the manner in which previous disciplinary situations have been handled will be taken into account by employment tribunals when considering unfair dismissal applications.

Let's consider two examples of this:

- A manager who claims that a dismissed employee was previously warned about the consequences of continued poor timekeeping will have to be able to produce the requisite records, the notes of disciplinary interviews and letters of confirmation to the employee concerned.

- In a case of poor performance, the manager will need to produce evidence that he or she reviewed the situation with the employee at regular intervals, communicated the standards of performance required, set realistic targets for improvement, provided the necessary support mechanisms to help the individual to improve, monitored the situation and kept records of subsequent performance before any decision to dismiss. Further, the manager will have to show that the messages given out to the employee at formal appraisal interviews did not contradict those issued in the disciplinary context.

All organisations, large or small, should have in place written disciplinary and grievance procedures and, we would recommend, a separate capability procedure to deal with poor performance and ill-health cases. In unionised environments, these documents must be agreed with the trade union(s). The procedures then form part of the conditions of employment within the organisation. The Advisory, Conciliation and Arbitration Service (Acas) Code of Practice 1: *Disciplinary and Grievance Procedures* 2009 gives guidance to employers on the content and operation of disciplinary rules and procedures, and the Acas Guide – *Discipline and Grievances at Work* – provides good practice advice for dealing with discipline and grievances in the workplace.

DISCIPLINARY RULES

We shall deal first with disciplinary rules. These set the standards of behaviour and conduct expected in the workplace. The contents of the rules vary greatly depending on the size of the organisation, the industry, management style, the history of employee relations, etc. It is likely, however, that they will refer to the following:

- general conduct
- health and safety
- security
- time-keeping and attendance.

Examples of disciplinary rules under each of the above might include:

- Disorderly conduct, threatening behaviour, skylarking, horseplay or loitering is strictly forbidden in any part of the works.
- Any defects in personal protective equipment must be reported immediately by the employee to his or her supervisor.
- Employees are strictly forbidden to take from the works any materials, tools, equipment, or other company property unless written permission is first obtained from their departmental manager.
- Under no circumstances is an employee permitted to deface his or her clock card, to clock any card other than his or her own, or to tamper with the clocks.

The type of organisation to which these rules might be applicable is not difficult to guess. What do you think – a small retailing outfit, a high-street bank or a heavy engineering concern?

Disciplinary rules help to ensure a consistent and fair approach to the treatment of employees. Managers obviously wish to have a disciplined workforce, but the majority of employees are likely to be just as keen to have a set of rules in operation so that their working lives can be reasonably orderly, and so that they are clear about the behavioural standards expected of them.

Breaches of disciplinary rules vary in their seriousness. It is always a good idea to consider whether an informal discussion is appropriate to resolve the issue before moving into the use of formal procedures. However, once a decision has been made to deal with an issue formally, then the types of action you should consider are:

- Minor infringements – eg an occasional late arrival at work – might merit a verbal warning.
- More serious infringements – eg failure to complete quality checks properly – might result in a written warning.
- Gross misconduct – eg theft, fighting, negligence or fraud – will probably result in summary dismissal (dismissal without notice or pay in lieu of notice).

You should always point out to an employee that failure to heed warnings by engaging in repeated breaches of the rules – eg continued poor attendance – may ultimately result in dismissal.

It has been mentioned that management must seek to be fair and consistent in applying the disciplinary rules. However, no two disciplinary incidents are ever identical. Thus managers must always ensure that they take into account the circumstances of the case before them. For instance, they are likely to deal less severely with a previously satisfactory employee whose poor attendance is due to temporary domestic commitments than with a newer employee who has already had some attendance problems. Depending on the circumstances of an employee's case, the manager may decide that disciplinary action is inappropriate and that an informal approach is more appropriate. This might include the manager's arranging for counselling to take place (see Figure 8.1 on page 226). Some may see this as a soft option (putting off the inevitable), but this approach is entirely consistent with the aim of disciplinary rules and procedures – ie assisting employees to improve their performance rather than providing the means for managers to dismiss employees legally.

We shall now consider disciplinary procedures. For more information on disciplinary and capability procedures and practices, refer to the book *The Employer's Guide to Grievance and Discipline Procedures* by Mike Parkin (details at the end of this chapter).

DISCIPLINARY PROCEDURES

We have seen that where standards of conduct are not met, management may decide to take some form of disciplinary action against the employee(s) concerned. Disciplinary procedures provide guidelines for adherence to the rules and a fair method of dealing with infringements.

The Acas Guide 2009 lists the following essential features of disciplinary procedures. Good disciplinary procedures should:

- be put in writing
- be non-discriminatory
- provide for matters to be dealt with speedily
- allow for information to be kept confidential
- tell employees what disciplinary action might be taken
- say what levels of management have the authority to take the various forms of disciplinary action
- require employees to be informed of the complaints against them and supporting evidence, before any meeting
- give employees a chance to have their say before management reaches a decision
- provide employees with the right to be accompanied

- provide that no employee is dismissed for a first breach of discipline, except in cases of gross misconduct
- require management to investigate fully before any disciplinary action is taken
- ensure that employees are given an explanation for any sanction, and
- allow employees to appeal against a decision.

The procedures should also:

- apply to all employees, irrespective of their length of service, status or number of hours worked
- ensure that any investigatory period of suspension is with pay, and specify how pay is to be calculated during such period. If, exceptionally, suspension is to be without pay, this must be provided for in the contract of employment
- ensure that any suspension is brief, and is never used as a sanction against the employee prior to a disciplinary meeting and decision
- ensure that the employee will be heard in good faith and that there is no pre-judgement of the issue
- ensure that where the facts are in dispute, no disciplinary penalty is imposed until the case has been carefully investigated, and there is a reasonably held belief that the employee committed the act in question.

The Guide also advises that all formal disciplinary actions should be confirmed in writing to the employee concerned. Further, when deciding on the level of disciplinary action (if any), managers should take account of the employee's record and any other relevant factors (often referred to as 'extenuating circumstances').

Acas is empowered by the Secretary of State for Business, Innovation and Skills to issue codes of practice such as the one referred to above. Failure to observe the provisions of a code of practice will not of itself render a person liable to any proceedings. However, a code of practice is admissible in evidence in any tribunal proceedings, and if any provision is relevant to any questions arising in the proceedings, it will be taken into account in determining that question. Furthermore, a failure to follow the Acas Guide can lead to an award for unfair dismissal being increased

The message here is very clear: regardless of the size of your organisation, you should ensure that you incorporate the 'essential features' listed above in your disciplinary procedure. Further, once disciplinary rules and procedures have been formulated in conjunction with interested parties, managers must ensure that the written procedure matches up with the actual practice within the organisation (or employees will have a head start in pursuing their claims at an employment tribunal).

Failure to follow the correct procedure is one of the most common arguments put forward (often successfully) by representatives of unfair dismissal applicants. Examples of such failures include:

- not distinguishing between misconduct and poor performance – eg a failure to achieve performance targets may be the result of inadequate training or poor supervision, rendering a disciplinary sanction inappropriate. Alternatively, the shortfall in performance may be due to a medical problem, in which case a capability procedure should be followed. (See the section on capability procedures on page 227)

- an incomplete or prejudiced investigation – eg managers ignoring the evidence of a key witness or failing to keep an open mind about the possible outcome of the enquiry

- the improper constitution of a disciplinary hearing – eg a supervisor on night-shift making a decision to issue a final written warning when he or she is not authorised to do so

- the absence of a person suitably independent to hear an appeal against a disciplinary decision – eg because the manager who should hear the appeal has been involved in either the investigations or the discussions leading up to the disciplinary decision

- an employee not being accompanied – eg because the manager assumed that the employee was familiar with this right and would make his or her own arrangements

- an employee not being reminded of the right to appeal and the procedure for so doing (this is an illustration of the importance of keeping accurate notes of all disciplinary hearings so that the validity of such an allegation can be checked).

ERA also states that employers must give new employees written particulars of employment within two months of their starting date, including dismissal and disciplinary procedures. The written statement must specify the disciplinary rules. (Please note that the term 'dismissal procedures' also applies to non-disciplinary terminations such as with capability cases or fixed-term contracts.)

Managers should not, however, assume that 'offending' employees are fully conversant with the contents and operation of the organisation's employment policies. It is often the case that our working lives are so busy that we are forced to adopt a 'need-to-know' approach regarding the information that we take in. Thus previously exemplary employees would have had no need to know intimately the workings of the disciplinary procedure.

So what can the employer do to bring the disciplinary rules and procedures to the attention of the workforce? There are several options – incorporate this subject into the induction programme, make copies readily available to all employees (using appropriate means, including the company intranet), or provide training for newly appointed line managers and refresher training for existing ones (organisations often wait for disasters to occur before doing this – eg a finding of unfair dismissal at a tribunal hearing). Further, if management decide to clamp down on certain activities – eg careless timekeeping, 'casual' sickness absence or private work during company time – they should publicise this by, say, including it on the agenda of team meetings, by issuing emails and by compiling reports highlighting statistical trends.

Now consider Activity 8.1.

ACTIVITY 8.1

Have a look at your organisation's disciplinary policy and rules. Are they clear and easy to follow? How are they brought to the attention of new and existing employees? How far do they contain the essential features identified by Acas? See if you can identify any changes needed, and discuss these with one of your learning sources.

We will now summarise the key elements in implementing disciplinary procedures.

Good practice in implementing a disciplinary procedure

It is advisable for disciplinary procedures to reflect the principles of the Acas Code of Practice and Guide and to ensure that the following guidance is adhered to:

- Disciplinary processes should be carried out promptly and consistently.
- All necessary investigation should be carried out to establish the facts.
- The employee should be informed of the basis of the problem and be given an opportunity to put his or her side of the story.
- The employee should be informed of the right to be accompanied by a work colleague or by a certified trade union representative or employed trade union official, and allowed to be so accompanied.
- The employee should be allowed to appeal.

It is important to note that wherever possible the different elements of investigation, putting the case to the employee and hearing their side of the story, and the appeal should be handled by different people. This avoids the possible criticism that a manager has prejudged the situation and is not, therefore, of an independent mind.

It is worth pointing out that in disciplinary situations, including dismissal, managers are not expected to prove that an employee is guilty of an offence (as in a court of law) but to establish, after a full investigation, a 'reasonable belief' that the employee committed the offence.

With regard to the first stage – that of investigation – you will need to collect evidence of the relevant acts, omissions or conduct under consideration and accompanying documentation. As well as the disciplinary procedure itself, you will need copies of relevant rules and company policies – eg health and safety, equality and diversity – and the employee's contract of employment and employment records on, say, attendance, training, appraisal and previous disciplinary incidents. Factual data such as production figures and cost or quality information may also be needed, along with physical evidence such as 'stolen property' and video recordings.

If you need to interview the employee during this stage, ensure that he or she is aware that it is an investigatory hearing and not a disciplinary hearing. Further, make sure that in practice this distinction is a clear one.

Next, if on the face of it disciplinary action seems to be warranted, you should write to the employee outlining the allegations made and inviting him or her to a disciplinary meeting to discuss the matter. You must then hold a meeting, for which detailed guidelines are provided in Table 8.3 on page 238.

With regard to the equally important stage of conducting the disciplinary appeal, the Acas Guide *Discipline and Grievances at Work* (2009) recommends that an internal appeals procedure should:

- specify a time-limit within which the appeal should be lodged
- provide for appeals to be dealt with speedily, particularly those involving suspension or dismissal
- wherever possible, provide for the appeal to be heard by someone senior in authority to the person who took the disciplinary decision and, if possible, who was not involved in the original meeting or decision
- spell out what action may be taken by those hearing the appeal
- set out the right to be accompanied at any appeal meeting
- provide for the employee, or a companion if the employee so wishes, to have the opportunity to comment on any new evidence arising during the appeal before any decision is taken.

See Case study 8.1.

CASE STUDY 8.1

Is it possible to get it right? One organisation – a charity – did. The organisation found that pornographic images were stored on an IT employee's computer and there was evidence to suggest that such material had been passed between the members of the department. There was a concern among the managers that if they were not seen to take decisive action, they might be viewed as condoning similar behaviour in the future as well as running the risk of receiving harassment claims and, possibly, a criminal conviction. After an investigation, the IT manager was unable to identify the guilty party or parties, and so reluctantly decided to dismiss all four employees in the department. One employee appealed, but the appeal was turned down and subsequently the same employee submitted an unfair dismissal claim.

In summarising the reasons for the finding of fair dismissal, the tribunal chair pointed out that:

- the organisation did have an established Internet and email policy that clearly

- specified what was 'acceptable use' and which actions were prohibited
- infringement of this policy was listed as an example of gross misconduct in the organisation's disciplinary procedure
- a thorough investigation had taken place, but the employer had not been able to discover which employee/s

were to blame, and so had dismissed all four employees on the grounds of a reasonable suspicion

- it was noted that the employees had been unhelpful during the investigations and there were no mitigating factors to be taken account of.

ACTIVITY 8.2

If you are inexperienced in handling disciplinary situations, ask if you could sit in on a disciplinary interview as an observer only. Try to identify good and bad practices (diplomatically, of course). Did you agree with the decision reached? If not, seek to discuss the reasons for the decision with the manager concerned.

We have now looked at the content and operation of disciplinary rules and procedures as well as the effect of relevant employment legislation. Before moving on to the issue of capability procedures, we must consider when disciplinary action is necessary. The flowchart in Figure 8.1 should help.

In Figure 8.1 we can see that although conduct is unsatisfactory in some manner, there may be extenuating circumstances that merit consideration and render disciplinary action unwise or unjustifiable. The manager may decide that counselling is a more appropriate option and either personally undertake this role or arrange for a 'specialist' to do so (see Chapter 12 for more information on counselling). In this process the manager is likely to have asked whether the unsatisfactory conduct is within the control of the employee or not. If not, then disciplinary action is rarely appropriate because there is an underlying assumption that the employee has the ability to change and the use of a capability procedure is generally more advisable. (See the CIPD *Policies and Procedures for People Managers* manual listed at the end of this section for in-depth advice on discipline and capability handling.)

Figure 8.1   Disciplinary action checklist

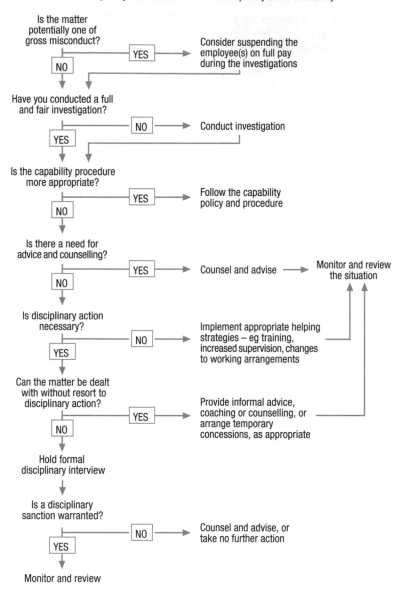

CAPABILITY

CAPABILITY PROCEDURES

These may be designed to cover poor performance and ill health. We will deal first with poor performance cases.

Poor performance

Employers are entitled to expect their employees to produce work of good quality and in accordance with sensible deadlines. Where an employee fails to meet the required standards, the manager concerned may decide to invoke disciplinary action. This would be appropriate if the employee is simply not trying and has the ability to change his or her behaviour. Our suggestion, however, is that poor performance is generally not a conduct issue, and a separate capability procedure would therefore be more appropriate.

The Acas Guide *Discipline and Grievances at Work* stresses the need to carry out a full investigation in seeking to identify the cause of the problem. It proposes the following actions:

- Ask the employee for an explanation – check this explanation, if possible.

- If the reason is lack of necessary skills, give the employee training and time to reach the required standard.

- If, despite encouragement and assistance, the required standard cannot be reached, consider finding the employee suitable alternative work.

- Issue an improvement note to encourage the employee to reach a satisfactory standard.

- Meet the employee to discuss the improvement note (and agree actions).

The advisory handbook also states that:

- An employee should not normally be dismissed because of unsatisfactory performance unless warnings and a chance to improve have been given, with additional training if necessary.

- If the main cause of the unsatisfactory performance is the changing nature of the job, employers should consider whether the situation may properly be treated as redundancy rather than as a capability issue.

Further, where poor performance may arise from a disability, consideration must be given to any reasonable adjustment that could enable the employee to reach a reasonable standard of performance. In an assembly environment, for example, a reasonable adjustment could mean providing special seating for an employee with back problems.

It is essential that the performance is monitored at all stages and that full records, including notes of meetings, are kept.

These good practice steps are demonstrated in Case study 8.2.

A company selling electrical goods had employed one sales executive for three years. He reported to one of four regional sales managers (RSMs) who, in turn, reported to the sales director. In the last six months, the RSM had issued the sales executive with two written warnings for minor incidents. One concerned the late submission of a report and statistics, and the other his failure to follow the notification of sickness absence procedure. More recently she issued him with a final written warning (FWW) because she couldn't contact him during working hours. The sales executive felt that he had been badly treated and lodged an appeal.

At the appeals hearing, which was conducted by the sales director, the sales executive said that his problems with his job had several causes. He hadn't told the RSM anything about them because he didn't get on with her and felt that she would be unsympathetic. The causes were:

- He had a number of personal problems, not least trying to gain access to see his children since his marriage break-up.

- There had been a change in the computer package used for his work and he was really struggling to adapt to it.

- He was feeling very stressed and insecure, and at the suggestion of his GP had been visiting a counsellor when the RSM had tried to contact him. He had a letter confirming his state of health from his GP, and pointed out that he had made up the time the following day.

The sales director concluded that this case had been inappropriately dealt with under the disciplinary procedure to date, although there were understandable reasons for this. She upheld the appeal and withdrew the FWW. Nevertheless, she informed the sales executive that his performance still needed to improve. In future, this would be handled in accordance with the company's capability procedure and the company would do its best to help him with regard to IT training and his personal and health problems.

Next we consider cases of ill health.

Ill health (long-term and short-term)

Case law suggests that disciplinary procedures are inappropriate in most circumstances relating to sickness absence, whether it is long-term or short-term. Ill-health capability procedures follow a rather different route from disciplinary procedures (although both may have the same conclusion – ie dismissal of the employee). The key elements of an ill-health capability procedure are:

- consultation with the employee – ie maintaining regular contact throughout the period of absence and fully involving the employee in the decision-making process. Remember that for meetings which may result in actions such as warnings, demotion or dismissal, the employee has a statutory right to be accompanied (see page 235). This right does not apply to informal or investigatory meetings or counselling sessions

- a medical investigation – ie gathering medical evidence on the likelihood of an early return to work and the suitability of the current position

- consideration, where appropriate, of alternative employment (and/or reasonable adjustments in the case of disabled employees) before any decision to dismiss (or retire) the employee.

In tribunal proceedings, the panel, in reaching their decision on whether a dismissal was fair or unfair, will consider whether these elements were provided by employers.

Unfortunately, there are other pitfalls in store for you in ill-health dismissals. You may have followed the above good practice guidelines, but what if the dismissal occurred during the employee's contractual entitlement to sick pay? In such a case the employee may have a claim for breach of contract if there is no express term to permit this. You should note the following approach to dismissing an employee on the grounds of sickness:

1 Check the contract of employment for relevant clauses and seek legal advice if there are ambiguities.

2 Ensure that you follow a correct procedure (see the key elements listed above).

3 Ensure that the provisions of the Disability Discrimination Act 1995 are taken into account before making your final decision.

We have mainly concentrated above on long-term sickness absences. What about short-term absences?

Sometimes we tend to forget that employees may genuinely be sick, and if these are infrequent occurrences where proper notification and certification procedures have been followed, then no further action is likely to be necessary. If the absences are genuine but frequent, you should follow the capability procedure as set out above.

On the other hand, if investigations show that absences are not genuine (for instance, an employee returning from a period of absence with a deep suntan might lead you to investigate more fully), you should follow the normal disciplinary procedure because this is a conduct issue. However, it is often the case that suspected 'casual' absences cannot be proven, so you should be wary of treating absences as misconduct. Do not despair, though, for unacceptable levels of attendance can be dealt with by ensuring a fair review of the attendance record, allowing the employee to make representations, gathering medical evidence (which could reveal genuine underlying causes), seeking to help the employee to improve his or her attendance record and warning him or her of the consequences should that improvement not occur. If there is no adequate improvement, dismissal should be a justifiable option.

SICKNESS ABSENCE MANAGEMENT TOOLS

Whatever the cause, duration or validity of sickness absences, it is undisputed that the cost to industry is very high. A survey of 642 UK employers conducted by the CIPD in 2009 revealed that UK employees are taking an average of 7.4 sick days off every year, at an average cost of £692 per employee per year.

According to the survey, a third of employers have an employee well-being strategy in place, in which the most common benefits are:

- access to counselling services
- employee assistance programmes
- support to stop smoking
- subsidised gym membership.

So what can you do to reduce sickness absence? You would be advised to adopt the good practice steps outlined above alongside a combination of absence management tools. You may wish to make your choice based on the conclusions of the CIPD survey, which looked at a range of absence management tools and drew conclusions on their effectiveness, as shown in Tables 8.1 and 8.2.

Table 8.1 The most effective tools for managing short-term absence

Most effective part of short-term absence management approach	Percentage of organisations specifying this as one of the most effective tools
Return-to-work interviews for all absences	64
Use of trigger mechanism to review attendance	29
Disciplinary procedures for unacceptable absence	23
Restricting sick pay	16

Source: CIPD (2009) *Absence Management* Annual survey report

Table 8.2 The most effective tools for managing long-term absence

Most effective part of long-term absence management approach	Percentage of organisations specifying this as one of the most effective tools
Occupational health professional involvement	44
Return-to-work interviews	17
Flexible working	16
Rehabilitation programme	15
Changes to work patterns or environment	12
Capability procedure restricting sick pay	10

Source: CIPD (2009) *Absence Management* Annual survey report

ACTIVITY 8.3

Consider your own organisation. Which absence management tools are currently used? How successful do you think they are? If you were to adopt a different approach, which tools would you recommend, and why? Discuss your thoughts with one of your learning sources.

Now we turn to grievance-handling.

HANDLING GRIEVANCES

Case law dictates that employees must be provided with a means by which they can officially raise complaints and seek redress. As with disciplinary procedures, ERA declares that details of the grievance procedure must be contained in the written statement of employment. It is good practice to have a written grievance procedure. Employers should encourage employees to raise concerns so that problems can be dealt with at an early stage before they start to affect other employees. Otherwise, the problems may escalate into more serious issues and can even result in industrial action. This is more likely if the grievance raised affects a large number of employees rather than just a handful. Nevertheless, it is difficult to predict which unresolved grievances could provide the trigger for industrial unrest – for example, a poorly handled redundancy selection programme affecting only one or two employees could have a disruptive effect on the motivation and productivity of the rest of the workforce.

In theory, then, managers should welcome grievances, but the experience of many employees is that management view those who raise them as nuisances or troublemakers. What is your view?

You should therefore ensure that employees are aware of the existence of the grievance procedure by publicising it through the induction programme for new employees, making copies readily available to all employees, making known the results of successfully resolved grievances and providing specialist training for all levels of management likely to be involved in handling grievances.

It cannot be stressed enough how important it is for grievances to be dealt with in an appropriate manner. If an employee has decided to make a complaint formal, it usually means that he or she feels strongly about the issue and will not, therefore, appreciate a manager attempting to trivialise the complaint. Further, if employees perceive that managers never seem to respond to formal complaints, the incidence of grievances may fall. This does not then mean that there are no problems, but that employees are too demotivated to raise them. It is unlikely to result in an energised and productive working situation.

Examples of issues likely to be raised under grievance procedures include:

- working conditions – eg lighting, heating

- use of equipment – eg poorly maintained tools
- personality clashes
- refused requests – eg timing of annual leave, shift changes
- shortfalls in pay – eg late bonus payments, adjustments to overtime pay
- allocation of 'perks' – eg Sunday overtime working
- the imposition of company policies or practices
- terms and conditions.

More serious matters would include:

- complaints about deductions from pay
- allegations of sex or race discrimination.

The type of issues included within the scope of grievance procedures vary from one workplace to the next.

We shall now look more specifically at the content of grievance procedures.

GRIEVANCE PROCEDURES

Grievance procedures are the means by which employees can formally raise complaints with management. The aim is to resolve these issues as near as possible to the location of the original complaint. Grievance procedures should be:

- equitable in the way in which employees are treated
- simple to understand
- rapid in their application.

Further, in the interests of natural justice, the investigation of a grievance should be conducted by an unbiased individual.

The outcome of a successfully handled grievance would be a solution that satisfies all the parties. For example, an employee with a justifiable complaint about the unequal distribution of overtime would probably be satisfied if a new written procedure was drawn up to avoid this in the future. Management are also likely to be happy, because this should minimise the likelihood of similar complaints in the future. Sometimes, though, there is no satisfactory solution available, so management's job becomes one not of problem-solving but of explanation and persuasion. Employees will often initially view the effect of a decision as unfair but will be more likely to accept it if they know why it was made. (See Chapter 12 for more information on the important skills of negotiating, persuading and influencing.)

As for the content of grievance procedures, the procedures often follow the stages set out below:

Informal stage – The employee should first raise the matter with his or her immediate manager, or a manager from another department if that is more appropriate.

Stage 1 – If the matter remains unresolved, the employee can raise the matter formally in writing with the relevant manager. A meeting will be arranged with the employee, the companion (if applicable) and the relevant manager. The decision will be confirmed in writing.

Stage 2 – If the employee wishes to appeal against the decision, a meeting will be arranged with the employee, the companion (if applicable) and the relevant senior manager. The subsequent decision will be confirmed in writing.

Stage 3 – If the employee wishes to appeal against *that* decision, a meeting will be arranged to include the functional director and the companion/union regional officer (if applicable). The subsequent decision will be confirmed in writing.

Note that:

- Each stage will be timebound so that a speedy resolution can be sought.

- In a smaller organisation, the grievance procedure may contain only two formal stages.

- In non-unionised organisations, it is likely that the decision given by the authorised officer at the final stage is a binding one – ie there is no further internal right of appeal.

- In unionised organisations, if there is a failure to agree at Stage 3, the arrangements outlined in the organisation's disputes procedure may come into play – eg independent conciliation or arbitration or, possibly, a ballot for industrial action. Thus the grievance procedure and the disputes procedure dovetail at the final stage. Any form of industrial action is precluded until all the stages have been completed and a failure to agree recorded – ie the procedure has been exhausted.

CASE STUDY 8.3

A company was faced with a grievance submitted by a female employee who had been nominated to attend a weekend training event. The employee did not want to go and approached her immediate manager to complain that she was only given two weeks' notice and would find it difficult to arrange for childcare. The line manager followed the procedure, met with the employee to clarify the problem and sought expert advice on a range of possible options. He realised that the training was necessary and would be expensive to cancel. He found it difficult to reach a decision that was satisfactory to all parties. In this instance, the employee was not satisfied by the response she received at this informal stage, but did agree to the compromise solution proposed at the formal Stage 1 meeting.

ACTIVITY 8.4

In carrying out his investigations, what questions did the supervisor need to find the answers to before reaching a decision?

Compare your response with the feedback given at the end of this chapter.

HR practitioners often feel that they are in a difficult position in handling grievances. Often, their only formalised role is to take receipt of grievances at Stage 1 and onwards. A good record-keeping system should assist them in determining whether any previous decisions have established precedents for handling similar grievances. Some HR practitioners will, however, initiate the investigations and discussions necessary in order to address grievances and may also attend grievance hearings. These actions will help them to keep a tight rein on such matters so that line managers do not seek resolutions to grievances without thinking through the consequences for the rest of the organisation.

For instance, in our previous example regarding the unequal distribution of overtime, it is unlikely that changes to overtime allocation arrangements within one department could be taken in isolation of all other departments. Dependent on the organisational position of the HR department (and personal standing of its members), HR practitioners will have varying degrees of success in seeking to influence such decisions.

WHISTLE-BLOWING

'Whistle-blowing' is the term used to describe a situation in which an employee perceives a wrongdoing at work and reports it to an outsider. The Public Interest Disclosure Act 1998 contains employment guarantees for employees who have made a protected disclosure so that they may not be dismissed or suffer detriment for so doing. The types of disclosure covered by the Act concern criminal offences, failure to comply with legal obligations, miscarriages of justice, health and safety risks, and environmental damage. If an employee feels safe and confident to raise the matters of concern with his or her employer, this is invariably to the employer's advantage. It may be that there has been a misunderstanding. But more importantly, it enables the employer to deal with the matter before other agencies become involved.

Employers must, of course, comply with the terms of the Act but could be more proactive by reviewing the arrangements that would be necessary to allow employees to raise these types of concern. It may be that the existing grievance procedure can simply be revised or that a separate policy and procedure should be implemented to reflect the greater sensitivity and seriousness attached to such matters. This can be particularly valuable in the care sector where a 'whistle-blower's policy' can protect employees who report those colleagues who are abusing vulnerable people. However, abuse of the policy itself (by malicious reporting) would result in disciplinary action.

BULLYING AND HARASSMENT

An employee relations issue that has been growing in importance and has had more attention given to it by employers over recent years is bullying and harassment. Both bullying and harassment can be very damaging in the workplace and can lead to a negative impact on individual health, levels of motivation and morale, the employee relations climate at work and individual relationships. It is an issue that must be taken seriously and be seen to be taken seriously by employers – it should not be tolerated in the workplace. In the Acas guide for managers and employers on bullying and harassment it is stated that those making a complaint often define bullying and harassment as something that has happened that is unwanted, unwelcome and has a negative impact on them. They advise that any such complaints should be treated as a grievance which must be dealt with. The normal grievance procedures should be used for this, although in many larger organisations there will be specific procedures for dealing with bullying and harassment. The legislation on discrimination (covered elsewhere in this book) also provides protection from harassment on the grounds of sex, race, disability, sexual orientation, religion or belief.

ACTIVITY 8.5

What sort of behaviours would you consider to be bullying and harassment? Do some further reading and research to see what behaviours are generally held to be bullying and harassment. How does your list compare?

For more information on grievances in the workplace, see the CIPD *Policies and Procedures for People Managers* manual listed at the end of this chapter.

THE RIGHT TO BE ACCOMPANIED AT HEARINGS

As we have already stated, the Acas Code of Practice on disciplinary and grievance procedures provides guidance on the statutory right for workers when they face certain disciplinary or grievance hearings to be accompanied by either a fellow-worker or a trade union official.

This right applies to any disciplinary hearing at which action may be contemplated against an employee. Thus it may be that it would not apply to an investigation, especially if that is solely concerned with obtaining facts. It would apply to a consultation on ill-health absence, if continuation of employment could be an issue – even though this is not a disciplinary matter.

With regard to grievance hearings, the right applies to meetings at which employers deal with complaints about duties owed by them to workers, whether the duty arises from statute or common law.

Your disciplinary and grievance procedures and practices should reflect these rights. Perhaps you should check to ensure that this is the case.

Before moving on to consider the case for employee involvement, we will deal with the skills necessary for successful disciplinary, capability and grievance hearings.

INTERVIEWING SKILLS

We have seen that HR practitioners and line managers need to acquire a great deal of knowledge in order to be competent in handling disciplinary, capability and grievance situations. They also need certain skills – written and oral communications, investigatory skills, persuasion, judgement, decision-making and analytical reasoning, to name but a few. At no time is the need for this knowledge and these skills more evident than when carrying out the disciplinary, capability or grievance interview, and we shall now examine accepted good practice.

Thorough preparation will help to ensure that interviewers are as professional as possible, regardless of their level of experience. It can safely be said that few managers actually relish the idea of conducting a disciplinary or capability interview: most, as has already been suggested, are more likely to view grievance-handling as an unpleasant chore than as a rewarding experience (a visit to the dentist might engender only slightly less enthusiasm).

Many of the skills required to carry out satisfactory selection interviews (see Chapter 5) are equally applicable to disciplinary and grievance interviewing – for example:

- preparing for the interview
- preparing the environment
- using open and probing questions
- active listening
- maintaining good eye contact
- using appropriate body language
- using silence
- keeping control of the subject matter and timing
- taking notes
- remaining unemotional
- providing clarification
- summarising.

There are obviously differences in the purposes of these types of interviews. It is good practice, in selection interviews, for instance, to establish a rapport with the interviewee. This generally involves a warm welcome and friendly exchange in an attempt to relax the interviewee so that he or she can perform at his or her optimum during the interview. Such behaviour is obviously not entirely appropriate in a disciplinary or capability interview, and also, to some extent, a grievance interview, although it is advisable to establish the appropriate degree of rapport to ensure trust and confidence as far as possible. If you are too familiar or too personal, there is a danger of not being taken seriously, or of possibly being drawn into arguments and straying into personality issues. A lack of perceived seriousness could:

- invalidate a disciplinary warning
- give sick employees the impression that their employment is not at risk if their absence continues, or
- lead employees with a grievance to the conclusion that their views are unimportant.

Conversely, an overly formal and impersonal style may seem to compromise reasonableness. Implementation of procedures in ways that are devoid of humanity is likely to lead to dissatisfaction and, in the case of dismissals, successful employment tribunal claims. You need to strike a balance between the two approaches.

In summary, the key points applicable to disciplinary, capability and grievance interviews are to:

- stay calm and in control
- be reasonable and objective
- be factual and unemotional.

There is no one correct and precise way to conduct a disciplinary or grievance hearing but you should find that Tables 8.3 and 8.4 provide useful step-by-step approaches.

Table 8.3 The disciplinary interview

Before	During	After
• Ensure that you are familiar with the disciplinary procedure – eg the disciplinary penalties, the limit of your authority, the employee's rights to accompaniment and to appeal. • Suspend the employee on full pay if this is a case of suspected gross misconduct. • Carry out a thorough investigation and gather facts. Record all the information you acquire in accordance with the requirements of the Data Protection Act 1998. • Consider any relevant precedents, and the employee's disciplinary record. • Inform the employee in writing of the time, date, location and type of hearing, the nature of the allegations and the right to be accompanied. Provide copies of evidence, such as witness statements, preferably prior to the meeting. • If the employee is disabled or English is not his or her first language, check whether any particular arrangements will be needed at any time during the procedure – eg access to facilities, a reader or interpreter. • Decide on the sequence or structure of the interview. Invite all the relevant parties – ie companions and witnesses – and arrange for their release from duties. Be prepared to agree a postponement to the hearing should individuals be unavailable. • Arrange a suitable venue for the hearing – ie a quiet place free from interruptions – and allow sufficient time in your diary. • Ensure that the hearing will be properly constituted according to the procedure – eg in a potential dismissal case, a senior manager must take the decision.	• Convene the disciplinary hearing and make the necessary introductions. • Explain the purpose of the hearing; present the allegations and the evidence. • Request that supporting witnesses give their statements and are prepared to answer questions from both parties, if appropriate. • Listen to the employee and/or the employee's companion as they give their side of the story, and allow them to call supporting witnesses. • Ask questions of the employee and the employee's witnesses (and allow your management colleagues to do the same). • Take comprehensive notes (or arrange for someone else to). • Seek clarification of the key issues. • Give the employee and/or the employee's companion the opportunity to reiterate any aspects that they wish to emphasise. • Adjourn the hearing to allow consideration of the points raised and any mitigating circumstances (or to allow further investigation). Agree an extension to the schedule for the hearing if necessary. • Consider the appropriate action to be taken. • Reconvene, and inform the employee of your decision and the reasons for it. Highlight the change in behaviour needed, if appropriate, and the consequences of a failure to improve in the future. • Specify a review date, if there is to be one. • Inform the employee of the appeals procedure.	• Confirm the decision to the employee in writing, and write up the notes of the interview. Provide the employee with a copy, and place copies of all the relevant documents on the personal file. Complete the disciplinary record. • Monitor and review.

NB: Halt the proceedings at any point where it is apparent that:
• the use of the disciplinary procedure is inappropriate and, say, counselling or the capability procedure should be used
• there is no case to be answered by the employee.

Table 8.4 The grievance interview

Before	During	After
• Ensure that you are familiar with the grievance procedure, any required time-scales and with what happens if you fail to resolve the grievance at this stage. • Request that the employee (or companion, if applicable) provide full details of the grievance in writing. • Carry out a full investigation. Seek to establish the facts – eg dates, times, places, witnesses. • Request details of the nature of any prior discussions from appropriate managers. • Question other parties relevant to the grievance. • Consider any information pertinent to the issue raised – eg policies and procedures, statistical information, custom and practice, notes of interviews, written statements, personal records, employment legislation, codes of practice. • Record all the information you have acquired, ensuring compliance with the Data Protection Act 1998. • Inform the employee, in writing, of the subject matter, time, date, location and nature of the interview, and of the right to be accompanied. • If the employee is disabled or English is not his or her first language, check whether any particular arrangements will be needed at any time during the procedure – eg access to facilities, a reader or interpreter. • Decide on the sequence or structure of the interview. Invite all the relevant parties – ie companions and witnesses – and arrange for their release from duties. Be prepared to agree a postponement to the hearing should individuals be unavailable. • Arrange a suitable venue for the interview – ie a quiet place free from interruptions – and allow sufficient time in your diary. • Ensure that the meeting will be properly constituted, according to the procedure.	• Convene the grievance interview. • Listen objectively to the employee's complaint. • Regardless of the eventual outcome of the grievance, thank the employee for bringing the matter to your attention. • Hear witness evidence and allow for examination and cross-examination, as appropriate, by both sides. Consider any documentation provided by the employee. • Be prepared to answer questions/ explain current practices, etc. • Seek clarification of the key issues, including any solutions sought. Summarise your understanding throughout the interview. • Arrange for comprehensive notes to be taken. • Allow time for the employee to confer in private with his or her companion at any point in the proceedings. • Adjourn the interview to allow consideration of the points raised, and the circumstances. If the case is particularly complex, or if further investigations are necessary, request and agree an extension to the time allowed before a response is expected. • Consider the appropriate action to be taken, if any, bearing in mind any relevant procedures and possible repercussions. • Reconvene, and inform the employee of your decision, giving your reasons and seeking agreement, if possible. If an immediate recommendation cannot be given, ensure that it is communicated to both parties within the appropriate time-scale, and confirmed in writing. • If a mutually acceptable agreement has not been/is not likely to be reached, inform the employee of his or her right to appeal at the next stage, and of the procedure for so doing, if the procedure has not been exhausted.	• Record the results and write up the notes of the interview. Arrange for confirmation of the decision to be sent to the employee and his or her companion. Depending on the nature of the grievance, in the interests of good employee relations, and bearing in mind data protection provisions, you may wish to publicise any resultant changes to all workers. • Monitor the situation by, for example, maintaining informal contact with the employee or arranging a formal review meeting (whichever is more appropriate). • Evaluate the success or otherwise of any actions that have been taken as a result of the grievance being raised.

We now turn to the role of employee involvement in employee relations

EMPLOYEE INVOLVEMENT

In this chapter we are using the term 'employee involvement' in its generic sense. This concept has a broad application and covers all communication, consultation and participation schemes – ie written and verbal, as well as those that are one-way or two-way and are directed top-down, bottom-up and laterally. The purposes of different approaches to employee involvement vary and can be represented on a continuum with 'receiving information' at one extreme and 'having a real say in strategic decision-making' at the other.

There are three main types of employee involvement scheme: direct, indirect, and financial. Direct involvement means that workers are directly involved in matters that affect them – ie they are communicated with or consulted with in their own right. On the other hand, indirect involvement means that workers are involved in decision-making via representatives. Sometimes, indirect involvement is split into representative and union-based involvement. Finally, financial participation offers workers a financial stake in the economic success of their employing organisation.

ACTIVITY 8.6

Decide whether the approaches to employee involvement listed below are examples of direct, indirect or financial schemes:

1. team meetings

2. newsletters and intranet bulletin boards

3. collective bargaining

4. profit-related pay

5. employee share ownership

6. quality circles

7. worker representatives on the board of directors

8. works councils

9. cascade networks

10. joint consultative committees.

If you are unfamiliar with any of these terms, look them up in appropriate reference sources before tackling this activity. Compare your responses with the feedback given at the end of this chapter.

Other examples of employee involvement are:

- direct – briefing or discussion groups, letters or emails to employees, attitude surveys, conferences and seminars, suggestion schemes and training
- indirect – health and safety committees, staff associations and problem-solving or focus groups
- financial – profit-sharing, target-related pay and gainsharing.

With so many choices at their disposal, there is a temptation for organisations to try 'a little bit of everything' in the hope that healthy employee relations or the ability to introduce change with the minimum of disruption will result. The implementation of any new approaches will, however, cost money, so it would be foolish to introduce them without first analysing whether they are suited to the organisational culture and circumstances.

There are a number of factors that you should take into account before selecting your choice of approach. These include:

- the presence of trade unions, and management attitudes towards them
- management attitudes towards consultation, participation and involvement generally
- trade union attitudes, if applicable, towards these concepts
- the aims and objectives of involving employees
- organisational characteristics, including its size and structure, activities, locations, history, industry sector, relationships between employees and their managers
- past experience of employee involvement initiatives
- the number and levels of employees to be included
- the costs of implementation and maintenance of the processes of involvement
- the need for education and training to support the implementation
- legal restrictions and requirements – eg the Trade Union and Labour Relations (Consolidation) Act 1992 on rights of consultation, the European Works Council Directive 1994, and the Information and Consultation of Employees Regulations 2004 (see National Works Councils below).

ACTIVITY 8.7

For the purposes of this activity, consider a small, recently established but rapidly expanding e-recruitment organisation, which is not unionised. The owner-manager is keen to increase the involvement of employees across all activities but wishes to retain full responsibility for all business decisions.

Select six approaches that are likely to be suitable for this company and identify which type of approach they represent as well as

their pros and cons. You can assume that the owner-manager has already complied with any legal requirements such as establishing a health and safety committee.

Consider whether the chosen approaches would be suitable for your own organisation. If not, why not?

Compare your response with the feedback provided at the end of this chapter.

NATIONAL WORKS COUNCILS

The Information and Consultation of Employees Regulations 2004 came into force in April 2005. They apply to undertakings employing at least 50 employees. The Regulations oblige employers to establish information and consultation (I&C) arrangements with their employees. Those who do not comply may be fined.

It is advisable for employers to be proactive in negotiating an I&C agreement with trade union or employee representatives. This ensures that such agreements will be tailored to the organisational circumstances and allows for more flexibility than those prescribed by the Regulations as a fall-back position. Note that Acas can provide assistance in ensuring compliance.

TRADE UNION INVOLVEMENT

The role played by trade unions, recognition arrangements, collective agreements and industrial action has already been covered in Chapter 3. Here we will be concentrating on the specific roles played by trade unions in the context of employee involvement in the workplace. Trade unions share in the decision-making within unionised organisations in five main ways:

1 Collective bargaining – this constitutes negotiations between employers (or employers' organisations) and trade unions. Traditionally, collective bargaining in the UK has centred on substantive terms and conditions of employment – eg pay, hours and holidays. In many cases there has also been bargaining over the allocation of work and job duties and the physical working environment. From time to time there may be negotiation over procedural matters – eg the criteria to be used for redundancy selection.

2 Statutory consultation – this covers areas where employers are obliged to consult with a trade union, where one is recognised. We mentioned these in Chapter 3. In addition, recognised unions can require the appointment of a safety representative or representatives who have wide powers to access the workplace and to table questions to which management has to respond.

3 Joint consultation – this complements the collective bargaining arrangements in unionised environments and involves managers and trade union/employee representatives meeting regularly to discuss items of mutual concern – eg health and safety, welfare, training, efficiency and quality.

4 Dispute resolution – as we have discussed, trade union representatives frequently accompany employees at disciplinary and grievance hearings and may also raise collective grievances.

5 Partnership arrangements – these are based on agreements between management and trade unions and are symbolic of a desire to move away from the old adversarial approach to employee relations (or industrial relations). Gennard and Judge (2002: 278–9) summarise six key principles on which partnership arrangements are based. These are paraphrased below.

- Both management and trade union are committed to the success of the enterprise and have a shared understanding of its goals.

- Each side has legitimate and separate interests.

- There is a joint responsibility to maximise employment security and improve the employability of employees via training and development.

- The quality of working life will be improved by creating opportunities for personal growth.

- There needs to be a real sharing of 'hard' information.
- Tapping into new sources of motivation, commitment and resources will 'add value' to the business.

We now turn to examine the psychological contract and its employee relations implications.

THE PSYCHOLOGICAL CONTRACT

In Chapter 3 we covered the legislation governing the contract of employment. It was pointed out that the contract terms may be explicit – ie written down and/ or agreed between the parties – or implicit – ie implied by statute, custom and practice, etc. An even more subtle feature of the employment relationship relates to the unwritten expectations that employers and employees have of each other. This is referred to as the 'psychological contract'.

What do we mean by this term? In the past, employers expected loyalty and obedience in exchange for providing employees with job security and regular pay increases. As 'jobs for life' (and inflation-linked pay increases) have become increasingly rare, the exchange of expectations nowadays tends to centre on factors such as the following:

Employers expect	**Employees expect**
commitment to goals and values	skill development to aid employability
hard work and flexibility	fair and respectful treatment
creativity and innovation	involvement in decision-making
team-playing capability	good working relationships

It is an inevitable fact that changes, minor and major, in the work situation will be necessary. Such changes frequently have an impact on the 'health' of the psychological contract. All of the above expectations are relevant to the management of change within organisations. Also, many conflicts within the workplace are related to the way in which change is managed. Forcing changes on individuals is not only bad practice but is likely to have detrimental consequences. Neglecting the psychological contract will inevitably impact on the state of employee relations within the organisation.

As Gennard and Judge (2002: 98) say: 'There is now overwhelming evidence that individuals work harder, and smarter, when the psychological contract is in a state of high maintenance.'

If you want to contribute towards an improved psychological contract in your organisation, you might like to give attention to the following:

- the expectations that are created at the recruitment stage – in advertisements, for example
- the expectations that are created on appointment, including the terminology used (some of these are created by the legal contract itself)

- the expectations created at the induction stage, and the extent to which there is fulfilment of some of the earlier expectations
- the extent to which all these expectations are realised as the job and employment unfolds
- the amount of trust shown in employees
- the extent to which openness and honesty is encouraged
- the attitude to mistakes – are they an opportunity for learning or an opportunity to blame?
- other related cultural factors (see Chapter 2).

We will now examine the role of HR practitioners in seeking to maintain harmonious employee relations in the workplace.

THE ROLE OF HR PRACTITIONERS

In the above text we have tended to concentrate on the role of line managers in implementing the rules and procedures applicable to discipline, capability and grievance-handling and in managing employee relations. As HR practitioners, you will obviously adopt the same role when dealing with your own staff but are also likely to carry out the following roles, depending on the circumstances in your organisation.

AN ADVISORY ROLE TO LINE MANAGERS

In this capacity your advice is sought when employee relations incidents occur or before disciplinary action is taken or grievances are addressed. This will help to ensure a consistency of approach across the organisation as, in this role, you need to be familiar with relevant employment legislation, case law and accepted good practice. You should also have an appreciation of how such situations have been dealt with in the past and the likely repercussions of decisions taken for the future, as well as being the 'authority' regarding the operation and interpretation of your own rules and procedures. (It has already been stressed that industrial action could result from poorly managed disciplinary and grievance situations – most managers would agree that troubleshooting is generally preferable to firefighting!)

AN OVERSEEING ROLE

In this you bring possible disciplinary infringements and performance problems to the attention of line managers for their action – eg following a periodic check on attendance records and/or sickness notification and certification records. This again serves to ensure a standardised approach to organisation-wide problems, but difficulties may arise when line managers use this as an opportunity to abdicate responsibility back to the HR department.

A SECRETARIAL ROLE

You often carry out this role in communication and consultation meetings as well as disciplinary, capability and grievance hearings to ensure that detailed and accurate records are kept. This is especially necessary in the event of appeals against disciplinary action or unresolved grievances that are progressing to the next stage and (every HR practitioner's nightmare) employment tribunal hearings. See the Appendix to this chapter for a checklist on taking notes of disciplinary interviews. (This checklist could also, with some slight adaptation, be used for capability and grievance interviews.)

A DECISION-MAKING ROLE

This concerns the action that should be taken in addressing an employee relations issue or a disciplinary situation, or in concluding a grievance application (hopefully) satisfactorily. The authority for this role must be stated in the appropriate procedures (except where, as an HR practitioner, you are acting as the line manager for your own staff). This role is more likely to be adopted in a smaller organisation where, for instance, the HR manager has the authority to dismiss, and the managing director reserves the independence of a third party of higher status in order to be able to hear any appeals.

A TRAINING OR EDUCATIONAL ROLE

This is to ensure that managers follow the procedures correctly and are trained to carry out interviews and to obtain other requisite skills such as counselling and negotiating. Training may be formal or informal, as appropriate. Most managers, unlike HR practitioners, do not have a wide experience of handling conflict situations; they may have undergone formal training some time previously but need some coaching to give them the confidence to lead an interview or meeting.

A PERSUADING, INFLUENCING OR NEGOTIATING ROLE

Depending on the job role, you may find that you need to:

- persuade managers that they must pay heed to your advice on employee relations incidents
- 'sell' the benefits of organisational changes or the results of disciplinary or grievance proceedings to appropriate personnel
- consult or negotiate directly either with individual employees or union/ employee representatives over a range of issues affecting the employment relationship
- 'set the tone' by the way you phrase correspondence, policies and other communications with employees
- manage expectations by influencing what is put in job advertisements or appointment letters, said at interview or outlined at induction.

See Chapter 12 for more information on the requisite skills. It is essential that the HR practitioner identifies which 'hat' (or 'hats') he or she is wearing in disciplinary and capability matters and grievance-handling. Employment tribunal cases regarding unfair dismissal claims have been lost by employers when it became apparent that the decision to dismiss was taken by someone other than the person named in the procedure as having sufficient authority.

SUMMARY

- You should now be familiar with the theory and practice of handling conduct, performance and grievance issues. We have looked at the content and operation of disciplinary rules and disciplinary, capability and grievance procedures, as well as their importance, relevant legislation and accepted good practice.

- We have also highlighted a range of absence management tools that organisations have found to be effective in reducing absenteeism and its associated costs.

- We have considered the purposes, types and factors that would determine the suitability of employee involvement initiatives in unionised and non-unionised environments.

- We then highlighted the need to take account of the psychological contract in seeking to manage employee relations.

- The knowledge and skills necessary for dealing with employee relations issues have also been examined, specifically with regard to the role(s) played by HR practitioners.

Finally, note that a list of legislative Acts is included within the *References and further reading* immediately below. Activities have been suggested throughout the chapter, and you are encouraged to complete some, if not all, of these Activities in order to reinforce and apply your learning. The Appendix checklist follows the Activities feedback at the very end of the chapter.

EXPLORE FURTHER

REFERENCES AND FURTHER READING

ACAS (2009) Advisory Booklet on *Managing Attendance and Employee Turnover*. Leicester: ACAS

ACAS (2009) Advisory Booklet on *Bullying and Harassment at Work: A guide for managers and employers*. Leicester: ACAS

ACAS (2005) Advisory Booklet on *Employee Communications and Consultation*. Leicester: ACAS

ACAS (2009) Code of Practice 1: *Disciplinary and Grievance Procedures*. Leicester: ACAS

ACAS (2009) *Discipline and Grievances at Work. The ACAS Guide*. Leicester: ACAS

– All these are available from the Advisory, Conciliation and Arbitration Service, ACAS Publications, PO Box 235, Hayes, Middlesex, UB3 1HF; tel.: 08702 429090. They can also be downloaded at www.acas.org.uk

The following are available from the Chartered Institute of Personnel and Development (CIPD), 151 The Broadway, London SW19 1JQ; tel.: 020 8612 6201:

CIPD *Policies and Procedures for People Managers* manual

CIPD (2009) *Absence Management*: Survey Report. London: Chartered Institute of Personnel and Development

CIPD (2005) Change Agenda – *What is Employee Relations?*

EVANS, A. and PALMER, S. updated by WALTERS, M. (2002) *From Absence to Attendance*, 2nd edition. London: Chartered Institute of Personnel and Development

FARNHAM, D. (2000) *Employee Relations in Context*. London: Institute of Personnel and Development

GENNARD, J. and JUDGE, G. (2002) *Employee Relations*, 3rd edition. London: Chartered Institute of Personnel and Development

PARKIN, M. (2009) *The Employer's Guide to Grievance and Discipline Procedures: Identifying, addressing and investigating employee misconduct*. London: Kogan Page

ACTS OF PARLIAMENT AND CODES OF PRACTICE

Disability Discrimination Act 1995

Employment Rights Act 1996

Public Interest Disclosure Act 1998

ACAS (revised 2009) Code of Practice 1: *Disciplinary and Grievance Procedures*. Leicester: ACAS (reproduced in full in the ACAS Advisory Handbook on *Discipline and Grievances at Work* above)

WEBSITES

Acas (code of practice): www.acas.org.uk/publications/pdf/cp01.pdf

Department for Business, Innovation and Skills (Employment Relations): www.berr.gov.uk/er/index.htm

Legislation: www.legislation.hmso.gov.uk

ACTIVITIES FEEDBACK

Activity 8.4

Before reaching a decision, the supervisor needed to answer the following questions:

- Does the contract of employment contain a clause referring to out-of-hours training?
- Which legislative acts are relevant – eg the Sex Discrimination Act 1975 (regarding indirect sex discrimination)?
- What has happened in the past in similar circumstances (ie custom and practice)?
- Has the employee been willing to attend previous training events?
- What is known about the employee's domestic circumstances (taking into account the employee's right to privacy)?
- Can the company provide any help and assistance regarding childcare?
- Can alternative arrangements be made to accommodate this training – eg rescheduling the event to weekdays, changing the attendance requirements?
- What are the likely repercussions of all the possible solutions?

Activity 8.6

Table 8.5 Approaches to employee involvement

Example	Type
Team meetings	direct
Newsletters and intranet bulletin boards	direct
Collective bargaining	indirect
Profit-related pay	financial
Employee share ownership	financial
Quality circles	direct (but could be indirect depending on the profile of the group)
Worker representatives on the board of directors	indirect
Works councils	indirect
Cascade networks	direct
Joint consultative committees	indirect

Activity 8.7

Table 8.6 Selecting suitable approaches to employee involvement

Approaches	Type	Pros	Cons
Emails	direct	Speedy means of imparting information	One-way in the main. Employees may suffer from information overload
Whole-company meetings	direct	Allows for probing, clarification, suggestions and comments	Time-consuming and will be more difficult to arrange as the company expands
Problem-solving groups (including reps from various functions)	indirect	Able to gain views from different levels and functions. Encourages an integrated approach. Synergistic benefits	Ideas may not get implemented. Attendance may be viewed as time away from the job
Staff council	indirect	Means of cascading information to all levels of staff while seeking their buy-in	Loss of control of the message – ie the 'Chinese whispers' effect. Reps may view this as paying lip service to employee involvement if they feel they are being told of decisions rather than being involved
Employee share ownership	financial	The time lags attached to the tax benefits of these schemes can encourage employees to stay with the company	Shares may increase or decrease in value. Employees will find it difficult to assess their individual contribution to company performance and share price
Attitude survey	direct	Confidential means for employees honestly to express their views and make suggestions	Increases employee expectations, so inaction following an attitude survey can lead to employee resentment

APPENDIX TO CHAPTER 8

CHECKLIST FOR TAKING NOTES OF DISCIPLINARY INTERVIEWS

The following checklist should assist you in ensuring that your written notes fully meet the need to:

- provide sufficient information for whoever is responsible for issuing the confirmation letter to the employee (if this is necessary)
- provide a useful justification and record of the action taken at this stage should the situation deteriorate further (possibly resulting in an unfair dismissal claim being heard at an employment tribunal).

Do the notes include: **YES/NO**

1 the date, venue, and start time of the interview?

2 an account of those attending the interview and their roles?

3 details of the allegations stated to the employee and of the supporting evidence – eg witness statements?

4 details of the employee's response and of the supporting evidence?

5 a record of any adjournments and approximate timings?

6 consideration of the employee's previous record?

7 the decision on whether disciplinary action was appropriate or not and the type of action taken with the appropriate time-scale?

8 the review date and a clear statement of intent if improvement does not occur?

9 reference to the right to appeal and the finish time of the interview?

10 reference to the note-taker's name plus a date and signature?

CHAPTER 9

Learning and development

LEARNING OUTCOMES

After reading this chapter you will:

- be able to distinguish between training, learning and development

- know how to identify learning needs arising from change, whether internal to or external to the organisation

- confidently plan a training programme incorporating a variety of learning experiences

- be able to implement learning activities.

INTRODUCTION

In recent years there has been an increasing tendency to talk about learning, rather than training. It emphasises a subtle but important difference in approach. Training is a process through which individuals are helped to learn a skill or technique. The emphasis is very much on the responsibility of the trainer or the employer to assist the employee. It implies that the process is effective (sometimes it is not) and that the employee can be a passive recipient in the process. The latter explains why training does not always succeed in its objectives. But when computer-based training (CBT) was developing, it became apparent that the user had to take responsibility for learning, not the computer for training. So learning switches responsibility and carries the further implication that the employee himself or herself can initiate the learning whether or not the organisation provides any specific assistance. Learning is very broad-based, encompassing minor and major pieces of information, skills, judgement and personal growth.

The opportunities for learner-driven, rather than trainer-driven, learning are increasing. Software can be learned through online tutorials (or often just the Help key) whereas conferences, forums and other forms of social networking are allowing us to learn (cautiously, it should be said) from the practical experience of others who we have never met and who we probably never will meet.

Training tends to focus on skills or techniques. These are areas where one person (the trainer) can more easily guide another (the learner) than ones where the learner might guide himself or herself. A skill may be primarily manual, as in using a keyboard, or essentially intellectual, such as negotiating a house sale. The latter is often referred to as a 'soft skill' since no 'hard' equipment is involved. Instruction is a very typical form of training, but there are many others. There is often an end point – perhaps the achievement of a specific data-entry speed.

Development places emphasis on the growth of the individual. It relates to acquiring a very broad range of soft skills through planned activities and experience. Management of people, handling work relationships and leadership are typical of broad ranges of skills that are developed. Success in all these areas requires maturity of judgement. There is no fixed end point to development, because individuals can continually improve, for example, their leadership skills.

This chapter is included because training, learning, or human resource development typically sits within a human resource department. In small organisations it may be the direct responsibility of the HR manager or officer. However, these responsibilities are often treated as a major function in themselves. So this chapter focuses on matters of interest to the HR practitioner rather than on the broader needs of a dedicated learning and development practitioner. The structure of this chapter follows the steps in the *learning cycle*, which we shall look at in a moment. First, though, we consider the importance of learning and development activities.

WHY ARE LEARNING AND DEVELOPMENT IMPORTANT?

We shall be looking at the unrelenting pace of change in the world and at its implications for learning needs. If our organisations respond to change early, they will prosper and gain rewards in terms of security, profit or attainment of their goals. Today, commercial products can be imitated – some almost immediately. So technological advantage may give one producer an edge over others, but these other producers can catch up quickly. In a free-market economy all organisations have similar access to capital, to customers and to employees. It is their effectiveness in operating, as organisations of people, that primarily distinguishes one from another. Key factors in operating effectively are the knowledge and skills of people.

In the commercial world, then, if we train our people and continually ensure that they have up-to-date knowledge and up-to-date skills, it follows that we shall be able to compete effectively, and reasonably expect to prosper. Few, if any, jobs today are protected from commercial realities. Even those not originally viewed as commercial organisations – for example, charities – now place considerable importance on obtaining well-trained professional people to run their operations.

As an HR practitioner you have an important role to play. You should be able to relate to commercial needs and your corporate mission, using them to help identify suitable learning. Like every other operation, learning and development has to be managed. HR practitioners need to acquire advanced skills and knowledge if they are to manage it effectively.

We shall commence with a look at the learning cycle, which helps identify the main principles involved in managing learning and development activities.

THE LEARNING CYCLE

Figure 9.1 describes how learning is managed. It is a continuous cycle. We shall look first at how learning needs are identified, usually referred to as 'learning needs analysis'. Then we shall look at how to plan a learning programme, highlighting the ingredients available to satisfy those needs that have been identified. When learning is designed and implemented, we must be aware of the different learning styles that individuals prefer, and we shall look at the four styles. Last, and not least, we shall look at how the effectiveness of learning can be evaluated.

Figure 9.1 The learning cycle

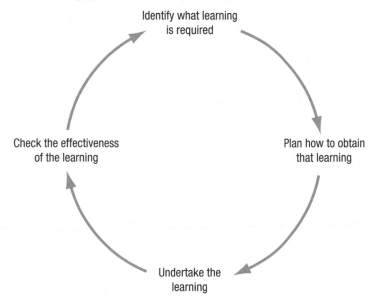

Consider how this might work in practice.

At an annual appraisal you decide that an improved knowledge of employment law would add to your effectiveness. You will want to assess what level of knowledge you need and the areas of knowledge that are important to your particular role, whether recruitment and selection, policies and procedures or employee termination matters. You should compare what you know already with what you need to know. This would identify the learning needed. You should set some objectives for the outcome of the learning.

Planning could involve discussions with colleagues, investigating short courses in employment law, private study, or even considering the CIPD Advanced Certificate in Employment Law. You will need to assess the appropriateness of the options, how much time would be involved, when you will be able to go, and what the cost will be.

You implement the learning by going on the course(s), doing the reading, completing any coursework.

Checking the effectiveness of the learning is often the most difficult. How effective has your learning been? Are you confident of actions that you might have previously referred to others? How does it match up to the original outcomes? Is this saving your organisation time, cost, disputes and grievances, exposure to tribunal claims, etc? It doesn't stop there, because as you review the learning you will probably uncover other learning needs – and the cycle continues.

ACTIVITY 9.1

Work through the learning cycle by using your own example, as below.

- Realistically identify some skill need(s) of your own – eg in using a previously unused facility in a software programme, perhaps using macros in Word. Set some objectives, and write them down.

- Plan how to satisfy that need, examining a range of options for achieving your objectives and selecting one or more possibilities.

- Undertake the learning and/or development that you have planned.

- When you have completed the learning and/or development, assess its effectiveness against your original objectives.
  - Have you achieved your objectives?
  - Did you learn as fast as you expected?
  - Were the options you chose the best?
  - Have you discovered additional skill needs?

Although learning is a continuous cycle, we shall look first at how learning needs arise.

LEARNING NEEDS ARISE BECAUSE THE WORLD CHANGES

Change is continuous; it affects the environment in which organisations operate and it exists within organisations themselves. Employees are affected by change and they must adapt, learn new skills, cope with different pressures, acquire new knowledge and forge new relationships. Learning brings additional resources to individuals to enable them to change and develop. When we looked at the organisational context (Chapter 2), we briefly identified the types of changes that affect the corporate environment. We shall now examine these in more detail and relate them to learning and development.

- In recent years *political change* has brought about the need for new management skills in many different industries. The government increasingly manages sectors of both the public and the otherwise private economy through regulations, inspections and standards. The extended government involvement in the banks and the standards to be met by care homes are particular examples where managers and employees have to learn how to respond to changes brought about by political philosophies. Politicians also seek to influence the participation of organisations and individuals in learning. This has led to initiatives such as National Vocational Qualifications (NVQs) and National Training Awards (NTAs).

- The *economic conditions* of the early twenty-first century favoured the creation of many small businesses encouraged by tax advantages, new technologies and a healthy economy generally. This created the need for wider business skills on the part of many people who had previously worked only as part of a larger enterprise. The subsequent recession placed further demands on those same people.

- *Social change* creates learning needs. For example, as mentioned before, as more people travel abroad and experience the high levels of customer service in North America and the Far East they become more demanding in their expectations for customer service at home. As a further example, in society we now acknowledge women's right to occupy jobs at the highest levels in companies and institutions. Both these examples indicate the need for learning: the first in customer care skills, and the second in management skills for women (to help redress the imbalance at senior levels).

- *Technological change* is relentless. The learning needs it creates in computer skills, in advanced technical skills and in new ways of doing things are widespread and substantial. The ability to develop and exploit software opportunities is critical for business and such new software means the need for learning. The Internet has far-reaching implications for the availability of information, for education, for retail trade and for many more activities. It has already changed the way we work and created many new businesses that support the technology. The development of social networking is continuing the process and will result in changes that are still difficult to predict. At the same time, all this provides new techniques for trainers and learners to use in the process of learning itself.

- *The law* changes continually as well, and HR practitioners are only too aware of the learning needs it creates for them. Keep in mind that employment is only one area affected by the law. Product liability, labelling of consumer goods and the regulation of financial services are just a few examples where the law creates learning needs for employers.

- *Environmental issues* are increasingly to the fore. Fair trade, organic foods and green products are responses to consumer choice. The need for re-use, recycling and reduced landfill is creating new industries. These changes create threats for some companies and opportunities for others. In many industries, environmental pollution can be reduced by the better training of operatives.

(The list continues.)

These changes lead to new products, services and standards of expected performance that, in turn, demand new skills and abilities. Organisations that can respond to these changes quickly by training their employees appropriately steal an advantage over their competitors.

Listening to and reading suitable media material and cautious social networking will raise your awareness of the corporate environment. We recommend:

- *People Management*
- other specialist training or learning publications
- quality daily or Sunday newspapers
- quality magazines covering business or current affairs
- BBC Radio 4
- the CIPD website
- a wide range of other websites on the Internet
- LinkedIn
- Twitter.

In respect of the last two on that list, this is written in 2010. In a changing world the best social networking sites will also change as some grow, others contract, and new ones with new ideas come onstream.

Individual learning needs also arise internally, directly or indirectly, as a result of external changes. Even without those external changes, learning needs will arise for employees who are new to the organisation, gain promotion, relocate, are redeployed, or are due to retire. So when looking at learning needs, we have to consider not only changes in the environment but also changes for individuals.

LEARNING NEEDS ARISE BECAUSE PEOPLE'S JOBS AND CAREERS CHANGE

Induction training addresses the needs of new-starters, and similar training is needed for all employees who transfer or are promoted within the organisation. We choose the term 'training' because the responsibility to initiate the learning here rests primarily with the organisation. Some special cases are considered below.

- School-leavers have much to learn about the world of work. They need to understand the level of commitment required and to be able to assess others' expectations of them. Working with adults will be a novel experience, and new attitudes must be formed. All this is quite separate from the actual mechanics of doing the job. Comparatively simple everyday tasks, such as answering the telephone, can be a major source of anxiety to those who have never been in employment before. (Perhaps you can remember your first day at work!)

- Young graduates, especially those who have not been in employment before, need similar induction to that for school-leavers, although they can be expected to learn faster. Most employers give special consideration to graduates, recognising that they may eventually become senior managers in the organisation. Building relationships with people in many departments of the organisation and having a broad understanding of what each function does is critical for those who seek a progressive career. Graduate learning schemes invariably recognise this, and graduates often spend time in different functions before settling into their chosen career path.

- New employees who already have experience elsewhere need to learn about the culture of your organisation – ie 'how things are done'. They need to meet, and begin to build relationships with, those with whom they will be in regular contact. Systems and routines will be different from those of their previous employer. At the same time, new employees usually bring alternative approaches that can benefit their new employer.

- Returners from maternity leave, a career break, or a period of unemployment need time and help to build up their confidence. For example, online commerce has radically changed the way in which many commercial companies do business and hence the way in which people work in such organisations. Given support to adapt and learning in new skills, returners usually regain their confidence rapidly.

- Employees who have moved from other departments, functions and sites also need time to acclimatise to their new situations. The building of new relationships and finding the right contacts can be encouraged by team-building events and by deliberate inclusion in social activities.

- With the possible exception of those from other departments, all these groups are likely to need to learn to use the corporate computer facilities.

Providing mentors and associates to aid all these transitions is a popular way to assist employees. Mentors, usually more senior than the employee, can provide encouragement and support and pass on their own skills and experience as well as lead by example. Associates may be peers of the employee, such as a graduate who joined with the last intake and who can relate easily to a new graduate entrant.

- Retirement calls for a new set of life skills, and responsible employers recognise the need for learning for this. They provide preparatory courses covering subjects such as health and financial planning, as well as introducing employees to pensioners' groups.

- Current employees who are not performing at the right level require specific diagnosis. The problem may lie in a lack of technical skills or in attitude, but very often other factors not directly related to learning needs may be diagnosed.

- Promotion creates learning needs. Surprisingly, this is often not recognised. It does not follow that the best operative is automatically an effective supervisor, that the best salesman is a natural manager, or that an experienced schoolteacher knows how to be a headteacher. The Peter Principle, which suggests that everyone is promoted to their level of incompetence, possibly reflects the lack of learning that most employees receive on promotion.

- Future potential is another reason for training and developing individuals. It particularly relates to those who are progressing to managerial or professional careers, where the responsibility for development of skills rests more heavily with the individual. 'Fast-tracking' is the term used when individuals are identified as having significant future potential. Such individuals are singled out for special development. Activities may include studying for professional qualifications, secondments to other sites, departments or companies, special project responsibilities, and mentoring from one or more senior managers.

- Organisations have to try to identify the capabilities that they will need in the future. This gives them the option of developing the talents required from within the organisation – talent management. The activities described above are equally appropriate, but the emphasis is on the needs of the organisation rather than just developing the potential of individuals (whose talents might not be those eventually required).

LEVELS OF LEARNING NEEDS ANALYSIS

When we look at analysing learning needs we shall see that learning is needed at three levels. These are the organisation, the job or occupation, and the individual employee.

THE ORGANISATION

Customer care is typical of a learning need that originates at the level of the organisation and is experienced by most, if not all, employees. It could arise from a board-level decision to change the organisation's image in this one regard.

JOB OR OCCUPATION

Learning in electronic 'point of sale' equipment (eg the scanners familiar at supermarket checkouts) is an example of learning that applies to everyone in a specific job – in this case, checkout operators.

INDIVIDUAL EMPLOYEE

Here there may be an opportunity for learning where an individual has a particular need or the organisation requires an individual to be trained in a particular area. For the HR officer, an employment law course or secondment to another organisation might be examples.

MAKING LEARNING NEEDS ANALYSIS COMPREHENSIVE

Jill Fairbairns has provided a model that emphasises three matters that must be addressed in making decisions about appropriate training and hence learning. We shall use this model to describe our approach to identifying where training should be concentrated. In part, it links the three levels above but it can also be applied to evaluating the suitability of learning solutions at each level. Because of its early development it refers to training rather than learning, but the principles are still highly relevant today.

Throughout our working lives we increase our levels of knowledge and skills in order to perform work activities well. The acquisition of relevant knowledge and skills opens up opportunities to individuals for increased job performance, career development and personal development. Organisations continually seek the best return on their limited funds, so it is necessary to be selective and to identify those areas that will be important in the particular job in question (Important in my job – see Figure 9.2).

Figure 9.2 Factors in the selection of training (Fairbairns' model)

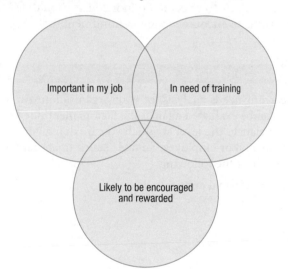

Most jobs today need a wide range of skills and knowledge: some are critical and others desirable for top performance. Job-holders usually have the majority of those skills and knowledge already, but for the reasons outlined above there will always be areas that can benefit from additional training (In need of training – see Figure 9.2). So at this point we would be looking for the overlap between importance in the job and need of training.

The third factor involves the culture of the organisation. We looked at culture in Chapter 2 and observed that businesses are characterised by different attitudes and priorities – ie the corporate culture. Learning knowledge and skills that do not fit comfortably with the corporate culture will either put the trained person at odds with that culture or, more probably, lead to the learning being rejected on the basis that 'it does not work here'. For example, learning in customer care may be misplaced if it is immediate additional sales (rather than repeat business) on which success is judged. Another example of a cultural factor is the attitude to NVQs or Scottish Vocational Qualifications (SVQs); some organisations are more enthusiastic about these than others. In an enthusiastic organisation an NVQ initiative will receive a better reception and more support from senior managers. Identifying the cultural direction in which your organisation is going will help identify the most relevant training (Likely to be encouraged and rewarded – see Figure 9.2).

HR practitioners will benefit from taking these three factors into account in selecting suitable learning activities. It is where such activities address the overlap between all three factors that the most benefits are likely to be realised (again, see Figure 9.2).

The person being trained is a further factor to be considered. Offering training can imply weakness or that an individual has a problem with some aspect of his or her performance. Unless individuals see training as a valuable learning opportunity or believe it is important in their jobs and relevant to their organisation, they are likely to reject it. So individuals should be involved in the plans for their learning to encourage their commitment to it.

GATHERING THE INFORMATION

To carry out a learning needs analysis for your organisation you will need information that can be evaluated against the factors mentioned above. The information must relate to the level at which you are doing your analysis: organisation, occupation or employee. Suitable source material for the analysis is likely to include some of the following:

- mission and values (formal culture)
- business plans
- succession plans
- competency framework
- views and observations about 'how we do things around here' (this is the informal culture, not necessarily the same as the formal culture)
- appraisal records
- evidence of competence for individuals (eg portfolios)
- opportunities for improvement (eg development opportunities)
- minutes of meetings (eg action points that highlight needs)
- questionnaires
- job descriptions
- performance targets
- observation of employees at work

- recorded conversations, such as on a customer care line
- relevant NVQs or SVQs
- interviews with:
  - managers
  - staff
  - subordinates
  - internal customers
  - external customers.

Using sources such as these is important because you start with the needs that relate to the business. Once you know what is needed, you can start to consider the best way to meet those needs.

When you have gathered the source material and feel well-informed, it is time to carry out your analysis. This could be at the level of the organisation, job or individual. To illustrate the process we shall consider examples at the job level.

You have to ask what job performance is needed in the particular situation. The answer should be in the form of a level of performance. This could be quantitative (for example, the number of calls handled per hour) or it may be qualitative (for example, all telephone calls are to be answered politely, competently and effectively).

Another way of defining the required performance may be to use an NVQ/SVQ standard or other competency framework that directly defines the competence – for example, to select candidates for jobs within agreed time-scales and budgets. Competencies can be invaluable in helping you decide on desired levels of performance. An accepted framework will provide a sound basis on which line managers and trainers can discuss what is needed.

We shall assume that in these examples learning is a suitable remedy. That may not be the case in all circumstances – for example, if operations are under-resourced, learning is an inappropriate solution.

Next you need to ascertain what performance or competence is being achieved at present. Perhaps applicants responding to a recruitment advertisement are kept waiting for a reply with no apology offered when the call is answered. Maybe the person answering does not understand how to handle some of the enquiries, or incomplete messages are taken. In the second example, selection of candidates may regularly overrun both time-scales and budgets. More critically, you may lose a good candidate. The difference between this and the level of performance needed is known as the 'learning gap'.

You may have to try to estimate what that 'gap' is costing the organisation, or the gain and benefits of closing that gap. We may be able to get information about sales lost owing to poor telephone technique, or estimate the costs of taking an extra day to fill a vacancy. This is important because these costs will provide the justification for the learning costs or, perhaps, lead to the conclusion that training is not justified in a particular instance.

A manufacturer of plastic pipes found that a market opportunity existed for providing not only pipes but also a variety of equipment associated with customers' use of them. The sale of a 'package of pipe and equipment' enabled higher margins since pipe had often been sold to an intermediary who then put its own package, and margin, together for industrial customers.

This diversification of its operations was a significant change for the manufacturer.

As a buyer of raw polymers the manufacturer was a major customer of the polymer supplier. Consequently, negotiations were carried out at a very senior level and favourable terms were the norm.

The change in product range meant that as well as processes the manufacturer was also carrying out assembly work. This created a learning need that was recognised. However, components had to be purchased from a variety of sources and by junior purchasing staff. Furthermore, the pipe manufacturer was not a significant customer so far as the individual component manufacturers were concerned. Delays began to occur. Deliveries for large orders of pipe were being held up because the equipment to be shipped with them was not ready. The equipment, in turn, was being held up because minor components had not arrived from local suppliers in good time.

Fortunately, the company recognised the problem as one of negotiation. It was not sufficient to get the best price for components – reliable delivery had to be part of the deal. Purchasing staff that had been treated well by large polymer manufacturers now had to learn to deal with owners of small engineering works. The process of learning how to work in these circumstances had to be accelerated and a training programme in negotiation skills was initiated.

The next phase is to plan the learning and development.

LEARNING AND DEVELOPMENT PLANS

Here a balancing act is required between available resources, which may be influenced by the benefits that have been estimated, and the identified needs. Achieving such a balance is a matter of skill. As we saw in the Fairbairns model (Figure 9.2), you will have to weigh up needs in the context of the political considerations, style and culture of the organisation.

Let's look at some of the factors that will have to be considered.

GOVERNMENT INITIATIVES

Successive British governments have recognised the need for training if Britain is to compete internationally. They have developed and supported initiatives to encourage employers and employees to take responsibility for training and learning.

Investors in People (IiP) provides a detailed approach to training and to its integration within the organisation thereby assisting thinking on policies, procedures and action.

IiP status requires an organisation to meet specific standards, to demonstrate that it is doing so and to submit to an inspection process. National Training Awards and vocational qualifications are other examples of initiatives designed to encourage learning. The UK government is keen to encourage these achievements, and there are invariably financial incentives such as grants and subsidies provided for organisations and individuals seeking these awards, and in some cases, financial rewards and publicity for achieving them. For many small and medium-sized organisations, Investors in People is the main route to government funds that assist with learning.

In addition there are government schemes on offer to encourage employment of particular groups such as school-leavers (ie Apprenticeships), and Train to Gain can help to fund employee training for organisations. What is available varies from time to time.

It is therefore wise to investigate the current availability of grants and subsidies for learning. You should approach the Skills Funding Agency Business Links, regional development agencies, universities, colleges or local authorities. In many cases funds for learning can come, via these bodies, from European sources such as the European Social Fund. You can explore all these initiatives using the appropriate websites at the end of this chapter. Networking with your learning sources can also reveal useful opportunities. At the same time you should assess the requirements placed on your organisation by such bodies as a condition of providing grants or subsidies. For example, you might be expected to train your HR administrator to an NVQ/SVQ standard and to train your HR officer as an assessor. While it may be worthwhile to do such training, it might be time-consuming. Even if no special conditions apply, it is still important to assess the amount of time you may need to spend on administration and documentation. Wise use of the funds has to be demonstrated to those who provide them, and this often means significant documentation.

THE INTERNAL LEARNING AND DEVELOPMENT RESOURCES AVAILABLE

You must understand the size of the budget and how it is structured. Structure can be important. For example, some budgets may apply only to amounts invoiced – thus the use of a supervisor to train call centre operators may well not be counted against such budgets. This does not mean that using the supervisor would be without cost, but it may save some of the budget for use elsewhere.

You may have some facilities available internally, such as a learning centre well equipped for craft learning, management learning, computer learning, or for all of these. On the other hand, there may be very limited facilities. Nonetheless, in most cases there will be equipment available that could be used for learning. Production departments, for example, may have idle production lines that could be used for learning purposes. Setting up a workstation for call centre learning or an additional computer on the corporate system may be straightforward.

Consider the availability and capability of specialists and trainers within the company. These may be increased by training supervisors in the techniques of instruction, for example. In addition, experienced employees may be available for training-based activities. At more senior levels, experienced managers may be willing to coach or mentor more junior managers or staff. This can be a valuable development activity for both the senior and the junior.

Another valuable development activity is secondment to another section, site or associated company. Equally, these locations and jobs themselves may provide project opportunities. A local non-competitor may have a good call centre operation and be willing to share expertise. Some organisations are very innovative and engage in formal partnership arrangements, sometimes including a training provider, to share employee development opportunities.

THE EXTERNAL LEARNING AND DEVELOPMENT RESOURCES AVAILABLE

Using external resources invariably has an opportunity cost. There will be absence from the workplace and, in consequence, temporary loss of production, sales, service or contribution to the business. Often these costs are hidden in that they do not appear in any financial calculations, but they are there nonetheless. In addition, there will be the cost of course fees, travel and accommodation. Such costs are rarely hidden and are likely to need justification. If there are grants or subsidies available, these may help. As we discussed above, you have to know the conditions laid down by the bodies providing them. Expect questions as to whether the external resources are in fact available internally or could be more economically provided internally. Investigate, also, the availability of grants and subsidies for external training from the bodies we mentioned above.

Finally, you need to evaluate the quality of such training, its relevance and its relationship to the culture of the organisation and to the quality standards demanded in the workplace. For example, a local telephone techniques course might not be sufficient to meet your expectations if you work in an international marketplace. Specified competencies can help you and any external provider identify appropriate learning objectives. A discussion that centres on these can help you and your training provider decide if they can, in fact, meet your expectations. You should also consider the relevance of learning to an individual's career. Qualifications, in particular, can be relevant to the needs of both the organisation and the individual – we look at these next.

QUALIFICATIONS

In many organisations it is important to have qualified people; in some cases, third parties may impose such requirements. Hospitals are obvious examples, where qualifications are necessary for doctors and nursing staff. In industry, accountants and engineers are examples of professional people who are frequently required to be suitably qualified. Even when not a statutory requirement, qualifications help to show that responsibilities are taken seriously. Health and safety qualifications, for example, indicate a responsible approach to an important issue – one for which a company may be held liable for injuries and occupational ill health.

Qualifications provide external verification of skills, competence or knowledge. This can be helpful, for example, where pay is related to level of qualification.

- Examination-based qualifications provide evidence of knowledge and ability to examine issues and solve problems. High performance in examinations may also imply judgement. However, such a guide is not always reliable, and furthermore, examinations rarely assess practical skills.

- Competence-based qualifications depend on providing evidence of ability to carry out specific tasks to the standard expected in the workplace. Evidence is assessed by a qualified assessor who judges whether it provides sufficient evidence of competence. Typical evidence might include documents prepared by the 'candidate', reports, copies of correspondence and witness testimony about carrying out activities to a specified standard. Competence can also be assessed by observation.

- NVQs and SVQs are nationally recognised competence qualifications. They provide detailed descriptions (standards) of vocational competencies, breaking them down into units of competence, then into elements of competence. Units of competence can be accredited individually, accumulating into a qualification. Elements of competence describe activities (such as leading a meeting) and have performance criteria against which competence in the activity can be judged (eg handling conflict). The detailed descriptions can be invaluable in preparing learning activities for specific skills and for checking achievement. Colleges and other local and national government bodies can help employers identify relevant NVQs/SVQs for their employees.

The use of competence-based workplace learning can involve the use of internal advisers and assessors. While these would naturally be supervisors and experienced employees, the cost of training advisers and assessors, of administering the system and of providing the learning may be substantial. One point of caution on competence-based learning and NVQs/SVQs: take care not to allow the collection of evidence to develop into a 'paper-chase', because this may obscure the need to develop skills and impart relevant knowledge – ie to help employees to learn – a point we take up now.

CHOOSING APPROPRIATE LEARNING EXPERIENCES

This choice should take into consideration the range of techniques available and individual learning styles.

LEARNING AND DEVELOPMENT TECHNIQUES

There is a temptation to associate learning with the provision of 'training courses'. In practice the majority of learning takes place outside such courses, is often 'on the job' and is frequently left to chance. Learning opportunities abound and the learning specialist should seek to manage these as effectively as possible. So 'learning and development techniques' include using naturally occurring or deliberately created learning opportunities. The examples of techniques and opportunities that we list here can also help you to address your own learning and development needs.

On the job

- job instruction
- coaching and mentoring
- work diaries and log books
- records of continuing professional development
- rotating a person's job with someone else at a similar skill level
- enlarging the job by providing more tasks or responsibilities at the same level
- enriching the job by adding tasks at higher level of responsibility
- group meetings
- projects and assignments
- NVQ/SVQ programmes
- computer help facilities, online and offline
- Internet information resources such as wikipedia
- networking forums such as those provided by the CIPD and others
- social networking.

Off the job

- seminars and workshops
- attending talks and presentations
- guided reading
- local discussion groups
- local meetings of professional bodies, such as the CIPD or Institute of Administrative Management (IAM)
- visits to other organisations
- business games
- delivering talks and presentations
- programmed learning in books, computers, interactive video, CD-ROM and the World-Wide Web
- computer simulation
- assignments prepared for a course
- Action Learning
- outdoor development.

ACTIVITY 9.2

Look at the lists of on-the-job and off-the-job learning techniques above. Are any of those listed unfamiliar to you? Discuss any that you are unclear about with a learning source and undertake further reading, as appropriate.

CASE STUDY 9.2

An assembly factory found itself continually running into problems meeting its delivery targets. It had a full manufacturing requirements planning system in place, good reliable suppliers and excellent industrial relations. On the face of it the planning system should have enabled the targets to be met comfortably – but it was not happening. The training officer became involved and he went to talk to the supplier of the planning system.

There was, it seemed, a familiar problem. The system worked, but senior people circumvented it. If a customer asked for a special delivery, an improvement on an existing delivery date or a change to the order, it would be granted – even if it meant tweaking the system. Any attempt to resist on the part of the planning staff would be referred to the managing director, who invariably supported the sales staff. Indeed, he tended to bypass the system himself. If the system were overridden for special circumstances, it clearly could not be blamed if delivery dates went awry.

To deal with this problem the computer supplier developed a computer simulation program. Rather like a flight simulator this provided the opportunity to experiment with the system and experience the effects of different options. The appropriate senior managers were persuaded to take part in a simulated exercise. Because it wasn't the real factory (any more than a flight simulator is a real plane) they could 'crash' the system again and again until they learned that if they followed the rules of the system, the planning worked. The process took several days but it convinced the managers that if the system was followed, and everything was put through the system, the delivery targets would be met.

LEARNING STYLES

In choosing appropriate experiences we need to acknowledge that individuals are different. In particular they learn in different ways. Honey and Mumford describe four learning styles that enable individuals to be categorised by their preferred approaches to learning. We have summarised these styles as follows:

Activists   Their approach to learning is very open-minded.

They thrive on activity and tend to decide first and learn afterwards.

They learn best from short 'here and now' exercises – eg business games, group work.

Reflectors   They gather and reflect on all available information before making a decision.

They take account of the wider picture.

They prefer to stand back, listen, observe and record information – eg diaries, time logs.

Theorists	They think problems through in a logical, step-by-step way.
	Their decisions tend to be 'black and white' – ie categorical.
	They use models, systems, concepts and theories – eg conventional science teaching.
Pragmatists	They are keen on practical approaches and on solving problems.
	They are down to earth: 'If it works, it works.'
	They seek to establish a close link between the subject matter and its practical application – eg projects, workplace learning.

For individuals, it is valuable to play to strong learning styles, although it is also useful to seek to develop the other learning styles. Groups of individuals may benefit from emphasis on a particular style, too: a group of supervisors is more likely to respond to a pragmatic approach, whereas a group of young science graduates would probably respond better to a theoretical approach. In choosing appropriate learning techniques and opportunities you should consider the preferences of the individuals. Learning that centres on a number of individuals will have to accommodate a variety of activities to cover the different styles of the participants.

ACTIVITY 9.3

Look back at the learning style descriptions. From these you should be able to decide who will benefit most from each of the following activities:

- 'having a go'
- taking a back seat in a meeting
- applying a new technique to a current problem
- an intellectual debate
- keeping a daily log
- being coached by an expert
- exciting experiences
- being cross-examined on a decision he or she has made.

Compare your views with those at the end of the chapter.

IMPLEMENTING LEARNING AND DEVELOPMENT ACTIVITIES

The key to successful learning activities is planning and preparation. In planning, it is helpful if you can regard people at events as participants in a learning process. Use of terms such as 'attenders', 'trainees' or even 'students' implies they are passive rather than actively involved in a learning process for which they have responsibility. One could, perhaps, refer to them as 'learners' at the risk of sounding patronising. Carefully consider each of the following:

- the learning objectives of the event (these can be broad or very specific, but the accuracy with which they have been determined will be a major factor in the success of the event)

- how many will be trained at any one time
- the length of your learning sessions and how much will be learned at each session
- how much time is available and how you will divide it up
- the likely preferred learning styles of participants
- the range of learning techniques available and their suitability
- how to involve participants in the learning process
- the pace of learning.

If you plan to run a workshop, seminar or training course you will also have to consider:

- the practical arrangements – room, layout, etc
- the use of support material – handouts, videos, PowerPoint slides, other visual aids
- the learning resources – flipchart, laptop, DVDs, data projection equipment, etc. Make sure you know how to use any technology!

CASE STUDY 9.3

The authors run workshops. Having identified the needs either generally or in conjunction with a client, their starting-point is a series of behavioural objectives. These are similar to those in the chapters of this book but typically also include specific objectives for skill development.

We set a limit of 12 delegates at a time. Sometimes the more delegates you have, the fewer questions are asked, and we encourage questions, so 12 works well. Most of our workshops run for six hours and we aim for blocks of about an hour and a half. These are not 'solid' blocks, but contain a mixture of approaches to cater for different learning styles.

We are keen also to provide pragmatic solutions, so we provide frameworks for 'having a word with an employee' or for a 'return-to-work interview'. These give delegates techniques that they can take away and use.

Invariably, there is some activity. Typically, we seek to reinforce knowledge and techniques with practical exercises, perhaps a role-play, or a brief presentation.

Because many of our subjects have a legal underpinning, there has to be some theory behind the techniques we advocate. So as to involve the delegates, the flipchart is a useful visual aid. As we said, we love questions because they help delegates to test out theories and models.

We usually ask questions as well as answer them, because pertinent questions can encourage reflection. Finally, we ask delegates to plan some actions that they will take subsequently, as a result of the workshop. This provides further opportunity for reflection.

Neither learning nor development activities need take place in a workshop or course environment, as we have already seen with the examples given in an earlier section. They should nevertheless have clear objectives, planned activities and appropriate support. Performance improvements should be reviewed against those objectives regularly, until the desired performance is achieved.

Development will be a longer-term process with a cyclical pattern of broad objectives, actions, review and further objectives. There should be a senior trainer, coach or mentor to oversee the programme, to help with review, and to ensure that individuals have access to developmental opportunities.

Tip: If you want to develop your ability to plan programmes further, read some of the books in the *References and further reading* section on pages 275–76. We find that the content of Siddons (1997) is very relevant to planning learning activities. The CIPD also offers a Certificate in Training Practice, and its college-tutored course is highly relevant to planning and delivering effective training.

ACTIVITY 9.3

Take learning or development needs at your place of work. Write some learning objectives for addressing a specific need. These may include behavioural objectives – for example: 'to be confident about "having a word" with a subordinate'. Decide the activities that might be available as options for the learning or development, and select suitable ones. Write out a plan that addresses the issues discussed in this section. Then discuss your plan with a learning source.

When we have implemented our training, there is one more task. It is not really the last task, because it is only one step in the learning cycle. It is appropriate for it to lead to the identification of further needs.

WHY SHOULD WE EVALUATE OUR LEARNING AND DEVELOPMENT?

It is important to remember that learning and development activities are not ends in themselves. The nineteenth-century biologist T. H. Huxley said: 'The great end in life is not knowledge but action.' Unless our activities result in some positive changes in the performance of our organisation, they have no relevant value. We should therefore evaluate the action that results from our learning, if we are to know whether it was worthwhile.

It is good practice to evaluate any business investment to learn lessons for the future. When we look at learning, some particular reasons to consider are:

- justifying the expense
- providing the trainer with feedback
- providing feedback on techniques
- establishing whether the needs and objectives of the learning have been met
- improving future programmes

- identifying further needs
- providing data for justifying further expenditure
- helping top management understand the broad costs and benefits of developing people.

We might be prompted to ask the question posed in the next heading.

WHY IS LEARNING AND DEVELOPMENT SO FREQUENTLY NOT EVALUATED?

Looking at the answers to this question helps to identify the practical problems.

- The benefits of learning and development are often intangible: effectiveness may improve, but in ways that are not immediately obvious. Development activities help people to grow, to improve their judgement and to increase their value to an employer. Such skill develops gradually and may not become suddenly apparent on completion of the activities.
- Sometimes the objectives of the learning and development have not been defined, or when they have, it may be difficult to measure whether they have been achieved.
- Even where measurable change exists, it is not always easy to establish a direct link between the learning or development and the results, because there are many other factors that may impinge on the same changes.
- It costs time and money to evaluate learning and development thoroughly, and that has to be weighed against what is learned from the process of evaluation. For instance, an in-depth evaluation of a management development programme that will be implemented across many parts of a large organisation is likely to be worthwhile (and essential in terms of justifying the expenditure). For a one-off training course for one particular person, a thorough evaluation is likely to be disproportionate.

The result is that evaluation is often confined to questionnaires completed by trainees at the end of a training course.

What we find particularly helpful in evaluating the effectiveness of training, and hence learning, is a model proposed by Hamblin and described by Reid and Barrington (1999: 257) – see Table 9.1 – in which there are examples of measures for assessing the true value of training at each of five levels.

If, on evaluation, a particular piece of training has achieved its objectives and made a significant contribution to the success of your organisation, you might consider applying for a National Training Award for your organisation (the awards are competitive). If successful, this accolade would provide substantial publicity: it would publicly recognise your success in following the learning cycle.

Table 9.1 Hamblin's levels of evaluation

	The levels	Methods of evaluation	
Level 1	Reactions of the trainees – to the content and methods of training, to the trainer, and to any other factors perceived as relevant. What the trainee thought about the learning exercise	Discussion Interviews Questionnaires Recommendations of trainees Desire for further learning	
Level 2	Learning attained during the training period Did the trainees learn what was intended?	*Behaviour*	Objectives obtained
		Knowledge and understanding	Examinations and other tests
		Skills	Analysis by observation of demonstrated skill Evidence of skills applied Projects or assignments
		Attitude	Questionnaires
Level 3	Job behaviour in the work environment at the end of the learning period Did the learning get transferred to the job?	Production rate Customer complaints Discuss with manager/subordinate/peers Activity sampling Self-recording of specific incidents Evidence of competence Appraisal	
Level 4	Effect on the department Has the learning helped the department's performance?	Minutes of meetings Deadlines met Stress indicators Quality indicators Interview other managers and superiors	
Level 5	The 'ultimate' level. Has the learning affected the ultimate well-being of the organisation in terms of business objectives?	Standing of the training officer Growth Quality indicators Stress indicators Achievement of business goals and targets	

ACTIVITY 9.4

Evaluation of a training programme, course or exercise should be measured against its objectives. The result of the evaluation may legitimately lead to improved objectives, but the training event itself should be reviewed against the original learning objectives.

Take a learning activity in which you have been involved recently – perhaps a group exercise on a Certificate in HR Practice (CHRP) programme if you are currently a participant. Investigate the objectives of the activity.

Then discuss with others who have followed a similar activity the effectiveness of that activity. Try to decide how that effectiveness might be measured at your place of work. Concentrate on Level 3 of Hamblin's model (see Table 9.1) and, if you feel it appropriate, Level 4 or even 5. Look for some tangible measures, remembering that it is actions that really count in the workplace. Relate these back to the objectives in order to make your decision.

THE ROLE OF HR PRACTITIONERS

Your role in learning and development activities will be largely determined by the structure and culture of your organisation. As previously discussed, an HR practitioner may be expected to take responsibility for learning and development activities. If so, then the content of this chapter will be especially relevant.

AN INFLUENCING ROLE

If you want to influence line managers towards better training decisions, you will benefit by learning to understand their needs. That means talking to them about what they are trying to achieve. You will then be in a position to make positive and helpful suggestions.

By becoming familiar with government initiatives and sources of grant support you will increase your own value and credibility and, hence, your ability to influence.

Remember that many organisations still give learning and development low priority. In the 1990s a prominent businessman, Sir John Harvey-Jones, suggested that British businesses rarely spend more than 2% of their total payroll budget on learning and development, and yet compete with businesses who regard 10–20% as a more appropriate figure. In the new millennium, has that percentage really changed? The 2009 *Learning and Development* survey from the CIPD suggested a spend per employee of just £220 per year, so perhaps not much has changed. Your most valuable contribution could be to research the true value of learning and development for your employer and make clear cost-justified cases for improvement. Remember that learning and development activities need to produce a return in a similar way to any other investment.

AN ADMINISTRATIVE ROLE

You take this on when you concentrate on making the arrangements for learning and for keeping the records. Significant costs from the budget can be saved by effective arrangements and diligent negotiation. Well-organised records on objectives and outcomes can provide valuable information for evaluating the true benefits of learning activities. In specific sectors – for example, health – records of certain training are needed for quality and safety inspection purposes. However, if you want to break out of the administrative mould, you should use your learning in this chapter and your unique access to learning records to move towards an influencing role.

A TRAINING ROLE

This comes into play when you are appointed an HR and learning practitioner. If you are so appointed, you will have clear training responsibilities. If this also involves delivering training on a regular basis, you may consider trying to specialise in either training or HR rather than spreading your skills and responsibilities too thinly.

Delivery of training and hence learning requires planning and thorough preparation. HR responsibilities often require you to respond to demands that arise suddenly and unexpectedly. The two responsibilities therefore do not always sit very comfortably alongside each other.

A DECISION-MAKING ROLE

Here you have the opportunity to make decisions about learning needs, about the response to those needs and about the effectiveness of the response. This chapter should have given you the basic understanding you require to start making decisions. If you are new to the task, commence slowly and build up your experience as you go round your own learning cycle.

AN OVERSEEING ROLE

This role requires you to keep in touch with all the learning activities in your sphere of responsibility, which will help you to influence others, as we discussed above. You may be able to pick out many ways of improving the relevance and effectiveness of learning.

SUMMARY

- We have looked at the steps of the learning cycle and used those to examine the management of learning and development. It is the changes in the environment in which a business operates, and people's job and career changes, that create the need for learning.

- Learning needs can be identified at the level of the organisation, job or occupation, and at the individual employee level. We have to consider not just what may require training but whether that is both important in the job and likely to be recognised or rewarded within the culture of the organisation.

- Learning needs are established by examining the gap between the performance that is sought and the performance currently being achieved. A wide variety of sources is available to help determine both the desired performance and current performance. Competency frameworks can be particularly useful.

- In formulating plans for learning and development it is important to examine the internal resources available, the external resources and the relevance of qualifications. We can select from a wide variety of techniques and opportunities, and should never restrict our concept of learning and development to training courses alone. Individuals have preferences for the ways in which they learn – their learning styles. The choice of learning activities should take this into account.

- To complete the learning cycle, we emphasised the value of evaluating training and learning, considered some of the practical obstacles, and identified a model that can help structure our evaluation.

If you have the opportunity to be involved in learning and development activities, we suggest you involve yourself with enthusiasm. There is much to be gained.

EXPLORE FURTHER

REFERENCES AND FURTHER READING

CHARLTON, J. (2008) 'Back off: how much does your organisation spend per capita on training?', *Personnel Today*, 13 May

EASTERBY-SMITH, M. and TANTON, M. (1985) 'Turning course evaluation from an end to a means', *Personnel Management*, April; pp.25–7

FAIRBAIRNS, J. (1991) 'Plugging the gap in training needs analysis', *Personnel Management*, February, pp.43–5

FINDLAY, J. (2004) 'Evaluation is no white elephant', *People Management*, 25 March; p.50

HACKETT, P. (2003) *Training Practice*. London: Chartered Institute of Personnel and Development

HARRISON, R. (2009) *Learning and Development*. London: Chartered Institute of Personnel and Development

HARVEY-JONES, Sir J. (1995) *All Together Now*. London: Mandarin

HONEY, P. and MUMFORD, A. (1992a) *The Manual of Learning Styles*. Maidenhead: Honey

HONEY, P. and MUMFORD, A. (1992b) *Using Your Styles*. Maidenhead: Honey

REID, M. A., BARRINGTON, H. A. and BROWN, M., (2004) *Human Resource Development: Beyond training interventions*, 7th edition. London: Chartered Institute of Personnel and Development

WHIDDETT, S. and HOLLYFORDE, S. (2003) *A Practical Guide to Competencies*, 2nd edition. London: Chartered Institute of Personnel and Development

Investors in People UK provides a number of publications, available through The Stationery Office (TSO) website.

There is a variety of information available on NVQs/SVQs: see the *Websites* below.

See also the Chartered Institute of Personnel and Development's Management Shapers and Training Essentials series, which cover all aspects of the learning cycle. In particular, see:

BOYDELL, T. and LEARY, M. (1996) *Identifying Training Needs*. London: Institute of Personnel and Development

BRAMLEY, P. (2003) *Evaluating Training*. London: Chartered Institute of Personnel and Development

SIDDONS, S. (1997) *Delivering Training*. London: Institute of Personnel and Development

National Training Awards publishes a brochure giving interesting case studies from award winners. For more information, contact National Training Awards Office, Moorfoot, Sheffield S1 4PQ; tel.: 0114 259 3419.

WEBSITES

BBC Education: www.bbc.co.uk/learning/adults

Chartered Institute of Personnel and Development: www.cipd.co.uk

Employer Solutions Ltd: www.employersolutions.co.uk

The Stationery Office: www.tso.co.uk/investors_in_people.html

Train to Gain: www.traintogain.gov.uk

Qualifications and Curriculum Development Agency: www.qcda.gov.uk/

National Training Awards: www.nationaltrainingawards.com/

People Management: www.peoplemanagement.co.uk

ACTIVITIES FEEDBACK

Activity 9.2

Activists like to 'have a go' and are unlikely to shrink from exciting experiences.

Reflectors are more likely to take a back seat in a meeting so as to absorb what is happening. Keeping a daily log is consistent with a tendency to learn from reflection.

Pragmatists like techniques that solve problems and should respond well to coaching (from those who know how to get tasks done – that is to say, not from a counsellor who may reflect the problem back on them).

Theorists will welcome an intellectual debate and are likely to be tolerant should their reasons for a decision be cross-examined.

CHAPTER 10

Information and communication technology in HR

LEARNING OUTCOMES

After reading this chapter you will:

- be aware of the importance of keeping accurate HR records

- be able to find some suitable computer applications for use in the HR function, including the role of databases and e-learning

- be able to respond to the main legal requirements for confidentiality, data protection and security of data

- recognise the implications of Internet and email use in an employer organisation

- be aware of some of the ways in which web-based technology is changing information management and appreciate what may be available on the web

- be able to contribute to discussions about the pros and cons of social networking, Wikis, and openness versus confidentiality in the management of information

- be alert to the opportunities provided by the read-write opportunities on the web.

INTRODUCTION

No other area of HR practice is changing faster than the use of technology in accessing information and in facilitating new methods of communication. In 2002 scarcely 50% of the UK adult population had access to the Internet, whereas today, well, readers can assess for themselves. At the outset of 2008 Twitter was virtually unknown, but by the end of 2009 it had about 50 million users.

Some of our readers may have been using databases for decades whereas for others the concept may be relatively new. Those working in education, the media or recruitment should be familiar with social networking. In commerce, small organisations or generalist HR, individuals' experience of social networking may be more personally based than work- or career-based. In writing this chapter we are addressing a diverse audience but our intention is to focus on the relevance of information and communication technology to HR. Occasionally, we refer to basic concepts for the benefit of those who may be unfamiliar with them.

In this chapter we will:

- examine some of the information of which HR is the nominal guardian
- highlight some of the technology that assists that task
- consider the legal position in relation to data protection and freedom of information
- discuss issues relating to email and the Internet
- highlight the increased access to information, to collaboration and Web 2.0 facilities.

A typical HR department is responsible for a substantial amount of information about the people employed in the organisation and needs to maintain accurate and largely up-to-date records. So let's start by examining why that should be so.

WHY RECORDS ARE IMPORTANT IN HR

We see seven main reasons why records are important:

- to satisfy legal requirements
- to provide the organisation with information to make decisions
- to record contractual arrangements and agreements
- to keep contact details of employees
- to provide documentation in the event of a claim against the organisation
- to provide information for consultation requirements
- for due diligence in the event of a business transfer.

There is an extensive body of legislation that regulates and controls the management of personal data and information. HR records have to satisfy a number of legal principles. We look first at the importance of records in more detail.

TO SATISFY LEGAL REQUIREMENTS

Government departments, including the Inland Revenue, can demand information on how many people you employ, what they are paid, what they have been paid over a number of years, and how many hours they have worked.

The Working Time Regulations and the National Minimum Wage Act each require certain specific records relating to hours of work and, in the latter case, pay.

TO PROVIDE THE ORGANISATION WITH INFORMATION TO MAKE DECISIONS

Knowledge and information are the lifeblood of good decision-making for organisations. For individuals, access to accurate, factual and dependable information that can be used for arguments and influence is a vital factor in their ability to achieve. In the past, financial information has been highly regarded and available to considerable levels of sophistication. HR information has been harder to obtain, but because computer software is becoming highly developed in this area, such information is becoming much better and more readily available.

It is also significant that in an era of high technology, products of all kinds are quickly and easily imitated. Consequently, products are becoming increasingly similar and therefore business is beginning seriously to value service. It is now frequently service that differentiates one supplier from another. This has led business decision-makers to appreciate the value of their employees more, because of the need for them to give good service to customers. In a healthy organisation, or in shared services, 'good service' includes internal customers (ie fellow employees and managers). In turn this places more emphasis on good HR information. For example, if you want to know the level of staff turnover in different departments, a good computer system will allow you to access it relatively easily. Having such information may aid in the identification of problems.

TO RECORD CONTRACTUAL ARRANGEMENTS AND AGREEMENTS

Agreements that are recorded are clearer and also easier to insist upon. It is not only a legal requirement to provide written particulars of employment, it is simply good practice to provide them. Employment problems are less likely to arise when all parties are clear about what has been agreed. Records are needed for reference purposes in the case of disputes and, as we emphasise below, for defence if, for example, claims are made to an employment tribunal.

TO KEEP CONTACT DETAILS OF EMPLOYEES

The simplest and most obvious reason for this is so that employees can be paid. It is not difficult to see other reasons, such as the need to call someone in at short notice to provide relief cover.

TO PROVIDE DOCUMENTATION IN THE EVENT OF A CLAIM

Employment protection rights demand that we keep records to protect ourselves, as employers, from claims that we have discriminated against or unfairly dismissed employees. Health and safety legislation demands that records are kept of accidents, exposure to hazardous substances, what training has been provided, and much more. Employers must be able to demonstrate responsible management of health and safety issues.

When employees feel their rights have been infringed, they may make claims to employment tribunals. Expectations on employers are increasing continually. Tribunal cases at which the employer is closely questioned by the claimant's barrister are becoming more common. If your employer needs to defend such a case in a tribunal, it will place heavy demands on the accuracy and comprehensiveness of HR records.

TO PROVIDE INFORMATION FOR CONSULTATION REQUIREMENTS

In Chapter 3 we outlined the requirements likely to be placed on larger organisations by the information and consultation regulations, which include information on developments relating to employment within the organisation. Even if your organisation is not within the scope of these regulations, there will still be many other areas where information for consultation is required. For example, if employees might be made redundant, there is a need to consult – and if they are to be transferred to another organisation (under an outsourcing arrangement, perhaps), there are similar requirements to consult. Information on alternative jobs, pay rates and skills needs as well as records of the consultations themselves will be important.

FOR DUE DILIGENCE IN THE EVENT OF A BUSINESS TRANSFER

In the event that an organisation or the activities of part of an organisation are transferred to another organisation (the transfer of an undertaking), the employees in that organisation, or part of it, normally have their employment transferrred to the new organisation. On transfer they are entitled to precisely the same terms and conditions (as a minimum) as they enjoyed with the previous organisation. This is a complex area of legislation not least because it creates complications for the transferee (the organisation that receives the employees) as they may have other employees on different, perhaps poorer, terms and conditions. The legislation is known as 'TUPE' – often pronounced 'chew-pea' or 'two-pea', depending on regional accents. Whether or not TUPE applies in any particular case has been the subject of much case law over many years. As a general rule, employees follow their jobs.

The reason for explaining this here is that the transferor (the organisation losing the employees) is required to provide the transferee (the organisation gaining the employees) with detailed information about the terms and conditons under which those employees were employed – for obvious reasons. The detail is known as 'employee liability information' and the requirements are laid out in the Transfer of Undertakings (Protection of Employment) Regulations 2006, from which the acronym TUPE is derived.

Finally, it is worth emphasising that good organisation of records is the key to efficiency and effectiveness, and to the credibility of the HR department.

ACTIVITY 10.1

Have a close look at the records in your department.

- Identify what is recorded, what duplications occur, what information is routinely sought, what information is aggregated.

- Is data recorded that is never used?

- How much time does it take to record the data?

- How easy is it to obtain information when it is needed?

- What routines exist to ensure that data is kept up to date? Do they work?

- Are your systems in 'real time'?

- If not, how do systems cope with current information required (such as number of employees) before current data has been recorded (such as new appointees)?

- How quickly could you access a record that an employee had attended an induction?

MANUAL AND COMPUTERISED RECORDS

You can see from the above that many records are kept and that some of these will be manual records – ie written or printed on sheets of paper – such as application forms, copies of qualification certificates and some everyday correspondence received about an employee.

Typically, these items will be in an individual employee wallet or envelope and kept secure from threats such as fire or theft. Thought needs to be given to the filing processes. Not only should records be easy to find when needed but also different records should be destroyed after different periods of time. Unsuccessful application forms may be destroyed after a few months whereas pension-related documents should be kept for 60 years or more. Guidance about the length of time records need to be retained can be found on the CIPD website.

Good document discipline is needed in HR departments – paper should not be left lying around for prying eyes, and a 'clean desk at night' policy should be mandatory. In an HR department the only flat surfaces on which papers can be placed should be personal desks.

Documents can be scanned into computers and their image stored as a computer file. The advantage of having scanned documents on computer is that they can then be accessed by means of a computer screen rather than by going to a filing cabinet. They can be forwarded easily to others who may need the information. Placed on a central server they can be found by search processes. They can also be assigned an expiry date so they are not kept longer than necessary. In many cases optical character recognition (OCR) software can convert text in images to electronic text for indexing or word-processing. Document management systems of this type are becoming commonplace.

CASE STUDY 10.1

In a medium-sized manufacturing company not many years ago, maintaining the records for – and calculating a redundancy payment for – an employee was a laborious process. The employee's earnings were held on a salary card contained in an envelope in a filing cabinet. Salary cards were updated annually after the pay settlement or when an individual's salary changed. This card (which had to be removed from the envelope) did not contain the date of commencement or date of birth of the employee. The latter information had to be looked up in a book of forms that maintained a list of employees in alphabetical order. When an employee joined, a new form with his or her details was inserted, and when one left, the form was removed to a 'former employees' book.

Length of service and age had to be calculated arithmetically from the respective dates. A week's pay was calculated from the salary. Statutory entitlement in terms of the number of weeks' pay (subject to a statutory maximum) could be determined from a printed ready-reckoner, and the correct weeks' pay calculated from the salary. There were also company enhancements that depended on service and age and on a week's pay but without the statutory maximum limit.

For reasons of confidentiality and responsibility, each calculation was performed by the HR manager and for accuracy was checked by the HR director. Typically, 20 minutes' work went into each calculation and almost as much again into the checking. The final result was written longhand on a paper form for discussion with the individual.

With hundreds of redundancies during the early 1990s, considerable time and resources were devoted to this relatively simple task. If it was necessary (as it occasionally was) to know the costs of a proposed redundancy programme, only an estimate could be made, because a precise figure could not be produced from the information in sufficient time.

Today the information (even for closing the whole company!) can be determined in seconds by the use of a few keystrokes on a computer keyboard, and it can be confidential, timely, accurate, well presented and administratively efficient.

DATABASES

Once a database has been set up for employees, you should be able to find who is due for a long-service award, who will retire next year, whose probationary period ends next week, whose salary exceeds £30,000 – all just by a few clicks of a mouse. Proprietary computer systems use databases in such fast and subtle ways that you may not even be aware of the search processes or the structure of the database. (See *Using databases* below.)

APPLICATIONS SOFTWARE ON COMPUTERS AND THE WEB

You will have noticed that we have referred to the use to which a computer is put as an 'application'. Drawing up an organisation chart may thus be considered an application, and there is a variety of proprietary software available to meet this purpose. Often applications are contained within other applications. For example, a word-processing package will probably include an organisation chart facility. For clarity, this software is usually referred to as 'applications software'. Matching organisation needs to applications software demands knowledge of both the needs and the software. In this section we look at some of the applications software that is available to meet potential business needs.

An increasing number of applications are available on the web. You may have used one of the route-planners available from motoring organisations (or the one on Google). You input the data (departure point, destination, etc) and your route is calculated on their computer, then fed back into your browser. Some HR administration and information systems are available as applications software on the web, as are employee policies and procedures. In these cases you would use the application but might not own the software. There are also remote facilities in which your applications are held remotely and accessed over the web, but where you own the software. Differing facilities are being developed all the time and you may need a basic understanding of how your system works because you may be responsible (and will almost certainly have to react) if it fails.

CASE STUDY 10.2

A few years ago, a large national baker maintained its policies and procedures in the company head office HR department. These were kept on paper and had been prepared in a variety of formats and by different people at different times. Some were part of negotiated agreements, others enhancements to statutory entitlements such as maternity leave.

Now all these policies and procedures are gathered in one place on the Internet. They can be accessed by all the 5,000 employees and their managers. The presentation reflects the status of the company, is consistent, and allows navigation from one web page to another. Employees and managers can search for keywords in the documents, print out relevant policies, link directly to government websites. The whole suite is kept continually up to date; there is no haphazard search for the latest copy or being unsure of its status when found. Routine forms, such as holiday requests, can be printed out directly by employees only when needed, and in time these will no doubt be completed online too.

As it was implemented, the HR manager commented: 'Our employees across the country will now benefit from a central source of valuable up-to-date information and guidelines.'

There is always a trade-off between the benefits available from a particular piece of software and the investment in time required to learn all the possibilities it provides or input all the data it needs. Some priority-setting is likely to be necessary. First let's have a look at just a few of the applications that you might use.

Word-processing

So commonplace now that it scarcely merits mention. But there is a huge range of facilities in any typical program. If you have specific needs, such as cross-referencing, or have more than one person needing to work on a document, then always investigate to see if there are facilities that would assist the task. Most of us use only a small fraction of the facilities available – even authors!

Using databases for primary employee records

The data here would typically be personal details such as name, address, date employment commenced, date of birth, National Insurance number, payroll number and salary. It could be used in its raw, unprocessed form to send out a letter, for example. In addition it could be processed to identify who is due to retire or to calculate salary costs for a department. Aggregating data for reports to managers is a valuable computer task. As with word-processing, there are so many facilities in a typical database that you will be unlikely to use them all – but investigating them often pays off.

Absence recording and analysis

This is a popular application. Because tangible financial savings can be identified from reductions in absence level, it is easy to make a cost case for this application. Only actions taken by managers and supervisors can bring the absence level down, but good records can help them to do that job. The HR department can also monitor the situation to see that the job is being done.

Administration

HR departments need to seek to reduce administrative burdens. Computers can help with many aspects of administration, of which recruitment administration is a particularly good example. The use of online forms, intranets and self-service access to employment details can further reduce the administrative burden by allowing employees to do much of it themselves. Because of the ease with which computers can communicate, this is an application that is easily outsourced to a shared service provider (see Chapter 2).

Diaries, organisers and workflow

Organisers can bring together the diaries of different managers, making it much easier to identify dates and venues. This can be invaluable for discovering when, for example, all members of a recruitment panel might be available.

CASE STUDY 10.3

HR personal assistants (PAs) in the past lived by their diaries. Every recurrent task would be entered under the date and time when it was to be done. Task lists would be prepared so as to check that all the activities – for a new starter, for example – were completed, and each activity would be ticked off as it was done. Typical tasks could be to confirm salary, send out an offer, check acceptance of a contract, confirm acceptance to the manager, notify payroll, notify security, prepare a salary card, etc. Probationary reviews, stages in the pay review process, retirements (employees used to retire at 60 or 65), long-service awards due are all examples of the information that would be entered. Irregular day-to-day activities would also be added. Great diligence was required to ensure that all activities were entered, all procedures followed and everything ticked off correctly when it was done.

Today's PA can rely on an HR database as an organiser. Task lists are less necessary because the system does most of them automatically. Ones that require manual action can be set up as an automatic list of actions to be prompted. New information will still need to be entered but actions can be brought to the PA's attention in advance. Tasks with relevant telephone numbers and addresses can all come onto the screen at the appropriate time. Actions not completed can be deferred to a later time. Memos, letters and emails can be written direct from the database and a record kept on the employee's file, cross-referenced to the memo, letter or email itself. Even telephone calls can be made directly from the database. These actions can each initiate history records which, with added notes, can easily be kept for future reference.

Instead of circulating information by means of paper memos, email can be used for most purposes. Reference information that many employees may want to access can be placed on an intranet or the Internet.

These applications can improve workflow around the organisation, ensuring that tasks are passed smoothly from one individual to another and keeping all people in the system informed of the progress of items, subject to any access restrictions.

Payroll

This contains much of the information held in primary records and for this reason there is a great temptation to amalgamate the two. Unfortunately, payrolls are designed for weekly (or monthly) calculations and for 'pay history' purposes. They do not often lend themselves well to the task of providing or analysing other HR information. It is nevertheless feasible to link payroll and HR systems, and the software that makes this possible is becoming more sophisticated.

Time and attendance

Systems such as these help manage flexitime and, when linked to payroll, pay. Clocking systems are linked to a central computer and can make considerable administrative savings. Care is needed over who controls the system to ensure that there is no abuse.

Organisation charts

Drawing organisation charts by hand is a long and tedious task and one that soon needs repeating if they are to be kept up to date. People outside the HR function often ask why HR practitioners never seem to be able to cope with what they see as an easy task. Fortunately, a variety of software now exists to make the task more manageable.

Candidate selection systems

These are a very different form of application, but there is an increasingly wide variety available. A number of purveyors of psychometric testing provide their own software; others sell selection systems to help identify suitable candidates from your own employees. They tend to be more relevant to larger organisations. See the cautionary notes, in the *Data protection* section below, about the logic in automatic systems.

The Internet is also being used for candidate selection. There is a wide variety of systems, some of which give the applicant immediate feedback on whether he or she really is a suitable candidate.

Specialised processing applications

Placing primary employee records onto a computer database provides in itself no more than a computerised reference system, valuable though that might be. Specific applications offer benefits by facilitating routine calculations. Complex calculations such as those for redundancy pay, pensions, labour turnover, salary trends and time to fill vacancies are usually included in proprietary packages. Furthermore, what-if calculations can be invaluable in assisting decision-making.

Other records systems

There are many other records that lend themselves to computerisation. Company vehicle records, Control of Substances Hazardous to Health records, risk assessments and equal opportunities monitoring are just a few such. With interrelational databases they can usually be cross-referenced to the primary employee records and to each other.

Expert systems

As specialised versions of reference information, expert systems can guide inexperienced individuals (by means of question-and-answer sessions) through otherwise complex decisions. One area in which they are used is medical diagnosis. In HR, such systems can be used to guide managers through disciplinary action and legal requirements, for example.

Interactive learning

Similar in principle to expert systems, these often use the Internet and DVD to enable learning. Typically, users choose answers to questions posed and the system takes the user through learning points appropriate to the answers they give. Systems use text and a variety of illustrations, and often incorporate substantial amounts of video illustration. Many larger organisations and training centres have set up learning centres where these facilities are available to their employees and often also to outsiders. In our experience they seem to be more successful when a learning centre manager proactively promotes them rather than when they are just left available for employees themselves to explore.

Podcasts, streamed and downloaded training

Podcasts are downloaded to iPods or other MP3 players and there is much material available for keeping pace with current affairs, for being up to date on technical subjects and for use in training.

Streamed facilities – of which BBC iPlayer and YouTube are examples – can provide training allowing you to hear presentations from leading experts and to access e-learning programmes over the Internet. The content can often be downloaded onto your own computer for viewing later or on repeat ocassions.

Self-service

Many large organisations are beginning to allow staff to access the information held in their HR records from their own workstation and to update their own personal details, such as change of address. Clearly, this frees the HR staff from a good deal of work of a minor nature and helps to meet many aspects of subject access as required under the Data Protection Act.

Other applications

Our list is not exhaustive: there is a huge range of applications, including many on the web (some of which we discuss later), that can help you and your department perform well. But for HR practitioners these are the means to an end. It is important not to lose sight of the end itself!

ACTIVITY 10.2

Seek out some new software that would be useful in your HR department, and investigate it. You should find many possibilities in HR magazines, on the Internet or by networking with colleagues on a college course.

Prepare the outline of a case for implementing one of your discoveries into your HR function.

For example, a document management system may have the potential of revolutionising the archiving of your HR records.

THE DATA PROTECTION ACT

This Act applies to personal data that is held in a 'relevant filing system'. This means that it applies to personal data held in manual filing systems as well as email, taped telephone conversations or websites. You must have legitimate grounds for processing such information. The Act places restrictions on the processing of personal data. Personal data is information that relates to an identifiable living person. It does not need to be 'confidential' or 'private' to be deemed personal data. An email describing an incident involving a named individual is 'personal data'. The same applies to information on successful and unsuccessful job applicants, agency and contract workers, individual customers (rather than businesses) or, for example, residents in a care home. Obtaining, recording or simply holding data is equivalent to processing it.

Depending on the purpose for which personal data is held, your organisation may need to notify the Information Commissioner. There is a ready check process for this on the Commissioner's website. Certain data is defined as sensitive information. This includes anything that relates to a person's racial or ethnic origin, political opinions, religious beliefs, trade union membership, physical or mental health or sexual life. Processing of such data requires the explicit consent of the individual (which usually means a signature freely given), unless the individual has himself or herself made it public. There are, however, some exceptions to this explicit permission where the data is to be used for health and safety purposes, for monitoring of non-discrimination in the workplace or for the protection of customers' property or funds, and for certain legal purposes.

It is also important to realise that data gathered for one purpose cannot be used for another. So, for example, if you gather information about union membership to deduct union dues (with explicit permission, of course), you cannot then use it in negotiations unless, again, you have explicit permission to do so. Workers (and others on which you might hold data) are entitled to know the purpose for which data on them is held.

STAFF HANDBOOKS

Employers are responsible for ensuring that they, and their staff, comply with the data protection principles. It would therefore be a good idea if the staff handbook and policy provided guidance so that staff know how to comply with the data protection principles. Staff and managers can only lawfully have access to personal data where there is a legitimate need.

Disciplinary rules must indicate examples of misconduct and gross misconduct in relation to data protection. For example, you would be wise to make it a disciplinary rule that references must be given only by a specified level in the HR department.

Your handbook could be a useful place to indicate what information is held on individuals, how it is obtained, how it is processed and to what purposes it is put. This would help to prevent staff requesting this information individually and creating a serious administrative burden. If your handbook is on an intranet, it will be easier to keep up to date. If you allow employees to access their own records, it will enable them to check the information held on them.

THE EMPLOYMENT PRACTICES DATA PROTECTION CODE

The Information Commissioner has produced a code of practice in four parts:

1 Recruitment and selection

2 Employment records

3 Monitoring at work

4 Information about workers' health.

The scope of this code and its various parts is wide. It often gives very specific information about how the matters in each area of employment should be handled. Its purpose is to act as a source of recommendations on how the legal requirements of the Data Protection Act can be met and good practice achieved.

DATA PROTECTION PRINCIPLES

As a data-user you have to comply with a set of principles that are designed to protect individuals from the misuse of data. These are examined, in summary, below. The purpose of this examination is to give general guidance about the principles. You should refer to the detail in the Code, or even the Act, before implementing actions.

The basic requirement of the Act is that the processing of both automated and manual data must comply with certain data protection principles.

- Firstly, data must be processed fairly and lawfully.
  Examples of fairness could be advising applicants that their records are being kept on file; making available the logic of any automatic selection processes; or giving candidates the opportunity to defend themselves against adverse information obtained from third parties. There are legal restrictions on the processing of sensitive data, as we have already seen, and unjustified disclosure of private information is likely to contravene the Human Rights Act.

- Secondly, personal data can be obtained only for specified and lawful purposes and not processed in any incompatible manner.
  You must have a legitimate need for obtaining information. This may mean assessing the pros and cons of what information you gather. For example, you may be justified in recording telephone conversations in order to be able to hear what happened in the event that a customer subsequently complains about a worker. However, if you use the same recordings as examples for training purposes in open class, that use might be incompatible. An unlawful purpose would be to require disclosure about spent criminal convictions (other than where provided for by law).

- Thirdly, the data must be adequate, relevant, and not excessive.
  In applications forms, for example, you should seek only information that is relevant for the job in question. Records that you retain should be based on a business need.

- Fourthly, the data must be accurate and, where necessary, kept up to date.
  In employment, one way to achieve this is to allow employees to check, and even update, their own records.

- Fifthly, data should not be kept longer than necessary.
  When it comes to employment records, there should be a clear and foreseeable need for retaining information. The need diminishes as time passes, so some data may be best destroyed after a few months (unsuccessful application forms, as we mentioned earlier, for example) whereas other data should be retained for many decades. Not keeping data longer than necessary may be simple when such data is kept on a computer and cross-referenced by date. However, manual records can pose a problem. An example of this is leavers' files. These may be filed more conveniently in alphabetical order than in the order of leaving. Indexing manual files to a computer system could provide an interim solution. Phasing manual files out altogether may provide the long-term answer.

- Sixthly, data 'shall be processed in accordance with the rights of data subjects'. Employees have a right to privacy, particularly in respect of their personal life. If private telephone calls that an employee makes are recorded, this would breach their rights (unless they clearly knew such calls would be recorded).

- Seventhly, data must be protected by appropriate security measures. There is quite a lot here for the HR practitioner to think about.

  How is data stored? Is it protected from computer failure, fire, intrusion, and unauthorised access? What happens when employees take information out of the organisation on laptops, on memory sticks or via PDAs? Are communications systems – such as email or remote-access – secure? It is particularly important that appropriate technical and organisational measures be taken against unauthorised or unlawful processing of personal data and against accidental loss or destruction of, or damage to, personal data. Data can be destroyed accidentally – and we look at the need to take security measures to protect computer data below. Other forms of data recording are not so easily duplicated, so there is a need to consider appropriate protection where manual data is held. So, for example, fire-proof safes may be appropriate. HR departments must be particularly careful about disclosure, especially when it may be unlawful. HR computer screens should not be visible to visitors to the department. Keep in mind that telephone calls from people purporting to be building societies, future employers or other plausible bodies may, in fact, be from private investigators.

- Finally, personal data must not be transferred to countries that do not provide an adequate level of data protection.
  If you are a small company you may need specific advice on this. Larger organisations are likely to have clear policies wherever this may apply.

SECURITY

This covers not just password protection but also long-term protection of data. The major threats are computer failure, viruses, fire and even sabotage. The main protection against all these is a regular programme of back-ups, anti-virus software and sound firewalls in place. Make sure your supplier or IT department addresses these issues with an approach that is done automatically by the system. You may need to change tapes daily and to update software. It is important that routines are in place where necessary. There should also be an off-site back-up kept. Also keep the following in mind:

- Back-ups must be capable of being restored to a different machine to cover machine failures.

- Viruses usually come from software that originates from an uncertain source, such as pirated software or software downloaded on the Internet.

- Fire and sabotage can be covered by using a fireproof safe for back-ups or by an off-site back-up (password-protected) at another location. If you are a 'belt and braces' person you will do both!

- Recognise that in most cases your IT department or supplier will also have access to your system and may take responsibility for passwords and access 'permissions' to various parts of your system. It is important to understand what is happening and who has access to what. If the supplier is external, your contract should specify how your data is still protected from unauthorised access.

ACTIVITY 10.3

Imagine that there was a serious fire at your place of work. Your office, archives and computer system were completely destroyed. What would happen? Are critical pieces of data protected? If no data is protected, then what *should* be? Even if back-ups were secure in a fireproof safe, would you be able to get access to key information (such as contact details) if access to the site was denied? Put forward recommendations to rectify any shortfalls.

WHAT ARE THE OTHER LEGAL IMPLICATIONS?

It is a criminal offence to hold personal data for certain purposes (educational records, for example) without notifying the Information Commissioner, and your employer could be prosecuted. The same applies if the data is obtained unlawfully or sold unlawfully.

Individuals have rights under the Data Protection Act. They include the right to have access ('subject access') to the information you hold on them (although not to any intentions, such as promotion, that you may have). This access includes access to details of the data being processed, to a description of the data being processed, to the purposes for which it is being processed, to the names or titles of any potential recipients of this data, and to information on the source of the data.

Case law suggests that the data thus protected has to be biographical to a significant extent and have the 'data subject' as its focus. It must also be in a 'relevant filing system'. The email we mentioned earlier would be in a relevant filing system if attached to the employee's record in a computer database, and in such a case it is possible that the email will be about the individual in some biographical way. But if there is merely mention of an employee in the minutes of a meeting, the employee is unlikely to have the right of access to it, either because the data will not be in a relevant filing system, because it will not have the data subject as its focus, or because it does not say much about them.

Where the data is processed automatically, and is likely to form the sole basis for any decision significantly affecting the data subject (such as a psychometric test used for short-listing purposes), the individual is also entitled to know the logic involved in the decision-making. It is your responsibility to supply the logic to any enquirer, so you will need to be careful to obtain it from test suppliers. You would also be wise to check that the logic is valid. Checking the validity of a test, even relying on data from the supplier, requires some understanding of statistics.

If you need to do this yourself, we suggest you read Roland and Frances Bee (see *References and further reading*, page 304).

Failure to comply means that the individual can complain to the Commissioner, who has a range of powers. Individuals can also request information to be corrected or deleted, and they can also sue for damages if they suffer financial loss (or physical injury) as the result of incorrect data.

This is an important Act. As we warned in Chapter 3, employment law is not an area in which issues are necessarily clear-cut. Quite frequently, the precise way in which the law is interpreted changes. So although we have explained key principles, you are likely to need further advice from more senior colleagues, the Advisory, Conciliation and Arbitration Service (Acas) or legal specialists.

ACTIVITY 10.4

Go onto the Information Commissioner's website and use the guidance there to check through for what purposes you need to notify and for which purposes you may be exempt.

OTHER LEGISLATION RELATING TO INFORMATION

THE FREEDOM OF INFORMATION ACT

This Act covers information in the public sector but also applies to the private sector where an organisation holds data on behalf of a public organisation.

The Act came into force in 2005 but it does not provide additional rights for employees or others to have access to employee records, although there may be exceptions. For example, in 2009 a disaffected soldier used the Act to obtain information on MPs' expenses and the information was subsequently published in the *Daily Telegraph*. Because the MPs held a public office, individuals' expenses were disclosed and a huge public outcry resulted that led to ministerial resignations.

If you are likely to need to respond to access requests under the Freedom of Information Act, you should be well briefed by your legal department. Where you are not – in a small private company holding public sector information, for example – you must take further advice. There is no dispensation for being inadequately prepared.

THE HUMAN RIGHTS ACT

The Act confers the right of respect for privacy on individuals and provides for employees in the public sector to take legal action against their employer if they consider that their rights have been infringed.

Employees in the private sector might claim constructive dismissal if they consider the intrusion into their privacy breaches trust and confidence (in their employer).

The Human Rights Act also protects individuals from you disclosing private information that you may hold as a result of employing them. Disclosure without consent could lead to a grievance and a claim of constructive dismissal.

The need to respect privacy may extend further. For example, you can be required, under the Data Protection Act, to disclose the content of a reference that you have received for an applicant (to the applicant) but you have to take steps to protect the privacy of the person who provided the reference.

THE REGULATION OF INVESTIGATORY POWERS ACT

There is no absolute right to privacy (some intrusion may be justified so long as it is proportionate to the circumstances) but care may be required when investigating disciplinary matters that intrude on privacy. You may be called on to show that you have a 'legitimate' and 'defined' purpose for such investigation.

THE INFORMATION AND CONSULTATION OF EMPLOYEES REGULATIONS

Employees, whether trade union members or not, have the right to be informed and consulted about matters that affect their employment. These were discussed in Chapter 3.

In summary, the issues relating to information legislation are complex and the various Acts interact to a significant extent. The important points for you as an HR practitioner are to be very careful about what personal information you obtain, how you obtain it, what you do with it, how you protect and manage it, and to whom you disclose it. The four parts of the Employment Practices Data Protection Code are a helpful guide (and also help you to defend your actions). In all areas of doubt, seek advice. The relevant legislation discussed in this chapter is:

- the Data Protection Act 1998
- the Human Rights Act 1998
- the Regulation of Investigatory Powers Act 2000
- the Freedom of Information Act 2000
- the Information and Consultation of Employees Regulations 2004.

EMAIL AND THE INTERNET

EMAIL

Email, in common with technology-based communication generally, has the huge advantage of being asynchronous. That is, the two (or more) parties do not need to be communicating at the same time. Most of us will have experienced frustration at attempting to speak with someone only to find they are in a meeting. How many times are we in the middle of some complex task (requiring us to keep things in our short-term memory as we do so) when someone interrupts us? If you need to communicate across time zones, synchronous communication can be very inconvenient. Three-way telephone calls can be handy and conference calls can save significantly on travel but the latter, particularly, need to be set up in advance and all parties need to be available at the same time. So unless we need an immediate response from someone it is usually better to use an asynchronous method.

The downside is that in many major companies employees spend four hours a day dealing with their inbox. There is a desire to reverse this trend. Whether or not newer concepts, such as those of Web 2.0 (which we discuss below), will succeed in doing so remains to be seen.

Emails are still relatively informal – salutations such as 'Hi Sarah' being quite acceptable in most quarters – but guidance might be given to employees. They need to know the policy on email use for personal purposes (mirroring the Internet guidance below), be clear about any rules on content (not attaching offensive material, for example), and make use of suitable disclaimers. Employees also need to know what disciplinary actions might be taken against them for breaches of the policy. Below are some examples of where HR practitioners, among others, must be vigilant:

- Email has the equivalence of a note on company headed paper. It is traceable and recorded on both your computer and the receiver's computer (as well as possible intermediate servers). Employees must realise the implications of this. For example, contracts, including employment contracts, could be established unintentionally by careless use of email.

- Email addresses can be easily disclosed inadvertently. Simply circulating email to everyone in your address book, as some virus warnings advise, could disclose the address of each of your contacts to everyone else in your address book, including (perhaps conveniently) the person who sent you the warning! An email address is also personal information, and this would be likely to breach privacy and to make unregistered disclosures. Data protection principles apply to email just as they do to any other form of storing personal data.

- Email started as an informal process and this has led to communications that are not always carefully phrased. And yet, as already said, it is recorded and traceable. Email should never be used for processes such as discipline, in which the parties must see each other. Emails that were not intended to be blunt can often seem so and be cited in claims of bullying. Where email has to be used for difficult subjects, it may be advisable to read, delay, re-read, delay, and re-read before sending the message. Strong language can have a devastating effect on the recipient and prompt serious reactions. It should not be used. Once an email is sent, 'the die is cast'.

THE INTERNET

As we have already outlined, this facility makes a wealth of information available at the desk of everyone connected to it. But as with email, employees need guidance. Here are a few specific issues that HR practitioners should consider.

A policy should specify the limitations and conditions of any use for personal purposes. Some organisations allow business-only use; others accept personal use in the employees' own time (after normal hours, for example); and a third alternative is to allow limited private use in work time (as might be allowed for private telephone calls, for example). Many organisations do not allow their employees to view Internet recruitment sites. It is important that employees know the rules, and also – especially if use is to be monitored – that they know that private matters may not remain private.

Social networking, which we discuss below, carries with it many implications for damage to the company, for breaches of confidentiality and other risks. Employees need to know what is allowed, accepted or even encouraged.

Some of the material obtainable is very offensive – in rare cases, illegal. Fortunately, most of the worst material can now be filtered out by technology. Equally, many employees may consider soft pornography relatively harmless. Guidance is needed on what is acceptable to view or circulate. Just as rules are established about what may be pinned up in an office, so they must be established for Internet usage. Almost all organisations make downloading of pornographic material a disciplinary offence, or even a gross misconduct offence. A well-communicated policy provides the best basis for justifying action.

CASE STUDY 10.4

In January 2000, Incomes Data Services published a study on Internet and email policies. Company policies vary considerably in their scope and detail, but the following provisions feature most often in codes:

- Personal use is either prohibited or allowed on a limited basis.

- Confidential information should not be transmitted by email, unless it is encrypted.

- External email messages should have appropriate signature files and disclaimers attached.

- Employees should be familiar with general housekeeping good practice (eg the need to delete email messages regularly).

- Employees should use appropriate etiquette when writing email messages; the use of capital letters, for example, is considered to be the equivalent of shouting.

- Inappropriate messages are prohibited, including those which are sexually harassing or offensive to others on the grounds of race, religion or gender.

- Employees should not send potentially defamatory email messages which criticise other individuals or organisations.

- Employees should not access or download inappropriate material, such as pornography, from the Internet.

- Employees should take care not to infringe copyright when downloading material or forwarding it to others.

- Employees should ensure that any information which is posted on a corporate website is accurate and updated regularly.

What can be downloaded may have to be restricted further. Copyright is an issue to consider both in respect of software and in respect of other material that might be printed or forwarded. Material from uncertain sources may contain viruses or assist hackers in gaining access to the organisation's systems. Information technology specialists should be involved in preparing guidance on downloading material.

MONITORING

Employers often have reason to want to know what their employees are doing. For example, they want to maintain standards of service (for instance, on customer care lines); they want to know if disciplinary rules are being broken; they may want facts to support a disciplinary action; and they may want to be sure that commercially valuable information is not leaking out of the organisation.

You will find appropriate references in the *References and further reading* section to help with preparing policies. However, what employers can monitor, and how, is an area of evolving law, and it is essential to obtain up-to-date advice if a new policy is being implemented or an existing one questioned.

ACTIVITY 10.5

Review Case study 10.4. This is over 10 years old now. How would you change it for 2010 onwards – what would you add or delete? Discover whether your organisation has an email and Internet policy. If it does, study it and compare it with what you think should be included. If your organisation does not have a policy, draft one and discuss it with an appropriate learning source.

CONFIDENTIALITY, OPENNESS AND WEB 2.0

Confidentiality and openness are complex areas that are often ethical and philosophical in their content. It is not our intention to provide direct guidance in these matters but rather to 'air' them so that you are aware of the need to consider them and of the need to be very careful in how you proceed.

CONFIDENTIALITY

Personal matters

As an HR practitioner it is inevitable that you will be party to confidential information. Some may include sensitive data of the type described above, some may be detail about management intentions towards individual employees, and yet more may be commercially sensitive information. For example, you might become aware that someone is HIV positive, or that an individual is being tipped for promotion, or you might know something about the true market value of an employee who is key to the business.

Most of us aspire to work in or create open, honest organisations whose 'mission' is one to which we relate and one which is full of people with good intentions towards each other. Reality is often different. Moods and feelings such as jealousy, envy, ambition, apathy, greed, fear, arrogance and insecurity can be found wherever significant groups of people come together. The extent to which they are present in any particular organisation is a matter of conjecture or opinion. Personal information about individuals is of great interest to those who seek to exploit the weaknesses of others and much of that personal information is in the hands of HR.

Senior managers are not immune to these feelings and moods and yet often have legitimate reasons for knowing personal information about individuals.

The question of confidentiality is therefore a complex one for HR, and one where the answers are not necessarily clear-cut. But your ability to keep confidential information and to keep information confidential – at least confidential to those who have legitimate reasons for having it – is a key HR skill. At times you will have to exercise judgement.

Corporate confidentiality

Confidentiality goes beyond the personal. As an HR practitioner you may know that re-structuring of the company is being considered, whether redundancies are likely or whether the business is being sold. All these can have a disturbing effect on morale within a company and senior managers will want to be able to deliberate on such critical matters without setting rumours running. Indeed, in some cases the law may require them to keep matters confidential. In other cases the law runs counter to some of these deliberations. For example, consultation on redundancies should commence as soon as they are contemplated, and should run for significant periods of time.

Contrary to this is the new era of the 'net-generation' with social networking, YouTube, Google and Web 2.0 developments threatening to blow secrecy and

---

CASE STUDY 10.5

◉ Storming success at Dell

Dell's social media platform, *EmployeeStorm*, culls ideas from its business units and fosters discussion among employees.

Its worldwide community of more than 80,000 employees post and discuss ideas on topics ranging from product upgrades and innovation to critiques of company policies, facilities improvements and benefits. Ideas submitted are routed to the right departments for conisideration.

Communications and leadership team members can join the discussion, keeping posters abreast of the status of the ideas they submit.

Dell has implemented nearly 200 of the 10,000 or so ideas that have been posted on *IdeaStorm* in under a year.

Reported in 'Conversations at your fingertips': see *References and further reading*.

much confidentiality apart. For example, when a disgruntled employee left Dell computers he published a blog entitled *22 Confessions of a Former Sales Manager*. When Dell tried, unsuccessfully, to have it removed, they drew even more attention to the article. Since then Dell has re-thought their whole strategic approach to control and openness. See Case study 10.5.

WEB 2.0

Martin, Reddington and Kneafsey explain that Web 2.0 differs from earlier web applications because it is a *read-write* medium 'providing a democratic architecture for participation, encouraging people to share ideas, promoting discussion and [it] fosters a greater sense of community'. Until a few years ago placing material on the web required specialist skills – for example, a knowledge of HTML, the basic language of the web. Now with Facebook, YouTube, blogs and many other facilities, almost anyone can put their own material there. We will look at some of these facilities as available in 2010, mindful that the area is ever developing and that new ideas may add to or replace older ones in a matter of years.

Collaboration

Most of us use Wikipedia without necessarily knowing how it evolved and how it continues to do so. In fact, it is a collaborative effort comprising tens of thousands of authors who each contribute in their own specialist area.

You too can prepare documents jointly with others by working on a single copy held on a central server or on a 'Wiki'. These facilities will record who has made a contribution, perhaps when it was made, and allow for comments to be posted. For example, the text for this book was prepared by the collaboration of three authors using similar techniques. Collaboration can be truly global – at one point one of the authors was in Chicago. Within HR, textual collaboration has application in preparing reports, policies and procedures, and employee communications.

Within the organisation itself collaboration can extend to decision-making, to research, and to project management, as just three examples. HR practitioners need to be alert to these possibilities and the implications for contracts of employment, reward, and intellectual property may all need to be considered by the HR management of the organisation.

Virtual offices are on the rise. Homeworking needs a health and safety risk assessment, and there are other issues about protecting confidentiality of company information (not just personal data). Nonetheless, it saves overheads, eases the job marketplace for parents and can increase motivation.

Wikis as meetings

Wikis may go further and allow for serious discussion of topics leading to sound policies or decisions. In a traditional formal meeting, minutes are written up afterwards, are circulated and then 'matters arise' at the next meeting for further discussion. In a Wiki the minutes *are* the meeting, and further discussion, corrections or amendments can follow immediately. Unlike informal face-to-face meetings, there is always a record (for good or bad).

Social networking

Facebook, LinkedIn, Twitter, and others that will probably develop over the life of this book, are further examples of collaboration, sharing information and exchanging experiences. They provide the opportunity to learn from others, to make valuable contacts, for research, to engage teams and existing employees and to recruit potential employees. Case study 10.5, referred to earlier, gives some examples of what can be achieved. Activity 10.6 encourages you to explore Web 2.0 further.

ACTIVITY 10.6

Visit an exhibition such as the CIPD HR Software Show held in London each year, and persuade exhibitors to show you their software in a free demonstration.

Agree an 'exchange' with a colleague on a college course, or an outside learning source. Spend half a day with them understanding how

they manage information, and spend a further half a day showing them your systems.

Log on to the CIPD website to find out how to audit your organisation's information systems using the Institute's action plan. Conducting an audit could be a valuable subject for a project.

Some risks

However large the organisation, leaked information about potential redundancies, or other sensitive matters, could be around your employees in minutes. So you should think carefully about confidential information to which you as an HR practitioner may be party. Guidelines for employees generally might be worth providing too.

Material placed on social networking sites is there *permanently*. What may seem fun after a few beers may not look so cool when you apply for promotion. As an individual, you may want to try to maintain separate identities for your social life and professional life.

A further risk, and conversely also an opportunity, is that social networking may help competitors to lure your best employees away. The converse is that you may be able to find employees yourself, including those who were not even thinking of moving – a double-edged sword.

As individuals it is easy for us to make contributions that we might later regret, so all contributions should be made with care. Not only may we research others on social networking sites but others can research us too. Too much frivolity could be a career inhibitor.

Social networking is not always accurate. Although discussions usually 'get there in the end', the end cannot be identified in advance. See Case study 10.6 for an example.

This is a summary of a typical exchange on a LinkedIn Group (HR Professionals UK) discussion in which one of the authors participated.

- An HR manager with a firm of solicitors posts a question to the LinkedIn Group: 'Do notice periods have to be reciprocal?'

- Almost immediately a human resources consultant confirms that they do not, followed quickly by two heads of employment law who also confirm this. There is some further comment that while notice periods are often reciprocal, it is a question of negotiation between employer and employee.

- Then another consultant makes the suggestion that an employee cannot be required to give more notice, but can give less. She also makes helpful remarks about good practice. However, she misquotes (see later) the statutory minimum notice periods.

- A director of consulting supports these contributions and comments on how business-critical employees are often offered extended periods of notice in return for the same obligation.

- The author then raises questions. He thinks that the statutory periods of notice have been misquoted and re-states the legal requirements. He also questions the assertion that the employee cannot be required to give more notice than the employer and asks the contributors where they are getting their information from.

- He is then supported on both counts by both a head of employment law and a consultancy director.

- Finally the original HR manager posts a big 'Thank you' for the comments.

This summary illustrates several points and in particular that not everything that you read on a social networking site, even a professional one as this is, is necessarily correct. Nonetheless, if you doubt the answer, you can pose your own query, and errors are usually corrected. Secondly, also note my request as to from where the information is coming: 'the authority'. It is easy for people to think they know the answer, but they may only be repeating something they have heard. Much better if they can point to an authority such as an eminent commentator, a statute or regulation, or a court case.

Note too that a great deal of helpful information emerged around the original question, and note the final 'thanks' from the person who started the discussion.

The CIPD website contains much useful advice on how to participate in a discussion.

Incidentally if they needed it for a practical matter, CIPD members could have reached the answer to this question in five minutes simply by calling the CIPD legal helpline.

Deciding whether, or how, to participate in these opportunities is both an individual decision for an HR practitioner and probably a corporate decision too. But the level of control that can be exercised over these opportunities is diminishing, as the example of Dell, above, demonstrates. Most organisations now have a policy on email and the Internet that includes social networking. It is likely to need continual review.

Beware addiction! There is a risk that social networking becomes so interesting and compelling that we, or employees, might do little else. In time we will probably all need to restrict or take control of our activities.

Avoidance is the converse – and if you haven't yet indulged in social networking with some enthusiasm, you are missing out. Think of it like any social interaction or business networking event. You don't know what you will learn or what you will gain until you go.

Information

If you wrote down everything that happened to you in your lifetime for every minute of the day, would that be of value? The information would be so unordered, and critical points would be so deeply buried in detail that they would be unlikely ever to be discovered. But type the same information on to a hard disk or a social networking site, and the answer could be very different. Search algorithms and massive data storage systems have transformed access to information.

An HR practitioner today has immediate access to legislation in the form of statutes and regulations, can get rapid access to comment and advice on case law, can research promising candidates on Google, LinkedIn and other social networking facilities, and can access information on any topic of interest.

Another area of value to HR practitioners is the numerous conferences, discussion groups and forums in our specialist field. For example, you may want to find out about good practice in dress codes. You can search authoritative literature through Google, including material from the CIPD. But you will find equally valuable information about practitioners' practical experience by searching discussion groups.

Social bookmarking services such as Delicious (formerly del.icio.us) enable you to store and organise websites that you might want to retrieve from another computer or wish to share with others. They can enable you to be updated daily or even minute by minute on developments (on employment law, for example) by using web-feeds such as RSS (on the BBC News website, for example).

The volume of information and detail out there is almost infinite, but by carefully selecting what is of serious interest it is easier to be well-informed than it ever has been.

ACTIVITY 10.7

'It is not the strongest of the species that survives, or the most intelligent; it is the one most capable of change,' wrote Charles Darwin. Review the publications by Martin, Reddington and Kneafsey and by Tapscott and Williams, and the article entitled 'Conversations at your fingertips' – all listed in *References and further reading* – and consider your own experiences. Perhaps discuss with your learning sources and then respond to this statement with reference to Web 2.0. Assuming those who can adapt to the opportunities of Web 2.0 will 'survive' better than those people who are simply more intelligent, how will you, or would you, change HR practices to take advantage of the new opportunities? If you are not already engaged in social networking, now may be the time to start so as to add your own experience in answering this question.

The importance of face-to-face communication

Information technology and communication have effectively merged. But as we explained in Chapter 2, it is important to remember that only a small percentage of communication in a face-to-face encounter is made up of the words used. Body language and intonation account for most of the rest. Remove body language (as in a telephone conversation) and less is communicated. Remove intonation (as in an email) and you are left with about 6% of what might have been communicated had your exchange been face-to-face. It is also easier for words to be misinterpreted and misunderstandings to arise.

In September 2001 Prime Minister Tony Blair crossed the Atlantic when no civilian airliners were doing so. Following 9/11 he considered an immediate face-to-face meeting with President George Bush to be crucial.

There are times when technology-based communication is inappropriate.

THE ROLE OF HR PRACTITIONERS

Information and communication systems are tools that you use to support line managers and to assist you with your other HR roles and activities. We can look at your role in five categories.

AN ADMINISTRATIVE ROLE

This involves keeping well-organised records and providing information. It is seen by some as the dull area of HR activities. However, the flow of information around an organisation is vital to effective decision-making. Providing the management of the organisation with high-quality HR information (ie pertinent, clear, timely and accurate) represents a major contribution to the business. At the same time, it is a substantial job for HR practitioners, and one that can be underestimated far too easily. Technology is a means to an end.

AN INFLUENCING ROLE ENHANCED BY NEW RESEARCH OPPORTUNITIES

In this role you are meeting the challenge of providing high-quality information that enhances the credibility of the HR function in your organisation. Researching HR principles and practice in using web and Web 2.0 technologies will assist you in being well-informed and enhancing your credibility, which leads to greater access to decision-makers. That makes your job more rewarding and may provide the opportunity to extend your role and influence into interesting areas.

A USER ROLE

This concerns being the user of computerised systems. Here you may become the customer of an IT department or of an external supplier. You will have a part to play in ensuring that the systems meet your needs for providing your own 'customers' with the information they in turn need. Making sure that computers, the available software and web applications assist rather than hinder this objective is a substantial task in itself.

AN ADVISORY ROLE TO LINE MANAGERS

It is quite possible that the issue of data protection in your organisation will fall to the HR department. In addition, the increasing use of email and the Internet means that you may be called on for advice on policy issues and the actions required if there is abuse of these facilities. If so, you need to know and understand the basics of the relevant legislation, and to know where to go to find more detailed information. We have already cautioned you in this chapter about the complexity of the legislation and when we looked at a similar role in relation to other employment law. It is crucially important that you do not overestimate your understanding of the law, so if you are in any doubt, always seek further advice.

A GATEKEEPER BETWEEN CONFIDENTIALITY AND TRANSPARENCY

We have examined the need for confidentiality but also highlighted the trend towards transparency and openness. Within people-focused areas HR cannot avoid a central role. Decisions are likely to be taken at a senior level in HR, but if you are a sole practitioner you will need to give thought to policies and procedures that guide employees and managers.

SUMMARY

- We have looked at the need to keep records, and you should now have a broad idea of the important reasons for keeping information. Most records and information can now be managed on computer systems and there is a wide range of applications software to assist in information management and HR tasks. We have also considered the requirements of the legislation in this area and noted the implications, for HR practitioners, of email and Internet use.

- Confidentiality is of crucial importance in HR and we have considered both this and the increased openness being fostered by Web 2.0 applications such as social networking. Web 2.0, and some of its other implications, has been looked at in its own right.

- HR practitioners must be familiar with computer software opportunities, the Internet and the communication of information, and now Web 2.0, in order for them to assess how the new read-write facilities can help in their HR responsibilities.

- You should take time to keep up with the trends in software, new applications, web-based opportunities and other new approaches to communications.

REFERENCES AND FURTHER READING

BEE, R. and BEE, F. (2005) *Managing Information and Statistics*. London: Chartered Institute of Personnel and Development

CHA (2009) 'Conversations at your fingertips: how HR professionals score as social networkers'. London: CHA Insideout Communications (see website below)

HAMMONDS (2004) *Data Protection*, 2nd edition. London: Chartered Institute of Personnel and Development

HOGG, C. (2002) *Internet and Email Use and Abuse*. CIPD Good Practice Guide. London: Chartered Institute of Personnel and Development

IDS (2000) *Internet and Email Policies*, IDS Study 682, January

THE INFORMATION COMMISSIONER, *Employment Practices Data Protection Code*. Available from The Information Commissioner's Office, Wycliffe House, Water Lane, Wilmslow, Cheshire SK9 5AF

MARTIN, G., REDDINGTON, M. and KNEAFSEY, B. (no date) *Web 2.0 and HR: A discussion paper*. London: Chartered Institute of Personnel and Development

TAPSCOTT, D. and WILLIAMS, A. D. (2008) *Wikinomics: How mass collaboration changes everything*. Great Britain: Atlantic Books

Articles in *People Management* (www.peoplemanagement.co.uk):

'Caught in the web', Jane Amphlett, 3 February 2000

'Insider information', Olga Aikin, 23 November 2000

'On peeking terms', Olga Aikin, October 2000

'Uncertain freedoms', Audrey Williams, September 2000

'How to monitor e-communication', Ellen Temperton, 22 June 2000

'Mind your own business', Hilary Larter, 16 September 2004

'Respondez PDQ', Hilary Larter and Jennifer Wotherspoon, 11 November 2004

'Too much information', Steve Smethurst, 25 November 2004.

WEBSITES

Information Commissioner: www.informationcommissioner.gov.uk

HMSO Legislation: www.legislation.hmso.gov.uk

Chartered Institute of Personnel and Development: www.cipd.co.uk

CHA Insideout Communications: www.chapr.co.uk

SOCIAL NETWORKING SUGGESTIONS

www.LinkedIn.co.uk

www.facebook.com

www.xperthr.co.uk/blogs/employment-intelligence

http://twitter.com

Follow Malcolm Martin at http://twitter.com/employersolutns

EXPLORE FURTHER

ACTIVITIES FEEDBACK

Activity 10.5

We would keep the current items, but be mindful that email is such a familiar medium today that some points may no longer need to be spelled out in great detail.

The earlier provisions make no mention of laptops, memory sticks or PDAs, all of which present a security risk and are now commonly taken off site.

Remote access and homeworking is now more common and this can link into the use of laptops, which may no longer need to retain company data. But it also makes password confidentiality and other security measures more important.

Social networking was not a major issue 10 years ago but now needs to be considered in any ICT policy. Employees need to know what they may or may not do. Some employees will have company identities as well as individual identities. A rule against bringing the organisation into disrepute via social networking may have to be brought to the attention of employees.

Activity 10.7

Answers to this question are to be found in numerous discussion groups, blogs, chatrooms, etc. Here a just a few suggestions:

- Build your own network of contacts. It used to be said that 'It is not what you know but who you know that counts', and while there is a need for some substance behind your expertise, this statement is still substantially true.
- Participate in intra-organisation communication facilities – or set them up.
- Participate in relevant groups and communities, posting discussion questions of interest to you and making constructive contributions to the discussions started by others.
- Find a career opportunity.
- Recruit new staff.
- Use the reference facility on LinkedIn to research candidates.

CHAPTER 11

Change in organisations

After reading this chapter you will:

- understand the importance of change and why it happens so frequently in organisations

- appreciate the importance of managing change and be familiar with some of the tools and frameworks available to support you

- be able to identify the key responses and reactions to change that you can expect to see in individuals affected by change

- be familiar with the different ways in which you can support people experiencing change.

INTRODUCTION

Change is becoming a constant activity in many organisations. Indeed, much research suggests that small-scale change is happening almost all the time while major change happens in organisations approximately every three years. Change may be voluntary and prompted by the organisation for positive business reasons, or forced, such as many changes seen during the current economic downturn. As such, change is a key activity for both managers and HR practitioners – who have responsibilities to achieve the desired change, manage any negative impacts of change, and manage the impact on people while keeping the day-to-day business running: quite a challenge!

HR practitioners can have a variety of roles in change processes, and these will often depend on the size and nature of the change being introduced. The introduction of a new organisation-wide pay system will necessitate a very involved role for HR – from devising and leading the change to supporting individuals through it. A departmental restructuring, on the other hand, will generally be led by the departmental manager with support from HR to guide the manager through the change and to give support to the employees affected.

In this chapter we consider the context for change in organisations – why it is important and why organisations need to change. We look at approaches to managing change to achieve a successful outcome and then move on to consider the impact of change on individuals and what you can do to support individuals through change.

WHY IS MANAGING CHANGE IMPORTANT?

Change is a process of moving from one state to another state. It affects all types of organisation – public and private sector, voluntary and charitable, national or local, large and small. It can also occur in any aspect of organisational life, from large-scale change that affects a whole organisation and the core purpose of the business to much smaller change, just affecting one business process or one team or activity. Most commonly, change can be seen in the areas of:

- organisational structure
- working practices and processes
- reducing costs
- mergers and takeovers
- business location and infrastructure
- organisational culture
- workforce profile, capability and terms and conditions.

Any change, however large or small, will impact on the people working in the area where the change happens, and one aim of all change processes will be to get 'buy-in' from the people affected – which is easier said than done. The type of change being introduced and the impact it will have on individual members of staff will affect the degree of this buy-in. Some change may be viewed positively and be welcomed by those affected by it – for example, introducing flexible working arrangements – whereas other change – for example, reductions in the size of the workforce – may be seen in a more negative light leading to resistance on the part of those affected. Every individual interprets and will respond to change in a different way depending on a number of factors such as their personal circumstances, how much the change affects them and their previous experience of change. Change in organisations often requires employees to change the way they work or to change their behaviour and attitudes – not something that everyone will be keen to do or have the capability to do. All of this can make change very unpredictable and difficult to manage.

A wide range of research shows that change is not always successful – according to the CIPD 2002 survey *Reorganising for Success* over 40% of change programmes fail to achieve their stated objectives. It is therefore very important to do everything possible to increase the chances of success.

WHY ORGANISATIONS NEED TO CHANGE

Change happens because organisations need to remain competitive in order to survive. Pressure for change may be internal – for example, because of increasing costs or a desire to enter new markets – or it may be external – for example, because of changing economic conditions or pressure from customers. To survive in a competitive business world or deliver highest quality and best value for money in publicly funded bodies, organisations need to be adaptable and agile. A wide range of factors, both internal and external, affect organisations and prompt the need for change. This can be seen by considering some well-known organisations/types of organisations and looking at some of the changes that have affected/are affecting them:

- BT
  Over the last few years we have seen huge changes in the nature of this organisation (and other similar organisations) as technology has developed and the market for their products has changed dramatically. We have seen a move into the provision of mobile phone networks, Internet broadband and other digital services. A BT switchboard operator from 20–30 years ago would not recognise the business of today.

- BBC
  A relocation of five key departments, including sport and children's services, from London to Salford is an example of the huge impact that moving a business to a new location can have. This move not only introduced new up-to-date technologies, potentially having an impact on working practices, but also required staff that wanted to remain in their jobs to move a significant distance – which can have a hugely unsettling effect not only on the individual concerned but also on the individual's family.

- utility companies
  Significant change over the last few years in this sector has included individual companies being established and moving out of public ownership into the private sector, the development of new technologies associated with renewable energy, and mergers and takeovers with companies in other European countries.

- motor manufacturers
  Here organisations have had to change and develop their business as new technology has developed while at the same time being significantly affected by the economic downturn. This has required the development of innovative solutions to reduce the size of the workforce and associated costs while not causing the loss of necessary skills and talent that will be required once recovery takes place.

- the NHS
  Changes in the legislation around working hours have had a significant impact on health services, particularly in relation to the working time of doctors in training. Hospitals have had to redesign shift and working patterns, increase staffing and extend the roles of other healthcare professionals to replace the input once made by doctors in training who worked extremely long hours.

Just from these few examples it can be seen that change in organisations is affected by a multitude of factors – developments in new technology; growing, contracting and changing markets; changing legislative requirements; the economic climate; and moving the business. Other factors also driving change in organisations include the arrival of new competitors, government policy, customer pressure and changes in the population. With so many factors having an influence, it is clear to see why change is so common in organisations striving for success.

ACTIVITY 11.1

Consider a change that has happened in your organisation in the last 12 months. Think about why the change was necessary and what the driving forces for the change were – note down your ideas. Then talk to some of the people involved in planning and managing the change to find out their views on why the change happened and what the driving forces were. How close are your views to the actual reasons?

APPROACHES TO CHANGE

Change can be viewed in a number of different ways, and many different models of, and approaches to, change exist. Sometimes change is deliberate and prompted by the organisation. This is often referred to as 'planned' change. Conversely, where change seems to evolve in a less structured and planned way it is often known as 'emergent' change. Such emergent change may result from apparently unrelated decisions and actions by managers, although these might be linked to assumptions that managers make about what is happening in the environment within which the organisation operates.

As well as considering whether change is planned or emergent, the extent and scope of change is often also considered – Ackerman (1997) distinguished three types of change – transitional, developmental and transformational.

The *transitional* model of change seeks to achieve a known future state that is different from the current situation. This transitional change model can be traced back to the work of Lewin (1951), who described change as a three-stage process involving:

- 'unfreezing' the existing situation
- moving to a new position
- 'refreezing' in the new state.

Developmental change is change that improves or corrects existing aspects of an organisation and often focuses on improvements to skills or processes – an improvement of an existing situation.

Transformational change requires a fundamental change in assumptions by the organisation and those who work within it. The outcome of transformational change can be an organisation that differs significantly in terms of structure, culture and strategy from the previous one. The change period is difficult to control and manage and may feel quite chaotic.

This short section has just provided an overview of two different ways of viewing the change process – there are many more. Reading some of the further reading references at the end of this chapter will provide you with more information.

We will now consider approaches to managing change.

MANAGING CHANGE

There are numerous different approaches to managing change in organisations. 'Change management' is the name usually given to a varied set of processes, tools and techniques, methods and approaches for managing the 'people' aspects of change and achieving a desired change. (The term 'project management' tends to be used to refer to managing the more technical, less people-oriented aspects of change.) Whatever tools and approaches are used in your organisation, the aim will be the same – to successfully achieve the goals of the change while minimising any negative impact of change. The CIPD tool for supporting change – *Approaches to Change: Key issues and challenges* – identifies one framework for change ('the 7 Cs of change') with a focus on seven key actions that will improve the chances of success. These seven actions are:

- *Choosing a team*
  It is very important to ensure that those involved in leading, managing and implementing the change have the required knowledge and skills to give the best chance of success. This may involve different people at different times and/or the use of external consultants to provide particular expertise or

Table 11.1 Key people and their responsibilities for change

Who	Key responsibilities
Top team	Aligning change with organisational strategy. Providing leadership to make change happen. Internal and external communication. Monitoring and evaluation after implementation.
Line management	Owning their part in change. Cascading communications. Preparing teams for implementation.
HR professionals/HR function	Championing the 'people' agenda. Redefining the roles, jobs and skills. Training and developing the staff involved. Adapting and refining HR policies – for example, careers, reward. Building learning on/knowledge of change. Communicating with and involving staff.
Programme and project managers	Establishing project capability and accountability. Communication. Management and implementation. Project planning. Engaging senior management and key stakeholders.

Source: CIPD (2006) *Approaches to Change: Key issues and challenges*

facilitation skills. Table 11.1, taken from the CIPD guide, shows the range of responsibilities that key people might have during a change.

- *Crafting the vision and path*
  In any change, a clear vision of what you are trying to achieve is needed along with an understanding of the things you have to do to get there – the 'what' and the 'how'. A popular tool to use for doing this is a 'roadmap' for change – which generally includes three stages: initial vision, ongoing project management and detailed implementation. Such a roadmap helps you to consider the actions you must take and what outcomes you are aiming for at each of the different stages.

- *Connecting organisation-wide change*
  It will improve the chances of success if the different aspects of the change are considered together. This will allow you to identify the connections between these different aspects – such as changes in ways of working, changes in any systems and processes, and changes needed in equipment and facilities.

- *Consulting stakeholders*
  In any change there are likely to be a range of different stakeholders – for example those with a stake in the outcome of the change and those affected by the change. The different stakeholders are likely to have different views and responses to change. It is important to try to anticipate these different views and respond appropriately.

- *Communicating*
  The different stakeholders will also have different needs when it comes to communication, so thinking about using existing and new channels of communication can help. At a minimum, communication needs to be honest, consistent and up to date.

- *Coping with change*
  Both organisations and individuals need to cope with the change. For an organisation the challenge is managing the change while keeping the day-to-day business running effectively. For individuals change can be very difficult and stressful and most will go through a cycle of emotions. This cycle of emotions has been looked at by many people and is often described as a change curve (or rollercoaster) – more detail on these individual reactions to change is featured later in this chapter.

- *Capturing learning*
  With the pace and frequency of change seen in most organisations today, it can increase the chances of success if organisations build their capability to manage change successfully. In part this will depend on capturing and sharing learning from previous change processes, an area in which HR practitioners can have a big impact through the development of processes to capture and share.

A range of other factors will also need consideration when embarking on any change process – such as project management, training, leadership and organisational culture.

THE IMPACT OF CHANGE ON INDIVIDUALS

Almost any change in any organisation will impact on the people who work in that organisation because all organisations are essentially human systems – made up of the people who work within them. In any consideration of change it is therefore important to consider the impact of change on individual employees. The impact that any given change will have on employees in an organisation will depend on a number of factors, including how significant the change is for the individual employee, the individual's personal circumstances and ability to cope with change, and whether the individual views the change positively or negatively. To a large extent the views of individuals are determined by how the individuals think in relation to the change. The way in which the change is put across to them can therefore be crucial to their reaction.

What is also important is to consider the reverse – the impact of individuals on change. Where a change is happening that has been driven by external factors rather than by the people affected and involved, it is unlikely to succeed unless some of the people affected are in favour of it. Individuals or groups in an organisation can resist and sabotage change to the extent that it either doesn't happen or fails to achieve the goals set. It is therefore helpful to think about the different individual positions people affected might take when faced with change. Peter Senge identifies the different positions individuals might take in response to change.

Table 11.2 The responses of individuals to change

Position	Response to change
Commitment	Want change to happen and will work to make it happen.
Enrolment	Want change to happen and will devote time and energy to making it happen within given frameworks.
Genuine compliance	See the virtue in what is proposed, do what is asked of them and think proactively about what is needed.
Formal compliance	Can describe the benefits of what is proposed and are not hostile to them. Do what they are asked, but no more.
Grudging compliance	Do not accept that there are benefits to what is proposed and do not go along with it. Do enough of what is asked of them not to jeopardise their position. Voice opposition and hopes for failure.
Non-compliance	Do not accept that there are benefits and have nothing to lose by opposing the proposition. Will not do what is asked of them.
Apathy	Neither in support of nor in opposition to the proposal, just serving time.

Source: Peter Senge (2006) *The Fifth Discipline*

For a change to succeed, not everyone needs to commit, but it can be helpful to think about the positions different individuals or groups might take and consider how support at the right level might be achieved.

ACTIVITY 11.2

For the purposes of this Activity, consider three independently owned businesses manufacturing double-glazing products. All have been affected by the economic downturn and they have decided to merge into one business to reduce costs. One is family-owned, and that family will be selling up. The ownership and management teams in the other two businesses will merge and run the three separate businesses as one. Two of the businesses are in the same town, while the third is in a neighbouring town. The new management will want to centralise operations in one place.

Now try to identify the different individuals/ groups of individuals that will be affected by this merger and think about what position they are likely to take in this change. What are the factors that will influence the positions taken?

Compare your responses with the feedback at the end of this chapter.

INDIVIDUAL RESPONSES AND REACTIONS TO CHANGE

Although the impact of change on people is subject to variation and individual reactions will be different, the first response people most often have to change is an emotional one. This will often also be a fairly self-centred reaction – 'What's the effect of this going to be on me and my job?' Depending on the nature of the change and what impact it will have for a particular individual, this emotional response may range from positive feelings such as excitement and anticipation to more negative feelings such as anger and cynicism. The emotional reaction to change is a well-researched area, many commentators using a variation on the 'change curve' to describe individual emotional responses to change. This change curve was originally described by Elisabeth Kübler-Ross in work she did on grieving, and it has subsequently been adapted by many people to reflect the stages an individual experiencing change goes through (see Figure 11.1 on page 314). The curve looks at an individual's emotions over time as change is happening.

Using the change curve in supporting individual employees through change can be very helpful – think about the emotions at play, how they might be affecting each individual's behaviour and how you might act to support employees through each phase. The individual reactions involved can include:

- *shock, denial and anger* – the initial reactions where people may be stunned by the news of the change and individuals may be thinking that the organisation is not really going to go through with the change or that the proposed change is a complete waste of time or money. Those who view the change negatively may have this emotion for longer than those who don't. At this stage of reaction employees often need information and communication. Although messages about change can be complex, you should think about what information is available to be shared, and when, and also how the messages can be kept as clear and simple as possible. Here employees are still absorbing the news about a change. It is helpful to communicate information as early on as possible so that employees can begin to see the need for change and the end point. At this stage, however, individuals are not yet ready to hear how things will be better

Figure 11.1 Kübler-Ross's change curve

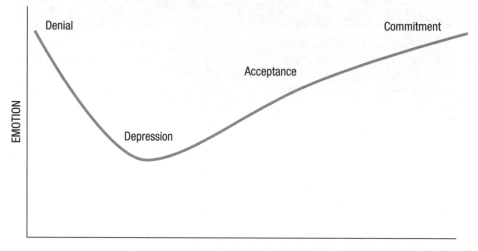

for them once the change has happened. It is useful to provide opportunities for individuals to discuss their feelings – where frustration and grievances can be aired constructively, the degree of bitterness and anger can be reduced. Even when angry or in shock, what individuals have to say must still be listened to and taken seriously – they may have legitimate concerns and what they have to say might affect the success of the change initiative.

- *frustration, fear, depression* – where individuals may start to grudgingly accept that the change is really happening but feel there is either nothing they can do about it or think about ways they might resist or frustrate the change process. During this phase employees need emotional and practical support in order for them to start thinking more positively about the change. It is important to acknowledge that emotions are important and real for people. It can be a challenge to get people to listen at this stage, so extra effort must be put into communication processes.

- *acceptance, understanding, exploration* – where individuals start to really acknowledge that change is happening and may start to see some of the positives in the change, appreciate the need for the change and be thinking about how they will move on. Here individuals will probably be in need of support and guidance about what the future holds for them. The challenges for managers and HR practitioners during this phase can be developing and maintaining a common understanding about the future state and ensuring that everyone feels involved. This is when it is essential to generate buy-in from all those affected by the change. Additional information will be needed at this stage to support employees in developing a real understanding of what the future looks like and how it will affect them. It can be useful here to set goals for individuals both to be involved in the change process and for the future once the change has happened as a way of taking ownership of the future state. It is during this stage that any benefits for individuals can really start to be discussed in a constructive way. Attention should be paid to any new teams that are going to be formed and facilitating them in coming together to discuss the future and working together. It can also be helpful in this phase to think about some quick wins that are achievable, and to ensure wide communication of these once they start to take place.

- *commitment and moving on* – where individuals may really start to embrace the change and think about how they can make it work for them. The challenges here can be about keeping up momentum, starting to really make the change happen and become embedded, ensuring that the whole organisation moves at a similar pace, and making sure that any unrealistic expectations of what the change might mean are managed. It can be helpful here to find ways for individual employees to test out the changes by supporting them in being creative and taking some risks in order for them to improve performance. It can also help to identify those employees who reach this stage earlier than others and to use them as advocates for the new way of doing things – having a colleague talking about the change positively can be much more powerful than a manager or HR practitioner doing so.

Although it can be very helpful to think about individual employees moving through this journey during a change process as a way of taking action to support them, you should always bear in mind that not everyone will react in the same way and that people will move at different speeds in their reactions and responses to change. Of course, if the change is viewed as positive by employees from the outset, then although reaction may still be emotional it is likely to be positive emotion rather than the more negative and potentially damaging emotions described above.

CASE STUDY 11.1

Two separate GP practices, both of which occupied old, inadequate accommodation, agreed to move to a new purpose-built building. One GP practice would occupy the ground floor of the new building, and the other would occupy the first floor. Although they would continue to operate as separate practices, there would be a shared waiting and reception area on the ground floor. The change was necessary because the old accommodation for both practices did not meet accessibility requirements under the Disability Discrimination Act and could not be easily adapted. One practice was considerably bigger than the other. Even during the earliest stages of discussion with staff in the practices about the move there was a lot of complaint, disagreement and anxiety about what the change would mean. This started to have an impact on staff morale, sickness levels

and relationships at work. Discussions with staff in both practices highlighted a range of emotions and reactions to the proposed move including:

- fear from staff in the smaller practice that this was a 'takeover' by the bigger practice

- worries about a new IT system that would be introduced as part of the move

- concern that a shared reception and waiting area would not work and would in effect mean the two practices becoming one

- concern that the new building would not be as close to patients' homes as the old buildings, making it more difficult for them to attend

- anger that what staff perceived as two

very good practices were having to change at all.

In order to deal with these responses to change and help the change process move more smoothly, a number of actions were taken. Opportunities for staff to discuss these reactions both individually and collectively were provided along with opportunities for staff from the two different practices to meet and get to know each other. Significant work took place to communicate the reasons for the change to staff and to seek and respond to feedback. A joint working group representing both practices was established to provide a vehicle for staff to be involved in building design. Joint training sessions for staff from both practices on the new IT system were introduced. Acknowledging the feelings of the staff affected, keeping them informed and providing opportunities for staff to discuss their feelings and get to know each other meant that staff felt much more involved in the change than they had expected to be, felt they were listened to, and felt they had some influence over the outcome. All of this worked well to ensure a smooth change process with staff acknowledging the benefits of the move to them and their patients.

In our experience of change processes, whatever the final outcome of change, employees more usually start with a negative than positive reaction and view the change as something undesirable and to be resisted. This is partly because negative effects are often very real and more immediate and in some cases individuals will suffer serious loss. Conversely, positive effects are invariably some way into the future and therefore less real and are not guaranteed. There are usually other factors at work too. We now move on to look at resistance to change.

RESISTANCE TO CHANGE

One of the common reactions you may see to change – often during the second phase of the change curve – is resistance to the change. It is a very human characteristic to resist change, generally based on the organisational culture we work in. Change can lead to people losing their jobs, having their career pathways blocked and having increased pressure to perform, to reach targets or to work longer hours. It can almost be an automatic reflex to resist change. Resistance emerges when there is a threat to something the individual values. This threat may be real or perceived; it may arise from a genuine understanding of (but disagreement with) the change or from misunderstanding what the change is really about. The resistance may stem from disagreement with the proposed change based on intellectual reasons, personal values or more deep-seated psychological reasons. Thus there are a number of reasons why people will resist change:

- loss of control or authority – the less in control people feel, the less they will be inclined to co-operate in change
- change has been imposed
- lack of understanding about the change or its implications
- fundamentally disagreeing with the proposed change

- uncertainty about what the change means or how it will be achieved
- fear about losing something they value – a way of doing things, their job, benefits or status
- worry about being able to cope with the change and learn new ways of doing things
- 'change fatigue' where change has been occurring all too frequently
- lack of trust and confidence in the managers leading the change
- having to move to a new team or get to know new colleagues.

Whatever the reasons for resistance, there can be a reasonably predictable pattern to how it emerges and affects performance – using the change curve depicted above can help you to think about this.

ACTIVITY 11.3

Consider your own organisation and think about any change that is in the early planning stages. How might this impact on individual employees? What sorts of resistance do you think might occur, and why? Come up with three ideas for how you might overcome resistance. Discuss these with one of your learning sources and see how appropriate and effective these ideas might be in your organisation.

CHANGE AND THE PSYCHOLOGICAL CONTRACT

The concept of the psychological contract has already been mentioned in previous chapters. It concerns the mutual perceptions the two parties to the employment contract (employer and employee) have about their obligations to each other. It is important because the 'health' of the psychological contract can impact on company performance. By its very nature the psychological contract is unwritten and hard to pin down, so any organisational change that affects the perceptions employers or employees have can have a significant effect, but without necessarily being clear and transparent. Traditionally, the basis of the psychological contract was an offer of stability and job security from the employer in return for commitment and loyalty from the employee. Much change in organisations affects this stability and security – from the introduction of new technology to changing market conditions to restructuring and redundancy programmes – and thus impacts on the psychological contract.

In the CIPD survey of organisational change in 2001, the findings indicated that contrary to popular belief, employees have a positive attitude to change because it is seen as a way of supporting employees to do their jobs better. However, some kinds of change are more likely to have a negative impact on employees' attitudes and this can impact on the success or not of a change programme. Whereas changes in job design, new technology and products and job responsibilities were viewed positively by employees, changes in HR policies, changes that resulted in redundancy programmes and large amounts of change were found to have a negative effect. Given that employees often have an emotional reaction to change and may seek to either passively or actively resist change, these findings show how important it is for the type of change and likely impact on employees to be considered carefully and plans made to specifically manage this.

SURVIVOR SYNDROME

This is a term you may come across if you are involved in any change that results in downsizing of the workforce or redundancy. It refers to those employees who remain with an organisation once the change has happened – the 'survivors' – and is about the attitudes, feelings and perceptions they have about what has happened. Generally, in a downsizing or redundancy situation a lot of attention will necessarily and rightly be paid to the people who will be losing their jobs. Far less attention is ordinarily paid to those who remain. In the same way that being involved in change creates a range of emotions, so being a 'survivor' of change can also lead to feelings such as fear, anger, depression, guilt and lack of trust. The impact of this in the workplace can include:

- lower levels of employee morale
- increased work pressure and stress on the survivors
- survivors feeling 'cheated' if those leaving get generous severance packages
- perceptions of fewer career development opportunities
- negative impact on the psychological contract.

SUPPORTING EMPLOYEES THROUGH CHANGE

By considering the impact change can have on individual employees as outlined above, you will be able to see how important it is for organisations to support all those affected by organisational change. There are a number of ways in which this can be done, including ensuring that communication and consultation processes are effective, putting in place employee support schemes such as employee assistance programmes and outplacement, and having effective policies for managing change in a consistent way. We will now consider each of these in turn.

COMMUNICATION AND CONSULTATION

There is no one right way to communicate effectively with employees during change. The effectiveness of communication will depend on the type of information to be shared, on the type of change concerned, on the individual preferences of those involved about how they hear information, and on ensuring that opportunities for employee feedback and involvement allow everyone to have a voice. It is important to know exactly what the change is trying to achieve so that this can be communicated clearly as a starting point for getting employee buy-in. Make sure you know exactly how things are changing and why, who is losing what, what is changing and what is not. It is also important to think about

Table 11.3 Communicating with and involving employees during change

Activity	Benefits
Involve employees	<ul><li>encourages ownership of the change</li><li>ensures that they hear the official information not just the rumours</li><li>provides opportunities for two-way communication and for employees to feel they have been heard</li><li>helps you to identify those in favour of change to use as advocates/champions for change</li><li>allows employees to influence and have input to the design of the new/changed processes</li></ul>
Involve trade unions	<ul><li>encourages ownership of the change</li><li>can help to stop rumours getting out of control</li><li>can help generate greater acceptance of the change from employees</li></ul>
Interview employees	<ul><li>helps you to understand employees' feelings about the change</li><li>gives you an insight into employee ambitions/preferences for the future</li><li>provides a confidential environment for employees to discuss their anxieties</li><li>provides a measure of how effective your communication processes are</li></ul>
Use those who are both negative and positive about the change	<ul><li>allows you to identify informal leaders – those who influence other employees</li><li>helps you to understand and respond to objections and concerns about the change</li><li>helps to reduce resistance to change</li></ul>
Over-communicate. Anticipate questions. Have answers where you can; be honest where you haven't	<ul><li>more likely that messages will be heard</li><li>makes the changes more visible and real</li><li>helps you to deal with rumours and misinformation more rapidly</li><li>fosters trust and understanding</li></ul>
Vary the medium	<ul><li>will be effective with more employees as people like to hear things in different ways</li><li>ensures greater thought is given to what and how to communicate</li><li>reinforces key messages</li></ul>
Consider timeliness, consistency and, as far as possible, simultaneous communication	<ul><li>people get the right messages at the right time</li><li>rumour and speculation is less likely and there is therefore less danger of distortions going through the grapevine</li><li>avoids bad news being delivered at inappropriate times (eg redundancy notices issued on Christmas Eve)</li><li>allows support processes to be put in place as news is given</li><li>ensures that key messages are not lost as they cascade through an organisation</li></ul>
Stay positive	<ul><li>will help develop a positive climate and culture whilst change happens</li><li>more likely others will stay positive too</li></ul>

methods of and channels for communication during change. We have all heard stories of employees being notified of change, including redundancies, by text or email – and have seen the negative consequences that can arise. We would always recommend making communication as personal as possible during change so that every employee feels that he or she matters. In unionised workplaces it can also be very helpful to involve the trade unions in the communication and consultation processes because this can help to stop rumours getting out of control.

Although there is no one correct way to communicate with and involve employees during change, the ideas outlined in Table 11.3 should help.

ACTIVITY 11.4

For the purposes of this Activity consider a restructuring and downsizing change programme in a mail-order business moving from three different offices 10 miles apart to one new purpose-built office building. Think about the different methods of communicating with and involving employees in change listed below.

- team meetings
- individual interviews
- newsletters

- hotlines
- bulletin boards
- e-discussion groups
- focus groups
- working groups
- employee surveys.

What do you think the benefits of each will be? Can you think of any other methods of communicating that will work in this environment with this change programme?

CASE STUDY 11.2

A large unionised organisation in the service sector was closing one of its service divisions because of technological developments that would enable it to deliver the service in a new way. The new service would be established 10 miles away from the existing service and would require 30 fewer employees in total. The organisation gave a lot of thought to the communication processes that would be appropriate for communicating the change to employees and involving them in planning the new service. The organisation planned the new service over a number of months, during which time they held a number of seminars and workshops to share information about the technological development with employees, about the likely changes it would mean in working practices, and to get employee input to developing a new way of working.

Once a final decision was made about implementing the change, a meeting was held with all employees, and their union representatives, in the service division affected to let them know that the change was now moving ahead. At this meeting the director responsible shared information with employees about what was happening and when, and talked about the process that would be followed to implement the change. An opportunity was provided at the end of the meeting for any questions, to which answers were forthcoming.

Despite the previous involvement of employees in developing the plans, there was still shock that the change was now really happening and that 30 employees would lose their jobs. Later that week, individual meetings were held with every employee in the division at which the trade union representative and the HR manager were present. These allowed employees to discuss their individual position, share any concerns and talk about their aspirations for the future and indicate whether they would be interested in the voluntary redundancy package on offer. Over the next few weeks during the formal redundancy consultation period, further team and individual meetings were held, newsletters were issued and an employee assistance and outplacement service was put in place to ensure that two-way communication channels were kept open. After the changes were implemented, both those employees who were made redundant and those staying in the organisation were asked for their views on the change process. Regardless of how the employees felt about the change and their personal outcome, they all indicated that they thought the communication and support aspects of the change had been effective, and that this had helped them cope with the change more easily.

Consultation

In certain change situations – for example, redundancy programmes – there are legal requirements to consult with trade union representatives. Information on formal consultation requirements has already been provided in Chapters 3 and 8 and you are advised to refer back to this when considering change in organisations.

EMPLOYEE SUPPORT

Employee assistance programmes

One way of providing practical and emotional support for employees experiencing change is to introduce an employee assistance programme (EAP). Although designed to provide support for employees with any issues – at home or at work – they can be a particularly valuable tool during times of change. EAPs generally provide a confidential counselling service, delivered by qualified specialists, who can address a range of issues from advising on personal and emotional problems to providing legal and financial advice. Organisations will generally buy EAPs from external expert providers and the services on offer are usually accessed online or by phone, but face-to-face sessions are often also provided if needed. For employees undergoing change – particularly where there is a risk to job security – they can provide an opportunity for employees to discuss their fears and anxieties in a safe and confidential way.

Outplacement

Outplacement services were first introduced for executives and senior managers facing redundancy situations, often in larger organisations. Now, outplacement is something that many more employees expect to be provided with. Outplacement typically provides practical support for people facing being/having been made redundant and can create structure for those faced with a very big change to their daily routine. The sorts of services offered include:

- help with CVs and applications

- job search support
- interview skills practice
- guidance on making decisions about the future
- career guidance and counselling
- a review of existing skills and capabilities.

Where a company is able to take a long-term view, they may provide support and training towards qualifications to better equip employees for the 'outside world'.

As well as providing individual employees with support, outplacement also offers organisations the opportunity to manage their employer brand for the future. If those leaving the organisation have as positive an experience as possible and feel that they were supported and treated well by the organisation, it becomes easier to attract people in when the organisation changes or grows in the future. Providing outplacement services can also send a positive message to employees not facing redundancy that your organisation cares about people and seeks to support them in difficult situations, which will help with the impact of any survivor syndrome.

Change policies

An increasing number of organisations, particularly large ones, have policies for managing and dealing with change. Having such a policy can provide useful guidance for managers leading change, can increase the degree of consistency seen and experienced by those affected, and can outline any formal consultation requirements.

ACTIVITY 11.5

Find out if your organisation has a policy or some written guidance on managing change. If it does, see if the policy covers everything you would expect it to in the light of this chapter. If your organisation doesn't have a policy, consider drafting one or alternatively some guidelines for managers involved in managing change. Discuss what you have found/written with one of your learning sources.

THE ROLE OF HR PRACTITIONERS

HR practitioners must adopt a range of different roles in any change process. This can include being involved in both supporting the management of change and supporting the individuals affected by change. In unionised environments there will also be a key role in liaising and communicating with relevant trade union representatives. It is likely that you will carry out some or all of the following roles.

AN ADVISORY ROLE

Managers may look to you for advice on handling any of the people-related aspects of change – including dealing with individual reactions and responses to change. Where the change is likely to impact on job numbers, you will be called on to provide advice on issues such as redundancy and other legal aspects of change. As well as managers seeking your advice, you may well find that individuals affected by change also seek your advice – on issues such as redundancy payments and CV-writing and applying for new positions.

AN ADMINISTRATIVE ROLE

When a large-scale change is happening, it can increase the chances of success to ensure that the whole change is managed in a co-ordinated way. Your skills may be called on to develop project plans or roadmaps, to monitor and keep track of the change while it is happening or to produce progress reports. In any change process there is also a great deal of work involved in making sure the personal records of any staff affected by change are up to date so that if the change affects aspects such as job descriptions and contracts of employment it is easy to check what the change means on an individual basis.

A SUPPORTING ROLE

You may be called upon to work with individuals to support them in coping with the change – particularly around the behavioural and emotional aspects of what is happening. This can involve being part of any individual interviews and discussions that take place with those affected to discuss the personal impact on them and their future and offering counselling and coaching for individuals about their future direction. It may also involve you in setting up more formal schemes for employee support, such as outplacement and employee assistance programmes.

SUMMARY

This chapter has examined various aspects of change – why organisations need to change, the factors to be considered in managing change through to a successful outcome, the impact of change on individuals and their reactions and responses to it, and the various options available to you and your organisation in supporting individuals affected by change. It is clear that getting individuals to change – their behaviours, work practices, etc – is key to success. In our experience the challenge of these people elements of change are probably the most difficult to deal with. The following quick checklist summarises key issues for you to remember:

- Give maximum warning of the change to allow people time to go through the emotional responses.

- Explain the reasons for change.

- Involve people in the planning and implementation.
- Communicate, communicate, communicate.
- Introduce change gradually if possible, with activities which will show quick results.
- Give appropriate consideration to training – offer people the chance to develop new, relevant skills.
- Sell the benefits – 'what's in it for them' matters more than the organisation.
- Take the present situation and personal circumstances into account.
- Always remember the impact on individuals – think of the change curve.
- Check on how individuals are coping, and remember to support them.

You should by now be clear about some of the key aspects involved in managing change and supporting individuals through the change process. You will have developed an awareness of what a complex and difficult area of work change is, but also how it is a fact of life in most organisations these days. Even if you have not yet had any experience of managing or supporting change in your organisation, it is still highly likely that you have been affected by change. Think about your reactions and how you coped with change, and about what support you got and what support you would have liked. This personal experience of change will be invaluable to you as you begin to work more in this area of HR practice.

EXPLORE FURTHER

REFERENCES AND FURTHER READING

ACKERMAN, L. (1997) 'Development, transition or transformation: the question of change in organisations', in Van Eynde, D., Hoy, J. and Van Eynde, D. (eds) *Organisation Development Classics*. San Francisco: Jossey-Bass

CIPD (2006) *Approaches to Change: Key issues and challenges*. London: Chartered Institute of Personnel and Development

CIPD (2005) *HR's Role in Organising: Shaping change*. London: Chartered Institute of Personnel and Development

CIPD (2002) *Reorganising for Success: A starting point for change*. London: Chartered Institute of Personnel and Development

DONKIN, R. (2004) *HR and Reorganisation: Managing the challenge of change*. London: Chartered Institute of Personnel and Development

GUEST, D. E. and CONWAY, N. (2001) *Organisational Change and the Psychological Contract: An analysis of the 1999 CIPD survey*. Research report. London: Chartered Institute of Personnel and Development

HUGHES, M. (2006) *Change Management*. London: Chartered Institute of Personnel and Development

KOTTER, J. and COHEN, S. (2002) *The Heart of Change: Real-life stories of how people change their organization*. Cambridge, MA: Harvard Business School Press

KÜBLER-ROSS, E. (2008) *On Death and Dying*. London: Routledge

LEWIN, K. (1951) *Field Theory in Social Science*. New York: Harper & Row

NEWTON, R. (2007) *Managing Change Step by Step: All you need to build a plan and make it happen*. Harlow: Prentice Hall

SAHDEV, K. and VINNICOMBE, S. (1998) *Downsizing and Survivor Syndrome: A study of HR's perception of survivors' responses*. Bedford: Cranfield School of Management

SENGE, P. (2006) *The Fifth Discipline*. New York: Random House

WEBSITES

Chartered Institute of Personnel and Development: www.cipd.co.uk

People Management: www.peoplemanagement.co.uk

ACTIVITIES FEEDBACK

Activity 11.2

The different groups of individuals likely to be affected include:

- the family in the family-owned business
- the owners of the other two businesses
- managers within all three businesses
- employees within all three businesses.

The range of factors that will affect the positions they take include:

- whether they are selling up or forming part of the new ownership team
- whether there will be any opportunities for career advancement for them
- where the new business will be located
- whether their job will be at risk of redundancy
- the culture and management style of the new merged business
- whether any working practices are changing.

CHAPTER 12

Personal effectiveness

LEARNING OUTCOMES

After reading this chapter you will:

- understand the concept of self-development and the need to take some risks in seeking to improve your own personal effectiveness

- appreciate the main concepts behind a range of skill areas – ie those under the broad headings of communication, negotiating, counselling, time management and assertiveness

- be willing to identify your existing strengths and development needs in these skill areas and plan to address the latter by proactively seeking out appropriate learning experiences

- be able to select and take appropriate actions to develop your skills

- plan to employ measures to improve your knowledge and skills continually, in compliance with the CIPD's continuing professional development requirements.

INTRODUCTION

The majority of the previous chapters contain sections on the role of the HR practitioner in, for example, recruitment and selection and in handling disciplinary matters or grievances. You may have been daunted by the multiplicity of roles performed by HR practitioners. This is not the end of the story, though, because in order to perform these roles, effective HR practitioners have to develop some broad skills that have wide-ranging applications. One prime example is interviewing skills. We have seen that HR practitioners have to possess well-developed interviewing skills for a variety of purposes: selection, discipline- and grievance-handling, appraisals, and a whole host of less formal situations.

Interviewing skills have been dealt with in the earlier chapters. In this one we shall be concentrating on the following broad skills areas:

- communication – report-writing, making presentations and making a business case for introducing change

- negotiating, influencing and persuading – in formal and informal situations

- counselling – in handling redundancies, early retirements, sickness absence and personal problems

- time management – inside and outside the workplace
- assertiveness – in work-related and personal situations.

This is not intended to be an exhaustive list, because we are sure that you can think of other useful skills that you utilise on a regular basis in your jobs as HR practitioners. Nor are the contents of this chapter intended to provide you with comprehensive reading in these areas. We do hope, however, that you will find this introductory guide a useful starting point on the road to personal effectiveness in your role as an HR practitioner, and in life in general. The important topics of self-development and continuing professional development (CPD) are also covered in this chapter.

Undoubtedly, you will have already acquired some of the skills listed above owing to your past experiences and innate abilities. Others you will need to work hard at developing by gaining as broad a range of experience as possible. Please note that we are not suggesting that you will ever reach the stage when your skills are honed to such a degree that everything runs smoothly. Life is not like that. In the context of your working life, the organisational environment is in a constant state of change (and, if you think about it, without some changes occurring, life would be rather dull). Further, you may find some situations more difficult than others and feel that you will never develop the full range of skills necessary. For instance, your job might entail notifying workers whose jobs have been made redundant, dealing with members of staff who appear to doubt your credibility and authority, or visiting the spouses of employees who have died in service to discuss pension details. The first time that you are confronted with these circumstances you may feel very inadequate. You will, however, through experience, learn how to effect tasks such as these in a sensitive and professional manner.

A key recent development relevant to the broad area of professional and personal effectiveness has been the introduction of the CIPD's HR Profession Map, which is a comprehensive view of the HR role at every level and specialism within the profession. It provides a detailed overview of what HR people do and it looks at the different areas of professional competence required and the behaviours necessary to be an effective practitioner. It also creates a clear and flexible framework for career progression, recognising both that HR roles and career progression vary. If you have not already done so, you would be well advised to look at the map on the CIPD website and consider how it relates to your role as an HR professional.

WHY IS PERSONAL EFFECTIVENESS IMPORTANT?

We saw in Chapter 6 on *Performance management* that 'effectiveness' means 'doing the right things' (whereas 'efficiency' means 'doing things right'). In the organisational context it has long been recognised that choosing 'the right things to do' at the individual level means performing those activities or attaining those targets that are in line with business or organisational goals. Thus as HR practitioners you should seek to determine which activities are the 'right' ones and then acquire the requisite knowledge and skills to perform them to a level that ensures the optimum result. Success then breeds success: a positive result will enhance your status and your credibility in the eyes of your co-workers. That is personal effectiveness.

If you are a member of the CIPD, you will find it useful to consult the CIPD Code of Professional Conduct and Disciplinary Procedures. The Code defines the standards expected of members aligned to achieving the objectives of the Institute – ie the promotion of the art and science of the management and development of people for the public benefit.

HR practitioners have a dual role in acquiring the knowledge and skills necessary to perform their tasks and activities effectively at work and to meet the exacting standards laid down by their profession.

We will now look at the skills areas listed above in the introduction and their importance to you.

COMMUNICATION

This is a vast subject, so here we shall be concentrating on two main topic areas: one in the field of written communications (ie report-writing) and the other (a classic example) in the field of oral communications (ie making presentations). These activities are both important and may often occur together, especially when, as an HR practitioner, you are engaged in project work. In fact, we should rarely rely on written reports alone if we wish to influence management decisions – the written word may be powerful but oral communications are much more effective in, say, persuading others to agree to a particular course of action.

The value of good written reports is that they often gain you access to more senior managers in the organisation and hence provide the initial route to influencing them. Writing a report also forces you to think through your ideas in a logical and structured fashion, which is invaluable if you then get the opportunity to promote your ideas in a formal presentation.

Let's take an example. You are involved in issuing an attitude survey to all staff prior to your organisation's being involved in a friendly merger with a former rival. The aim is to gauge the feelings of staff about the merger with a view to gradually bringing about a culture change that ensures as smooth a transition as possible. You present your analysis of the attitude survey results, other research evidence and your proposals for the future in a written report. Regardless of how well written and presented the report is, it is unlikely to 'sell' itself (after all, you would be dependent on senior managers' reading it thoroughly, which not all managers have the time to do). It would therefore be advantageous for you to make an oral presentation. This would afford you the opportunity personally to 'sell' your ideas and influence decisions, and will have more impact than the written report on its own. A presentation also lends itself to two-way communication, especially if you incorporate a question-and-answer session to address concerns. Brief guidelines on successful report-writing and making presentations are provided below.

REPORT-WRITING

Reports are written for a variety of reasons. Often, they are based on research into a particular subject and are intended to convey information and ideas and get buy-in from others. Reports may lead to action because they help managers to take decisions. There are no rigid rules governing the art of report-writing, but there are well-accepted guidelines, summarised below.

A Terms of reference

Before you commence any analysis, you must be very clear about your terms of reference:

- What is the subject matter of your report (eg sickness absenteeism in Company XYZ)?
- Why is the report necessary (ie what is its purpose – eg to get buy-in to a project to decrease the level of sickness absence)?
- Who will read the report, what prior knowledge do they have and what information do they need to make decisions (eg XYZ's senior management team and a college tutor)?

B Plan your report

It helps to plan your report before you start writing it so that you can be clear it will include everything it needs to and will address the target audience appropriately. Things you will want to consider include:

- how long the report should be and whether there are any specific requirements or limitations
- creating an outline of your report, thinking through the key messages and a logical sequence for the information you need to present (see suggestions below for report layout)
- how you will gather and collate information for the report – what information is needed, what do you have already, and what will you need to find out? Once the information is available, you will want to check what the key messages are and whether they support what you are trying to achieve
- what style you are going to use for the report – will it be first- or third-person, are there any 'house-style' rules in your organisation?
- whether to write an outline report first containing the key messages and checking that structure and content look appropriate before doing a full write-up.

C Title

The title page should contain the title, the name of the author, the organisation's name (if appropriate) and the date. Simple as it may sound, the title should be concisely stated and self-explanatory – eg 'A review of sickness absence in Company XYZ' is not as informative as 'A proposal to decrease the levels of sickness absence within Company XYZ within the next 18 months'.

D Layout

Informed opinion is generally in agreement on the following sequence:

1 Title page

2 Summary (abstract or synopsis)

3 Acknowledgements

4 Contents page

5 Introduction

6 Main body of text

7 Conclusions – ie research findings

8 Options

9 Recommendations, including a costed implementation plan and a cost/benefit analysis

10 Appendices

11 References and bibliography.

(NB: Not all these features need to appear in every report. You should select such sections as are appropriate for the length and complexity of your material.)

Checklists

Two checklists are provided in the Appendix at the very end of this chapter to give further assistance on the process up to and including the writing up of your report. Like most things, practice makes perfect!

ACTIVITY 12.1

Approach one of your internal learning sources and ask for help in choosing an HR issue that is topical within your organisation but that has not yet been tackled. Carry out some research by studying information available internally – eg statistical data, minutes of meetings – and externally – eg legislation and journal articles. Write a short report to your learning source and other appropriate members of management. In your report, examine the issue and put forward proposals on how the organisation should respond. Follow the guidelines provided in this chapter on effective report-writing.

MAKING PRESENTATIONS

The more inexperienced you are in this area, the more likely you are to be filled with dread at the thought of standing up in front of a group of people to make a formal presentation. There are two main ways of attempting to control your nerves:

- Never do it.

- Take a risk and have a go!

If you take the former route, you will never conquer your fear and may impede your career as, more and more, managers and professionals are expected to be able to make effective presentations. Indeed, many recruitment processes now require candidates to make a presentation as part of the selection process, so becoming more confident in this area may well help you with future job applications you may make. If you follow the latter route, you will find that your nervousness will create adrenaline that will help you to perform, and that with good preparation, the use of relaxation techniques and more experience you will find the fear diminishes. Never expect to become completely laid back at the thought of making a presentation: even very experienced presenters may find the prospect of presenting to an unknown audience a daunting one, but their experience helps them to keep their fears under control.

We recommend that you do take a risk and get into the habit of volunteering to make presentations. (Sometimes you will be nominated anyway by well-meaning bosses or colleagues.) Inevitably, you will improve your presentational skills in both formal and informal situations. For instance, you will become more adept at succinctly expressing your point of view in a meeting, even at short notice. You will also increase your profile within the organisation.

We shall now look in more detail at the two stages to making presentations: planning and preparation, and delivery.

Planning and preparation

1 The approach

You must establish answers to the following questions:

- Who? – the audience   **A**
- Why? – the purpose   **P**
- When? – the time   **T**
- Where? – the place
- What? – the subject
- How? – the means.

In a word, your presentation must be APT.

2 The subject matter

There are four stages:

- Do your research.

- Arrange the information logically – eg introduction, main theme, summary, and conclusion.

- Prioritise and prune to suit your

  > Audience

  > Purpose

  > Time.

- Prepare concise notes and visual aids. As for notes, cue-cards containing bullet points of information are much easier to use and look more professional than scripts on A4 paper. Further, it is very tempting to read out the latter in full and thus break eye-contact with your audience. As for visual aids, each type has advantages and disadvantages – but the bottom line is that they should all be aids and not distractions. They should be big, bold and simple to be really effective.

3 Plan delivery

This will help you to overcome your nervousness.

- Be thoroughly prepared; carry out at least one full dress rehearsal.

- Make sure you know how to operate any equipment you might be using – eg laptop and projector.

- If possible, get feedback on your rehearsal.

- If you know that you tend to get a dry mouth, arrange to have water available.

- If you know that you get a blotchy neck, wear appropriate clothing.

- If you know that your hands tend to shake, don't hold your papers but place them on a table in front of you.

- Adapt the content of your presentation as necessary to ensure that it will be APT.

- Practise deep breathing.

Delivery

You will have heard the maxim:

Tell them what you are going to say.	*Introduction*
Say it.	*Main theme*
Then tell them what you have said.	*Conclusion*

Depending on the length of your talk (and it is important to stick to the time allotted, including time for questions and answers), you will be able successfully to present only a limited number of key points. Pick these points carefully and deliver them effectively by:

- being enthusiastic about your subject
- being yourself, with your own style
- speaking naturally, with only minimal reference to notes (if you are well prepared, your cue-cards and visual aids will provide the necessary prompts)
- monitoring reactions – ie watch out for body language to gauge interest and understanding
- asking questions to keep the audience on their toes.

So how well do you understand delivery? Try answering the following questions. Should you:

a) start with an apology because you feel that you are not an expert?
   Or state your credentials for giving this presentation?

b) start with a joke to lighten the atmosphere if you are inexperienced or do not know your audience?
   Or outline what you are going to tell them?

c) speak quickly in order to get the talk over with?
   Or speak at a deliberate and measured pace?

d) focus on one friendly-looking person to the exclusion of all others?
   Or make gentle eye-contact with every member of the audience?

e) switch off all the lights and hide behind the laptop/projector?
   Or stand directly in front of your audience with no barrier between you and them?

f) not allow time for questions in case you do not know the answers?
   Or periodically invite the audience to seek clarification or further details?

g) read straight from comprehensive reference notes to ensure that you do not miss anything out?
   Or use brief notes to ensure that you cover your key points and not worry if you miss some details?

h) keep your head down because you are worried that if you look up you will see everyone is bored (or has left the room)?
   Or look at your audience so that you can check their body language for comprehension and interest?

i) make extensive use of a whiteboard or flipchart because it provides an opportunity to turn your back on the audience?
   Or make occasional use of differing visual aids to provide variety?

j) nail your feet to the floor and not move your hands and arms?
   Or trust your own body language?

k) try to copy the style of someone you admire?
   Or be yourself?

NB: As you'll have realised, the preferred answers to all these questions are the second ones!

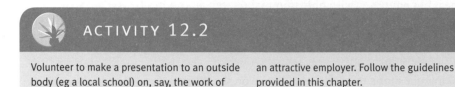

MAKING A BUSINESS CASE

It is likely that when writing reports or making presentations you are seeking to influence managers to agree to some sort of change. In the section that follows we look at the need for HR practitioners to develop the skills of negotiating, influencing and persuading. These skills are obviously critical to success if you wish to be proactive in seeking improvements or responding to the need for change.

Here we are concentrating on those factors you should consider if you wish to strengthen your business case. There is no exact science in determining which are the most appropriate ones because this will depend on the organisational culture. Your learning sources may be able to help you to select wisely from the suggested list below:

- Legislation – is the proposed change necessary to comply with existing or forthcoming legislative requirements?
- Good practice – is there a case for suggesting that the organisation goes beyond minimum legislative compliance and adopts good practices, perhaps in response to competitive pressures?
- Risk – what are the risks associated with not making the change – eg employment tribunal claims, loss of key individuals, theft of commercial knowledge, industrial disputes, safety issues, etc?
- Employee engagement – can you demonstrate the benefits that would result from your proposals in terms of increased attraction, retention and motivation?
- Productivity, profitability and growth – are there strong arguments to suggest that successful implementation of your plans will bring about discernible improvements in company performance?
- Customer care – can you show that the quality of customer service will improve if your proposals are adopted?

As you are no doubt aware, decision-makers are less interested in views and beliefs and more interested in facts. To convince them, you invariably require evidence. You firstly need to make it clear where your arguments are backed up by research evidence – eg workforce profiles or employee attitude survey results.

Secondly, managers will not be swayed by vague promises of future benefits, so you will need to translate your proposals into credible and realisable financial benefits. Very few business decisions are taken without being backed by a clear financial case. Below are a few hints to help you to identify the relevant cost/benefit information:

- Use plausible estimates – familiarise yourself with some typical costs such as average salaries for different grades of staff. Then take account of the fact that people are employed for more than their salary cost because in addition to direct employment costs there are indirect ones such as office space and the cost of providing employee benefits.

- Remember opportunity cost – when they are not engaged in normal day-to-day activities, employees will not be contributing to organisational performance in the usual way, so there is an opportunity cost to, say, being on a training course or being absent through sickness – eg lost sales, lower production.

- Distinguish between 'one-off' and ongoing costs and benefits – eg absence management policies and training may cost several thousands of pounds to prepare and implement, but this is a one-off cost whereas the resultant benefits of reduced absenteeism should continue year after year. Further major investment is unlikely to be necessary although there will be some annual 'maintenance' costs attached to managing absence.

We hope that you find the above guidelines useful in seeking to improve your communication skills and in making a business case, both verbally and in writing. We now consider the associated skills of negotiating, influencing and persuading.

NEGOTIATING, INFLUENCING AND PERSUADING

As an HR practitioner, you are likely to find yourself in situations, formal and informal, that require you to use negotiating skills in order to reach an agreement. Further, you will find it difficult to promote your ideas, affect decisions and 'sell' changes without well-developed influencing skills. Both of these need to be backed up by powerful persuasive techniques and assertive behaviour (the latter subject will be discussed in a separate section later in this chapter).

There are several definitions of 'negotiation', but we shall use that provided by Alan Fowler (1998):

> Negotiation occurs whenever there is an issue that cannot be resolved by one person acting alone; it occurs when the two (or more) people who have to be involved begin with different views on how to proceed, or have different aims for the outcome.

Negotiations do not have to result in win/lose outcomes but may lead to win/win results. For example, if I have an orange that you and I both want, and we negotiate, there are various possible outcomes:

- I keep the orange.   *I win, you lose*
- You get the orange.   *You win, I lose*
- We cut the orange in half.   *I win, you win (compromise)*
- We divide the orange so that

  I keep the peel for baking a cake, and

  you get the fruit to decorate a drink.   *I win, you win (collaboration)*

Fowler (1998) also provides us with definitions of 'influence' and 'persuasion':

> Influence is a broad concept, involving the effect on each person of the whole context in which the discussion takes place, including the quality of past and present working relationships as well as each participant's unspoken ambitions or fears. Persuasion involves all those skills of argument and discussion that can be used by one person to obtain another's agreement.

Thus as HR practitioners you will frequently be in situations, ranging from formal meetings to chance corridor discussions with other parties, when you will need to use influence and persuasion to reach an agreed outcome. For instance, we mentioned in Chapter 8 that sometimes there is no satisfactory resolution to a grievance. In such cases you will need to persuade the employee(s) concerned to accept that there is no point in continuing to pursue the grievance to the next stage, because the answer there will be the same.

Fowler describes the range of influencing factors that are used in such circumstances and points out that:

- you should be aware of them so that you are not unduly influenced by them
- you should use them to your own advantage when they apply in your favour.

You should therefore compare yourself with the other party in a negotiating situation by examining the following influencing factors:

- the personal relationship – ie past history
- any status differences
- connections with sources of organisational power
- the formality of the location and the negotiating situation (and whose style this suits best)
- the level of information and experience
- gender, race and age differences
- reputations – for success or failure
- expectations about outcomes
- timing – duration and deadlines
- work pressures.

Once you have carried out this analysis, you can use some of these factors to your advantage and resist the temptation to be adversely influenced by those that favour the other party – or you may positively take action to counter them. Let's now consider Case study 12.1 in order to demonstrate this last point.

CASE STUDY 12.1

In an earlier section in this chapter we considered a situation in which you might wish to influence the outcome of a management decision under discussion at a meeting. This case study concerns a meeting at which the topic for discussion was the reduction of car parking spaces due to the erection of a Portakabin for contract workers. The car park was used by technical and office workers during the day and at night by shopfloor workers and a small number of technical staff who worked nights on a rotational basis.

The administrator for the technical department was due to attend a staff consultative committee meeting, and saw that this item was on the agenda circulated. The topic had been the subject of considerable discussion within the department and the administrator was concerned at the effect that it would have. There was already pressure for spaces at night-time because the shift for the technical staff commenced after that of the shopfloor workers. He carried out an informal analysis which showed that 90% of the technical staff brought their own cars to work, and all would have concerns for their safety and that of their cars if they had to park further away from the main building at night-time. The administrator decided on two possible solutions: to designate three spaces for the use of the technical staff at night-time (but he was not confident that this would be adhered to) or to relocate the Portakabin.

The administrator knew that the chairperson would normally introduce such a measure as a *fait accompli*, and he realised that there were several influencing factors that acted in the chairperson's favour: he was senior in status and had more influence with important members of senior management. Further, he was known to be fairly dogmatic in outlook but was also under a lot of work pressure at that time.

The administrator completed his research, considered alternatives and decided to put forward proposals, backed up by sound reasoning. He also decided to canvass support from one of the engineers present at the meeting (thereby discovering that the engineers' 'on call' system would provide them with similar problems). He successfully gained some 'air time' and in 'making his business case' the administrator highlighted those factors (listed above) that would help to strengthen his arguments – eg the safety issues – as well as putting forward the cost-benefits of the alternative proposals. The *pièce de résistance*, from the chairperson's point of view, is that he then offered – on the condition that the committee accepted his proposal – to talk to the chief engineer and health and safety officer to decide on an alternative location for the Portakabin.

The chairperson, faced with sound reasoning and someone prepared to take responsibility for the problem, was much less inclined to make the influencing factors work in his favour. The administrator, on the other hand, had not only resisted the urge to be daunted by those factors but had found a way of working around them!

Let's return to your powers of persuasion. Fowler (1998) provides an excellent self-assessment questionnaire to investigate this. Analyse the range of negotiating situations that you are currently involved in before responding honestly to the statements in Table 12.1. Think of situations that are formal and informal, and that take place inside and outside the workplace.

Table 12.1 Assess your powers of persuasion

	Rarely			Always		Rate yourself on a scale of 1 to 5
	1	2	3	4	5	
1 I adopt a positive and collaborative style.						
2 I am successful in avoiding confrontation.						
3 I assess the other person's viewpoint.						
4 I adapt my position to reflect the other person's viewpoint.						
5 I encourage a dialogue and do not set out all my case immediately.						
6 I do not interrupt the other person when they make statements I disagree with.						
7 I am a very attentive listener.						
8 I use questions, not statements, to probe or challenge the other person's case.						
9 If I need time for thought, or for emotions to cool, I seek an adjournment.						
10 I first introduce proposals for compromise or concession on a no-commitment basis.						
11 I link my proposed concessions to moves by the other person.						
12 I emphasise the benefits to the other person of proposed compromise.						
13 I use summaries to ensure mutual understanding and move the discussion on.						
14 I take the initiative in bringing the discussion to a constructive close.						
15 I ensure that any agreement includes details of how it will be implemented.						
16 I ensure that any agreement is mutually understood and is not ambiguous.						
17 I observe body language for clues about attitudes and intentions.						

Obviously, you are aiming to develop your powers of persuasion so that you will eventually be able to award yourself a rating of 5 on each criterion. To be realistic, this may never happen, but in the meantime the results will show which areas you should start working on.

We have now looked at the three areas of negotiating, influencing and persuading, and have seen how interlinked they are. Another connected behavioural style is assertion, which is dealt with later in this chapter.

Let us now turn to another important communication skill – counselling.

COUNSELLING

What do we mean by 'counselling'? We will commence by stating what counselling is *not*:

- giving advice

- giving opinions

- sympathising

- giving practical help – eg taking over the problem and solving it.

Counselling is not better than these helping devices, but it is different from them and more suited to certain situations. In fact, in one meeting you may need to use a range of helping devices. For instance, when discussing early retirement options with an employee, you will need to:

- counsel the employee to help him or her decide whether to retire early or not

- give practical help by providing the pensions calculations.

In any situation where you are being called upon to undertake counselling, you should always consider whether it is appropriate for you as an HR professional to do so, or whether the issue would be best dealt with by an employee's line manager, or indeed whether the issue is one on which the employee should really seek more expert support. This is often a judgement call and you will become more practised in making good decisions about this as you gain more experience.

Counselling is about – in simple terms – *helping people to help themselves*.

Thus a professional counsellor aims to assist 'clients' in exploring their problems, considering the range of options available to them, and deciding on their chosen course of action. Professional counsellors are generally independent third parties with no vested interest in the outcome of the process. As an HR practitioner this may not be the case, because it is often the actions of the organisation that you represent that have led to the need for counselling. For instance, a potential applicant for early retirement would perhaps not have considered this option if the organisation had not recently announced a major restructuring exercise that may greatly change his or her job role in the future. Thus the HR practitioner should aim to counsel the 'client' following the tips described below, though inevitably with one eye on the organisational circumstances – ie the need to equip the organisation with new skills to meet future market needs.

Counselling is a complex subject, as is evident from the number of professionally trained specialists in the field. As an HR practitioner you will increasingly find that managers and employees expect you to be the person responsible for dealing with those problems that require counselling as the helping style. You should always question whether this is appropriate in your role and ensure that a request for such intervention from a line manager is not motivated by them wanting to abdicate their own people management responsibilities. However, there will be occasions where it is right for you to undertake such tasks and this will to some extent depend on usual practice in your organisation and the role(s) agreed for

HR professionals. We do not wish to suggest that after a little practice you would be competent in dealing with every possible situation requiring counselling skills in the workplace. As the saying goes, a little knowledge can be a dangerous thing. You should seek to develop your counselling skills so that you are able to help some employees in some situations, even if it is only in a very limited way. If you have a tendency to try to avoid dealing with employees who you know have particular problems, you will be seen as an unapproachable and uncaring employer. You may even lose good employees because you did not take the appropriate action at the time.

CASE STUDY 12.2

One story worth relating is that of a young brother and sister who lost their father. Both went straight back to work on the day after the funeral, but each had rather different experiences.

On her return to work, the sister was invited into the office of the HR officer, who expressed his sympathy (he had previously sent a note signed by the young woman's colleagues together with flowers from the company). He reassured her that if she felt she could not cope with coming back to work so soon, she should just inform him and he would make the appropriate arrangements with her manager.

On the other hand, when the woman's brother returned to work, nothing was said by his supervisor at all, although he had known why the young man had been absent. In fact, a couple of days later, when he was feeling very disheartened, his supervisor said to him in the hearing of other workers, 'It's about time you pulled yourself together.'

Can you guess which employee remained longer with the employer?

There are a number of commonly occurring situations that you may be expected to deal with personally. These may include problems between an employee and his/her manager, redundancy, early retirement, sickness absence, work-related problems and some personal problems. In fact, organisations often have in place formalised counselling procedures to deal with such situations. In such cases the counselling procedure replaces, or runs in parallel with, other procedures. (See the Acas publications *Discipline and Grievances at Work* and *Redundancy Handling* for further details.)

It is not our intention to provide a comprehensive guide to suit every occasion, but a few simple tips are offered below. These should be read and implemented in the context of each situation that you deal with and in accordance with the appropriate organisational procedures.

TIPS

- Listen actively.
- Show empathy – ie non-critical, non-judgemental acceptance.
- Reflect back and paraphrase what has been said.
- Use open questioning.
- Ask questions to ensure that the client focuses on the problem.

- Prompt (but do not direct) exploration of a range of options.

- Provide summaries throughout of what has been said or agreed.

- Encourage the client to find his or her own solution and set his or her own goals.

- Agree an action plan.

- Summarise at the end.

- Monitor and review (if appropriate – ie if you are dealing with work-related issues).

A word of caution here: don't expect too much from a 30- to 60-minute counselling session. Counselling takes time, because clients are often trying to work through complex problems. Don't, though, be tempted simply to allocate a larger chunk of time on the next occasion, because short sessions with 'thinking time' in between are usually more fruitful. If you have practised good counselling skills, your client can leave the meeting better equipped to think through the options before reaching a decision on what to do next. He or she may decide not to do anything, but as a result of the counselling may feel better equipped to deal with the situation than before.

TIME MANAGEMENT

Like all busy managers, HR practitioners are likely to find that there appears to be a serious mismatch between their volume of work and the time they have to do it in. This is especially so when a large part of each day seems to be taken up dealing with queries from employees and other parties. A lot of people attend courses in order to learn about good time management techniques. They often get very enthusiastic about how they will revolutionise their working (and personal) life by employing these techniques at the conclusion of the training course. The problem is that when they get back to the workplace, nothing (and no one) else has changed, so they find that they lack the time to try out any new ideas or to develop the necessary skills. In fact, 'it takes time to save time' initially because good time management involves more planning and preparation; it is often easier to slip back into old habits and react to emergencies and crises rather than thinking ahead to try to avoid them.

It is also difficult to initiate the application of good time management skills at home because if this involves persuading other family members to take more responsibility for, say, certain household chores, they may be inclined to be uncooperative, because the benefits to them are not immediately apparent. Here we can see the link between the previous section on negotiating, influencing and persuading and good time management, as well as a link with the following section on assertiveness. It is necessary to use and develop all these skills if you really want to change your time management habits.

As we have already said, developing skills usually means changing behaviour. With time management in particular you are attempting to change patterns of behaviour that have been ingrained over many years, so don't expect a miracle cure. The good news is that once you begin the process and start to see the benefits, you will be greatly encouraged to carry on. The new patterns of behaviour in the workplace will start to spill over into your personal life as you gain the confidence to try to change others' behaviour along with your own.

First, let's examine some fallacies about time management (see Table 12.2).

Table 12.2 Time management

Fallacies	The truth
Time management will mean that I have to work efficiently all the time.	Time management will help you to work efficiently, but only when you want to. You may choose to work efficiently for just some of the time – for example, on priority tasks.
Time management will mean that I'll be so busy that I'll miss out on things like gossiping with colleagues or taking my time over a favourite job.	Time management helps you to choose the right things to do and to work through them more quickly. You will then free up extra time and you can decide how to spend it.
Time management will mean that I can no longer be spontaneous – eg agree to help out a colleague or accept an invitation from a friend.	Time management will help you to avoid crisis management but should not remove spontaneity. You can choose which aspects of your life you wish to retain.
Time management will mean that I have to work a lot harder overall.	Time management should mean that you do less work overall because you will decide which tasks are the important ones – ie the ones that contribute most to your goals. **You will work smarter, not harder.**

A fundamental stage in time management is to decide on our goals and priorities and then choose to work on tasks that help us to achieve them. Those tasks that do not fall into this category will then either come lower down our list of priorities or cease to be performed at all. In discussing time management we are referring to the distinction between efficiency and effectiveness: efficiency is doing things right; effectiveness is doing the right things.

These memorable definitions help us to remember that we should always aim to be effective rather than efficient. Many people pride themselves on being efficient, but that may mean that they are simply working hard to achieve tasks rather than working towards goals. Thus they may be wasting a lot of their time and will probably see other (more effective) people being promoted over them.

Good time management results in:

- more productivity
- more control
- more time for leisure

- less stress
- more effective decision-making
- success.

We shall now consider the most common time-wasters for HR practitioners and suggest some time management techniques for you to try out – see Table 12.3. Some of our suggestions assume that you have responsibilities for staff and can therefore delegate some tasks. We have suggested alternative techniques where this is not the case or where delegation is not appropriate (see below for guidance on this latter point).

Table 12.3 How to avoid time-wasters

Time-wasters	Techniques
Interruptions (telephone calls, drop-in visitors)	<ul><li>Operate a limited 'open door' policy.</li><li>Remove yourself to work undisturbed elsewhere.</li><li>Stand up when answering the telephone; tell the caller that you will call him or her back at a mutually convenient time.</li><li>Get someone to screen your calls and callers – either an assistant or a colleague (in the latter case you could set up a reciprocal and mutually convenient arrangement to cater for periods of intense pressure from work deadlines).</li><li>Make deals with your boss about availability and priorities.</li><li>Reschedule impromptu meetings for more convenient times.</li></ul>
Poorly conducted meetings	<ul><li>Have a personal agenda covering what you want to achieve during the meeting and work towards it.</li><li>Be assertive and suggest time limits for each item.</li><li>Gather support to suggest changes to the meeting – eg limited duration, less frequent, more informative/participative.</li><li>Meet in other people's offices; it is easier to leave!</li><li>In your own office have two clocks, one you can see and one your visitors can see.</li></ul>
Too much paperwork	<ul><li>Keep a tidy desk and tackle one task at a time (do not 'grass-hop' between different tasks).</li><li>Speed-read; you won't need to remember every detail of the communication – just the gist of it.</li><li>Adopt a simple filing system and stick to it.</li><li>Thin files out periodically to save time when referring to them.</li><li>Handle pieces of paper once only using the RAFT system (Refer it – Act on it – File it – Throw it away).</li><li>When possible, reply with short notes/memos/telephone calls rather than long-winded responses.</li></ul>

Time-wasters	Techniques
Poor delegation	• Delegate finite or routine tasks. • Ask for regular status reports. • Resist the temptation to get involved in the minute detail of a task.
Reverse delegation (when staff offload their tasks on to the boss)	• Listen to the problem but resist the urge to take it over. • Insist that staff present problems and some suggestions to solve them. • Support your staff in making their decisions.
Poor work-scheduling	• Use an 'organiser' to list your 'to do' tasks, and keep it up to date. • Set your own deadlines and priorities and stick to them; whenever feasible, don't allow other people's priorities to override your own. • Always allow for some undisturbed time during the day, and use it for thinking time or work on major projects (preferably when your energy levels are at their optimum).
Perfectionism	• Attention to detail has its place, but don't allow it to get in the way of achieving the task. • Allow yourself to produce the standard of work that is appropriate to the circumstances (and helps you to achieve your goals).
Poor use of technology	• Get up to speed with time-saving technology – eg word processing, spreadsheets, database packages. • Use telephone memories/answering facilities/divert systems. • Listen to self-development tapes while driving.
Lack of leisure time	• Schedule in leisure time/treats to your day. • Resist the temptation to use your leisure time to meet other needs – eg to complete a large project. • Keep fit: a healthy body helps you to perform better mentally.

Remember that you will need to take time out initially to decide on your goals and priorities and to plan how you will achieve them. Don't try to implement everything at once: practise one or two new techniques at a time to see which ones work for you.

DELEGATION

The following list shows those activities that you can or should delegate:

• work that you don't have to do yourself

• work that others can do more efficiently or more effectively

• whole jobs

• more demanding tasks that you closely supervise in order to pass on skills or knowledge.

Compare this with the following list which shows those activities that you should *not* delegate:

- work entrusted to you personally
- your own work that has gone wrong – eg a mistake has been made
- mundane routine work that is not a whole task
- critical tasks where mistakes cannot be tolerated
- work that you do not understand (because you will not be able to judge the outcome)
- staff and team roles and responsibilities
- confidential matters.

We have covered several aspects of this important skill here. Now you need to take time to do some further reading around this subject, making use of self-assessment questionnaires to determine your strengths and weaknesses in this area. Plan next to do something specific in order to improve your time management. It can be done: many others have been successful before you.

We shall leave this section with the following five steps to developing good time management habits:

1 *Recognise* the difficulty in changing.

2 *Develop* a better way.

3 *Launch* the new habit strongly.

4 *Practise* the new way often.

5 Allow *no exceptions*.

ACTIVITY 12.3

Make a log of your activities over a period of a few days. There are numerous formats you could use, but a simple record of activities and duration would be a good start. Then analyse your log by designating each activity as

   A   important and urgent

   B   important but not urgent

   C   not important but urgent, or

   D   neither important nor urgent.

and calculate the proportion of time spent on each category.

Ideally, at least two-thirds of your time should come into the B category, and only a fifth to a quarter into the A category. All being well, a minimal amount of your time will be spent in category D. But do not be dismayed if these figures do not reflect your distribution of time. Apply some of the time management techniques in this chapter and then repeat this exercise.

ASSERTIVENESS

Assertiveness is probably the most useful skill of all. Developing it will have an immediate impact on your working and non-working life. Assertiveness is clear, honest and direct communication that pays heed to our own needs and the needs of others. It is best described by comparing it to the two extremes of submissive and aggressive styles of behaviour – see Tables 12.4 and 12.5 (both adapted from Back K. and K. (1986)).

Table 12.4 Behaviour styles

Assertive	Submissive	Aggressive
Communicates impression of self-respect and respect for others.	Communicates a message of inferiority and results in lowered self-esteem.	Communicates impression of superiority and disrespect.
Our wants, needs, and rights are viewed as equal to those of others.	Allows the wants, needs, and rights of others to be more important than own.	Puts own wants, needs, and rights above those of other people.
Achieves own objectives by influencing, listening, and negotiating. Others are able to co-operate willingly.	Ignores own rights and needs in an attempt to satisfy the needs of other people.	Achieves own objectives by not allowing others a choice. Violates the rights of others.
Behaviour is active, direct and honest.	Anger towards others is directed inwards.	Behaviour is domineering, self-centred, and self-enhancing.
I'm OK . . . You're OK	**I'm not OK . . . You are**	**I'm OK . . . You're not**

Table 12.5 What are the differences?

Assertive	Submissive	Aggressive
Verbal		
'I' statements that make it clear you are speaking for yourself – eg 'I think', 'I would like', 'I feel'.	Few 'I' statements, and those often qualified – eg 'It's only my idea but . . .'.	'I' statements that are boastful or too numerous, and the use of the royal 'we' when it is really 'I' – eg 'We don't want to do that.'
Distinctions made between fact and opinion – eg 'As I see it . . .', 'My opinion is . . .'.	Opinions qualified with such words as 'maybe', 'perhaps', 'I wonder', 'possibly'.	Opinions expressed as facts – eg 'The scheme's crazy.'
Statements or questions that acknowledge disagreement and seek to resolve it – eg 'We have a disagreement on this, so how can we move it forward?'	Statements that downplay a disagreement or pretend that it does not exist – eg 'Well, having aired that one, I think it's best if we move on.'	Statements that inflame or keep disagreements going – eg 'Anybody with an ounce of common sense can see that won't work!'

Assertive	Submissive	Aggressive
Voice		
Tone – steady, firm, clear.	Tone – apologetic, wobbly, dull, monotonous.	Tone – harsh, sarcastic, blaming, challenging.
Volume – not overloud or quiet; may be raised to get attention.	Volume – quiet, dropping away at the end.	Volume – overloud, rising at the end.
Body language		
Gestures – open hand movements used with firm, measured pace to emphasise or demonstrate. Arms open or lightly crossed.	Gestures – covering mouth with hand, tight and nervous hand movements – eg fiddling with pen.	Gestures – dismissive hand movements. Pointing with finger/pen, thumping table, 'steepling' (ie fingertips pressed together as sign of supcriority), arms crossed high (ie unapproachable).
Posture – upright but relaxed, moving slightly forward.	Posture – shoulders hunched, huddled over papers.	Posture – head in air, chin thrust out, leaning far back, hands behind head.
Eyes – direct, relaxed gaze.	Eyes – averted.	Eyes – glaring, hostile

Once you are familiar with the differences between these three behavioural styles, you should note the following three essential skills of assertive behaviour, summarised by Anne Dickson (1984: 22) as follows:

1 Decide what it is you want or feel, and say so specifically and directly.

2 Stick to your statement, repeating it, if necessary, over and over again. (This is commonly known as the 'broken record approach'.)

3 Assertively deflect any responses from the other person which might undermine your assertive stance – ie acknowledge the response but do not allow yourself to become sidetracked or involved in an argument – eg 'I know that you're tired as well, but I still want you to help with the housework'; 'I know that you're disappointed, but I still have to say no.'

Successful assertive behaviour is demonstrated in Case study 12.3.

From personal experience we have found that the approach above can work very effectively and have recommended it to others. Recently, a colleague was finding that she had taken on more than she had realised when she agreed to do some tutoring on an open learning programme. She hadn't realised that some students would require additional support from her, either face-to-face or on the telephone or via email correspondence. The tutor was paid by the hour for running workshops and was paid a set amount for marking assignments. There was no provision for student support outside these provisions.

Initially, the tutor was happy to provide the support because she was committed to the programme and wished to give the students as much assistance as possible. Gradually, however, she became more and more resentful and thought about withdrawing from the programme, even though she enjoyed the work. Luckily, she took our advice before taking this step and talked to the programme manager. She decided what she wanted and explained the position, having kept a record of her recent contacts with students. The programme manager was sympathetic to her case. They agreed that in future the tutor would ensure that she acted assertively in seeking to limit the tendency for some students to become overly dependent on her advice. However, where the additional support was warranted, the tutor could make a claim for any additional hours worked. Several months on the tutor has found that setting ground rules for student contact has reduced the additional demands made on her time and the working relationship between the tutor and programme manager continues to be a happy one.

We can see in Table 12.5 that assertive behaviour involves lots of 'I' statements. It also involves the use of the word 'no', which can be a very difficult lesson for us to learn. If, for instance, a colleague asks you to help out with some salary calculations so that she can meet a deadline for a report on anticipated labour costs, your first inclination is likely to be to agree. This is acceptable so long as:

- your own work does not suffer

- you know that your colleague will be glad to return the favour at a later date

- you do not feel that your colleague is taking advantage of your better nature (and is only in this predicament through her own fault).

However, if any of these preconditions is not valid, you should seriously consider saying no. Remember that by saying no you are refusing the request, not rejecting the person. You will find that if you say no assertively, the person concerned will not consider that you have let him or her down or hurt his or her feelings. It will instead be clear that you simply cannot help him or her to solve this particular problem. So, in appropriate circumstances, practise saying no clearly and definitely without excessive apology or excuses and directly without lying or letting the other person down.

As an HR practitioner you will be dealing with all sorts of people in a variety of emotional states – eg upset, nervous, under pressure, angry, dogmatic, inconsiderate. There will be occasions when you feel that submissive or aggressive behaviour is more appropriate than assertive behaviour. An example of the former situation might be when you are not as interested in the outcome of a discussion as the other party and so allow their views to override your own.

An example of the latter might be when you use aggression in a controlled way to indicate that you really have come to the end of the road in a negotiating situation.

The choice of behavioural styles is always open to you. However, by practising assertive behaviour you are ensuring that you do consciously choose a particular style rather than rely on whichever behavioural style is your natural tendency.

We will now move on to look at self-development and continuous professional development.

SELF-DEVELOPMENT

Pedler, Burgoyne and Boydell (2006) define self-development as:

> personal development, with the manager (or employee) taking primary responsibility for her or his own learning and for choosing the means to achieve this.

They state that other commonly held views on the meaning and purposes of self-development include career development and advancement, improving performance in an existing job, developing certain specific qualities and skills, and achieving total potential – ie self-actualisation.

So in aiming to improve your personal effectiveness, you will inevitably have to get involved in some self-development exercises. These should include an initial analysis of your strengths and development needs in order to highlight areas that require further development. A plan to concentrate on these development needs can then be put into effect through:

- self-assessment questionnaires
- role-playing 'difficult' situations in a safe environment and carrying out a review of performance, possibly using one or other of the last two points below
- setting up real experiences such as secondments, projects and work-shadowing (see also the section on page 350 on increasing your personal profile)
- project work requiring the production of written reports and verbal presentations
- observation and feedback from a trusted third party
- self-analysis of experiences through techniques ranging from diary entries to observation of closed-circuit television recordings of real or simulated situations.

In general terms, you will need to experiment with new behaviours and would be well advised to follow the simple stages of Kolb's learning cycle in order to gain maximum benefit from the learning experience (see Figure 12.1).

A general point to note is that attempting to improve skills will usually involve a change in behaviour and will often require you to take a risk (of failure). For

Figure 12.1 Kolb's learning cycle

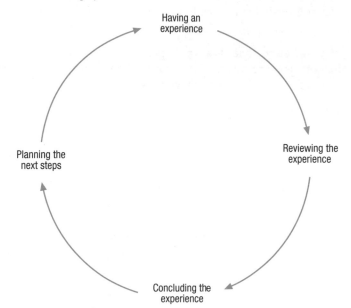

Having an experience

Reviewing the experience

Concluding the experience

Planning the next steps

instance, if you wish to influence the outcome of a particular management decision that is on the agenda of a meeting you are attending, you will not succeed by sitting quietly and taking no part in the discussions. You will, however, have an improved chance of success if, after carrying out some research, you are able to present your findings logically and put forward proposals that are backed up by sound reasoning. This could be done by way of a written report or an oral presentation. Regardless of the outcome, you should then seek honest feedback on your performance from people whose judgement you trust. (We saw earlier in the section on negotiating and influencing that, at a more advanced level, you may first decide to canvass support from other parties at the meeting to ensure that your ideas get a fair hearing.)

There are two further tips for self-development worthy of comment that will assist you in travelling down the road to enhanced personal effectiveness:

- Carry out an analysis of how you learn and make use of this information to plan your learning in the future (Honey and Mumford's Learning Styles Questionnaire is probably the best-known in this field – see Chapter 6 and the *References and further reading* section at the end of this chapter).

- Increase your personal profile inside and outside your employing organisation by being proactive. At work 'walking the floor' helps you to get to know a large number of employees and, probably more importantly, to become known by them. Also, volunteering to take part in activities that extend your normal range of duties – such as taking notes at meetings, involvement in working parties, project work and making presentations – will have the same effect of increasing your profile. If you do not take up such opportunities, you may be respected for your work but you will have less chance of really impressing 'onlookers'. Further, a 'backstage worker' approach may mean that someone else gets all the credit for your hard work – for example, the person whose name ends up on your report, or your boss when he or she presents your proposals to a senior management meeting. Outside work you should set time aside for networking through, for example, getting involved in your local CIPD branch activities, and attending seminars, meetings and other events designed to facilitate networking. You never know: at the next event you could end up sitting alongside your future boss!

Before moving on to enlarge our understanding of the specific skills areas listed above, it is worth again bringing to your attention *A Manager's Guide to Self-Development* by Pedler, Burgoyne and Boydell (2006). This excellent book covers a vast number of areas and provides several exercises and questionnaires aimed at an initial self-assessment. Please also take time to read *Personal Effectiveness* by Diana Winstanley (2005). This book covers many of the same topic areas as this chapter and provides a range of innovative activities and exercises to enable you to practise the skills and apply the knowledge to your own life.

CONTINUOUS PROFESSIONAL DEVELOPMENT

Two terms are commonly used when discussing personal effectiveness: they are 'continuous development' and 'continuing professional development' (CPD). The first term basically means learning from real experiences at work on a continuous basis – eg not assuming that a two-day skills training programme will provide delegates with all they need to become fully competent in the skill concerned. Thus learning continues throughout our working lives through formal events such as training programmes, but also through our day-to-day experiences, planned and unplanned.

The second and connected term is increasingly being adopted by professional bodies such as the CIPD to reassure outside parties that members of the Institute are fully competent in today's working environment – ie that they did not put all their books and journals away on qualifying but take great pains to keep up to date with legislation and other developments in the field of HR management. CPD is therefore a requirement for Chartered Member status of the CIPD, and evidence will be required at the time of upgrading membership and on a random selection basis at any time.

Records should show a mix of learning activities, such as courses, seminars, conferences and self-directed or informal learning, including reading, networking, special projects or indeed anything that develops your professional abilities. Ideally, it will not all be directly work-focused and will include reference to activities that take place outside work. Most importantly, you must include a synopsis of how the learning has been used or will be used in future activities. This, for example, could be the writing of a policy or a specific change in the way in which you will do your job or approach a particular situation in the future.

Your development plan encourages you to commit to future learning by specifically focusing on areas where you wish to develop your skills and knowledge and/or achieve your goals.

The CIPD Policy on CPD states five essential principles:

- Development should be continuous in the sense that the professional should always be actively seeking improved performance.

- Development should be owned and managed by the individual learner.

- CPD is a personal matter and the effective learner knows best what he or she needs to learn. Development should begin from the individual's current learning state.

- Learning objectives should be clear and wherever possible should serve organisational or client needs as well as individual goals.

- Regular investment of time in learning should be seen as an essential part of professional life, not as an optional extra.

The main message here is that the acquisition of skills is not a finite exercise. We can never be fully effective in all situations and are constantly thrown into new experiences that promote new learning.

Useful and comprehensive information on continuous professional development for HR practitioners can be found on the CIPD website at **www.cipd.co.uk/cpd/guidance**. This features further information on managing and recording your CPD, provides a template for use in recording CPD, gives examples and case studies, and outlines the benefits of CPD.

ACTIVITY 12.4

If you have not already done so, obtain the CIPD's information pack on CPD. Use it to set up a record of your CPD and a development plan. Discuss your development plan with one or more of your learning sources in order to gain their support in putting some of your action plans into effect.

SUMMARY

- In this chapter we have looked at a range of topics pertinent to your role as an HR practitioner. We have not tried to provide a comprehensive coverage, either in range or content, but an introductory guide to a number of skills areas. As your career progresses, you will find that you need to develop these skills in order to perform tasks and activities in as professional a manner as possible.

- We chose the skills and techniques of report-writing and making presentations as prime examples of communication skills that help you to 'sell' your ideas and proposals. We also considered the connected skills of negotiating, influencing and persuading and their application in both formal and informal situations. Next we examined the counselling skills necessary to deal with the vast range of problems that are likely to face members of your workforce as well as the vexing problem of managing your time. If you cannot manage yourself, it may be difficult to convince others that you are worthy of promotion to a position in which you will also be managing others.

- Finally, we proposed that assertive behaviour is appropriate in nearly every role played by the HR practitioner in the workplace (and in many other situations occurring outside it, too). It is an important skill that backs up the others necessary for you to achieve personal effectiveness. We ended with assertion because – of all the skills areas we have considered in this chapter – this is one you cannot afford to ignore. Assertive behaviour is enormously powerful and, used correctly, helps to build your credibility in the workplace. Try it at work and at home – you'll be amazed by the results.

Completion of a number of appropriate Activities, referred to throughout the chapter, will provide you with a useful starting point before you undertake some further reading into those skill areas that you decide are priorities for you. You should by now be aware of the importance of self-development and the need continually to keep up to date and seek further to improve your skills and knowledge in order to warrant the title 'HR professional'. You should aim continuously to develop yourself throughout your working life.

We wish you every success!

ACTIVITY 12.5

Buy a book on one of the topics covered in this chapter – eg negotiating, time management or assertiveness. Apply the techniques that you learn about to any important situation that you are currently facing. Use any self-assessment exercises and questionnaires provided in the book to begin the process of increasing your self-awareness.

EXPLORE FURTHER

REFERENCES AND FURTHER READING

ACAS (revised 2009) Advisory Booklet on *Redundancy Handling*. Leicester: ACAS

ACAS (revised 2009) Advisory Handbook on *Discipline and Grievances At Work*. Leicester: ACAS

BACK, K. and K. (1986) 'Assertiveness training for meetings', *Industrial and Commercial Training*, Vol.18, No.2, March/April; pp.26–30

BACK, K. (2005) *Assertiveness at Work: A practical guide to handling awkward situations*. Maidenhead: McGraw-Hill Professional

BORG, J. (2007) *Persuasion: The art of influencing people*. Harlow: Prentice Hall

BOWDEN, J. (2008) *Writing a Report: How to prepare, write and present really effective reports*. London: How to Books

BRADBURY, A. (2006) *Successful Presentation Skills*, 3rd edition. London: Kogan Page

CIPD (updated 2008) *Code of Professional Conduct and Disciplinary Procedures*. London: Chartered Institute of Personnel and Development

CIPD (2009) *HR Profession Map*. London: Chartered Institute of Personnel and Development

FORSTER, M. (2006) *Do It Tomorrow and Other Secrets of Time Management*. London: Hodder & Stoughton

FOWLER, A. (1998) *Negotiating, Persuading, and Influencing*. London: Chartered Institute of Personnel and Development

FRANKLIN, L. (2003) *An Introduction to Workplace Counselling: A practitioner's guide*. Basingstoke: Palgrave Macmillan

HONEY, P. and MUMFORD, A. (1992) *The Manual of Learning Styles*. Maidenhead: Peter Honey

JACKSON, T. (2000) *Career Development*. London: Chartered Institute of Personnel and Development

MEGGINSON, D. and WHITAKER, V. (2007) *Continuing Professional Development*, 2nd edition. London: Chartered Institute of Personnel and Development

PEDLER, M., BURGOYNE, J. and BOYDELL, T. (2006) *A Manager's Guide to Self Development*. London: McGraw-Hill

WINSTANLEY, D. (2005) *Personal Effectiveness*. London: Chartered Institute of Personnel and Development

WEBSITES

BBC Education: www.bbc.co.uk/education/home/

Chartered Institute of Personnel and Development: www.cipd.co.uk

People Management: www.peoplemanagement.co.uk

APPENDIX TO CHAPTER 12

CHECKLIST: THE MECHANICS OF REPORT-WRITING

Terms of reference

- Are you clear about the purpose of your report?
- Have you specified its aim and objectives?
- Are you clear about who will read your report and their level of knowledge?

Collecting information

- Have you used a workable recording system?
- Have you collected information from as many sources as possible?

Organising information

- Is your report presented in clear sections?

- Are the sections logically sequenced and easy to follow?
- Do you provide signposts (subheadings, for example) for the reader?

Grammar and style

- Are your paragraphs short, clearly defined in material and easy to read?
- Have you chosen simple, unambiguous wording?
- Have you checked sentence construction, spelling and punctuation?
- Is the style appropriate to the content of the report, your organisation and the reader(s)?

Checking your work

- Have you checked structure and language?
- Have you asked for a third person's comments?
- Have you proofread your final draft?

Layout

- Have you presented your report in the accepted organisational format?
- Are the sections numbered and headings highlighted consistently?
- Are quotes/illustrations/appendices/cross-references all referred to correctly?

Final presentation

- Have you chosen the most suitable form of presentation and distribution?
- Have you allowed enough time for these final stages?

CHECKLIST: THE LAYOUT/CONTENTS OF YOUR REPORT

Title page

- Does the report have a short, self-explanatory title?
- Does the title page contain other appropriate identification data – eg name of organisation, name of author, date of completion?

Summary

- Does it give the reader a framework showing the main features of each section?
- Does it include any conclusions reached?
- Is it self-contained and self-explanatory?

Acknowledgements

- Do they record a debt for help or use of facilities?

Contents page

- Are section/page numbers clear and accurate?

Introduction

- Does it refer to the terms of reference, limitations or constraints, scope, and the research method(s) you have adopted?
- Does it contain appropriate background information (depending on the needs of the reader(s))?

Body of the report

- Do you provide an analysis of the perceived problem and include the research findings?
- Does the discussion lead naturally on to the conclusions and recommendations of the report?

Conclusions

- Do you summarise your main research findings?
- Do you state clearly your interpretation of these results?
- Do they lead logically to the recommendations you are intending to make?

Options

- Have you considered the pros and cons of a number of alternatives before deciding on your final recommendations?
- Do they address the issues identified in your conclusions?

Recommendations

- Have you written clear recommendations that identify specific actions and assigned responsibility for those actions?
- Are they supported by good reasoning that is provided either here or earlier in your report?
- Have you costed them and made some assessment of the benefits?
- Have you included time-scales?

Appendices

- Do they contain lengthy or technical information?
- Are they correctly referenced in the report?

References

- Has a consistent referencing system been used?
- Have you included full details: surname, initials, title of article/book/journal, date of publication, volume/issue/page numbers?

Bibliography

- Do you acknowledge other works used and those for useful further reading?

Index